The
Golden Age
of
Melodrama

TO
REBECCA

BY THE SAME AUTHOR

Three Melodramas	(Samuel French Ltd)
Three More Melodramas	(Samuel French Ltd)
It Gives Me Great Pleasure	(Samuel French Ltd)
Make 'Em Laugh	(Wolfe Publishing Ltd)

SBN 7234 0514 X

Printed in Great Britain by
THE STELLAR PRESS HATFIELD HERTS

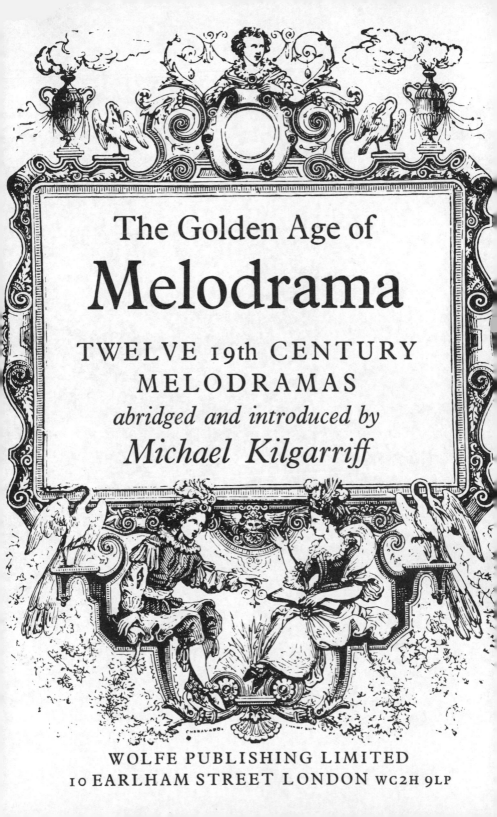

The Golden Age of
Melodrama

TWELVE 19th CENTURY MELODRAMAS

abridged and introduced by

Michael Kilgarriff

WOLFE PUBLISHING LIMITED
10 EARLHAM STREET LONDON WC2H 9LP

Frontispiece: The Restive Pegasus. Or, the Dramatic Author foiled in his Attempt to ascend Parnassus. (*British Museum*)

...TIVE PEGASUS.

...d in his Attempt to ascend Parnassus.

Contents

(continued overleaf)

7

List of Illustrations

9

Preface

This volume is intended for the casual enquirer; I make no claims to original research, although perhaps some of my conclusions may be novel. In the section headed 'Rise and Fall of the Melodrama' I have endeavoured to present a clear and straightforward (though necessarily brief) account of its origins and causes, uncluttered by copious extracts or numerous illustrative examples. In an attempt to avoid obscurity and prolixity, therefore, the facts follow thick and fast without corroborative evidence or piledriver repetition – an unscholarly procedure, but as I have said, I am not aiming at the specialist. The reader must take my word for it that the facts are accurate; my comments thereon I accept as being open to argument and rejection.

The plays have been selected as representative in respect of themes, authors and decades of the nineteenth century. I have included more biographical material than is customary in publications of this kind and have also included contemporary press notices which has not, so far as I am aware, been attempted before. These innovations will, I am sure, give the reader a much more authentic feel and flavour of the times than any ramblings of mine can suggest. The abridgements have, I hope, maintained the style and construction of the originals; my cuts have been chiefly confined to filleting the long speeches, and I have made no alterations of any other kind.

Appendix A consists of Planché's deliberations on the breaking of the Patent Houses' charter. I have quoted this at length since it shows the attitudes of informed opinion at the time (although there were many who held dissenting views) and outlines a complicated subject with exemplary clarity. Appendix B is also from Planché, and is an interesting apology for plagiarism.

My thanks are due to the following: to Dr Booth and Barrie & Jenkins for permission to quote from *English Melodrama*; to the administrators of Jerome K Jerome's estate for the extracts from *On The Stage – and Off*; to Samuel French Ltd for allowing me to use their precious copy of *Trilby*; to A & C Black Ltd for the passages from H G Hibbert's *A Playgoer's Memories*; and to Stanley Paul & Co Ltd for the reminiscence from H Chance Newton's *Crime And The Drama*.

MICHAEL KILGARRIFF
EALING, JULY 1973

Preamble

Melodrama's essential melancholy and Gothic romanticism were exactly suited to the moods of that strangely dark and passionate age, the nineteenth century. Propriety of sentiment and gloomily joyful denouements, gimcrack sensations and reach-me-down plots, empty bombast and florid declamation – not much of an evening's entertainment there, we might think.

But we must remember the frustrations of strong emotion and a rigid moral code, the repressions of poverty and degradation at one end of the social scale and extreme wealth at the other, setting up tensions that found some measure of release in the satisfying inevitability of the melodramatic last-scene climax – it might not be too far-fetched to describe it, in this context, as quasi-orgasmic.

Liberalism as we understand the term today was almost non-existent, and even the near-equivalent virtue of charity was in short supply throughout the era; our most celebrated national characteristic of hypocrisy inspired a savage envy of those who broke the accepted canons of behaviour – in public, at least – and showed itself in an hysterical condemnation of those with the courage or foolhardiness to do their own thing. Dress, mode of speech and accent, deportment and most of all sexual conduct were minutely regulated at both ends of society. Only in the businesses of making money and prostitution was all fair, the former provided it was pursued on a gigantic enough scale and the latter with discretion.

The didactic sermonising of the melodrama was dedicated (albeit unconsciously) to the maintenance of this status quo, which meant Papa's continuing dominance over property, wife and servants – the lower orders had to be dealt with firmly lest they got above themselves and started talking dangerous rubbish about 'democracy' (wasn't Britain already a democracy?), 'equality', or even 'republicanism'.

In a dismal attempt to ape their superiors the bourgeois and labouring classes gradually assumed the posture of respectability with all its concomitant attitudes of social, sexual and political rectitude. The desperate pathos of this demeaning mimicry is underlined by an appreciation that for the lower orders life was scarcely less 'nasty, brutish and short' that it had been for their Georgian fathers and grandfathers – and in many cases, more so.

(continued on page 14)

The Monster Melo-Drama
Published for the Satirist, *December 4th, 1807*

*Behind the four-footed monster are the theatres of Covent Garden (l.)
and Drury Lane (r.), the latter topped by its headless statue of Apollo.
The tail is enscribed* A Tail of Mistery; *a masked Harlequin's head is
protruding from the centre of the creature's back, the fore part of which
is clothed in Harlequin's coat; behind an old man or woman is driving a
flock of geese (the public ?) past Covent Garden.*

*Richard Brinsley Sheridan is saying 'Ha, ha, ha'; John Philip Kemble
('Black Jack') is expostulating 'Oh ! ! ! ! !' – hardly surprisingly, since
he has a dagger stuck in his neck; and the third of the front heads is the
great clown Grimaldi, who the previous year (1806) had come to
prominence in the pantomime* Mother Goose. *His balloon reads 'Nice*

moon' which may have been a catch-phrase of the time.

The figures under the monster represent popular contemporary authors, who may be identified by the titles of the plays on which they stand (the monster itself is standing on approved authors). Thus, Frederic Reynolds is standing on The Caravan – *or rather his dog is, M G Lewis (dressed inevitably as a monk) is upon his* Wood Daemon, *Thomas Holcroft (in spectacles and suckling from the monster) is standing on* The Road To Ruin; *the dilettante Sir Lumley Skeffington Bart (in striped trousers) stands on his* Sleeping Beauty, *and on the extreme right William Dimond stands on his* Hunter Of The Alps.

13

Want, harsh working conditions and miserable wages, rapacious employers and extortionate landlords should have given the great British Unwashed a more healthily unsubmissive attitude to the ruling élite. But no; no matter how much our masters sneered at us, patronised us, oppressed us, exploited us, enslaved our children and prostituted our women, at a smile and a word we doffed our caps, shuffled our feet, and blushed.

It is true that there were one or two anti-Establishment figures like Dick Turpin and Jack Sheppard whose exploits were romanticised on the melodrama stage, but these equivocal heroes had to pay the price for their contumacy on the scaffold. The prototype lovable rogue was of course Robin Hood, but even he turned out to be a peer of the realm – as did Tarzan of the Apes, which goes to show that nothing is new.

So the melodrama conspired to keep us in thrall by showing us all our prejudices and persuasions satisfyingly confirmed. Melodrama was rarely intentionally propagandist, it merely reflected our current convictions and helped to perpetuate our British way of life with all its hypocrisies, its unction and its snobbery. And it gave us romance, thrills and spectacle as well, both complimenting and complementing the social milieu.

It is by no means easy to distinguish a melodrama from a drama, for there is no specific technical difference between the two. One possible distinction might be that a melodrama was solely concerned with action and a direct appeal to the heart, whereas a drama was also concerned with the examination of an idea or ideal and an appeal to the intellect. But both used incessant musical accompaniment (as do movies today) and both made use of the asides which we find so absurdly dated – although we are still prepared to accept Shakespearean soliloquies without smirking.

My own attitude to melodrama is ambivalent. I love its idealisation of Life but mistrust its sanctification of traditional values; I am attracted to its Greek inevitability but repelled by its phoniness; its ingenuousness is endearing but its prejudices are not; its humour is appalling but its robust theatricality is glorious.

This book is described as a survey, a word which, as Humpty Dumpty said, 'means just what I choose it to mean – neither more nor less'. The result is therefore an entirely personal assessment of melo-drama. Broadly speaking, I have tried to separate opinion and fact into this Preamble and the following chapter respectively. Whether either is of any value I leave the reader to judge.

Rise and Fall
of the Melodrama

Historical background

The eighteenth century saw the steady decline of the drama as a serious art form in this country, a decline which was not to be arrested until Bernard Shaw, despairing of the British theatre ever producing an Ibsen or a Tchekov, began his own extraordinary career as a playwright in the eighteen-nineties. This represents a gap of some two hundred years since the previous 'Golden Age' of dramaturgy – the Restoration – during which time only a handful of plays by Sheridan and Goldsmith can be admitted to illumine the darkness.

Why was this? What are the reasons for this great chasm in our literary heritage? Why was it that though these two centuries gave rise to countless enduring works by men and women of genius in the fields of painting, sculpture, music, architecture and the humanities, the art of the dramatist withered and all but died? Even theatrical commentary was better served than the drama itself by such figures as Hazlitt, Lamb, Leigh Hunt, Coleridge and Archer; but in nearly two centuries there emerged not one single playwright whose works display the timelessness and universality of vision, the breadth of humanity, the beauty of language and the basic knowledge of stage-craft which might entitle him to a place in the pantheon of the world's great artists.

I shall not embark upon a history of the British theatre since 1700, but it may be of interest to try to discern the groundswell of taste and fashion which produced that debased form of theatre we know as melodrama. The word, derived from the French *mélo-drame*, music-drama, tells us nothing, being merely a convenient nomenclature.

We might begin, therefore, with the masques, pageants and ballet-spectacles of the seventeenth century whose huge casts, lavish settings and mechanical ingenuities were to be emulated in the increasing number of public auditoria being built to accommodate a rising population. While the drama still retained some pretensions to a high style, the aristocracy continued to patronise the theatres both publicly and privately – the Augustan age of neo-classicism was at its height.

However, the grandeur of Racine and Corneille and the felicities of

Molière, Dryden, Vanburgh, Congreve, Wycherley and Farquhar had little appeal to the newly affluent, semi-educated middle classes. This potential new audience had to be served, and so a simpler, more directly emotional and overtly sentimental type of play appeared, allied to spectacle and sensationalism.

This new form of drama was given impetus by the Romantic movement, and by the end of the eighteenth century had crystallised into the melodrama, a species of entertainment based upon the concept of man as an individual rather than an abstraction of ideas or philosophies. The Age of Reason, the new view of man in relation to society expounded by Diderot and Rousseau, brought about a softening of attitudes, a humanitarianism and egalitarianism which signified the approach of modern man at last beginning to shed his medieval savagery and blind intolerance. The Unities and the classical models were discarded: emphasis was now laid upon the protagonist as a personality with whom an audience could in some measure identify, while the story-line became more important than the language of expression.

Burlesque, extravaganza, 'realism' – this was the taste of the new bourgeoisie, as were plays which presented 'ordinary' people in domestic situations, strong plots, violence and broad humour, villainy confounded and happy endings. Materialism conquered art; rationalistic hedonism permeated down to the boards of our theatres, and left them impoverished.

Debility of the drama

What further reasons may be offered to account for the all-pervading mediocrity of the drama in those days? What were the prevailing conditions which inhibited the emergence of a dramatist of acknowledged stature?

The increasing size of public theatres, built without the benefits of modern lighting equipment and with little regard to acoustic principles encouraged the dominance of the personality actor with a consequent coarsening of style. Thespian despots of the day could be relied upon to destroy the balance of any play whose central role was not in their opinion central enough – whole scenes would be cut and transposed to accommodate these giant egos.

Allied to the uncertainty attendant upon the presentation of any play was the extra hazard of the claques, those bands of hired men and boys paid to applaud one piece and/or to boo another. Added to these bizarries were the antics of the Press, as egregious then as now. To be fair, the twentieth century critic expects little more than a couple of free seats and a drink or two now and again, but in the late eighteenth and early nineteenth centuries a play stood little chance of a favourable puff unless hard cash had changed hands.

Nor must we overlook the activities of the examiner of plays.* His sensitivities were increased ten-fold by the advent of the French Revolution which caused him ruthlessly to emasculate any tendencies to radicalism, real or imagined, in works laid before him for his imprimatur. Hand in hand with respect for authority went respect for religion – established religion, that is. No taint of free-thinking was permissible, for atheism was but another manifestation of the revolutionary philosophies sweeping Europe.

The prudery of the age also conspired against the playwright's freedom of expression. However notorious the private life of the governing classes (the Duke of Clarence† had no fewer than ten illegitimate children by Mrs Jordan, an actress) the general public had to be protected from any possible source of corruption – and indeed, the general public was happy to be so protected. Any theatrical management foolish enough to present anything on its stage offensive to the current moral code would find a riot on its hands; the proprieties had to be observed, and so erring husbands must die, villains must be foiled, duplicity must be unmasked.

A further and by no means unimportant consideration regarding the stultifying of the British drama was the monopoly of the Patent Houses. Until 1843 only the Drury Lane and Covent Garden Theatres (and later the Haymarket) and the various Theatres Royal in certain fashionable provincial towns were officially permitted to mount what we would today designate as 'straight' plays.‡

Finally, there was a lack of financial incentive for the erstwhile playwright which made publication of novels and poems a far more attractive proposition. It was not for many years that adequate copyright protection was to be enjoyed by playwrights, and even then it was very imperfect.

So the lyrical writers of the nineteenth century contented themselves with their odes and idylls and closet dramas (intended solely for private reading); exposure to the perils of commercial staging and the scrutiny of the mob laid the sensitive author open to the risk of public derision and private mortification, not to mention lampoons in the journals and the inevitable burlesques.

The theatre, therefore, was proscribed, with no self-respecting bellettrist bothering himself with the drama beyond heaving the occasional deep sigh for the splendours of the Elizabethan era. This desertion of the stage by a nation's literati left the way clear for the hacks,

---

*From 1841 the licensing of plays was brought under the control of the Lord Chamberlain

†Reigned from 1830 until 1837 as William IV. He was Victoria's immediate predecessor

‡See Appendix A for full details

17

the adaptors, the translators, the arrangers, the re-write men – those parasites and parasites of parasites whose greatest achievement was to evolve a form of presentation which will be forever equated with the banal, the superficial, the shoddy and the plain ridiculous. Trite sentiments, artificial pathos, circumscribed characterisation, and second-hand plots trotted out time and time again must have made playgoing a painful experience for the quality – much as Striptease or Rugby League football are looked down upon today by the more genteel elements in our society.

It would be wrong of me to imply, however, that the classical tradition was entirely lost, just as it would be wrong to term as melodrama all plays written in the first three-quarters of the nineteenth century. Joanna Baillie, Sheridan Knowles, Robert Browning and Lord Lytton would have been highly incensed at their plays being included in this category. These and other missionary-writers continued in a worthy attempt to revive the poetic drama. Successful as they were at the time (Lytton especially so) their dull earnestness and yardage of clumping, if highminded, poetry preclude any chance of a revival of their plays today. Less successful, even at the time, were Wordsworth, Keats, Shelley and Byron – all poets whose merits do not need to be elaborated by me, but whose talents did not extend to the stage. True, Tennyson's *Becket* was one of Irving's most popular roles to the end of his career, but even this tragedy was billed as 'adapted for the stage by Henry Irving'.

The sad conclusion is that, despite occasional endeavours, the collective genius of English poesy failed to bring about a new glory to the British stage, and all we remember of nineteenth-century drama today are half a dozen melodramas, and a handful of plays by Shaw, Pinero, and Wilde.

Sources

Until the very end of the century critics were complaining of the number of translations from the French which occupied British stages* – a complaint which goes some way to explain the remarkable fertility of the early melodramatists and farceurs such as Planché, the Dibdins, Burnand, H J Byron and J B Buckstone.† Authors regularly travelled to Paris to view and buy copies of the latest successes, usually by Guilbert de Pixérécourt, Eugène Scribe or Cuvelier de Trie. These would be rapidly translated (sometimes during the journey home) and put into production in London within a matter of days. From Germany, Goethe, Schiller and August von Kotzebue also provided much material for British 'play-

---

*Shaw's well-known gibe about 'Sardoodledum' is apposite

†It should be appreciated that burlesques, operettas, farces, etc, were generally of short duration, lasting for only one act – say, forty-five minutes or so

18

wrights' in bowdlerised and vulgarised versions. Not that this traffic was all one way. Continental dramatists would visit London on the same piratical mission, and it was by no means rare for translations of translations to reappear in the country of origin.

This wholesale plagiarism can partly be accounted for by the lack of any copyright provisions for plays in performance (not until 1833 were dramatists protected by Act of Parliament within this country, and not until 1887 was a form of international agreement reached) and by the shortness of runs, which were reckoned in days rather than weeks. A resident writer, therefore, in order to maintain his quota of two dozen or more pieces annually had to grub around for ideas and inspiration wherever he could find them. The frontispiece shows a threadbare dramatist with a huge load of stock ingredients trying ineffectually (despite his two whips and triple spurs) to force the Ass of Melodrama up the foothills of Art. The rider's desperation shows that the search for material was a matter of survival, and for the dramatist without the comparative security of a regular weekly wage the situation was even harder.

Novelists were fair game: Scott and Dickens, Dumas père et fils, and Hugo, were perhaps the most popular – in 1819 six separate versions of *Ivanhoe* were mounted and the following year *Kenilworth* was dramatised by no fewer than seven authors. Even opera libretti – scarcely the most promising bases for plays – were pressed into service. Not that the novelists lost out entirely by this mass rape of their works, for the interest thus aroused stimulated sales just as televised 'classics' do today.

Early Greek and Roman writings were also rifled to provide plots – only Holy Writ remained inviolate due to the religious sensibilities of the time. Nor have I been able to discover any early adaptations of Jane Austen's novels for the stage, but then her style is so anti-Romantic and her plots so enclosed that they must have defeated even the most practised hack's attempts to throw in the odd cliff-top rescue or educated horse.

Staging

All accounts of the eighteenth century theatre, and for long after, indicate that a play performance was more akin to a recital. If one admits entrances and exits to Handelian oratorio (itself an opera form designed to circumvent the prohibition on impersonation of Scriptural figures) and imagines the dramatis personae speaking instead of singing, the manner of staging plays at this time is, I believe, approximated.

Lighting, such as it was, remained full up both on stage and in the auditorium; long speeches were delivered as arias down-stage centre where was suspended the largest candelabrum; costuming made only the slightest concessions to character or period – even Garrick, considered a radical in many ways, played Brutus in a bag-wig.

Scenery consisted basically of a back-cloth and side wings set in grooves parallel to the footlights. Cloths were struck in the usual manner, by being raised and lowered or wound up on a roller; the wings were simply slid in and out of their grooves, which were fixed overhead as well as at stage level. The tables and chairs and other dressings were set and struck by breeched and bewigged footmen, whose presence was by convention regarded as non-existent – the notion of dropping a house-curtain between acts or a front cloth between scenes to hide changes came in response to the demand for more 'realism'.

Gas-lighting and the limelight began to appear in London theatres, first in the auditorium and then on stage, in the 1820's;* electricity, first employed wholly to light a theatre in this country at the Savoy in 1882, saw the introduction of the noisy, smoke-and-fume belching arc-light as well as chances for hitherto impossible lighting effects. Not that gas-lighting was inflexible by any means. Irving, whose productions were celebrated for their beauty and imaginative use of lighting, preferred it by far to electricity, and on returning from his first American tour to find electric lighting installed at the Lyceum had gas reinstated. But in those days of cheap labour he could afford to employ as many as *forty* gasmen as well as the usual small army of scene-shifters.†

Explosions, noises off, coloured fire, 'engines', trap-doors, flying-wires and gauzes were all part of the stock-in-trade of melodrama, besides distracting from the tattiness of the scenery. Contemporary accounts are full of complaints concerning the use of stock scenes time and time again, year after year, so that whatever merit they might have possessed (and the excellence of scenic artists in England was acknowledged throughout Europe) would be obscured by finger-marks, candle-soot and the grime of ages. The Palace Scene, Castle Scene, Cottage Scene, Forest Scene, etc., etc. would all be achingly familiar to habitueés of a particular play-house.

But improvements in lighting, the dawning concept of direction and ensemble playing, longer runs and an ever-increasing demand for realism and 'truth', a growing sophistication on both sides of the proscenium and innovations in mechanical effects; all these caused stage-management to reach its apotheosis in the staggeringly ornate settings of Irving and Tree, by which time the pendulum had swung so far over that the text was often swamped by the *mise-en-scène*.

---

*Although Drury Lane boasted full gas illumination throughout in 1817

†It was Irving who first questioned the value of footlights (or 'floats', so-called from the floating of burning wicks in a trough of oil), and instituted the practice of darkening the auditorium completely during a performance, thus putting into operation Nicola Sabbatini's suggestions of over three hundred years earlier

Planché's reforms of stage dress, décor and design were enthusiastically taken up by Charles Kemble, Charles Kean, Charles Mathews and Madame Vestris (Mrs Mathews), but it was not until the end of the century that the minor London and provincial theatres accepted that the provision of period clothes and accessories should be the responsibility of the management and not at the charge of the wretchedly under- (and irregularly) paid actor. In the provincial repertory movement in this country it was not until 1970 that British Equity finally convinced managements that they should provide modern dress for their contract artists also.

The performance of melodrama

A live performance, whether it be opera, music hall, ballet, circus, recital or play, is virtually impossible to recreate in print no matter how experienced the observer and no matter how fine his penmanship. For in a criticism, commentary or memoir the performance is offered at second-hand, filtered through another's attitudes, preconceptions, prejudices. Max Beerbohm's celebrated theatre columns are a joy to read,* but at the same time the reader is aware of an impish, mischievous scepticism which is perhaps at times more than a touch unfair to the plays and players whose efforts he was recording.

This is, I am aware, a commonplace remark, but I make it here to explain my disagreement with the current inclination to dismiss all nineteenth century acting as unintelligent, overemphasied, self-indulgent and creakingly slow. In a word: ham. But I would like to posit that there were ever good actors and bad actors, and to proceed on the assumption that the performance of melodrama was an enterprise capable of excellence of execution as much as any other.

Laboured delivery of dialogue in an over-elocuted manner did indeed occur very often, perhaps in a pathetic attempt by third-rate provincial actors to ape the speech of polite society; the slow speed and careful separation of syllables may in some measure be accounted for by inadequate lighting and the lack of microphones in large auditoria – all actors know that audiences to a large extent lip-read and that lines delivered off-stage have to be given at a slower pace and with extra clarity.

Irving's Hamlet at first disconcerted by its underplaying, but the breadth of the conception became apparent as his intellectual vision unfolded and his emotional resources were slowly revealed. 'Well might the people shout, for an ideal Hamlet had been found at last . . . there could be no question of the success, for here was such a Hamlet as had never been seen before, and only vaguely dreamed of . . . in a word, no

*Some of these are collected into *Around Theatres*, 1924

such actor and no such performance have been seen in our time'.* This was no ham.

The manner of play presentation in those days may seem to us now to be primitive, but this need not invalidate the stature of the great names of the past. They were artists worthy of the name, true for their time and age. A parallel may be drawn with music-making. An orchestral performance in, say, 1800 would seem to our ears a sorry affair. There would be no conductor, the woodwind intonation would be excruciating and the string bowing unco-ordinated. Just as in the theatre, rehearsals were minimal, and the result not infrequently led to total disarray. We do not know with absolute certainty what tempi the great composers of the past intended for their works – we cannot even be sure of the pitch in which they were performed. But if we are willing to accept that instrumental players of genius existed in the past, why should we not admit the possibility of a supreme stage player or two? If a great figure looms sufficiently large above the surrounding mediocrity, the world will beat a path to his door – even if he has the proverbial mouse-trap maker as his landlord.

If we were to see Irving act today we should possibly find him slow, mannered and painfully obvious in his striving for 'points' – but I am convinced that we should not care, for we should be coerced into willing acceptance of any technical extravagances by the power of the actor's rock-hard certainty of purpose. A superhuman will-power would envelope and vanquish us, and we would submit with a sigh.†

To be exposed to a psyche of such stature is an overwhelming and humbling experience. I have never really recovered from first seeing Richardson's transcendental performance in *Flowering Cherry*. Quite what he did and how he did it I cannot say, but I came out of the Haymarket a changed man. Such an actor has seemingly been allotted a larger quantum of humanity than is the ordinary mortal's portion; such an actor, whether it be in Greek tragedy or Transpontine melodrama,‡ gently unites us into a form of communion with each other and with his

---

*This quotation is from *Henry Irving, a Biographical Sketch* (1883), the first of several books by Austin Brereton on Irving and his family. Brereton does not give the name of the critic, simply describing him as 'well-known'

†The 1888 cylinder recording of Irving speaking Lewis's *The Maniac*, recently discovered in the bowels of Broadcasting House by Richard Bebb and Bennett Maxwell shows, however, that Irving's delivery was remarkably modern in its speed and understatement

‡Transpontine – across the bridge. A reference to the theatres on the South Side of the Thames famous in the early nineteenth century for their melodramas, principally the Surrey in Blackfriars Road and the Royal Coburg in Waterloo Road

own universality of spirit; for a magical hour or two we are invited to take our place on Olympus and to share in a mystical rite: the examination of and judgement upon a fellow-creature – albeit one whose existence is insubstantial, but a creature very real to those of us fortunate enough to be in the presence of a great actor as he fleshes out a role and gives it life. He is a god at such times, and we can share in his divinity for the price of a ticket.

Am I pitching it a little strongly to imply that this level of achievement can be reached in the performance of poor, slandered, traduced melodrama? Perhaps so, but if we take the argument down a notch or two I think it is relevant. In *On The Stage – and Off* (1883) Jerome K Jerome speaks of the time he was a member of a third-rate stock company in a small East Anglian town. A star (yes, the term was in use then) joined them as guest artist for one week.

'He infused a new spirit into everybody, and, when he was on the stage, the others acted better than I should ever have thought they could have done. It is the first time I have played with anyone who can properly be called an actor . . .' Who this actor was and what were the plays performed Jerome does not tell us, but the point is made that a great or even a good actor can illuminate a poor text and surmount an indifferent production, so let us not sneer too readily at the memory of the player of melodrama.

Decline of the Melodrama

It must be admitted, however, that the very word 'melodrama' is nowadays used as a term of contempt, not without justification, for anything which appears excessively full-blooded and without logical motivation. Today we look for truth, naturalism, reality in our dramas (and in our comedies, for that matter) forgetting that to a Georgian audience the new genre of play which we now derogate as melodrama *was* valid for the very attributes just cited, *viz.* truth, naturalism and reality. Melodrama presented ordinary people in ordinary milieux, even if the plots were unnaturally enlivened by untoward and arbitrary violence, crime, catastrophe or war – but without these ingredients, it was argued, there would be no conflict and therefore no play.

Latter-day tastes have improved, we believe. We now have a much truer insight into and understanding of the human condition. Freud has made amateur psychologists of us all, so now we demand identifiable persons in credible situations rather than cyphers in mechanically event-ridden plots. But the lack of any elevating influences allowed the meretricious tendencies of melodrama to become so entrenched as to be virtually immutable, suffering the inevitable atrophy of any fixed principle. In the late eighteenth and early nineteenth centuries the world of letters missed the opportunity, as we have discussed, to engender a new Golden Age in the British Theatre, and so the melodrama, instead of being just a passing aberration, became a century-long watershed in our dramatic culture. Had Shaw been born a hundred years earlier the story might have been very different.

So I do not for one minute attempt to deny the divers shortcomings of the genre – it would be foolish to attempt to do so – nor am I pleading for a return to the egregious drama of the nineteenth century, but I am sure that I am not alone in professing an occasional hankering for the simple, unabashed twopence-coloured entrancement of the sensation-play. As Michael Booth says in his *English Melodrama* (1965): 'As long as people enjoy uncomplicated characters, thrilling situations, throbbing emotions, and happy endings, as long as they are willing to lose themselves in a dream world of the imagination corresponding to their own reality, melodrama in one form or another will never cease to appeal.'

One feature of melodrama which I will pass over rapidly is its humour. The height of wit seemed to have been ignorance in rustics and the all-conquering pun. Puns by the bucketful, delivered in heavy slogging rhyme were rained down upon British audiences, who, it must be admitted, seemed to enjoy them. The humour was very decorous too, of course, which makes the tedium even more insupportable when reading the plays today. The final word on this painful subject I will leave to one of the most popular and successful nineteenth century writers of comedy, farce and burlesque, James Robinson Planché. This short quotation says it all:

> '*And I do not regret that upon every occasion I endeavoured to point a moral, though my abilities might not enable me to tell a tale*'. ('Recollections', *vol ii, pp 147*)

One significant event leading to a breach in the wall of neo-Eliza-bethan poetic dramas, bowdlerised Shakespeare and catchpenny melodramas was the breaking of the Patent Theatres monopoly in 1843, which allowed our classical drama past, present (for what it was worth) and future (for what it might become) to be freed from the hands of all those well-meaning but amateurish boards and committees, and the vulgarian commercial managers such as F B Chatterton at Covent Garden, Augustus Harris at Drury Lane, and, earlier, the notorious Alfred Bunn who for a time controlled both houses. Harris's productions were the most overblown, crudely splendid melodramas and pantomimes ever; had the legitimate drama's shackles not been loosed before his rise to power, the classical theatre in this country might have sunk without trace.

Queen Victoria's enthusiasm for and encouragement of the theatre (at least until Albert's death in 1861); the disappearance of the pit and its attendant rowdiness; the perennial fires which led to a plethora of LCC safety regulations, in turn leading to much rebuilding and refurbishing of theatres in accordance with the latest ideas of elegance, fashion and comfort – these were three more contributions to the renaissance of the serious drama.

Nor should the influence of Irving be underestimated. Despite all his well-rehearsed deficiences as a regisseur – notably by Shaw* – he remains unquestionably the greatest figure on the nineteenth century British stage. His cast-iron integrity and artistic probity commanded respect and reassured the cultured elements of society that the theatre could once again be respectable. His standards of discipline and concept of the dramatic performance as an ensemble enterprise, although anticipated by Planché, Boucicault and Charles Kean, helped very materially in bringing a resurgence of educated interest in and reacceptance of the drama as a valid art form.

The association of T W Robertson and the Bancrofts also represents a milestone in the history of 'stage-management' with their carefully orchestrated and minutely rehearsed 'cup-and-saucer' comedies.† In their day, *Caste, Ours, Society, Home, Play, School*, were regarded as the ultimate in stage realism – melodrama's realism existed merely in real waterfalls and real horses, a realism much easier by far to achieve and culturally valueless. Robertson's plays, and to a lesser but still important extent those of Tom Taylor, were the first to examine a theme, to pose a problem, and – provocatively for the times – to strike an attitude. All of these developments paved the way for Ibsen and Tchekov, stoutly championed by Shaw, to be eventually admitted to our stages, and the modernist movement was under way.‡

Conclusion

Not that melodrama succumbed without a fight. Quite the reverse, it became more and more extravagant. But the colossal spectacles at Drury Lane and the excesses of the Melville Brothers at the Standard, the Terriss, the Elephant and Castle, all appear now as the frantic convulsions of a dying giant. Like the dinosaur, melodrama was finally overcome by its own size and unwieldiness.

And now the melodrama, with its directness, its self-assurance, and its unblushing theatricality, is dead, regretted by many but mourned by few. When such titles as *The Worst Woman in London, The Girl Who*

---

*Shaw respected Irving as an actor, however, and intended *The Man Of Destiny* for him, a role which Irving unfortunately never played

†W S Gilbert, who deserves an honourable place in any account of stage-management, regarded Robertson as its founder

‡Although by no means without opposition. In 1891 Clement Scott wrote in the *Daily Telegraph*: 'Our literary drama may be as bare as Mother Hubbard's cupboard but we would sooner have none than any feeble imitation of *Ghosts* . . .'

Wrecked His Home, *The Monk And The Woman*, and *The Bad Girl of The Family* started to appear on London's playbills, the end was in sight, and the last desperate agony was mercifully not prolonged.

Was the melodrama totally devoid of intrinsic value? Was it wholly beneath contempt? Despite its falsity, its bombast, its cheapness, its rhodomontade, I think not. Nature, we are assured, abhors a vacuum; we had the theatres, the actors and a public demanding diversion. What we did not have were the playwrights, and so melodrama rushed in where poesy feared to tread.

The hunger for dramatic expression is as old as man. In our own times we can see primitive tribes in remote jungles performing re-enactments of ancestral legends, just as our own classical drama is founded in the religious observances of Attica in honour of Dionysius. To some extent we can still regard the melodrama in performance as a quasi-religious experience. In both the language is stiffly rhetorical and archaic, the format circumscribed, the outcome pre-ordained. Even the objectives are the same – to uplift the spirit, to inculcate Christian ideals, and to reinforce belief in the Divinity. The 1870's saw this surreptitious religiosity burst out in a rash of hothouse sanctimony, often spiced with sexual undertones, with such breathlessly titled plays as *The New Magdalen*, *The Golden Ladder*, *The Tempter*, *Michael And His Lost Angel*, *Saints And Sinners*, and of course *The Sign Of The Cross*. These dire dramas of flabby Christianity demonstrate how directly the stage hero had become identified with the Saviour, the heroine with His Bride (i.e. the Church and its members), and the villain with Satan.

Can the melodrama be taken, therefore, as a last gesture of Christian defiance in the path of creeping scepticism, materialism and agnosticism? It is significant that the demise of melodrama coincided with a growing apathy towards religion in the West – we are more concerned with humanity than spirituality; we no longer care if a heroine loses her honour yet lives happily ever after; we are no longer obsessed with the notion that behaviour is either good or bad, for we now recognise that there is an infinity of shades between these two extremes.

The rubrics of Church and melodrama both offered warmth and heart's-ease, security and comfort, and, in equating the cathartic release of the melodrama's last-act climax with the recurrent climax of the Eucharistic ritual, an opportunity for sublimation of the passions.

For Man needs ritual. The dismay among the Roman Catholic laity over the dismantling of their traditional rite of the Tridentine Mass shows how deeply ingrained this need can be; we all want to be reassured of our reality and meaningfulness as individuals in a society. To do this we must join with our fellow-creatures in some form of corporate ceremony of witness in which together we can reaffirm the order of things and the validity of our existence.

This the melodrama provided, and it was a not ignoble service.

A Tale
of Mystery

THOMAS HOLCROFT

Thomas Holcroft, by
John Opie, R.A.
(*National Portrait
Gallery*)

THOMAS HOLCROFT (1745/1809)

The Gothic ingredients of *A Tale of Mystery* were very much to the
taste of the late Georgian times. The novels of Horace Walpole, Ann
Radcliffe and Matthew 'Monk' Lewis were full of haunted castles, craggy
mountains lit by flashes of lightning, sinister forests enveloped in gloom,
and horrors of the most blood-curdling description set against a vaguely
Calabrian background. These thriller stories were runaway bestsellers
in England, and were enthusiastically adapted for the stage in Germany
and France, thus giving rise to a whole new dramatic idiom which
returned to England as the melodrama.

Holcroft's *A Tale of Mystery* is generally taken to be the first of the
genre in this country, and is itself an adaptation of *Coelina; ou, L'Enfant*

28

du Mystère by Pixérécourt, who might be described as the father of melodrama. Holcroft, according to Allardyce Nicoll*, recognised in Pixérécourt's work not so much a new form of the drama as a perfection of what he and others had been aiming at for some years. This 'perfection' was the combination of thrilling plot (often involving the supernatural), rudimentary character types and basic conflict between the forces of light and darkness, plus virtually continuous musical accompaniment.

Thomas Holcroft was born in Leicester Fields, London; his father (also Thomas) was a shoemaker-cum-itinerant peddlar. Thomas junior worked as a stableboy, cobbler, and at one time attempted to set up as a teacher with his own school, having somehow acquired an education. His voracious appetite for learning led to the study of literature and languages (he was competent in French, German and Italian) and to the world of journalism. He wrote for numerous journals and published several novels, tracts, poems and narratives of all kinds. His celebrated *Memoirs* were completed after his death by his close friend William Hazlitt and published in three volumes in 1816.

His involvement with the stage was due to a chance introduction to Charles Macklin, who engaged him as prompter at a Dublin theatre in 1770. Returning to England the following year he acted with a number of provincial strolling companies until 1778, when he obtained an engagement at Drury Lane as an actor at £1 per week. Here in the same year his first piece for the stage (he was to write some 30 in all) was performed. This was a comic opera entitled *The Crisis; or Love and Fear*, to music by T Attwood, which received but one solitary performance. His first success as a dramatist came six years later when, as Paris correspondent for the *Morning Herald* he saw Beaumarchais' *Mariage de Figaro* a sufficiently frequent number of times to be able to offer a memorised translation to Covent Garden, where it was enthusiastically received on December 14th, 1784, under the title of *The Follies Of A Day*. Holcroft himself played Figaro – due to the absence of the leading actor – but this would seem to have been his last appearance on stage. From *Follies* Holcroft received £600 as well as a substantial sum for the publishing copyright. His best and most celebrated play, *The Road To Ruin*, was produced at Covent Garden in 1792 and became a stock piece – it was still being revived over a century later. Although the evils of gambling were the overt target in this tragi-comedy, its prologue extolled the freedom of man and equality of all classes and races.

Holcroft was a political animal and one of Nature's radicals. Although opposed to violence he embraced the principles of the French Revolution, and in 1792 joined the Society for Constitutional Information which led to his imprisonment two years later, along with Thomas Hardy and ten others, on an indictment for high treason. After two months in Newgate gaol, he was brought up at the Old Bailey and discharged with-

* A History of English Drama, vol iv, p 81

ADVERTISEMENT

For the first published edition of *A Tale of Mystery* **1820**

There are few pleasures so great, or so pure, as that of being able, by a well told tale, to fix the attention, rouse the passions, and hold the faculties in anxious and impatient suspense. This pleasure is increased in proportion as the Spectators of a Drama, or the Readers of a Narrative, are known to be numerous. When multitudes agree in sentiment, and sympathise in feeling, when they pronounce with equal fervor, and applaud with unanimous warmth, the enjoyment of such general praise becomes intoxicating. In the Drama, forgetting how many Claimants there are, who must divide among them the merit that is due to the whole, the Poet is but too apt to attribute to himself effects, which are the result of a great combination of talents

Had not the applause bestowed by the Public on the following Piece been uncommon, such a train of thoughts would scarcely have occurred. Ready, however, as an Author may be, to think too highly of himself, I hope this error, in the present instance, has not been egregious. I cannot forget the aid I received from the French Drama, from which the

out trial. The notoriety surrounding his name caused several of his pieces to be advertised and published without his name, and in 1799 he left the country for four years. It was during this self-imposed exile that *A Tale Of Mystery* was first seen at Covent Garden (with Thomas Busby's music), and was pronounced by Genest to be 'the first and best of those *mélo-drames* with which the stage was afterwards inundated'.*

The non-speaking character of Francisco would have been familiar to contemporary audiences, due to the patent houses monopoly of the legitimate drama. Other theatres were obliged to present only plays which included vocal music and/or dances in the action – a rough assessment of the minimum permissible quantity would be five songs per act, thus satisfying the law by converting the piece into an opera or burletta.† Alternatively a management could circumvent the law by presenting mime plays. The Royal Circus (later renamed the Surrey Theatre) in particular was renowned for its dumb-show plays, essential

---

*An Account Of The English Stage (1832) vol vii, p 579

†See Appendix A

principal incidents, many of the thoughts, and much of the manner of telling the story, are derived. I exerted myself to select and unite masterly sketches, that were capable of forming an excellent picture; and the attempt has not failed.

I can as little overlook the Performers, the Composer of the Music, the Scenery, and the Dances; all which, in representation, have so essentially contributed to success. I acknowledge their respective aid with pleasure. The performers, especially, have displayed uncommon brilliancy of talent: but, however grateful my thoughts, I dare not venture to mention individuals, lest the persons not named should think themselves neglected. Beside, in order to be just, he that praises must examine and discriminate; and this is not the place for a dissertation on the dramatic Art. I, therefore, can but repeat my sincere tribute of commendation to all, and thankfully avow the efficacy of the support I have received.

I should be tempted to say something of the nature, powers, and scenic effects of the Melo-Drame; but that my thoughts must necessarily be given with too much brevity and haste. Other Dramatic writers will certainly produce these effects in a much more mature and perfect state; and of the pleasures they yield I shall be happy to partake.

dialogue being indicated to the audience by the use of captions painted on large scrolls displayed at the appropriate time.*

Holcroft returned to England in 1803 and set up a printing business with his brother-in-law; this was a complete failure, but with unabated energy he poured out plays (mostly comedies), adaptations, translations, biographies, travel diaries, novels, essays, articles and poems. Much of his fortune was dissipated by rash speculation and by a mania for 'picture-dealing' so that he was in a permanent state of financial embarrassment.

Thomas Holcroft married four times. His son by his second wife, William, committed suicide at the age of sixteen after robbing him of £40. One of his two daughters, Fanny, wrote several novels and translations, and his widow, Louisa Mercier, married the dramatist James Kenney. He appears to have been a stern and irascible but conscientious man, and Charles Lamb described him as 'one of the most candid, upright, and single-minded men' he had ever known. He died after a long illness at Clipstone Street, Marylebone, on March 23rd, 1809 at the age of 63.

---

*See Michael Booth's *English Melodrama* pp 69–73

Charley Farley as Francisco in 'A Tale of Mystery'.
Samuel de Wilde. (*Enthoven Collection*)

A TALE
OF MYSTERY

Dramatis Personae

First performed at Covent Garden
November 13th, 1802

Bonamo by Mr Murray
Romaldi by Mr H Johnston
Francisco by Mr Farley
Stephano by Mr Brunton
Montano by Mr Clermont
Michelli by Mr Blanchard
Malvoglio by Mr Cory
Piero by Mr Simmons
Exempt by Mr Beverly
1st Gardener by Mr Abbot
2nd Gardener by Mr Trueman
Selina by Mrs Gibbs
Fiametta by Mrs Mattocks
Peasants
Musicians
Dancers

The Music by Dr Busby

The Dances by Messrs Bologna *jun,* Dubois, *and* Byrnes

The Scenery by Messrs Phillips *and* Lupino

The Dresses by Mr Dick *and* Mrs Egan

A TALE OF MYSTERY

Act 1

Scene 1
A hall in the house of Bonamo. Music, to express discontent and alarm

Enter Selina and Fiametta

Selina You seem hurried, Fiametta?
Fiametta Hurricd, truly! Yes, yes; and you'll be hurried too.
Selina I?
Fiametta Fine news!
Selina Of what kind?
Fiametta A very bad kind. The Count Romaldi—
Selina (*Alarmed*) What of him?
Fiametta Is coming.
Selina When?
Fiametta This evening.
Seleina Heavens! What can he want?
Fiametta Want? He wants mischief. We all know he wants you to marry his son, because you're a rich heiress.
Selina Surely, my uncle will never consent?
Fiametta Your uncle and all Savoy fear him.
Bonamo (*Calling without*) Fiametta!
Fiametta I am here, sir.
Bonamo But I want you here.
Fiametta Lord, sir, I am busy.
Selina Go, run to my uncle.
Fiametta It's a shame that he should not think of marrying you to his own son; when he knows how dearly you love each other.
Bonamo (*Without*) Fiametta, I say!
Fiametta (*Going*) Coming! (*Exit*)

Enter Stephano, with his fowling-piece, net, and game

Selina Why are you so late, Stephano? I had a thousand alarms.

35

Stephano   Forgive me, dear Selina. The pursuit of game led me too far among the mountains.

Selina   Do you know –

Stephano   What?

Selina   I almost dread to tell you. Count Romaldi is coming.

Stephano   Romaldi!

Selina   I shudder, when I recollect the selfishness of his views, and the violence of his character.

Stephano   Add, the wickedness of his heart

Enter Bonamo and Fiametta

Fiametta   I tell you again, sir, it is uncharitable, it is cruel, it is hard-hearted in you.

Bonamo   Have not I a right to do as I please in my own house?

Fiametta   No, sir; you have no right to do wrong anywhere.

Stephano   What is the dispute, sir?

Fiametta   He has ordered me to turn the poor Francisco out of doors; because, forsooth, the house is not large enough to hold this Count Romaldi.

Selina   Think, my dear uncle, how grateful and kind is his heart!

Stephano   And that he is a man of misfortune.

Bonamo   Folly and misfortune are twins: nobody can tell one from the other.

Selina   His manners are so mild!

Fiametta   I'll be bound, he is of genteel parentage!

Bonamo   Who told you so?

Fiametta   Not he, himself, for certain; because poor creature he is dumb. But only observe his sorrowful looks. What it is I don't know, but there is something on his mind so –

Bonamo   You certainly know more, concerning this man?

Fiametta   Since it must be told, I do.

Bonamo   Then speak.

Fiametta   It is now seven or eight years ago, when, you having sent me to Chambery, I was coming home. It was almost dark; every thing was still; I was winding along the dale, and the rocks were all as it were turning black. Of a sudden, I heard cries! A man was murdering! I shook from head to foot! Presently, the cries died away; and I beheld two bloody men, with their daggers in their hands, stealing off under the crags at the foot of the mill. I stood like a stone: for I was frightened out of my wits! So I thought I heard groans; and, *afeared* as I was, I had the sense to think they must come from the poor murdered creature. So I listened, and followed my ears, and presently I saw this very man –

Selino   Francisco?

Fiametta   Weltring in his blood! To be sure I screamed and called loud enough: for, what could I do by myself? So presently my cries *was*

36

heard; and honest Michelli the miller, with his man, came running.

Bonamo   I now remember the tale. The poor man recovered; and everybody praised Michelli.

Fiametta   So they ought; he is an honest good soul! What then, Sir, can you suppose I thought, when, about a week ago, I again saw Francisco standing before me; making signs, that he was famished with hunger and thirst. If you had *seen* his clasped hands, and his thankful looks, and his dumb notes, and his signs of joy, at having found me! So turn him out of doors, if you have the heart.

Stephano   Fiametta, you wrong my father.

Bonamo   I'll hear his story from himself.

Fiametta   He can't speak.

Bonamo   But he can write.

Fiametta   I warrant him. I'm sure he's a gentleman.

Bonamo   Bring him here: if he prove himself an honest man, I am his friend.

Fiametta   I know that, or you should be no master of mine. (*Exit*)

Stephano   His kind attentions to Selina are singular.

Selina   Every morning, I find him waiting for me with fresh gathered flowers; which he offers with such modest yet affectionate looks!

Fiametta returns with Francisco

Bonamo   Come near, friend. You understand his gestures, Fiametta; so stay where you are.

Fiametta   I intend it.

Bonamo   (*To himself*) He has a manly form, a benevolent eye! (*Aloud*) Sit down, Sir. There is pen, ink, and paper: when you cannot answer by signs, write; but be strict to the truth.

Francisco   (*With dignity points to heaven and his heart*).

Bonamo   Who are you?

Francisco writes; and Stephano, standing behind him, takes up the paper and reads the answers

Francisco   'A noble Roman!'

Bonamo   Your family? –

Francisco   'Must not be known'.

Bonamo   Why?

Francisco   'It is disgraced'.

Bonamo   By you?

Francisco   (*Gesticulates*).

Fiametta   (*Interpreting*) No, no, no!

Bonamo   Who made you dumb?

Francisco   'The Algerines'.

37

Bonamo   How came you in their power?
Francisco   'By treachery'.
Bonamo   Do you know the traitors?
Francisco   (*Gesticulates*).
Fiametta   (*Eagerly*) He does! He does!
Bonamo   Who are they?
Francisco   'The same who stabbed me among the rocks'. (*A general expression of horror*).
Bonamo   Name them.
Francisco   (*Gesticulates violently, denoting painful recollection; then writes*) 'Never!'
Bonamo   Are they known by me?
Fiametta   (*Interpreting*) They are, they are!
Bonamo   Are they rich?
Francisco   'Rich and powerful'.
Bonamo   Astonishing! Your refusal to name them gives strange suspicions. I must know more: tell me all, or quit my house.

Enter Piero

Piero   Count Romaldi, Sir.
Francisco   (*Starts up, struck with alarm*).
Stephano   So soon!
Bonamo   Shew him up.
Piero   He's here (*Similar music*).

Romaldi suddenly enters, as Francisco is attempting to pass the door: they start back at the sight of each other. Romaldi recovers himself; and Francisco, in an agony of mind, leaves the room

Bonamo   What is all this! – Where is he gone? – Call him back, Fiametta!

Exeunt Fiametta and Stephano; both regarding Romaldi with dislike

Romaldi   (*With forced ease*) At length, my good friend, I am here. I have long promised myself the pleasure of seeing you. Your hand. How hearty you look! And your lovely niece! My son will adore her.
Selina   (*To her uncle*) Permit me to retire, sir.
Bonamo   Go, my child; go.
Selina   (*Aside*) Grant, oh merciful heaven, I may not fall the sacrifice of avarice! (*Exit*).
Bonamo   And now your pleasure, count?
Romaldi   Nay, I imagine, you can guess my errand. The care you have bestowed upon your niece, her education, mind, and manners, and

38

the faithful guardian you have been, both of her wealth and person, well deserve praise.

Bonamo   If I have done my duty, I am greatly fortunate.

Romaldi   She is a lovely young lady; and you are not ignorant of my son's passion: to which your duty toward your niece must make you a friend. I therefore come, with open frankness, to propose their union.

Bonamo   Your rank and wealth make the proposal flattering: but there is a question still more serious.

Romaldi   What can that be?

Bonamo   One which my niece only can resolve.

Romaldi   Inexperience like hers should have no opinion.

Bonamo   How, my lord! Drag the bride, by force, to that solemn altar, where, in the face of heaven, she is to declare her choice is free?

Romaldi   Mere ceremonies!

Bonamo   Ceremonies!

Romaldi   Ay: you are a moralist; a conscientious man. Your son is reported to have designs on Selina.

Bonamo   My lord!

Romaldi   No anger: I speak as a friend. Her fortune is tempting: but you disdain to be influenced. The wealth and rank of our family –

Bonamo   Surpass mine. True; still my niece, I say, must be consulted.

Romaldi   Indeed! (*Sternly*) Then my alliance, it seems, is refused?

Bonamo   By no means: I have neither the right to refuse nor to accept. If Selina –

Re-enter Selina with a letter

Selina   (*Presenting it to Bonamo*) From the unfortunate Francisco.

Romaldi   What, that strange fellow I met as I came in?

Selina   (*Aside*) He knows his name!

Romaldi   I forgot to ask you how he got admittance here?

Bonamo   When you came he was relating his adventures, which have been strange. The mutilation he has suffered; the wounds he received, not a league from hence; the –

Romaldi   (*Alarmed*) Did he name – ?

Bonamo   Who? The monsters that gave them? – No: but they are not unknown to him.

Romaldi   That – that is fortunate.

Bonamo   I was amazed to learn –

Romaldi   What?

Bonamo   That they are rich and powerful. But I forget: the story can have no interest for you.

Romaldi   (*Eagerly*) You mistake: I – (*Recollecting himself*) my feelings are as keen as yours.

39

Bonamo But what has he written ? (*Offers to open the letter*).

Romaldi If you will take my advice, you will not read. Doubtless, he has more complaints, more tales, more favors to request. Be kind and hospitable; but do not be a dupe.

Bonamo Of which, I own, there is danger.

Romaldi (*Seizing the letter which Bonamo carelessly holds*) Then let me guard you against it.

Selina (*Snatches the letter back*) This letter, my lord, was given in charge to me: I promised to bring an answer; and I respectfully intreat my uncle will read it.

Bonamo Well, well. (*Reads*) 'Friend of humanity, Should I remain, the peace of your family might be disturbed. I therefore go; but earnestly intreat you will neither think me capable of falsehood nor ingratitude – Wherever I am, my wishes and my heart will be here – Farewell'. He shall not go. Fly, Selina; tell him I require, I request, him to sleep here to-night, that I may speak with him to-morrow.

Romaldi (*Aside*) That must not be.

Selina Thanks, my dear uncle! you have made me happy. (*Exit, in haste*)

Enter Piero

Bonamo What now, Piero ?

Piero Signor Montano is below.

Romaldi (*Alarmed and aside*) Montano!

Bonamo I'm very glad of it, for I wanted his advice. (*To Romaldi*) The best of men!

Piero Please to come up, sir.

Romaldi With your permission, I will retire

Enter Montano

Montano I beg pardon, good sir, but –

(*Music loud and discordant at the moment the eye of Montano catches the figure of Romaldi; at which Montano starts with terror and indignation. He then assumes the eye and attitude of menace; which Romaldi returns*)

Montano Can it be possible!

Romaldi (*Returning his threatening looks*) Sir!

Montano You here!

Romaldi Not having the honor of your acquaintance, I know not why my presence should please or displease you.

Montano (*Addressing Bonamo*) Good night, my friend; I will see you to-morrow (*Exit, suddenly*).

40

Bonamo (*Calling*) Nay, but signor! Signor Montano! Are the people all mad? I must speak with him. Excuse me for going.

Romaldi Why in such haste? I have heard of this Montano: a credulous person; a relater of strange stories.

Bonamo Signor Montano credulous! There is not in all Savoy a man of sounder understanding. Good night, my lord; I will send your servant: that door leads to your bed-room. Call for whatever you want; the house is at your command. (*Exit*).

Romaldi What am I to think? How act? – The arm of providence seems raised to strike! – Am I become a coward? shall I betray, rather than defend myself? I am not yet an idiot

Enter the Count's Servant, Malvoglio

Malvoglio Your lordship seems disturbed?
Romaldi Francisco is here.
Malvoglio I saw him.
Romaldi And did not your blood freeze?
Malvoglio I was sorry.
Romaldi For what?
Malvoglio That my dagger had missed its aim

Selina, entering and hiding behind the door, overhears them

Romaldi Where is he to sleep?
Malvoglio There (*Pointing*).
Selina They mean Francisco!
Romaldi Obstinate fool! Since he will stay –
Malvoglio He must die.
Selina The monsters!
Romaldi I heard a noise.
Malvoglio (*Looking*) He's coming.
Romaldi Let us retire and concert –
Malvoglio Then, at midnight –
Romaldi When he sleeps –
Malvoglio He'll wake no more!

(*Exeunt. The stage dark: Fiametta enters, with Francisco. She regards him with compassion, points to his bed-room, and retires. He round looks with apprehension, goes to the chamber-door of Romaldi, starts away with horror, recovers himself, and sits down to write*)

Enter Selina, who gently pulls the sleeve of Francisco: he starts; but, seeing her, his countenance expands with pleasure

Selina   (*In a low voice*) Dare not to sleep! I will be on the watch; your life is in danger! (*Exit*)
Francisco   (*Greatly agitated draws a pair of pistols, lays them on the table, and seats himself to consider if he should write more*)

Romaldi and Malvoglio appear

Romaldi   Wretched fool! Why are you here?

(*Music; terror, confusion, menace, command*)

Francisco   (*Starts up, seizes his pistols, points them towards Romaldi and Malvoglio, and commands the former, by signs, to read the paper that lies on the table*)

(*Music ceases*)

Romaldi   (*Reads*) 'Repent; leave the house. Oblige me not to betray you. Force me not on self-defence'. Fool! Do you pretend to command? (*Throws him a purse*) Take that and fly.
Francisco   (*After a look of compassionate appeal, spurns it from him; and commands them to go*)
Romaldi   (*Aside to Malvoglio*) I know him; he will not fire

(*Music. They draw their daggers; he at first avoids them; at length they each seize him by the arm, and are in the attitude of threatening to strike, when the shrieks of Selina, joining the music, which likewise shrieks, suddenly brings Bonamo, Stephano, and servants*)

Selina   Uncle! Stephano! Murder!

(*Romaldi and Malvoglio, at hearing the noise behind, quit Francisco, and feign to be standing on self-defence*). (*Music ceases*)

Bonamo   What mean these cries? Why, my lord, are these daggers drawn against a man under my protection?
Romaldi   Self-defence is a duty. Is not his pistol levelled at my breast?
Bonamo   (*To Francisco*) Can it be?
Francisco   (*Inclines his head*).
Selina   Sir, you are deceived: his life was threatened.
Romaldi   (*Sternly*) Madam –
Selina   I fear you not! I watched, I overheard you!
Bonamo   Is this true?
Romaldi   No.
Selina   By the purity of heaven, yes! Behind that door, I heard the

42

whole; Francisco must quit the house, or be murdered!

Romaldi (*To Bonamo sternly*) I expect, sir, my word will not be doubted.

Bonamo My lord, there is one thing of which I cannot doubt: the moment you appeared, terror was spread through my house. Good seldom accompanies mystery; I therefore now decidedly reply, to your proposal, that my niece cannot be the wife of your son; and must further add, you oblige me to decline the honor of your present visit.

Romaldi (*With threatening haughtiness*) Speak the truth, old man, and own you are glad to find a pretext to gratify ambition. Selina and Stephano; you want her wealth, and mean in that way to make it secure. But, beware! Dare to pursue your project and tremble at the consequences! To-morrow, before ten o'clock, send your written consent; or dread what shall be done

(*Exeunt Romaldi and Malvoglio*)

Bonamo Dangerous and haughty man! But his threats are vain; my doubts are removed. (*To his servants*) Make preparations for rejoicing: early tomorrow, Stephano and Selina shall be affianced

(*Music of sudden joy, while they kneel*)

Stephano My kind father!
Selina Dearest, best of guardians!
Bonamo Francisco shall partake the common happiness.
Fiametta (*As they are all retiring*) Dear, dear! I shan't sleep to-night

(*Exeunt: Bonamo expressing friendship to all, which all return; Francisco with joy equal to that of the lovers. Sweet and cheerful music, gradually dying away*)

Act 2

Joyful Music

Scene: a beautiful garden and pleasure grounds

1st and 2nd Gardeners. Piero and his companions; all busy

Piero Come, come: bestir yourselves! The company will soon be here.

1st Gardener Well; let them come: all is ready.

Piero It has a nice look, by my fackins!

1st Gardener I believe it has, thanks to me.

Piero Thanks to *you!*

2nd Gardener And me.

Piero And *you?* Here's impudence! I say it is thanks to me.

1st and 2nd Gardeners You, indeed!

Enter Stephano

Stephano What is the matter, my honest friends?

1st Gardener Why, here's Mr Piero pretends to dispute his claim to all that has been done.

Piero Didn't you say to me, Piero, says you –

Stephano Ay, ay; each man has done his part: all is excellent, and I thank you kindly. Are the villagers invited?

Piero Invited! They no sooner heard of the wedding than they were half out of their wits! There will be such dancing and sporting! Then the music! Little Nanine, with her hurdy-gurdy; her brother, with the tabor and pipe; the blind fidler, the lame piper, I and my jew's harp! such a band!

Stephano Bravo! Order every thing for the best.

Piero But who is to order? Please to tell me that, sir?

Stephano Why, you. You shall be major-domo for the day.

Piero You hear. I am to be—do—drum-major for the day!

Stephano To your posts

They conceal themselves by the trees and bushes

Enter Bonamo, Selina, and Fiametta

Bonamo (*Looking round*) Vastly well, upon my word!
Selina I fear, Stephano, you have slept but little?
Bonamo Sleep indeed! He had something better to think of. Come
come; we'll breakfast here in the bower. Order it, Fiametta.
Fiametta Directly, sir. (*She goes*).
Bonamo How reviving to age is the happiness of the young! And
yet – (*Sighs*) – thou hast long been an orphan, Selina. Would thou hadst
less wealth, or I more!
Selina And why, my dear uncle?
Bonamo Evil tongues – this Romaldi –
Selina His menace – before ten o'clock – oh! that the hour were
over!
Bonamo Come, come; we'll not disturb our hearts with fears. To
breakfast, and then to the notary. Come, sit down

*They seat themselves. Sweet music. Stephano gives a gentle clap with
his hands, and the peasants all rise from their hiding-places, and suspend
their garlands, in a picturesque group, over Bonamo, Selina, and
Stephano. (Music ceases)*

Piero What say you to that, now?
Bonamo Charming! charming!
Piero I hope I am not made a major for nothing?
Bonamo (*To Francisco, who enters with Fiametta*) Come sir, please
take your seat.
Piero Here! dancers! pipers! strummers! thrummers! to your
places. This bench is for the band of music – mount!

(*Here the dancing, which should be of the gay, comic, and grotesque kind;
that is, the humorous dancing of the Italian peasants. In the midst of the
rejoicing the clock strikes; the dancing suddenly ceases; the changing
music inspires alarm and dismay*)

Enter Malvoglio

He stops in the middle of the stage: the company start up

*Malvoglio then presents a letter to Bonamo, with a malignant assurance,
and, gratified by the consternation he has occasioned, retires. Bonamo
opens the letter and reads with great agitation*

Bonamo Oh, shame! dishonour! treachery!
Stephano My father! –
Selina My uncle!

Bonamo (*Repelling her*) I am not your uncle.

Selina Sir!

Stephano Not?

Bonamo She is the child of crime! of adultery.

Stephano 'Tis malice, my father!

Bonamo Read.

Stephano The calumny of Romaldi!

Bonamo Read.

Stephano 'Selina is not your brother's daughter. To prove I speak nothing but the truth, I send you the certificate of her baptism'.

Bonamo 'Tis here – authenticated. Once more read.

Stephano (*Reads*) 'May the 11th, 1584, at ten o'clock this evening was baptized Selina Bianchi, the daughter of Francisco Bianchi.

Francisco (*Utters a cry, and falls on the seat*).

Selina Is it possible! my father!

Francisco (*Opens his arms, and Selina falls on his neck*).

Stephano Amazement!

Bonamo Sinful man! Not satisfied with having dishonoured my brother, after claiming my pity, would you aid in making me contract a most shameful alliance? Begone! you and the off-spring of your guilt.

Stephano Selina is innocent.

Francisco (*Confirms it*).

Bonamo Her father is – a wretch! Once more begone.

Francisco (*During this time has held his daughter in his arms; he now rises with a sense of injury, and is leading her away*).

Bonamo Hold, miserable man! (*To himself*) Houseless – penniless – without bread – without asylum – must she perish because her father has been wicked? (*To Francisco*) Take this purse, conceal your shame, and, when 'tis empty, let me know your hiding-place.

Francisco (*Expresses gratitude, but rejects the purse*).

Selina Spare your benefits, sir, till you think we deserve them.

Bonamo Poor Selina!

Stephano (*Eagerly*) What say you, sir?

Bonamo Nothing – let them begone.

Selina Stephano! farewell.

Stephano She shall not go! or – I will follow.

Bonamo And forsake your father! ungrateful boy! (*To Francisco*) Begone, I say. Let me never see you more. (*To the Peasants*) Confine that frantic youth

Stephano escapes, and suddenly hurries Selina forward, to detain her: after violent efforts, they are again forced asunder; and, as they are retiring on opposite sides, with struggles and passion, the Scene closes

Scene: The house of Bonamo

Bonamo, Stephano, brought on by the Peasants; who then leave the room

Bonamo   Disobedient, senseless boy!
Stephano   (*Exhausted*) Selina! Give me back Selina, or take my life!
Bonamo   Forbear these complaints.
Stephano   None but she shall be my wife.
Bonamo   Your wife!
Stephano   To the world's end I'll follow her!
Bonamo   And quit your father? Now, when age and infirmity bend him to the grave?
Stephano   We will return to claim your blessing.
Bonamo   Stephano! beware of my malediction.
Stephano   When a father's malediction is unjust, heaven is deaf

Enter Fiametta

Bonamo   I no longer wonder Count Romaldi should advise me to drive such a wretch from my house.
Fiametta   Count Romaldi is himself a wretch.
Bonamo   Fiametta! –
Fiametta   I say it again: a vile wicked wretch! and has written –
Bonamo   The truth. The certificate is incontestible.
Fiametta   I would not for all the world be guilty of your sins.
Bonamo   Will you be silent?
Fiametta   I won't! I can't! Poor Stephano! And do you think he'll forbear to love her? You may hold him to-day, but he'll be gone to-morrow. He'll overtake and find his dear forlorn Selina; and they will marry, and live in poverty.
Bonamo   For the last time, I warn you –
Fiametta   I know the worst: I have worked for you all the prime of my youth; and now you'll serve me as you have served the innocent wretched Selina: you'll turn me out of doors. Do it! But I'll not go till I've said out my say: so, I tell you again, you are a hard hearted uncle, an unfeeling father, and an unjust master! So now I'll go, as soon as you please

Enter Signor Montano, hastily

Montano   What is it I have just heard, my friend? Have you driven away your niece?
Bonamo   She is not my niece.
Montano   'Tis true. But where did you learn that?

47

Bonamo   From these papers.

Montano   Who sent them?

Bonamo   Count Romaldi.

Montano   Count Romaldi, is – a villain.

Stephano   You hear, Sir!

Fiametta   I hope I shall be believed another time.

Bonamo   Silence, woman! – By a man like you, such an accusation cannot be made without sufficient proofs.

Montano   You shall have them. Be attentive. Eight years ago, before I had the honour to know you, returning one evening after visiting my friends, I was leisurely ascending the rock of Arpennaz.

Fiametta   So, so! The rock of Arpennaz! You hear! But I'll not say a word.

Montano   Two men, wild in their looks, and smeared with blood, passed hastily by me, with every appearance of guilt impressed upon their countenances.

Fiametta   The very same! Eight years ago! The rock of Arpennaz! The –

Bonamo   Silence!

Fiametta   I'll not say a word. Tell all, Sir; I am dumb.

Montano   They had not gone a hundred paces before he, who appeared the master, staggered and fell. I hastened to him: he bled much, and I and his servant supported him to my house. They said they had been attacked by banditti, yet their torn clothes, a deep bite, which the master had on the back of his hand, and other hurts appearing to be given by an unarmed man, made me doubt. Their embarrassment increased suspicion; which was confirmed next day by Michelli, the honest miller of Arpennaz; who, the evening before, near the spot from which I saw these men ascend, had succoured a poor wretch, dreadfully cut and mangled. I no longer doubted I had entertained men of blood; and hastened to deliver them up to justice: but, when I returned, they had flown. Imagine my surprise and indignation, yesterday evening, when I here once more beheld the assassin! I could not disguise my emotion; and I left you with such abruptness to give immediate information. The archers are now in pursuit: I have no doubt they will soon secure him, as they already have secured his accomplice.

Stephano   Malvoglio?

Montano   Yes, who has confessed –

Stephano   What?

Montano   That the real name of this pretended Romaldi is Bianchi.

Bonamo   Just heaven! Francisco's brother!

Montano   Whose wife this wicked brother loved. Privately married, and she pregnant, Francisco put her under the protection of his friend here in Savoy – your brother, Signor Bonamo.

Stephano   My uncle! His sudden death occasioned the mystery.

Montano   But the false Romaldi decoyed Francisco into the power

48

of the Algerines, seized his estates; and, finding he had escaped, attempted to assassinate him.

Fiametta   Now are you convinced! He would not 'peach this brother of abomination! I told you Francisco was an angel!

Bonamo   (*Slowly; earnestly*). Pray, good woman, hold your tongue.

Fiametta   Repent, then! Repent!

Bonamo   I do repent!

Fiametta   Then I forgive you. (*Sobs*) I wont turn you away. You're my master again.

Bonamo   But where shall we find Selina?

Fiametta   Oh, I know where!

Stephano   (*Eagerly*) Do you?

Fiametta   Why, could you think that – (*Her heart full*) Follow me! Only follow me. (*Exeunt hastily*)

Thunder heard, while the Scene changes. Music

Scene: the wild mountainous country called the Nant of Arpennaz; with pines and massy rocks

The increasing storm of lightning, thunder, hail, and rain becomes terrible

Enter Romaldi from the rocks, disguised like a peasant, with terror

Romaldi   Whither fly? Where shield me from pursuit, and death, and ignominy? (*Dreadful thunder*) The heavens shoot their fires at me! Save! Spare! Oh spare me! (*Falls on the bank*) (*The storm gradually abates. A very distant voice is heard.* [Holla!]). They are after me! Someone points me out! No den, no cave, can hide me! (*Looks the way he came*) I cannot return that way. I cannot. It is the place of blood! A robbed and wretched brother! 'Tis his blood, by which I am covered! Oh, Cover me earth! Cover my crimes! Cover my shame! (*Falls motionless again*)

Michelli is seen coming toward the bridge, which he crosses

Michelli   'Tis a fearful storm! One's very heart shrinks! It makes a poor mortal think of his sins – and his danger.

Romaldi   I am known; or must be! – Shall I yield; or shall I – (*Points his pistol at Michelli, then shrinks in hesitation whether he shall or shall not murder*) How to act?

Michelli   (*Perceiving Romaldi*) Now, friend!

Romaldi   Now, miller!

Michelli   (*Observing his agitation*) You look –

49

Romaldi	How do I look?
Michelli	I – What have you there?
Romaldi	Where?
Michelli	Under your coat?
Romaldi	(*Leaving the pistol in his inside pocket, and shewing his hands*)

Nothing.

Michelli	Something is the matter with you.
Romaldi	I am tired.
Michelli	Come in, then, and rest yourself.
Romaldi	Thank you! (*Moved*) Thank you!
Michelli	Whence do you come?
Romaldi	From – the neighbourhood of Geneva.
Michelli	Did you pass through Sallancha?
Romaldi	Sallancha! Why do you ask?
Michelli	You have heard of what has happened?
Romaldi	Where?
Michelli	There! At Sallancha! One Count Romaldi –
Romaldi	What of him?
Michelli	Justice is at his heels. He has escaped: but he'll be taken.

The executioner will have him.

Romaldi	(*Aside*) All men hate me! Why should I spare him?
Michelli	I saved the good Francisco.
Romaldi	You! Was it you?
Michelli	I.
Romaldi	Then – live.
Michelli	I will, my friend, as long as I can; and when I die, I'll die

with an honest heart.

Romaldi	Miserable wretch!
Michelli	Who?
Romaldi	That Count Romaldi.
Michelli	Why ay! – Unless he is a devil, he is miserable indeed.

(*Music, quick march*) He'll be taken; for, look, yonder are the archers.

Romaldi	(*Aside*) They are here! I am lost! (*Retires*)

(*Music*). *The Archers come forward*

Michelli	Good day, worthy Sirs.
Exempt	Honest miller, good day. We are in search of Count

Romaldi, whom we are to take, dead or alive. Do you know his person?

Michelli	No.
Romaldi	(*Aside, and out of sight of the Archers*) Thanks, merciful

heaven!

Exempt	(*Reads*) 'Five feet eight' (*etc. The description must be that of*

the actor's voice, size and person: to which add) 'with a large scar on the back of the right hand'.

Romaldi	(*Thrusting his hand in his bosom*) 'Twill betray me!

Exempt   We are told, he is among these mountains.

Michelli   Oh, could I catch him by the collar!

Exempt   Should you meet him, beware: he's not unarmed.

Michelli   There is no passing for him or you by this valley after the storm; the mountain torrents are falling. You must go back.

Exempt   Many thanks. We must lose no time.

Michelli   Success to you

(*Archers reascend the hill*)

Romaldi   Death! Infamy! Is there no escaping?

Michelli   The day declines, come in; pass the evening here: recover your strength and spirits.

Romaldi   (*With great emotion, forgetting and holding out his hand*). You are a worthy man.

Michelli   I wish to be. (*Feeling Romaldi's hand after shaking*) Zounds! What? Hey?

Romaldi   (*Concealing his confusion*) A scar –

Michelli On the back of the right hand!

Romaldi   I have served. A hussar with his sabre gave the cut.

Michelli   Humph! It may be!

Romaldi   It is.

Michelli   At least it *may* be: – and the innocent –

Romaldi   Ay! Might suffer for the guilty.

Michelli   (*After looking at him*) Rather than that – I will run all risks. I am alone; my family is at the fair, and cannot be home tonight. But you are a stranger; you want protection –

Romaldi   (*With great emotion*) I do, indeed!

Michelli   You shall have it. Come. Never shall my door be shut upon the houseless wretch

(*Exeunt to the house*)

Francisco and Selina approach the bridge. The Miller, supposed to hear a noise, comes to enquire, sees Francisco, and they run into each other's arms

Michelli   Welcome! A thousand times welcome!

Selina   Ten thousand thanks to the saviour of my father.

Michelli   Your father, sweet lady?

Selina   Oh yes! Discovered to me by his mortal enemy.

Michelli   The monster Romaldi?

Selina   Alas!

Michelli   For your father's sake, for your own sake, welcome both.

Romaldi   (*Half from the door*) I heard my name!

Michelli   Come. I have a stranger –

Selina   (*Seeing Romaldi, shrieks*) Ah!
Francisco   (*Falls back and covers his eyes, with agony*).

(*Romaldi retires*).

Michelli   How now?
Selina   'Tis he!

(*Music of hurry, terror, etc*)

Michelli hastily ascends to cross the bridge in search of the Archers. Francisco intreats him back in vain. Romaldi, in terror, enters from the house presenting his pistol. Francisco opens his breast for him to shoot, if he please. Selina falls between them

Romaldi   No! Too much of your blood is upon my head! Be justly revenged: take mine!

Music continues as Romaldi offers the pistol; which Francisco throws to a distance, and intreats him to fly by the valley. Romaldi is met at the edge of the hill by several Archers, and maintains a retreating fight. Fiametta, Bonamo, Stephano, Montano and Peasants follow the Archers. When the combatants have descended the hill, Romaldi's foot slips, he falls, and Francisco intervenes to guard his body. The Archers forbear for a moment; and the music ceases

Selina   Oh, forbear! Let my father's virtues plead for my uncle's errors!
Bonamo   We all will intreat for mercy; since of mercy we all have need: for his sake, and for our own, may it be freely granted!

The Curtain falls to slow and solemn music

FINIS

THE PRESS

The Times, November 15th, 1802:

After the new comedy of Delays And Blunders, *a* Melo-Drame, *in Two Acts, called* A Tale of Mystery, *was brought forward on Saturday evening.*

An Entertainment more distinguished for novelty and interest, more happily composed of fable, incident, dialogue, music, dancing and pantomime, and more decidedly sanctioned by the approbation of an audience, has never been produced on the English Stage. The Author, Mr Holcroft, is indebted for the subject to the French School, and the original, Seline; or, The Maid of Savoy, *has been received at Paris with universal plaudits by overflowing houses. In justice to Mr. Holcroft, it is, however, necessary to observe, that the subject only can be considered as the property of another. In the management of it he has essentially deviated from the original; several of the incidents are new, and the dialogue is, with very few exceptions, his own.*

The title of Melo-Drame, *until the present instance unknown to our Drama, will justify a few remarks on its origin and nature. The* Drame *of the French Stage was first introduced by the celebrated* La Chausée, *who, by intertwining the tragic and the comic in the same production, and selecting for his Muse subjects of domestic misfortune, was the Author of that new species of composition in France called* La Commédie Mixte; ou, Drame. *Although the invention occasioned innumerable attacks from the Critics of the day, and was roughly treated, as a scandalous corruption of the art, yet it has stood the test of more than half a century, and still triumphs over the feelings of the audience, in those affecting Pièces of La Chausée –* Le Préjugé à la Mode, Mélanide, La Gouvernante, *and* L'Ecole des Mères. *The satires and epigrams to which they gave rise are all forgotten, and they are never acted at this moment without exciting tears. This kind of composition, which is unequal to the province of Tragedy in producing pity or terror, and inferior to that of Comedy in calling forth pleasantry and amusement, has given birth to the* Melo-Drame, *which strengthens the mixed composition we have noticed, by the powers of music, initiating at once both passion and action, and its success is the best proof of its influence over the human mind.*

[There then follows a lengthy outline of the various aspects of the plot, which] – *all combine to produce an effect that has not been surpassed by any mixed combination of a similar nature since the English Drama has attained to its present improved state.*

The Fable is, indeed, as it should be, the main string not only of all the grand and striking incidents, but it also warrants, in opposition to the most fastidious criticism, the introduction of those gay and pleasing embellishments that relieve the sombrous, however natural, and prevent the mind of the auditor from being overwhelmed by the calamities of the scene.

While we have so many just causes for satisfactions, we think it of little importance, that a few trifling defects and errors should present themselves. It would be captious to submit them to the public, since they are so destitute of weight, as not in the least to interrupt the business, or to impair the consistency of the whole. The sentiments are appropriate to the occasion, and the dialogue is natural and characteristic. There is no extravagance of idea – no laborious research after simile and metaphor – no display of pomp and inflated expression: the thought seems to arise from the moment, and the works appear to be suggested by the circumstances which pass under the eye of the spectator. In short, were the story dramatized as it is now, even without the assistance of all the fascinations which it possesses, we have no hesitation to say, that it would in an eminent degree attract the attention and admiration of the public.

The Music is equally entitled to notice for its natural connection with the business of the Drama, its intrinsic merits, and the novelty of the experiment. It is the production of Dr Busby, whose reputation for science and taste has already been so fully established by his Oratories of the Prophecy *and* Britannia, *his Ode called* Ocean, *the Music introduced in Mr Cumberland's* Joanna of Montfaucon *and many other effusions in the higher species of vocal composition. But however high his merits as a Composer may rank in the opinion of those acquainted with his former productions, the judgement and felicity with which he has executed this new, arduous, and critical task, confer on him an additional claim to their estimation.*

[There follows here a long analysis of the overture, continuing]

When the business commenced, expectation was not disappointed. The hurry and perturbation of the scene were forcibly depicted by the agitated notes of the orchestra, and this new adjunct to the interest of the drama was immediately felt by the whole audience. The arduous task of the Composer was fully accomplished in elucidating and enforcing

54

the various passions and situations. No province of the art could require more skill, or a nicer discrimination, than some of the incidents which depended on musical illustration; and where the Author relied with the greatest confidence on the Composer, there the latter seemed to have been uniformly studious to evince his talents, and to prove himself to the novelty and importance of the experiment entrusted to his care. Dr Busby has certainly evinced science and taste, which are calculated to give a degree of true and natural interest to an acting drama, superior to that which has marked its state for many years.

We do not recollect any piece, to the success of which the merits of the Performers have so materially contributed as to that of A Tale of Mystery. *To the feeling, judgement and versatility of voice and actions displayed by Mr H Johnston, the Author is particularly indebted. It is from the commencement to the conclusion a* chef d'oeuvre *which we despair of seeing equalled. His deportment and gesticulations were admirably varied to the transitions of the scene, and the boldness and rapidity of his attitudes and actions evinced a perfect knowledge of this difficult branch of the art. He had many obstacles, many prejudices to surmount, yet such was the natural force and energy with which he represented the cruel and remorseless* Romaldi, *that he extorted reiterated bursts of applause.*

Farley, under whose direction the piece has been brought forward, is entitled to peculiar encomium. To the merits of a skilful Superintendent, he adds those of a finished Performer in this line. His Pantomime was so very correct as to indicate the passions by which his bosom was actuated. He was in the words of Claudian, who has had occasion to extol a celebrated Performer in dumb shew, during his time, at Rome:

'Notu manisbusque loquax'

Murray, in Bonamo, *Brunton in* Stephano, *Blanchard in the honest Miller* Michelli, *and Cory in* Malvoglio, *exerted themselves with the happiest effects for the success of the Entertainment.*

Mrs Gibbs gave to Selina *every possible degree of interest; and* Fiametta, *in the possession of Mrs Mattocks, was spirited and impressive.*

The part of Piero, *the principal Gardener, performed by* Simmons, *is too trifling for the general subject of the scene. His jests are trite and contemptible. It is a wretched imitation of* Harry, *in* The Maid of the Oaks, *and might be altogether omitted.*

Mr Harris has, in his choice of a Composer, in the scenery, dresses, and decorations, evinced his accustomed judgement, taste, and liberality, and

A Tale of Mystery *promises to be as attractive as any piece that has been brought out at this Theatre for many years.*

The dancing by Mrs Wybrow, young Bologna, Dubois, King, and little Byrnes produced universal plaudits. In the rural preparations for the wedding of Selina *and* Stephano, *much appropriate taste and variety were displayed, and the march of the archers through the mountains was grand and picturesque.*

The House overflowed in every part at an early hour, and the approbation which attended the performance was cordial and unanimous.

The Monthly Mirror, December 1802:

A TALE OF MYSTERY

A Melodrame *by Thomas Holcroft, Esq*

By Melodrame we suppose is meant a drama, in which the language, situations, and passions are accompanied and heightened by music. We have had a slight specimen of what might be produced by this conjunction, in Lodoiska, *and it constituted one of the charms of that interesting romance. When the Tartars are attacking the castle, the agitation of* Baron Lovinski's *mind is expressed by the music, which, during the intervals of his soliloquy is introduced with the most pleasing effect. In this melodrame, the principle is more strongly applied. The composer tells the story as well as the author. The characters are introduced with appropriate melodies; the progress of the scene is illustrated in a similar way; and every incident and feeling is marked by correspondent musical expression. In addition to this, the subject of the* Tale of Mystery *demands the aid of* pantomime, *and there is also an opportunity for* spectacle, *and a* dance; *so that beside the charm of novelty, this entertainment exhibits a combination of every thing that is calculated to please the eye and the ear, and, we may add with strict justice, to gratify the taste, and powerfully to interest the feelings of the public.*

The story is so extremely interesting, that we think our readers will be pleased with a more particular account than we usually think it necessary to give. The original piece is French, and written by an actor in Paris. Its title there was Seline, or the Maid of Savoy; *but we understand that the alterations and improvements made by Mr Holcroft are so numerous, that it would be injustice to consider him in the light of a mere translator. Indeed we know that nothing can be transferred from a foreign stage to ours, without as much, and sometimes with more, trouble to the adapter than frequently attends an original production.*

[Here follows an extremely lengthy account of the plot]

We cannot too much admire the ingenuity with which this plot is conducted. There seems to be nothing superfluous, nothing deficient. The interest continues without interruption to the end. The mystery indeed is so far developed on the appearance of Romaldi, *that we know the author of* Francisco's *misfortunes; but we are unacquainted with the motives which induced him to persecute, betray, and mutilate his unhappy brother. Nay, this discovery rather increases the mystery of the tale in representation, for we are the more anxious to learn the particulars of an event, the consequences of which have been so fatal to* Francisco, *and to watch the various circumstances which gradually lead to the detection and punishment of a wretch whose crime is so enormous that even its miserable victim refuses to name it. It may be urged that the patient forbearance of* Francisco *under such accumulated injuries, is an improbability to which we cannot easily be reconciled. But we do not think it exceeds the licence of dramatic fiction; and is surely not so very difficult to believe, that a principle of family pride, and a noble generosity of nature, strengthened by fraternal affection, may impel a man to endure the utmost distress, rather than prefer an accusation, which must conduct his brother to an ignominious death. The instance certainly may occur; and if it be not beyond credibility, such a character is a fit subject for the stage, and worthy of our admiration. That a sense of family honour will prevail in great extremities, appears from the conduct of* Francisco, *the unhappy* Tyrolese, *now under sentence of death for firing a pistol at a tradesman in Lombard-street, who, if we may trust the newspapers, refused to mention the name of a brother who lives in high respectability in this city, and whose interference might possibly have been the means of saving him.*

The embellishments which the Tale of Mystery *has received from the liberality of the manager are of the most elegant and splendid description. The scenery is rich, and romantic. The last scene in particular has a most striking effect; the trees are represented in actual motion from the storm which, with the accompanying music, is well suited to* Romaldi's *state of mind, whose dreadful guilt has made him a fit object both of earthly and divine vengeance. The actors merit the most ample praise. Mr H Johnston in* Romaldi, *was admirable. His attempt to conceal his confusion, upon the unexpected appearance of* Francisco, *and afterwards of* Montano; *the expression of guilty compunction in the first scene with* Malvoglio; *his spirited action throughout; and especially his perturbation and terror in the last scene, were all of the most masterly kind. Mr Farley's* Francisco *was highly animated and affecting; and he* 'spoke his wrongs without a tongue' *with an eloquence that was irresistible. In short all the performers were particularly successful:– Murray in* Bonamo; *Brunton in* Stephano; *Cory in* Malvoglio; *Blanchard in*

57

the Miller; *Claremont in* Montano; *and particularly Mrs Mattocks in* Fiametta, *whose blunt fidelity and loquacious benevolence serve as a happy relief to the serious complexion of the drama. Mrs Gibbs in the heroine appeared to great advantage, and proved a powerful support to the interest of the scene.*

The costume *of the dresses and decorations is extremely accurate, for this the piece is indebted to Mr Farley, under whose sole superintendance the* melo-drame *was produced, and who, by his taste and judgement, has rendered every justice to the department entrusted to his management. The* music *is by Dr Busby.*

The length of these observations testifies our sense of the merit of the entertainment. It is the most captivating which the stage has for many years exhibited.

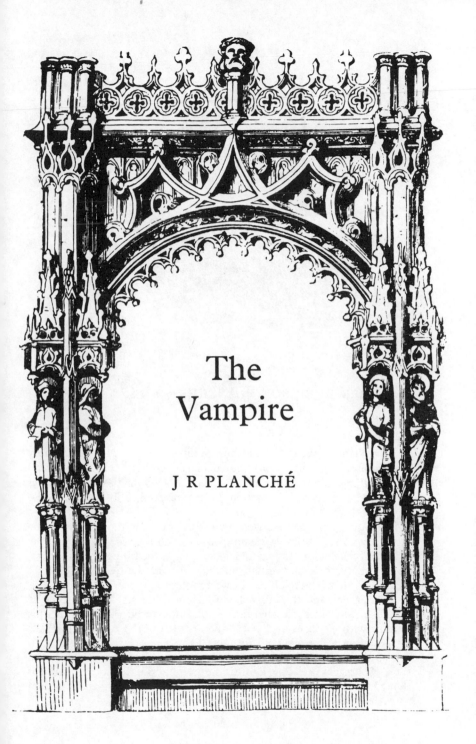

The
Vampire

J R PLANCHÉ

J R Planché, from the Illustrated London News 1880 (*Victoria & Albert Museum*)

JAMES ROBINSON PLANCHÉ (1796/1880)

J R Planché was one of the most prolific of playwrights in a notably prolific age. Well over two hundred pieces of every conceivable kind flowed effortlessly from his pen, and his two volumes of *Recollections* (1872) are a mine of information for any researcher into the period – including the present writer.

His interests extended well beyond the world of the theatre, for he was a recognised authority in antiquarianism, a founder member of the British Archaelogical Association, an expert (at the time the *only* expert) on British costume and armaments, and in 1867 he became Somerset Herald; on all of which subjects he wrote voluminously.

Of French ancestry, Planché had an untiring zest for whatever he turned his considerable energies to. He introduced the revue to this country with *Success; or A Hit If You Like It* at the Adelphi in 1825; extravangaza with *High, Low, Jack And The Game* at the Olympic in 1833, and opera bouffe with *Orpheus In The Haymarket* at the Haymarket in 1865. He was also a leading figure in the promotion of the Copyright Bill of 1833; he wrote a libretto for Weber, and had an abortive collaboration with Mendelssohn.

His monumental *History of British Costume* (1834) had its origins in his researches and designs for John Philip Kemble's production of *King John* at Covent Garden as a vehicle for Charles Young. This marked the first occasion that an attempt had been made at complete historical accuracy for all costumes in a stage work (although Garrick had made some innovations in this field half a century before) and received great acclaim. Not that the production revolutionised stage-costuming overnight, for the experiment was expensive – despite the fact that Planché himself was not paid for his work. Not that he minded, it seems:

> '*When the curtain rose and discovered King John dressed as his effigy appears in Worcester Cathedral, surrounded by his barons sheathed in mail, with cylindrical helmets and correct armorial shields, and his courtiers in the long tunics and mantles of the thirteenth century, there was such a roar of approbation, accompanied by four distinct rounds of applause, so general and so hearty, that the actors were astonished, and I felt amply rewarded for all the trouble, anxiety and annoyance I had experienced during my labours*'. (Recollections, *vol i, pp 56-57*)

Planché was engaged by Madame Vestris and her husband Charles Mathews for the 1839-40 season at Covent Garden as 'Superintendent of the Decorative Department', a position he revelled in and which he subsequently held at various theatres. Boucicault's *London Assurance* (Covent Garden, 1841) was especially praised for its scenery and costumes.

James Robinson Planché was born in Old Burlington Street, on February 27th, 1796. His parents were first cousins of French stock, their ancestors being refugees from the Huguenot persecution (Garrick had similar origins). His father was a well-established watchmaker at the time of his birth, but James was not enthusiastic about entering his father's business. He was an art student for a short while, but when his teacher died he was apprenticed to a bookseller at his own request. It was about this time that he began to interest himself in amateur theatricals, and wrote a burlesque called *Amoroso, King of Little Britain*. A mutual friend showed it to John Harley, the manager of the Theatre Royal Drury Lane, who happened to be looking for just such a piece. The first that Planché knew of its submission and acceptance was when he saw it advertised on the bills; its favourable reception decided him to be a dramatist in earnest. The next two years were furiously active ones for the young playwright, during which he produced 'several dramas of various descriptions at sundry theatres', including *The Vampire; or, the Bride of the Isles* at the English Opera House on August 9th, 1820. Concerning this production, Planché wrote:

> '*Mr Samuel James Arnold, the proprietor and manager, had placed in my hands, for adaptation, a French melodrama, entitled* Le Vampire,

the scene of which was laid, with the usual recklessness of French dramatists, in Scotland, where the superstition never existed. I vainly endeavoured to induce Mr Arnold to let me change it to some place in the east of Europe. He had set his heart on Scotch music and dresses – the latter, by the way, were in stock – laughed at my scruples, assured me that the public would neither know nor care – and in those days they certainly did not – and therefore there was nothing left for me but to do my best with it. The results were most satisfactory to the management ... The trap now so well known as the 'Vampire trap' was invented for this piece, and the final disappearance of the Vampire caused quite a sensation. The melodrama had a long run, was often revived, and is to this day a stock piece in the country. I had an opportunity many years afterwards, however, to treat the same subject in a manner much more satisfactory to myself, and, as it happened, in the same theatre, under the same management ...' (Recollections, vol i, pp 39-40)

'Many years' was in fact nine years, for it was in 1829 that Planché wrote the English libretto for a German operatic version of the same French original, with music by Heinrich Marschner. In this opera Planché was at last able to send his vampire back to Hungary, where he rightly belonged. He considered the piece superior in many respects to his first attempt, and that it was '*extremely well sung, and the costumes novel as well as correct...*'

The legend of the vampire remains to this day a staunch favourite as a Gothic theme for plays, films and novels. The year 1820 also saw a version by W T Moncrieff; some of the others include *The Vampire Bride* by George Blink (1834), *The Vampire* by H Young (1846), Boucicault's *The Vampire* (1852) which he altered ten years later into *The Phantom*, and Hamilton Deane's dramatisation of Bram Stoker's novel *Dracula* which is still regularly revived.

James Robinson Planché was a gregarious and clubbable man, who despite his self-important manner and rather snobbish tastes was well-liked and respected. In 1821 he married Elizabeth St George who herself wrote a handful of plays. He was awarded a civil list pension of £100 in 1871 for his scholarly work in the fields of heraldry, British armoury and costumes. He died at his home in St Leonard's Terrace on May 30th, 1880, and was survived by his two widowed daughters.

THE VAMPIRE

Dramatis Personae

First performed at the English Opera House
August 9th, 1820

In the vision

Unda, Spirit of the Flood, by Miss Love
Ariel, Spirit of the Air, by Miss Worgman
A Vampire by Mr T P Cooke
Lady Margaret by Mrs Chatterly

In the melo-drame

Ruthven, Earl of Marsden, by Mr T P Cooke
Ronald, Baron of the Isles, by Mr Bartley
Robert, an English Attendant on the Baron, by Mr Pearman
M' Swill, the Baron's Henchman, by Mr Harley
Andrew, Steward to Ruthven, by Mr Minton
Father Francis by Mr Shaw
Lady Margaret, Daughter to Ronald, by Mrs Chatterly
Effie, Daughter to Andrew, by Miss Carew
Bridget, Lord Ronald's Housekeeper, by Mrs Grove

Retainers
Peasants
Bargeman, etc, etc

THE VAMPIRE

Introductory Vision

The Curtain rises to slow Music, and discovers the Interior of the Basaltic Caverns of Staffa; The Moonlight streams through and partially reveals a number of rude Sepulchres. On one of these, Lady Margaret is seen, stretched in a heavy Slumber. The Spirit of the Flood rises to the Symphony of the following incantation

Unda Spirit! Spirit of the Air!
Hear and heed my spell of power;
On the night breeze swift repair
Hither from thy starry bower.
Chorus Appear! Appear!

(Music – The Spirit of the Air descends through the Chasm, on a Silvery Cloud, which she leaves and advances)

Ariel Why, how now, sister! wherefore am I summoned?
Unda Spirit of the Air! thy sister Unda claims
Thy powerful aid; Look here.
(Pointing to Lady M.)
Ariel A maiden, and asleep!
Unda Her name is Margaret, the only daughter
Of Ronald, the brave Baron of the Isles.
A richer, lovelier, more virtuous lady
This land of Flood and Mountains never boasted.
Ariel How came she in this den of death and horror?
Unda Chasing the red-deer with her father Ronald,
A storm arose, and parted from her train,
She sought a shelter here – calmly she sleeps,
Nor dreams to-morrow's hymeneal rites,
Will give her beauties to a Vampire's arms.
Ariel Say on.
Unda Beneath this stone the relics lie
Of Cromal, called the bloody. For his crimes,

65

His spirit roams, a Vampire, in the form
Of Marsden's Earl; – to count his victims o'er,
Would be an endless task – suffice to say,
His race of terror will to-morrow end,
Unless he wins some virgin for his prey,
Ere sets the full-orb'd moon.
Ariel And with this view
He weds the Lady Margaret.
Unda Aye, Ariel;
Unless our blended art can save the maid.
Ariel What can be done ? – our power is limited.
What can be done, my sister ?
Unda We must warn
The maiden of her fate. Lend me thine aid,
To raise a vision to her sleeping sight.
Ariel Let us about it

(*They perform Magical Ceremonies to the Symphony of the following Charm*)

Ariel and *Unda* Phantom, from thy tomb so drear,
At our bidding swift arise;
Let thy Vampire-corpse appear,
To this sleeping maiden's eyes. (*Thunder*)

Chorus – Appear! Appear! Appear!

(*A Vampire succeeds from the Tomb of Cromal, and springs towards Margaret*)

Vampire Margaret!
Ariel Foul spirit, retire!
Vampire She is mine!
Ariel The hour is not yet come.
Unda Down, thou foul spirit; – extermination waits thee: Down, I
say

(*Music – The Vampire sinks again, shuddering, and the Scene closes*)

66

THE VAMPIRE; or, THE BRIDE OF THE ISLES

Act the First

Scene 1

A Hall in the Castle of Lord Ronald. M' Swill and a group of retainers in hunting dress are seated round a table, drinking

Enter Bridget and Robert – M' Swill gets under the Table

Bridget Very pretty doings upon my word! Here's our poor mistress, the Lady Margaret, been lost for nearly the whole night in the forest; and no sooner is she by good fortune found again and trying to get a little rest in her own apartments, but you make all this noise, as if on purpose to disturb her.

Robert Nay, Mrs Bridget, don't be angry with them. They've been celebrating my lady's return.

Bridget Return! Don't tell me – They never want an excuse to get drunk – out of the castle directly – don't stand ducking and scraping there – go along directly, when I tell you. (*Exeunt Retainers*). Where is that rascal, M'Swill? he's at the bottom of all this; – but if I – (*M'Swill attempts to steal off*) Oh! oh! there you are, sir – come here, sir. (*Seizes him by the ear, and brings him forward*) Down on your knees directly, and ask my pardon.

M' Swill I do, Mrs Bridget.

Bridget Here has poor Robert been running through the forest all night, seeking my lady, and peeping in all the holes of the grotto, whilst you –

M' Swill The grotto, Mrs Bridget! Good guide us! O, dear! O, dear! the ignorance of some people – but you're an Englishman, and that accounts for it. Why, didn't you know that the grotto was haunted.

Robert Ha! ha! ha!

M' Swill Aye! aye! laugh away, do – but I can tell you its full of kelpies and evil spirits of all sorts; only ask Mrs Bridget.

Bridget It's very true, Robert, and you shouldn'y laugh, for they always owe a grudge to any body that jests about them.

M' Swill Did you never hear the story of Lady Blanch?

Bridget Hush! don't talk so loud.

M'Swill You know it, Mrs Bridget.

Bridget No! but Lord Ronald is very angry with every body who circulates stories of that description – so speak lower, if you are going to tell it.

M'Swill Well, then – once upon a time –

Robert Ha! ha! ha! – Mother Bunch's fairy tales.

M'Swill Well, isn't that the proper way to begin a story?

Robert Well, well, then – Once upon a time – what happened?

M'Swill Once on a time, there lived a lady named Blanch, in this very castle, and she was betrothed to a rich Scotch nobleman; all the preparations for the wedding were finished, when, on the evening before it was to take place, the lovers strolled into the forest –

Bridget Alone?

M'Swill No; together to be sure.

Bridget Well, I think it was highly improper.

M'Swill Well, they were seen to enter the grotto, and –

Robert And what?

M'Swill They never came out again.

Robert Bravo! – an excellent story.

M'Swill But that isn't all. – The next morning the body of the lady was found covered with blood, and the marks of human teeth on her throat, but no trace of the nobleman could be discovered, and from that time to this he has never been heard of; and they do say, (I hope nobody hears us) they do say that the nobleman was a *Vampire*, for a friar afterwards confessed on his death bed, that he had privately married them in the morning by the nobleman's request, and that he fully believed it some fiend incarnate, for he could not say the responses without stuttering.

Robert Better and better!

M'Swill Moreover, I've heard that these horrible spirits, call'd Vampires, kill and suck the blood of beautiful young maidens, whom they are obliged to marry before they can destroy. – And they do say that such is the condition of their existence, that if, at stated periods, they should fail to obtain a virgin bride, whose life blood may sustain them, they would instantly perish. Oh, the beautiful young maidens! –

Bridget Of beautiful young maidens – merciful powers! what an escape I've had. – I was in the cavern myself one day.

M'Swill Lord, Mrs Bridget, I'm sure there's no occasion for you to be frightened.

Bridget Why, you saucy sot, I've a great mind to –

(*A bell rings*)

I declare there's my lady's bell – no occasion, indeed – an impudent fellow; but men, now-a-days, have no more manners than hogs. (*Exit*)

M'Swill There's a she devil for you. I don't think there's such another vixen in all Scotland. She's little and hot, like a pepper-corn.

Robert All old ladies have their odd ways.

M'Swill Pray, Mr Robert, as you've been in London with Lord Ronald, do you know who this Earl is that the Lady Margaret is to be married to?

Robert I only know that he is the Earl of Marsden, and master of the castle on the coast facing this island.

M'Swill What? where the pretty Effie, your intended lives?

Robert Exactly.

M'Swill He'll arrive just in time, then, to be present at the wedding.

Robert I hope so.

M'Swill That will be glorious! two weddings in one day – such dancing, such eating, such drinking –

Bridget M'Swill! (*Off*).

M'Swill Ugh, choak you, you old warlock! what's in the wind now, I wonder?

Bridget M'Swill, I say!

M'Swill Coming, Mrs Bridget. (*Exit M'Swill*).

Robert Yes, as soon as the Earl arrives, I shall certainly take an opportunity to request him to honour the wedding with his presence – how pleas'd my dear Effie would be. Charming girl, I shall never forget the hour when we met – (*Sings to the tune of 'The Lass of Patie's Mill'*)

Exit Robert

Scene 2
Apartment in the Castle

Enter Lady Margaret and Bridget

Bridget Oh! my lady, you must not tell me; I'm sure the fright and the fatigue you have undergone has made you ill.

Lady M. Indeed, no – I feel quite recovered, I assure you, my good Bridget.

Bridget But I know better, my lady; that smile is not like your usual ones – something ails you –

Lady M. Something certainly troubles me, but my health is not affected. I would confide the cause of my uneasiness to you, but fear you will laugh at me when I tell you. It is a dream I have had.

Bridget A dream! for heaven's sake tell me, my lady.

Lady M. A horrible one, Bridget. Last night, as I was endeavouring to join the hunters, from whom, in the hurry of the chase, I had been separated, I wandered near the famous Basaltic Caverns, to which the vulgar attack so many strange traditions. The storm grew violent. By the strong flashes of lightning I discovered the opening of the grotto; I entered it for shelter, and overcome with fatigue, fell asleep upon one of the rocky tombs. On a sudden, a sepulchre opened, and a phantom approached me. I trembled. But an invisible hand seemed to prevent my flight. I could not even turn mine eyes from the apparition. To my surprise the countenance was that of a young and handsome man, but it was pale and woe-worn. His eyes, fix'd upon mine with the most touching expression, seemed to implore my pity. He uttered my name, and had nearly reach'd me, when a beautiful being stood between us, and check'd his progress. Then, Oh horror! the features of the spectre grew frightfully distorted; its whole form assum'd the most terrific appearance, and it sunk into the tomb from which it had issued with a shriek that froze me.

Bridget Mercy preserve us! I tremble all over.

Lady M. I awoke. The moon stream'd into the grotto, and I sprung into the open air. I heard the voices of those who sought me here. I answered them as loudly as I was able. With shouts of joy they surrounded me, and bore me safely hither.

Bridget I shall never sleep in peace again. Oh, my dear young lady!

Enter Lord Ronald

Ronald Well, my dear daughter. – What, up and dress'd again already. Come, this is a happy omen. Bridget, order my henchman to ascend the turrets of the Keep, and give notice of the Earl of Marsden's approach. (*Exit Bridget*). This day, my dear Margaret, will be one of the happiest of my life. But what's the matter? You appear sorrowful.

Lady M. Ah! my dear father, the nearer the moment approaches of his arrival, the more I feel uneasy.

Ronald Why this agitation, Margaret? I have never wished to force your inclination. I certainly desire his alliance most ardently; nevertheless, if you dislike him –

Lady M. I do not know that I shall. But you, sir, who wish me to accept him, do not know him personally.

Ronald 'Tis true; but if he resembles his brother, you cannot fail to love him. – Alas! poor Ruthven.

Lady M. I have heard you say he sav'd your life, and for that reason I revere his memory myself. But are you sure he no longer exists?

Ronald Alas! the fatal scene of his death is ever present to my imagination. When called, as you know, by the sudden illness of my now lost son to Athens, I found Lord Ruthven, with whom he had contracted an intimacy, hanging over his sick couch, and bestowing on him the attentions of a brother. Such behaviour naturally endear'd him to me; and after my poor boy's death, his lordship seem'd destin'd to fill that place in my affections which had become void by my son's decease. I shew'd him your miniature. – Never shall I forget his emotion on beholding it. 'By heavens!' he exclaim'd, ' 'tis the precise image my fancy has created as the

70

only being who could ever constitute my happiness'. We were on the point of returning to Scotland to learn your sentiments on the subject, when one evening – after a short excursion, we were attack'd by some banditti. I was disarm'd. Ruthven threw himself before me, and received the ruffian's sabre on his own breast. Our attendants, however, succeeded in overcoming the villains. I threw myself into the arms of my expiring friend – he press'd my hand – 'Lord Ronald', said he, 'I have sav'd your life – I die content – my only regret is, that fate has prevented me from becoming your son'. Gallant, unfortunate Ruthven! what a destiny was thine to fall in a foreign land, in the flower of thy youth, deprived of sepulchre.

Lady M. How! deprived of sepulchre!

Ronald An extraordinary circumstance prevented my fulfilling that last melancholy duty. In his dying agonies he conjur'd me to quit the spot, lest the assassins should return in number. I left the body to collect our servants who were in pursuit of the defeated villains, and 'ere we could return to the spot, it had disappeared.

Lady M. Remov'd for plunder, doubtless.

Ronald I ne'er could ascertain. The stains of the grass sufficiently mark'd the spot were I had lain him; but all search was in vain. On quitting Greece I heard Lord Marsden was in Venice. To him I sent his brother's property, and amidst it he found your picture which, in my desire for his alliance, I had given Ruthven. The Earl proposed immediately to replace the loss we had sustained in his brother, and nothing, I am confident, remains to complete our happiness but his arrival

Re-enter Bridget

Bridget The Earl has arrived, my lord.

Ronald Come, Margaret, let us haste and receive him.

Lady M. My dear sir, I cannot see him yet; indeed I cannot.

Ronald Retire, then, for awhile to your apartment. Bridget, attend your lady.

(*Exeunt Lady Margaret and Bridget*)

Enter Servants

I'll fly to meet the earl. – Ha! he is here

Enter Lord Ruthven

My Lord, the honour you have done me! – Heavens! what do I see ?

Ruthven Do I re-call the memory of a friend, Lord Ronald ?

Ronald His voice too! – Ruthven!

Ruthven Such was my name till the death of an elder brother put me in possession of my present title.

71

Ronald Can I believe my senses! Ruthven, my friend! But by what miracle have you been preserved to me?

Ruthven Unexpected, but powerful assistance, re-called my fleeting spirit. When sufficiently recovered to join you, you had quitted Greece. The news of my brother's death reach'd me. I wrote to you under my new title, and arriving in Scotland to take possession of my paternal estate determined to give you this pleasurable surprise.

Ronald Oh, happy hour! Be sure, Ruthven, that my daughter would only have become your brother's bride, to acquit me of the debt I owe to you.

Ruthven My generous friend, but think you I shall be fortunate enough to gain the lovely Margaret's affections?

Ronald I cannot doubt it – she has pitied your misfortunes – she has wept over your fate. She comes. (*Exeunt Attendants*) What will be her astonishment –

Re-enter Lady Margaret

My dear, behold that generous friend, whose loss we have so long deplor'd. 'Tis Ruthven claims your hand.

Lady M. My Lord, duty to a beloved parent will –

(*She raises her eyes slowly to his countenance – starts and falls, with a shriek, into the arms of Lord Ronald*)

Ronald Margaret! O, heavens! she is ill. Help there!

Lady M. (*Shuddering, and aside*) That countenance! The phantom of last night. (*Relapses into insensibility*).

Ruthven What can have occasioned this emotion?

Ronald Alas! I know not. Margaret! my sweet child!

Lady M. (*Reviving*) Pardon, my lord, this weakness – the effect of last night's adventure.

Ruthven Last night!

Ronald We hunted late yesterday. My daughter lost her way, and suffered much fatigue.

Ruthven Beautiful Lady Margaret, how am I to interpret this emotion?

Lady M. The surprise of seeing one whose death we were even now deploring.

Ruthven Is it possible, that without knowing me, the recital of my misfortunes alone, could thus have interested you?

Lady M. I am the daughter of Lord Ronald, and my heart, touched with gratitude – (*Aside*) I dare not look at him.

Ruthven With gratitude? and what will be my gratitude, if you but deign to approve your father's generous designs. Tell me, oh, tell me you confirm them; or never, never will I rise from your feet. (*Kneeling and seizing her hand*).

Lady M. (*Aside*) Heavens! how strange a thrill runs through my frame.

Ruthven (*Aside*) Then she's mine. O, my friend, join your supplications to mine.

Ronald My daughter is well aware of my wishes.

Ruthven Speak, dearest lady, I conjure you.

Lady M. (*Aside*) What spell is it that moves me thus? (*Aloud*) My lord, my father has never yet found me disobedient to his will.

Ruthven You consent, then?

Lady M. Pardon me, my lord; a strange confusion, a wild emotion overpowers me; let me retire. (*Exit Lady Margaret*).

Ronald Ruthven, the wish of my heart is gratified; you are my son.

Ruthven Dearest sir, I have still a boon to ask. Let our marriage be celebrated without delay.

Ronald It is my intention; and to-morrow –

Ruthven To-night, my friend; business of the utmost importance re-calls me to London. To-morrow's dawn must witness our departure.

Ronald Well, if my daughter makes no objection, I will go, plead your suit. Rest assured I feel for you all that a father's heart can feel. (*Exit Ronald*).

Ruthven Still must the fearful sacrifice be made! and suddenly; for the approaching night will find my wretched frame exhausted – and darkness – worse than death – annihilation is my lot! Margaret! unhappy maid! thou art my destined prey! thy blood must feed a Vampire's life, and prove the food of his disgusting banquet!

Enter Robert (*timidly*)

Robert My lord!

Ruthven What would you?

Robert I am a servant of Lord Ronald's, and would fain request your lordship's patronage.

Ruthven In what respect?

Robert I am betrothed, an please your lordship, to Effie, your steward's daughter; and as I hear it is your lordship's intention to visit your estate, I –

Ruthven (*Eagerly*) Betrothed, say you?

Robert Yes, my lord.

Ruthven And when is the marriage to take place?

Robert This evening, my lord.

Ruthven I will be there (*Half aside*).

Robert Oh, your lordship has made me so happy!

Ruthven What distance are we from my castle?

Robert The sea is calm, my lord – we may row there in a few minutes.

Ruthven Order the barge instantly, then.
Robert Yes, my lord. (*Exit*)

Enter Ronald

Ronald All is arranged to your wishes.
Ruthven (*With joy*) Your daughter consents ?
Ronald She does; and I have ordered the chapel to be prepared by our return.
Ruthven You go to Marsden with me, then ?
Ronald Certainly; your stay is so short, I will not leave you for a moment

Re-enter Robert

Robert The barge is ready, my lord.
Ruthven Away! Away!

(*Hurried music*). (*Exeunt*)

Scene 3
Garden of Lord Ruthven's Castle; the Sea in the back ground

Andrew and Effie discovered, surrounded by Village Lads and Lasses, dressed as for a fête.

Effie What can be the reason Robert does not arrive ?
Andrew Something has happened to detain him; he will be here soon. What is that to the right, there ? It is a boat; and making for the castle, too.
Effie Hark! father, hark!

(*A Boat is seen at Sea, which gradually approaches to the Symphony of the following Boat-Song, growing louder and louder as the Boat nears*)

BOAT SONG
Tune – 'Ye Banks and Braes'

Row on – Row on – across the main
So smoothly glides our bark to shore,
While to our boat-song's measur'd strain,
So truly dips the well tim'd oar.

Row on – Row on – in yonder Isle,
Impatient beauty chides our stay,
The head-land past – her sweetest smile
Our labour richly will repay

(*Shouts without*)

Enter Robert

Effie My dear Robert –
Robert My sweet Effie!
Effie What has kept you so long?
Robert Oh, I've news for you. Lord Ronald has come with me, and who do you think beside, father-in-law?
Andrew Nay, I'm sure I can't guess.
Robert Lord Ruthven.
Andrew Lord Ruthven! why he has been dead these twelve months

Enter Ruthven, Ronald, and Attendants

Merciful Providence, it is my young master!
Ruthven Yes, my good Andrew; behold me restored to you.
Andrew Thank heaven! Thank heaven!
Ruthven Let me not interrupt your felicity: – you are about to celebrate a marriage, I think?
Andrew Yes, my lord. – Here's my daughter, Effie, whom your lordship remembers a little girl.
Ruthven You must allow me to give the bride her dowry, and patronize the whole ceremony.
Andrew Oh, my lord, this is such an honour. Well, then before the dance commences, neighbours, let us go and arrange the supper-table, where we will drink our good lord's happy return.
Robert Away with you, then

Exeunt Andrew and Peasants

Ronald I must leave you a moment, Ruthven, to give some directions to my bargemen

Exeunt Ronald and Attendants

Robert Come, Effie, let's follow our neighbours. (*Going*).
Ruthven (*Detaining Effie*) Fair Effie, I would speak with you.
Effie If Robert has no objection, my lord –
Robert How, you silly girl, when his lordship does you so much honour. – You'll find me with Andrew

Exit Robert

75

Ruthven Come nearer, charming maid.

Effie My lord, I – I dare not, my lord.

Ruthven Fear nothing. (*Aside*) Yet, she has cause to fear. – Should I surprise *her* heart, as by my gifted spell I may, Margaret may (at least a while) be spared. How delightful 'tis to gaze upon thee thus! – My heart ne'er throb'd but for one woman, and you have just her features. This morning the flame of love was extinguished in my soul; but now, now it burns with redoubled ardour.

Effie But the lady whom you admir'd, my lord? –

Ruthven She is dead!

Effie Dead!

Ruthven Yes, dead, Effie: – but in you she lives again.

Effie What do I hear!

Ruthven Oh, Effie, can you not conceive the happiness of once more beholding the object we adore.

Effie See me no more, my lord, if that has occasioned your uneasiness. (*Going*).

Ruthven Stay! Effie, it is in your power to console me for all I have lost. Love me. – Nay, start not; mine you must and shall be.

Effie My lord, I'll hear no more. – If Robert –

Ruthven Think not of him; my bride thou art – no power on earth shall tear thee from me: say, Effie, that you love me (*Taking her hand*).

Effie (*Starting*) Mercy on me! – My lord, I – I know not what to say. My heart beats so that – Oh, pray leave me, my lord. (*Sobbing*).

Ruthven This instant let me bear thee to the priest.

Effie My lord, for pity's sake –

Ruthven You plead in vain: – Effie, thou art mine for ever

Bears her off

Re-enter Robert

Robert How long she stays – Not here! Why, (*Effie shrieks*) Heav'ns! what do I see – borne off, and struggling. – Villain, loose your hold!

(*Draws a pistol, and runs after them*)

Enter Andrew and Lord Ronald

Ronald Why, Andrew, said you not the Earl was here?

Andrew 'Twas here I left him but just now, my lord

(*A pistol is fired without, and Effie shrieks, 'O save me! Save me!'*)

Andrew My daughter's voice!

Rushes out, as Lord Ruthven enters wounded

Ronald Ruthven!

Ruthven *(Falling)* I die!

Ronald What murderous hand –

Ruthven Exclaim not. I have but a moment to live. – Ronald, swear by the host of heaven to obey my last commands.

Ronald I do, I do. – I swear by all that is most dear and sacred to honour and to man, to fulfil your last desire.

Ruthven Conceal my death from every human being, till yonder moon shall be set this night; and 'ere an hour shall elapse after I have expired, throw this ring into the waves that wash the tomb of Fingal.

Ronald I will, I will, Ruthven! – Dear Ruthven.

Ruthven Remember your oath. The lamp of night is descending the blue heavens; when I am dead, let its sweet light shine on me. – Farewell. Remember – Remember your oath. *(Dies)*

(Solemn Music. Ronald lays the body of Ruthven on a bank in the garden, and kneels mournfully beside it)

End of the First Act

Act the Second

Scene 1

The Tomb of Fingal in the Caverns of Staffa. – The Sea. – Moonlight. – A Boat enters the Cavern with Andrew, Robert, and Effie. – They land. – (Music)

Andrew Here, Robert, you may rest concealed till Lord Ronald's anger shall have subsided. Here is sufficient provision for the short time I hope you will be forced to remain. And so now bid Effie good-bye for a while; I'll look out in the mean time, and see if the coast be clear for our return

Exit

Robert Come, cheer up, Effie, all will be well yet. It was in defence of innocence I fired, and therefore that act will never be a load on my conscience.
Effie But if Lord Ronald should get you into his power!
Robert I will put it to Lord Ronald's self to say, whether a man should stand tamely by, and see the wife of his bosom dragged to misery and dishonour. – Come, come, kiss me, Effie, and farewell till better times

Effie and Robert sing to the tune of 'Down the Burn, Davie'

(During the last verse, Andrew has returned; he places Effie in the Boat, and they Exeunt)

Robert And now to find some hole for a bed-chamber. Rather sorry accommodations, I fancy; but a man with a clear conscience may rest anywhere

Exit into Cavern

(Music. – A Boat is seen at the Entrance, with Lord Ronald and two Attendants in it. – Lord Ronald lands)

Ronald Give me the torch, and wait without the cave till you see me wave it thus. (*Exeunt Attendants, with Boat*). How solemn is this scene.

Here is the ring – what am I about to do – what horrible suspicion flashes across my brain. Ruthven, mysterious being, what mean these ceremonies ? Before when I supposed him dying, he bade me place his body in the light of the then rising moon; and now again. And wherefore make me swear to conceal his death till the moon be set ? – But let me not reflect or pause. Unhappy Ruthven! thy friend performs his promise

(*Throws the Ring into the Water; a Peal of Thunder is heard; after which the Voice of Ruthven,* Remember your oath!)

Ronald It is his spirit speaks. Ruthven! my friend, my preserver!

Re-enter Robert

Robert What voice was that, Lord Ronald!
Ronald Ha! by heaven, justice hath given the murderer to my vengeance. (*Draws*).
Robert Hear me, my lord; Lord Ruthven would have wronged me.
Ronald Would'st thou asperse the dead! – Down, villain, down. (*Attacks him*)

(*They Fight; Robert is Disarmed. – Ronald plunges him into the Waves*)

Ronald Ruthven thou art revenged! Away! Away!

(*Ronald leaps into the Boat. – Robert reaches and clings to the Rocks; and the Scene closes*)

Scene 2
An Apartment in Lord Ronald's Castle

Enter Lady Margaret, meeting Bridget

Lady M. Bridget, I was looking for you; I am so happy.
Bridget Happy, my lady! and Lord Ruthven and your father not returned, 'tis ten o'clock, and they were to have been back again 'ere sunset.
Lady M. You may dispel your fears, then; Lord Ruthven has this moment announced to me my father's return.
Bridget Lord Ruthven!
Lady M. On opening the casement just now, I saw him by the moonlight crossing one of the walks. I call'd to him, and he will be here directly, that the ceremony may commence. We must depart for London 'ere day-break.

Bridget So soon?

Lady M. Yes; he has explained the reason to me. The King of England wishes him to marry a lady of the court, and he has no other way of avoiding the match, but by presenting me immediately as his wife.

Bridget And here comes your father, I declare. Well, my lady, I'll away and see that every thing is ready

Exit Bridget

Lady M. I can hardly account for my sudden attachment to Lord Ruthven, especially after the shock his introduction gave me

Enter Lord Ronald

Well, sir, is Ruthven coming?

Ronald Ruthven! Alas!

Lady M. You sigh; what troubles you, my dear father?

Ronald Nothing. (*Aside*) What shall I say to her?

Lady M. Every thing is prepared for the ceremony. – You do not listen to me – why, father, what's the matter?

Ronald My dear Margaret, we must think no more of this union.

Lady M. Think no more of it!

Ronald Question me not; I cannot answer you.

Lady M. Good heavens! and Ruthven, who not a moment ago, so warmly urged –

Ronald (*Starting*) Ruthven, not a moment ago – what mean you?

Lady M. You frighten me; but Ruthven will soon be here, and –

Enter Lord Ruthven, behind

Ruthven (*Aside*) Remember your oath.

Ronald (*Starting*) Can the grave give up its dead! Spirit what woulds't thou?

Ruthven Ronald, my friend, what means this wildness?

Ronald My brain turns round; – I saw him fall – I heard his dying groan – Fiend! – Phantom – hence, I charge thee.

Ruthven Alas, he raves!

Lady M. My father! my poor father!

Ronald Touch him not, Margaret! Fly the demon's grasp!

Ruthven How dreadful is this wildness. – Ho! within there!

Ronald I am not mad. Ruthven's dead! I saw –

Ruthven (*Aside*) Your oath

Enter Two Servants

Ruthven Your master is not well, his brain is wandering; secure

80

him, and let aid be sent for instantly

Servants take hold of Ronald

Ronald Stand off, slaves! 'tis a fiend in human shape. – I saw him perish; twice have I seen him perish.
Ruthven (*Aside*) Your oath!
Ronald Margaret, promise me you will not marry till the moon shall set; then, fearful fiend, I am no longer pledged, and may preserve my child.
Lady M. Oh, my poor, poor father!
Ruthven Remove him gently – suddenly, I say.
Ronald No, I will not quit my child an instant; horror overwhelms me! I know not what thou art; but terrible conviction flashes on my mind, that thou art nothing human. A mist seems clearing from my sight; and I behold thee now – Oh, horror! horror! – a monster of the grave – a – a Vam –

(*Falls into his Servants' arms, who bear him off*)

Lady M. Alas! How wild a fancy seized him, that you were dead; and his request too, not to marry till the moon had set. – Well, I will not.
Ruthven (*Aside*) Ha! (*Aloud*) I reverence your motive; but if you love me, Margaret –
Lady M. You cannot doubt it.
Ruthven Upon that love then, my repose, my happiness, my life depends; swear to me, dearest Margaret, to forget these idle terrors, and to be mine – mine only – for ever.
Lady M. I do, by Him who reads all hearts, to be thine, and thine only, for ever.
Ruthven Oh, happiness! receive this ring, and let it be a sacred pledge between us. (*Places it on her finger*).
Lady M. Ha!
Ruthven (*Smiling*) Her fate is seal'd, she cannot now retract. – You shudder; what ails my love?
Lady M. A strange sensation runs throughout my frame – Methinks my father's voice still rings in mine ears, 'Wed not before the moon shall set'.
Ruthven (*Aside*) The hour approaches; no time is to be lost. (*Aloud*) Think no more, I beseech thee, of these wanderings of the imagination, but let us hasten to consecrate the ties which unite us. Every arrangement must, by this time, have been made. Retire, my love, to your chamber; compose your spirits; and Ruthven then will lead thee to the altar. (*Music*)

Exeunt Ruthven and Lady Margaret

Scene 3
Distant View of Lord Ronald's Castle, by Moonlight

Enter Andrew and Effie, supporting Robert

Robert Nay, nay, do not trouble yourselves; I have sustained no injury. – But what made you come back to me so soon ?

Effie We saw the boat pass with Lord Ronald in it, and we feared some mischief.

Andrew So we lay-to till he left the cavern, and returned just in time to render you assistance. Yonder is the castle; are you still determined to seek him ?

Robert Yes; he has been imposed upon; and 'ere now, I am sure, he regrets having drawn upon me. I will lay open Lord Ruthven's villainy to him; and I know his noble nature too well, to fear a continuance of his anger

(*M'Swill sings without*)

Andrew Soft; who comes here ?

Robert By his gait it should be M'Swill, the Baron's toping henchman

Enter M'Swill

M'Swill My master's gone mad – there's a pretty job. If he had been going to be married, instead of the Earl, I shouldn't have wonder'd so much; but for an old man to go mad, who can sit and drink all day, without any one to snub him for it, is the most ridiculous thing that ever came under my observation. Old mother Bridget never lets me drink in quiet at home, so I carry a pocket pistol about with me. (*Pulls out a Flask*) Now this is what I call my 'Young Man's Best Companion;' it's a great consolation on a night excursion, to one who has so respectful a belief in bogles and warlocks, as I have. – Whiskey's the only spirit I feel a wish to be intimately acquainted with.

Robert (*Slapping gim on the Shoulder*) M'Swill!

M'Swill (*Dropping on his Knees*) Oh, Lord, what's that!

Robert Why, how now, booby; where have you been at this time of night ?

M'Swill Been! Oh, I've been for Father Francis; – my lord's gone crazy, and the Earl of Marsden sent me.

Robert and *Effie* The Earl of Marsden!

M'Swill Yes, to be sure; he's in the Castle there, and just going to be married to my Lady Margaret.

Robert Fool! the Earl of Marsden is dead.

M'Swill Nay, now you're mad. My master's been telling the same story this half hour; but the Earl says it's no such thing; that he is not dead, and never was dead; that my master's out of his wits; – and off he sends me for Father Francis, to come and talk to my master, and marry my mistress.

Robert What mystery is this? There is some foul play towards – At any rate, the Lady Margaret must know her danger. Is the friar gone?

M' Swill Oh yes, he's there before now.

Robert Les us haste, father; we may foil the villain yet

Exeunt Robert, Andrew, and Effie

(*M' Swill sings to the tune of 'Fy, let us awa' to the Bridal'*)

Scene 4

The Chapel. – A large Gothic Window, through which the Moon is seen Setting. – Lord Ruthven discovered, with Priest, Vassals, etc, etc. (*Music*)

Ruthven All is prepared; o'er the great fiend once more
I triumph! 'Ere yon orb shall kiss the wave,
The tributary victim shall be paid.
Bow, ye less subtle spirits – bow abashed
Before your master.
– Margaret!
'Tis Ruthven calls thee. Hasten, sweet, and crown
Thy lover's happiness. (*Music*)

Enter Lady Margaret and Bridget

Ruthven Lady, to the altar.

Lady M. I follow you, my lord – and yet –

Ruthven (*Impatiently seizing her hand*) Come, Margaret, come!

(*Distant Thunder. A loud gust of Wind shakes the Casement*)

Lady M. What noise was that?

Bridget 'Tis but the wind, my lady; we shall have another storm I think, when the moon sets.

Lady M. When the moon sets! – Ah, my poor father! See, 'twill set soon, my Ruthven; let me again beseech you to delay, till then, the ceremony!

Ruthven (*More impatiently*) Nay, this is folly, Margaret. – Father, commence the rites

83

Enter Lord Ronald, preceded by Robert, and followed by Andrew, Effie, and Attendants

Robert Make way! make way, I say! Lord Ronald shall be heard!
Ronald My daughter! my daughter!
Ruthven (*Aside*) Confusion! – Ronald!
Ronald Where is she? – Give me my daughter.
Lady M. My dearest father, be calm. What would'st thou with me?
Ronald Ha! do I again embrace thee. Follow him not – he drags you to the tomb.
Ruthven (*Furiously*) Margaret, we are waited for.
Ronald Barbarian! I forbid the ceremony. You have no right over her – I am her father.
Lady M. You are – you are my loving, tender father: – I will not wed against his will.
Ruthven I'll hear no more! – she is my bride betrothed: this madman would deprive me of her.
Ronald (*Loud Thunder. Another Gust of Wind blows open the Casement*) See! see! the moon already rests upon the wave! – One moment! – but one moment! –
Ruthven Nay, then thus I seal my lips, and seize my bride

(*Ruthven draws his Poignard: rushes on Ronald – Robert throws himself between Ruthven and Ronald, and wrenches the Dagger from his grasp*)

Lady M. Hold! hold! – I am thine; the moon has set.
Ruthven And I am lost!

(*A terrific Peal of Thunder is heard; Unda and Ariel appear; a Thunder Bolt strikes Ruthven to the ground, who immediately vanishes. General picture*)

THE CURTAIN FALLS

The Vampire, engraving by J Findlay showing tartans and Fingal's cave. (*Enthoven Collection*)

THE PRESS

The Times, August 10th, 1820:

ENGLISH OPERA-HOUSE

A new dramatic romance, called The Vampire; or the Bride of the Isles, *was brought out last night at this theatre. It is one of those productions which, uniting dialogue, and music with scenery of more than ordinary splendour, aided likewise by some admixture of pantomime, pass in the theatrical nomenclature under the title of* melodrames. *Its name will readily suggest that it is built on a well-known superstition, which is said to be yet prevalent in some parts of the Turkish dominions. We are informed, however, that it is nothing more than a free translation from the French, and that the original has met with unprecendented success amongst our neighbours. The only instance in which the translator has departed from his foreign model is, we think, rather an unlucky specimen of his judgement. He has removed the scene of his fable from those regions where the superstition is familiar, to the Western Islands of Scotland, and introduced a new guest to the bogles and warlochs, their ancient natives. Now the popular belief in matters purely imaginary is a very decisive mark of the character and manners of a people; and if we are to adhere to strict propriety, it is manifest that the author might as well have interwoven a portraiture of druidical rites with the representation of a pilgrimage to Mecca. On such an occasion we must not look for any regular congruity of incident, or preservation of character; but if we can forgive the sin just mentioned, (and in this respect we are of the same disposition as the audience), there may be found in it a very lively exhibition of those horrors which retain their hold on the ignorance and credulity of the Levantines. The* Vampire *in the new piece is a chieftain who, we may guess, probably lived in the time of Fingal; for his spirit appears to reside near that hero's tomb, and the number of his resurrections is undefined. Having acquired the epithet of 'the bloody' during his natural life, he afterwards assumed other characters, and continued to renew his existence, and avoid the dreadful gulf of annihilation, by winning, in a given time, some virgin for his prey, from whose veins he uniformly extracted the life-blood. In the person of* Earl Marsden *he gains the friendship of* Lady Margaret's *father,* Lord Ronald of the Isles, *is killed in his defence, and whilst* Lord Ronald *is preparing to*

86

receive his brother as a fit substitute on whom his daughter might bestow her hand, re-appears, and offers to have been but slightly wounded. He then commences his mysterious operations, which he is under the necessity of expediting because, unless he is married before the moon is set, his charter will have expired. Notwithstanding this necessity, however, he entangles himself in a fresh difficulty, is again killed, and, by the aid of potent spells, again revives, and within the time appointed for claiming his bride or determining his destiny. The eyes of Lord Ronald *are at length opened; he proclaims his intended son-in-law to be a demon incarnate; by his violence rather than his reasoning he causes the nuptials to be postponed till the moon has vanished, and the* Vampire *then drops into final extinction. Such is the plot or rather the subject matter of the piece. It has but little pretension, and calls not for a rigorous judgement. The decorations are suitable, if not magnificent; and the incidental music consists of a selection of favourite Scottish airs. One of the duets was executed with infinite sweetness and taste by Miss Carew and Pearman. The performers engaged exerted themselves with considerable effect, and the whole drama met with a most encouraging reception. It was to have been produced on Monday last, but the death of the Duchess of York led to a suspension, for two days, of all theatrical entertainments.*

From Leigh Hunt's *Dramatic Essays*:

THE VAMPIRE

The new Dramatic Romance (or whatever it is called) of the Vampyre is, upon the whole, the most splendid spectacle we have ever seen. It is taken from a French piece, founded on the celebrated story so long bandied about between Lord Byron, Mr Shelley, and Dr Polidori, which last turned out to be the true author. As a mere fiction, and as a fiction attributed to Lord Byron, whose genius is chartered for the land of horrors, the original story passed well enough: but on the stage it is a little shocking to the feelings, and incongruous to the sense, to see a spirit in human shape, – in the shape of a real Earl, and, what is more, of a Scotch Earl – going about seeking whom it may marry and then devour, to lengthen out its own abhorred and anomalous being. Allowing for the preternatural atrocity of the fable, the situations were well imagined and supported: the acting of Mr T P Cooke (from the Surrey Theatre) was spirited and imposing, and certainly Mrs W H Chatterley, as the daughter of his friend the baron (Mr Bartley), and his destined bride, bid fair to be a very delectable victim. She is, however, saved in a surprising manner, after a rapid succession of interesting events, to the great joy of the spectator. The scenery of this piece is its greatest charm, and it is inimitable. We have seen sparkling and overpowering effects of this kind before; but to the splendour of a transparency were here added all the harmony and mellowness of the finest painting. We do not speak

87

of the vision at the beginning, or of that at the end of the piece, – though these were admirably managed, – so much of the representation of the effects of moonlight on the water and on the person of the dying knight. The hue of the sea-green waves, floating in the pale beam under an archway of grey weather-beaten rocks, and with the light of a torch glaring over the milder radiance, was in as fine keeping and strict truth as Claude or Rembrandt, and would satisfy, we think, the most fastidious artist's eye. It lulled the sense of sight as the fancied sound of the dashing waters soothed the imagination. In the scene where the moonlight fell on the dying form of Ruthven *(the Vampire) it was like a fairy glory, forming a palace of emerald light: the body seemed to drink its balmy essence, and to revive in it without a miracle. The line,*

'See how the moon sleeps with Endymion,'

came into the mind from the beauty and gorgeousness of the picture, notwithstanding the repugnance of every circumstance and feeling.

Luke
the Labourer

J B BUCKSTONE

J B Buckstone
(*Enthoven Collection*)

JOHN BALDWIN BUCKSTONE (1802/1879)

Like Douglas Jerrold, J B Buckstone was placed on board a man-of-war at the age of ten, but, unlike his fellow-dramatist, he was soon released and allowed to return to school through the influence of a relative. He was articled to a solicitor, but much preferred amateur theatricals to studying the law; at about the age of eighteen he turned professional and for three years worked in the provinces, during which time he met Edmund Kean, who encouraged him in his new calling. Rapidly acquiring a reputation as a low comedian, in 1823 he made his first London appearance at the Surrey. From 1824–1827 he was with the Coburg Theatre, and then joined the Adelphi company to appear as Bobby Trot in his own *Luke The Labourer*. This first play had in fact been produced the year previously, but the manager of the Adelphi, a Daniel Terry, had lost the name and address of the author (the piece had been submitted by a friend of Buckstone's without his knowledge) – W S Gilbert's career in the theatre had a similar beginning.

At the Adelphi Buckstone met Sir Walter Scott, a meeting which inspired him to further his ambitions as a playwright. He was to produce well over one hundred pieces (including some under the name of H Younge), although few have any especial merit despite their success. He wrote principally for the Haymarket and Adelphi theatres, and churned out melodramas, farces and burlesques on all the usual themes of the day, including an adaptation of Bulwer-Lytton's novel *Last Days of Pompeii* (1834), a version of the ever-popular Jack Sheppard highwayman story (1839), and the play by which he is perhaps best remembered today *The Green Bushes* (1845) which was burlesqued relentlessly by many hands including Buckstone's own, and which includes the delicious stage-direction: '*Jack sits on a burnt stump and plays "Zip Coon" on the fiddle . . .*' How many actors of today could do that!

The following is a quotation from the *Dictionary of National Biography*:

Buckstone was not what is sometimes called an objective actor. To a great extent he was Buckstone in every character. It might be objected that on occasions his acting was somewhat too broad; but this defect was lost sight of in his infectious self-complacency and overflow of fun. Added to a countenance peculiarly fitted to express humour in all its varieties and transitions, he had an evident enjoyment of the droll conceptions he was embodying, which enhanced that of his audiences. He had sometimes a way of pausing before he uttered a joke, and, when he had wound up the house to expectancy, of discharging it with a rapidity and elation that were irresistible. As a man he possessed the abundant geniality which he threw into his acting. He was never more at home than at a weekly club which he founded at the Haymarket Theatre. In 1853 he became manager of the Haymarket, and remained in that capacity until within three years of his death.* His control of the theatre was in every way creditable. He was scarcely better known as an actor than as a prolific dramatist. Of his stage productions, amounting to between one and two hundred, scarcely one was a failure, while many were unusual successes. He had great knowledge of stage effect, much humour, though of a broad kind, nor was he deficient in pathos, or in such characterisation as commends itself to audiences. Buckstone was also a very humorous speaker. His addresses at the dinners of the Theatrical Fund and on his own benefit nights were always attractive. At one time he contributed a few papers to the periodicals. A sketch in the New Monthly Magazine *describing the career of an optimist perverted into a misanthrope by his experience of life, shows in its cynicism of tone and gravity of intention qualities far different from those which he displayed as an actor. In 1859*

---

*Irving appeared at his testimonial benefit on his retirement in 1876

he wrote a preface to the Rev Henry Bellows's Claims of the Drama. *After quitting the stage he sank into gradual decay, and died on October 31st, 1879*

Luke the Labourer is a drama (with the then newly fashionable domestic background) unusual in that, despite the last-minute rescue of the heroine from a fate worse than death at the hands of the Squire, his accomplice, Luke, is not only from the lower orders but is shown to have a degree of motivation for his villainy. The original Philip was another ex-seaman, T(homas) P(otter) Cooke, *qv*, who three years later was to consolidate his reputation as the finest stage matelot of them all in Jerrold's *Black-Eye'd Susan* at the Surrey, in which J B Buckstone appeared as *Gnatbrain*.

Luke The Labourer. Frontispiece from Cumberland's edition
(*British Museum*)

LUKE
THE LABOURER

Dramatis Personae

First produced at the Adelphi Theatre
September 17th, 1826

Squire Chase by Mr Foster
Farmer Wakefield by Mr Elliott
*Philip, His Son – in the First and Second Acts a Boy about Ten Years
of Age, by* Miss Daly *and* Mr T P Cooke
Aaron Mordica, A Jew Pedlar, by Mr Yates
Thomas Fillmug, Landlord of a Public-house, by Mr Phillips
Charles Maydew by Mr S Smith
Luke the Labourer by Mr Terry
Bobby Trot, A Country Lad, by Mr Salter
Michael, An Old Gipsy, by Mr Sanders
Dick, A Postillion, by Mr Lambert
Recruiting Sergeant
Corporal
Mrs Wakefield by Mrs Daly
Clara, Her Daughter, by Miss Taylor
Jenny, A Country Girl, by Mrs Hughes
Maria, Luke's Wife, by Mrs Yates

Villagers
Servants
Gipsies
Gamekeepers
Reapers
Wrestlers
Etc

Scene: a village in Yorkshire

Time of representation, three hours

LUKE THE LABOURER

Act 1

Scene 1
A village scene

Enter Farmer Wakefield, followed by Maria

Maria But, Farmer, only for a few days.

Wakefield No, I tell you, I will not. Hav'n't I repeatedly given him employment, and has he not as repeatedly neglected?

Maria He will not again – I'm sure he won't.

Wakefield This is the old story. For your sake, I've forgiven him, more than once, twice, or thrice. Does he not after receiving his wages, instead of going like others to his home, spend it in drink with his dissolute companions?

Maria Alas, too true!

Wakefield Do not think me hard-hearted – I am not. Your father and myself have toiled together in the field. We rose gradually to opulence together, and but for your marriage – would you had never seen him!

Maria Would I had not, indeed; but he is now my husband, and, as a lawful wife, 'tis my duty, whate'er his faults, to darken them to the world.

Wakefield On one condition I will again employ him.

Maria Oh, name it!

Wakefield That, should he again deceive me, you quit him then for ever! – (*A pause*) – and, for your father's sake, yourself shall in my house find a friendly home.

Maria Quit my husband – he whom at the sacred altar I have sworn to live and die with? No, never!

Wakefield Well, I consent once more to employ him. If he deceives me, your only resource is then the workhouse!

Enter Luke

Luke What bee'st doing here?

Maria I have solicited the Farmer to employ you again, and he consents.

Luke What didst ask him for? Ye might ha' stayed till to-morrow.

Wakefield Luke, come to your work! I forgive what's past. For your wife's sake, I –

Luke What ha' she to do wi' I?

Wakefield Luke, I wish to be your friend. Come to your work this day, or I have done with you for ever!

Exit Farmer

Luke (*Aside*) I will work this day – yes, for revenge.

Maria (*Taking him round the neck*) Come, Luke, we shall again be happy.

Luke Dom him!

Maria Nay, you wrong him, you do, indeed. Now, Luke, be persuaded.

Luke Well, for thy sake – but not to-day, to-morrow.

Maria Nay, why not directly?

Luke I can't. I'll tell 'ee why. I be going to wrestling match. (*She bursts into tears*) What ails 'ee? Come, come, Maria; all will be well. I shall work, I love 'ee, I tell 'ee, come – come. (*A loud noise without. Villagers, Gipsies, etc, pass across the stage*) Dang it, they be going to the wrestling match, and there'll be Mike the Gipsy. I want to speak wi' him.

Maria He is no companion for you.

Luke (*Not regarding her*) Ho, Mike! Stay, I want to speak wi' you (*Kisses her*) Good-bye to 'ee.

Scene 2
Inside of Wakefield's house

Mrs Wakefield and Philip discovered

Philip Why, mother, how can you be so hard-hearted towards Luke?

Mrs W. You mistake, my dear boy, I am not hard-hearted. Myself, as well as your father, would do anything to serve him, for his wife's sake.

Philip Then do ask father to let him come to work.

Mrs W. Philip, your father acts as a man – as a friend. He strives to win him from folly – to reclaim him. (*A knock at the door*).

Philip There's father come home!

(*Runs and opens the door, and Aaron puts his head in*)

96

Aaron Ah, my young master, vares your mother? I've got a new stock I vonts her to see. (*Perceiving Mrs Wakefield, he comes in*) I beg your pardon, I come as I go by, to ask before I leave, and go away, vot you like to pye. Only look here. Here is the latest new French toys, all come from the t'other side de vater.

Mrs W. I don't want any this time, Aaron.

Aaron You'll never have so great a chance again. If you don't pye now, to-morrow dey will be all gone. Dare, my little master, I vill give you that for a keepsake. (*Gives a book*) It's an almanack. Tells you all you don't know, and more as you will never learn.

Mrs W. Well, when the Farmer comes home, I'll ask him, and if he has no objection –

Aaron Oh, he will have none, I'm sure! Is there nothing else I shall leave for him to look? I can call as I come back from the wrestling. Dare – dare is a ring. Says I to myself, as I came across the fields, says I, Aaron – Aaron Mordica, dis ring is just the thing for Mrs Wakefield. There, you shall have it – a bargain for one pound one.

Mrs W. Is that the lowest, Aaron?

Aaron Vhy, you don't think I stole it. By the father Abram, it cost me almost all the money. But I must go, I will call as I comes back. I am very much obliged. I wish you a good day – good day to you, young master. (*Is going out, but starts back*).

Mrs W. Philip, go as far as the gate with Aaron.

Philip Yes, mother! Come, Aaron!

Aaron I thank you. Good tay!

(*Bows to Mrs Wakefield and Philip conducts him out*)

Scene 3

Represents the ring formed for wrestling. Luke in the ring, a man under him, as if just thrown. Loud huzzas by the spectators. Luke walks about the ring in high glee. Michael throws his hat in, and follows it. The Mob exclaim, 'Mike the Gipsy. This will be a good match, etc'. The men shake hands and go to work. Michael is thrown as the Scene closes them in

Scene 4

A front view. Village in distance

Villagers dance across. Then enter Michael dejected

Michael Curse Luke's better fortune; but for him I should have gained the prize! No matter, I'll be even with him. What he spoke of concerning Wakefield's child; he little knows Mike, or he'd ne'ar have –

97

Enter Luke, elated

Luke Mike, here they are – four crowns. I arn't had so much money many a day. Hark'e, Mike, you know what I said to 'ee ? This night I'll do 'ee; but come, we'll take some ale. Come, lad, I ha' gotten the money – come!

Michael I'm thinking it no easy matter to secure him; and then the risk I run!

Luke I know every inch of the house. You shall remain outside. I'll bring him to 'ee.

Michael You say Wakefield has wronged you ?

Luke Wronged me ? He ha' been a serpent stinging me all my days! He poured his poison into Maria's father's ear, and steeled his heart against me; but for him, old man would have left her all, and I'd ha' been a mon – a mon of might!

Michael The boy must be taken far from hence, so the reward you will receive from us cannot be much.

Luke Much! I do not care for that! Hav'n't I ha' gotten money? Loads on't – four crowns! You'll be true – ne'er speak on't to any mon, woman, or child ?

Michael Our tribe are bound on oath to be secret on all occasions, and where interest is concerned, it makes the oath more binding.

Luke Gu' us your hand then; there – there's the grasp of truth! (*Takes his hand*).

Michael I have felt his wrath, and for what ? Only because I and my fellow slept within his barn. The night was stormy – the rain fell in torrents – the lightning flashed around us, and the thunder seemed to threaten destruction – the very barn was shook with its horrid roar.

Luke Oh, that night! – never shall I forget it! The only child heaven deigned to bless us with in that fell night, were lost to us for ever! The roof of the house were beaten in by the storm, and our child that lay sucking at its mother's breast in peace, were killed by the rafter that fell upon its head. Methinks I see it now. Oh, the sight on't drives me to madness! Do na' – do na' name that night.

Michael You know what it is to lose a child, and yet you will take one from its parents' arms.

Luke That's right! Why, what ails you ? You are not half so bold as when you were wrestling wi' I. Come, the ale will rouse your spirits! Now don't be long, for I be dry. Come – come – come

Exit Luke

Michael Yes, I have committed many an act contrary to law, but never robbed a parent of its child; nor would I assist now, but that Wakefield's cruelty to me and my fellows drive me to it. For what were I imprisoned ? For what taken from my friends ? Because we were hid within his barn, and one solitary hare and pheasant found within my bag. Yet, for this did I toil three long months. I have sworn revenge! I'll keep my oath! But I will not harm the boy – not a hair of his head! No, no, no!

Exit

Scene 5

Outside of a village Ale-house. Luke, Gipsies, villagers, etc, discovered drinking

Luke Bravo, bravo, my boys! Come, drink; it's not every day we ha' gotten the money. Fillmug, what ho! (*Calls aloud*)

Enter Fillmug

Fillmug Why, Master Luke, you make more noise than all the other customers put togeather.
Luke Do I? Well, I can pay for what I call for, I reckon. Come, a full quart, and quickly.
Fillmug Well, well, you shall have it. (*Sings*)
To grieve in this life is a folly,
So, wrestlers, fill bumpers of ale

Enter Michael, Fillmug enters at the same time with a full tankard

Fillmug Here it is, Master Luke – the regular home brewed.
Luke Take it, Mike, and drink, lad.
Michael With all my heart! (*Takes the mug*).
Fillmug This makes nine quarts, besides the bacca and pipes.
Luke Well, and it were nineteen I'd pay for it.
Fillmug Oh, I don't doubt it; but long reckonings make short friends!

(*The villagers call*).

Villagers Fillmug, some more beer!
Luke Come, stir your stumps. Don't ye hear you're called?
Fillmug Yes, but –
Luke Don't stand scratching your head, but pay attention to your customers. (*Pushes him away. To Michael*) Well, here's success to our plans. (*Drinks*) Lord bless you, we are sure to succeed.
(*Aaron Mordica without*)
Aaron Who'll pye – who'll pye? I have got a new set of shop goods. Now's your time. I'll sell 'em all cheaper than nothing. (*Enters*).
Luke I tell you what I want.
Aaron Vot's that? (*Shows his box*).
Luke My dinner. We've got some pork chops frying. Will you pick

99

a bit with us ? (*They all laugh. Drum and fife heard without*).

Luke (*Rather inclined to dance*) Why, it be the Sergeant recruiting. He be a 'nation good fellow. I ha' had many a glass at his expense, and now I ha' gotten the money he shall drink at mine

(*The drum and fife keep playing till the Sergeant and his party come on*)

Sergeant, I'm glad to see you. Here, drink, mon.

Sergeant With all my heart. Here's the King. (*Drinks*).

Luke The King! Come my lads, upstanding, with three hip, hip, hip, huzza, huzza, huzza!

Sergeant Now's your time to make your fortune, and to serve the King you love. Who'll be a soldier? Remember this is the time for glory – to bring home the Spanish gold. Plenty of clothes and good provisions, and no scarcity of grog. Now, my lads, now's your time. Here's a shilling for the first brave fellow that likes to take it.

Luke (*More elated with drink*) Mike, I ha' a great mind to be a hero. Come, lads, what say you one and all, to defend our King, drink his grog, and load our pockets with the enemy's gold.

Michael Let them go that like – I shall remain here.

1st Villager So shall I.

2nd Villager I have a great mind; but I don't like to go alone.

Luke And thee sha'n't – I'll go with you! Come, Sergeant, give us a shilling. (*Staggers over to him*).

Sergeant There, lads – there's his Majesty's picture for you (*Gives money to Luke and 2nd Villager. The Corporal puts ribbons in their hats*).

Luke And I'll spend it to drink his health. Here, Fillmug, half a gallon of the best. I say, Moses, will you be a soldier?

Aaron Not to go abroad. But if the enemy vos to come here, I would fight for all the world as if I vos Sampson

Enter Fillmug, with a can of beer

Fillmug Here, my lads, here's a can big enough to swim in.

Luke Give it the Sergeant. I'll give you a toast. Here's, may every true born Englishman – Englishman – when he – he –
(*The Jew, as Luke staggers, by accident pushes against him*).
Dom, thee, you Jew thief – what's that for?
(*Throws the can at him, the contents of which go into his box*).

Aaron There, I declare, he has spoilt all my goods. I'll take the law at top on him, if it cost me all the profits of my pack. If it vos not for that, I'd knock him down.

Luke Now then, knock me down

(*Luke is coming towards him when Maria enters*)

Luke What ha' brought thee here ?

Maria Finding you had not been to the Farmer's, I came here to seek you. (*Sees the ribbons in his hat, and screams*) Why, Luke, you sure have not – Oh, good heaven, speak!

Luke Why, I be going to fight for glory and my King.

Maria You will not leave me, Luke – no, you do not mean it.

Luke Leave thee – no. Thee shalt go wi' me.

Maria No, no, no, you shall not go. Come, come, dear Luke – come to thy work; we can be happy at home.

Luke Noa, noa, I cannot work. Besides, Sergeant knows I mun go – But here arc three crowns; take 'em, girl. Go home and be merry (*The Sergeant comes down*)

Maria Oh, sir, do not, I implore, tear from a doating wife the husband of her heart. 'Twas folly – all. He would not have enlisted had he not been elated with his drink.

Sergeant I must perform my duty.

Luke Noa, noa; to be sure, I mun go.

Maria Is there no hope – no way to save him ?

Corporal There's one way, my girl.

Maria Oh, for mercy sake tell me, then!

Corporal Pay the Sergeant the smart money, and he'll release him.

Maria Willingly. Here, take it. (*Offers the three crowns*).

Corporal Here's not enough – five shillings short.

Maria Five shillings short. Oh, with five shillings I could be happy – could reclaim my husband! (*Cries*).

Aaron That's a great sum. Ah, but Aaron Mordica cannot see the tears of beauty trinkle down that lovely face, and not say here is a crown piece to wipe them dry. Dare, take it – take it – (*Gives it*) – and I hope de father Abram will repay me.

Maria Thanks – thanks, my kind, my generous preserver. Here, Sergeant – here is the money, and now my husband is free.

Sergeant He is!

Maria Now, Luke, you are free, and we shall be happy

(*Luke, scarcely knowing what he does, as she comes to him, thrusts out his arm, and she falls senseless into the arms of the Jew. The instant he has done it, he shows the utmost agitation and remorse as the act drops*)

Act 2

Scene 1

Outside of Wakefield's house. Thunder, lightning, rain, etc

Luke and Michael enter cautiously. Luke with a ladder, which he rests against the wing

Luke Softly, mon! There's a light still burning. If we are seen –

Michael (*Rain and thunder*) Hark!

Luke What ails ye, mon? It's only the thunder! Come, be bold and resolute, you see I be –

Michael Do you think I fear the storm then; no, but should they by chance detect us –

Luke Don't speak on't! I tell you they'll soon retire for the night (*Thunder, rain, etc*) Noa we'll ha' the boy, and though we get well drenched, the thought of what we make his father suffer will gladden our hearts and make 'em beat with joy.

Michael True, but I wish it were done and the boy safe away. (*The light at the window goes out*)

Luke See the light be out. Now then for our prize! (*Takes the ladder and puts it to the window, and is about to ascend*) Why, what ails me? My limbs refuse their office, and a numbness seized on every sinew. What were that? (*They both start*) Methought I heard a voice exclaim, 'Luke, forbear; proceed no further!'

Michael (*Frightened*) Come, let us return.

Luke What, afore we ha' gotten him? No; 'twas only a thought, mon – no more. What a fool were I to be thus chicken-hearted! (*An immense peal of thunder and lightning*) Never heed it, mon. 'Twill assist us. The noise, should he awake, will prevent his being heard. You stay here, and I'll bring him to you

(*Luke ascends, and goes in at the window motioning to Michael*)

Michael I would I had ne'er consented to entrap the child. Can Luke think because I am of a gipsy tribe, that I am callous to the feelings of humanity? He shall not harm him. No; rather than that, I would confess the whole! Shame, let me not think on't, I have sworn, and my oath must be kept!

Scene 2

A bedroom in Wakefield's house. Philip in the bed. Luke seen coming in at the window

Luke Save the thunder, all's as still as death. There he sleeps; 'tis so dark I cannot see his face, and 'tis well I don't. I do feel my heart beat, in spite of my boasted manhood, with some degree of pity for the youth. (*The lightning flashes on the bed so as to discover the features of the boy to Luke*). That face of innocence! Such had been my child, had it not been for that tremendous night. Ah, and shall my enemy possess his, and I alone be childless? Noa! This night's storm reminds. My poor child's fate rushes on my mind, and plunges me in grief I cannot conquer. 'Twas Farmer's fault, had he ha' kept the cot in repair, the roof had not fell, and I had still been a father. He's a parent. The child's at my mercy. Yes, I'll do't

(*Music – takes out his knife and goes towards the bed, and as he is in the act of stabbing the boy, steps are heard. Luke starts, puts back his knife, and conceals himself behind the bed curtains*)

Enter Mrs Wakefield with candle

Mrs W. How sweet is the sleep of youth! (*Kisses him*) Good, night dear boy, may the tempest ne'er disturb thy rest

Exit Mrs Wakefield. Luke comes from his hiding-place, listens that all is quiet

Luke She kissed her child, I have no child to kiss. Yet to murder hers. Shame, Luke, to harbour such a thought! No, no, no; if I bear him away, I sting 'em into madness. I'll do't, but I will not harm him. No, no!
Michael (*From the window*) Luke!
Luke Hey! Who calls? I thought I heard my name! Oh, it be Mike! (*Sees him*) Softly mon I are coming. Hence all vain fears – I discard them. Woman's tears avaunt! I am steel, rock, marble!

(*Music – Luke motions to Michael to remain quiet, listens at every avenue, then goes to the bed, and with great caution, takes up Philip in his arms. Pauses with fear, then goes towards the window, and resigns him to Michael. The Boy still sleeping. Luke is getting out of the window as the scene closes him in*)

Scene 3

A front wood

Enter Michael, dragging the boy, who resists

Michael Nay, it is useless – no tears can avail. Yet, fear not – your life is safe – I have sworn it.

Philip (*Kneeling*) Have compassion – return me to my dear father and beloved mother.

Michael He thaws me in spite of my fixed resolve, but my oath! Ah, I dare not think on't – be hushed, vain fears – (*beats his breast*) – adamant be firm!

Philip See my flowing tears – think on my poor parents! Oh, mercy – mercy! I never injured you, nor any living being! Pity my poor parents' feelings, if you cannot pity mine! Mercy, mercy! (*Falls at his feet exhausted*)

Michael 'Tis true he never injured me – (*Pauses*) – but he's the child of Wakefield, and what am I? Ah, what indeed? The despised outcast Mike, the Gipsy – he whom no one pities – who the world condemns as a hardened villain, and this act verifies the truth

Enter Gipsies

1st Gipsy What ha' kept you thus long? We have waited till we are tired. Come, no coward's fear – give us the boy – all is ready – we have sold him to a captain, who within this hour sails to a foreign land, and thus all traces end.

Philip No, no; you will not let them; you – you – (*Falls down again*)

Enter Luke

Luke I thought the boy were gone. Why do 'e keep him? Take e'n, lads, take e'n! Mike, what ails you?

Michael Nothing. (*After a struggle*) Away with him! (*Gives him to the Gipsies*) Luke, I have sworn; we are mutually wronged – this is payment. Keep thy own counsel, fear not mine. Away, away!

(*The Gipsies bear off the boy, and Michael rushes out*)

Luke He be gone; the father – mother – will never see him more. Farmer, thee and I are childless. Mine be dead, and thine be lost – lost to thee for ever. We are equals. How will thy heart feel? I know, by my own, it will throb with anguish, will beat with pain; its strings will tug, tug, but will not snap. I prayed that mine might burst, burst; I must away. I ha' been from home. Maria, she be ill, and I ha' let her wait for me. I will go. My revenge satisfied. I am now a mon; not one bad thought remains; no, not one – not one –

Exit

101

Scene 4

Luke's cottage. Maria discovered seated by a miserable fire

Maria Night approaches with rapid strides, and still Luke returns not. Can the Sergeant have been false? I dare not think it. Oh, Luke, what have I not endured for thee! Cold, poverty, starvation, my father's dying curse. (*Rises*) Till this day I never murmured. A blow! Was it real? Did, indeed, my Luke – Oh, heaven support me! I faint with hunger – my brain is heated (*Runs forward*) See my father beckons me to follow – my mother's ghost fleets before my eyes – now the bright clouds enclose her – I hear their voice. Mother – father – your Maria comes – comes – comes –

(*She is falling, when Luke rushes into the cottage, and catches her in his arms*)

Luke Maria, Maria! Oh, God. She dies, and for me. Oh, villain, villain! Maria! Maria – wife – partner of my soul, awake; let me but once more hear thy voice. Ah, she struggles in the arms of death! Speak, my own Maria! Oh, God, my cruelty has murdered her! Maria!

(*She, in the last struggle of nature, feebly raises her head and looking wildly around, seizes Luke round the neck, and frantically kisses his lips*)

Maria Luke – that blow – my husband!

(*Her frame becomes convulsed, and she expires in his arms*)

Luke But you forgive me, Maria? (*Takes her hand, then lets it fall*) Cold, cold! 'Tis the chill of death!

Enter Wakefield, Mrs Wakefield, and villagers

Wakefield Luke, we come to – (*They all stand amazed*)
Mrs W. He hears us not! Luke!
Wakefield Luke, thee sure hast not killed thy wife?
Luke (*Looking round*) Killed her! Is it thee? What dost want? Thee canst not restore her; but you might ha' saved her – a few crumbs of bread would have preserved her, and ye would not g'e it! See, see the corse of her I love lies before me! Hush! Maria, I hear you! Demons avaunt. I am your victim – 'tis I – I alone am mate for thee! Maria – Maria – Maria!

(*Falls beside his wife as the drop falls to slow music*)

*TWENTY YEARS ARE SUPPOSED TO ELAPSE
BETWEEN THE SECOND AND THIRD ACTS*

Act 3

Scene 1
A village, with a group of villagers discovered, celebrating the Harvest Home. An Alehouse and Luke seated at the door

Enter Charles

Charles This is all as it should be, my lads; everything is prepared for you in my cottage; but, as I am a bachelor, you must elect the prettiest lass among you to preside. So away with you, and be as happy as you ought
(*The villagers go off, singing*)

Enter Clara, hastily. She perceives Charles, and stops

Charles You appear to be travelling post haste, Clara. I was in hopes we should have had you with us at our harvest home.
Clara I have to attend to duties, sir, which should be considered before pleasures, however I might wish to indulge in them.
Charles Sir! You speak very cooly to me, Clara. Have I not known you long enough to be called Charles ?
Clara You are now growing rich, and, I hear, likely to become our landlord, so I thought – I thought –
Charles Be assured, Clara, it is not through pride that I have offered to purchase your father's cottage of Squire Chase. Though I have been so fortunate as to raise myself from a poor farmer's boy to what I now am, I shall never forget that the first week's wages I earned were paid me by Farmer Wakefield.
Clara Ah, sir, my poor father has been sadly unfortunate since that time!
Charles You are a good girl, Clara; I always said you were. But how is my old master, Farmer Wakefield ?
Clara He has not been out for some time, sir.
Charles Indeed! Not ill, I hope ?
Clara Only in mind, sir.
Charles But he should take some exercise. It would assist in driving away thought. Why don't he join us now in the evening, as he used to do ?
Clara Oh, sir – (*Bursting into tears*) – don't – don't ask me!

(Luke rises, and Clara, on perceiving him, utters a faint shriek)

Charles What is the meaning of this? What have you done, Luke, to cause this alarm?

Luke Why, you see, her feyther owed me a bit o' money, and when I wanted it, he wouldn't pay it, and so I thought –

Charles You'd put him in a gaol for it, eh? *(Aside)* It is as I suspected *(Aloud)* How much is the debt?

Clara Oh, sir, a very great sum!

Charles But tell me the amount!

Clara Nineteen pounds, sir!

Luke Nineteen pound, six shilling –

Charles Well, Luke, you need not be so exact!

Luke Some folk ha' been exact enough with me, before this time, and now it be my turn.

Charles Luke, I know you to be a needy man. How could Farmer Wakefield become your debtor in that sum?

Luke Why – for vally received.

Charles In what?

Luke Why, for a stack o' wheat. Ah, you may stare! Poor Luke, who never owned an acre, measter of a stack o' wheat. You see some folk can get as well as other folk.

Charles Well, well –

(A shot is heard without)

Luke Here comes squire. He be at work among the partridges already.

Clara The Squire? *(Crossing)* Good day to ye, Mr Charles!

Charles Nay, Clara, do not go yet; I wish to speak with you alone

Enter Squire Chase and Dick

Luke A dutiful good day to ye, Squire!

Squire Ha, the pride of the village here! The very lass I wished to meet – and Mr Charles, too! Glad to see you, my honest fellow! *(Charles slightly bows)* Well, Clara, and how is your father?

Clara He's very – that is, but poorly, sir.

Squire Come hither, Clara; let me speak to you alone. *(The rest retire)* Your father is in difficulties, I understand!

Clara He is, indeed, sir!

Squire I'm very sorry; but if you will come to the manor-house this evening, I shall be at leisure and will give you my assistance and advice.

Clara Ah, sir, assistance and advice have long been needed!

Squire Keep up your spirits, Clara, and fail not to come!

Clara At what time, sir?

Squire About half-past eight, or nine – say nine.

Clara It will be dark before I can return; and I am very timid since I saw my father taken to – Can't you make it earlier, sir?

Squire Not very conveniently; but a servant shall see you safe home. Luke!

Luke Here, Squire!

Squire (*Aside*) Follow me, I want you. (*To Clara*) You'll not fail?

Clara I shall be punctual, sir.

Squire (*Aside*) Now, Luke, we shall accomplish it

Exit, followed by Luke

Charles What was it the Squire said to you?

Clara He wishes me to go this evening to the manor-house.

Charles For what purpose?

Clara He has promised to assist my father in his difficulties.

Charles Take my advice, Clara, and don't go.

Clara Why should I not?

Charles Umph! Here is a pocket-book that I have no particular use for; and, as I know you are fond of reading and making memorandums, will you accept it?

Clara You are very kind. (*Taking the book*).

Charles When I am gone, open it; it contains nothing but what you are freely welcome to.

Clara Nay, Charles, I –

Charles I insist upon it

Exit

Clara What can he mean? Charles, I guess your object. (*Opens the book*) There's nothing here – no – Ha! Pockets – papers in them. Banknotes! One, two, three, four, five – another five – that's five, and five is ten – and ten's twenty. Twenty pounds! Kind, generous Charles! But for me to be so mean as to take it! No, I'll – I'll return it to him. But my father is in prison, and this would make him happy! What shall I do? I'll but borrow it, and I'll work night and day to get it together again. Oh, my poor father! I'll fly immediately to the gaol, and will not return home but with him!

Exit

Enter Bobby Trot with a bundle

Bobby Well, here I be once more, ready to start for Lunnun! This makes the fourth time as I've had my Sunday clothes on, and my bundle at my back, when, somehow, summut have always happened to make I turn whoame again. But now I wool go, come what may!

Enter Luke, hastily, with a letter

Luke Bobby, lad, come hither, I want thee!
Bobby Eh? Oh!
Luke (*Aside*) The work ha' now begun, and this will complete it. (*Aloud*) I ha' been looking for thee, Bobby.
Bobby Dang it! I shall be stopped again.
Luke I've a job for thee to do. Come, lad, listen to me! You know Measter Charles?
Bobby What, young Farmer Charles?
Luke Yes! You go look for him, and give him this letter.
Bobby Very well!
Luke You know Ripley, twenty miles off, where his brother James do live?
Bobby Ees, I do!
Luke Doan't you tell him I give you this letter, but say you be just come from Ripley, and brought it from his brother there, who be vary ill, and like die; when you ha' found un, come to me, and you shall be paid double postage.
Bobby Shall I, though? But where shall I find ye, Measter Luke, if I start at night. Shall you be at this alehouse?
Luke Alehouse? Noa, at the Squire's! Somebody be coming. It be he, for sarten. Now, lad, mind thy P's and Q's, and you're a made man!

Exit

Bobby Oh, I'll go to Lunnun now, for sarten! If a great ugly chap loike Measter Luke do keep company wi' squires, what shall a smart lad loike I do, when I get among lords and dukes!

Enter Charles

Sarvant, Measter Charles.
Charles Well, Bobby, what news?
Bobby Very bad, sir! I ha' gotten a letter.
Charles For me?
Bobby Ees, zur!
Charles (*Reading*) 'Dear brother, – This comes, hoping you are in good health, which I be not at present. I be very ill, and doctor do say I be dying. Dear brother, do come without fail, when you get this letter from your loving brother till death. – James Maydew. Postcript. – A neighbour ha' wrote this, I be so bad.' – Poor fellow! Who gave you this?

Bobby A mon.

Charles My brother's man, I suppose?

Bobby He – he – wasn't a woman.

Charles Here, Bobby, here's sixpence for you, and should you see Farmer Wakefield's daughter, tell her what has happened, but say I shall return early in the morning, if possible, and call at her father's on my way home

Exit

Bobby Oh, sly! I see how things do stand. If Measter Charles bean't her sweetheart, I know nout o' the matter. Oh, I be a main cute lad, and, if Lunnun doan't make me fortin, she doan't know how to vally a genus. (*Jenny is heard without, crying violently*) My stars, here be a stoppage now, for sarten. I'd better run for it

Enter Jenny, she catches him by the collar

Jenny I've cotched you at last, have I now? Bean't you a sad parjury fause lovier? Harkye, Bobby, if you go to Lunnun, I'll follow you, if I walk every step o' the way barefoot.

Bobby Now, Jenny, listen to me. I've told you, often and often, I was determined to see Lunnun some day, so hadn't I better go now I be a single man and you a single 'oman, than walk away some time when you ha' gotten a dozen young 'uns.

Jenny Now, I tell thee what, Bobby; if thee woan't go, you shall come to my mother's, and have as much cold pudding for supper as ever you can eat (*Coaxing him*).

Bobby He, he, he! I – I think I wool.

Jenny (*Pulling him along gently*) Come.

Bobby He, he, he! You know how to do't.

Jenny (*Chucking him under the chin*) I know you wool, Bobby.

Bobby He, he, he! I'll be shot if Lunnun temptation be onything to this!

Exeunt

Scene 2
A kitchen

Enter Mrs Wakefield

Mrs W. Where can my poor girl be? I be sore afraid when she do stay so long away. My poor husband in prison, and the young hope of our days fled from us when he wur but ten years old. Hey, bless me, this is a sad world for the helpless and unfriended!

Clara (*Without*) Mother, mother!

Mrs W. My child's voice! Bless us, what can be the matter?

Clara rushes in

Clara He's coming – he's coming!

Mrs W. Who, child?

Clara My father!

Enter Farmer Wakefield, who rushes into his wife's arms

Wakefield (*After a pause*) My warm, my comfortable fireside, do I again see thee? Oh, dame, dame, no man truly knows the blessings of his home, but he who has been shut out from it.

Mrs W. George, I've looked for this day, but never expected to see it.

Clara Sit, father – sit. How pale and changed you look.

Mrs W. But who have done this?

Clara A friend, mother.

Mrs W. Bless us, what friend?

Clara Charles.

Mrs W. What, Charles Maydew?

Wakefield Grateful boy! If ever it be in my power to return thy kindness – But what are hopes to me? Am I not ruined? No farm, no land!

Clara Father, I hope you have one comfort left. (*Embracing him with affection*)

(*A knock at the cottage-door, Wakefield starting*)

Clara Nay, father, don't stir. Sit still, sit quiet. I'll open the door. It's some friend, perhaps.

Mrs W. Mayhap Mr Charles

Clara opens the door cautiously, Luke walks in, but stops suddenly on perceiving Wakefield

Wakefield Well, sir, your business here?

Luke I ha' noa business particular, I ha' noa – only a – How came you out o' gaol?

Wakefield That be no affair o' yours, the keeper of the prison will answer that. And now your business?

Luke Why, you see, I be comed fra' Squire. He heard you were misfortunate, and wished your daughter to come to him, when he were at whoame this evening, and consult wi' him upon the business.

Wakefield The Squire be very good, certainly; but it be all settled now.

Luke But, Miss Clara, as t' Squire said he would do summut for thee, mayhap it may be better for you to see him. He be very civil, and who knows but he may set thy feyther on his legs!

Wakefield I should think it be of little consequence to you whether I stand or fall.

Luke Nay, not so. I be a friend o' the family, bless you! I bears noa malice.

Wakefield Then why be so hard upon me, when I caouldn't pay you at the time promised? And why did you tempt me to buy it wi' your false words of 'Any time would do to pay?' But I see through you; you be a scoundrel!

Luke You turned me away, and I had no character, because you said I was a drunkard. I were out o' work week after week, till I had not a penny in the world, nor a bit o' bread to put in mine er my wife's mouth. I then had a wife, but she sickened and died – yes, died – all, all along wi' you.

Clara Oh, Luke, Luke, for mercy's sake, no more! Forgive him.

Luke (*After a pause*) I were then quite ruined! I felt alone in the world. I stood looking on her white face near an hour, and did not move from the spot an inch; but, when I *did* move, it were wi' my fist clenched in the air, while my tongue, all parched and dry, cursed a curse, and swore that, if I had not my revenge, I wished I might fall as stiff and as dead as she that lay before me.

Clara Oh, Luke, I beseech you, I implore you, forgive my father! (*Falling at Luke's feet*)

Luke Ha, ha, ha! This is a great sight, the daughter at my feet!

Wakefield Get up, Clara, I'll not see it! I'll not see thee beg to any man! Obey me, girl!

Luke You ar'n't the man you were once. You are not that Farmer Wakefield that stood almost as high as t' Squire. Noa, noa!

Wakefield Do you abuse me on my own hearth? Now, Luke, heed me. If you don't instantly go out, I'll lay hold o' thee by the neck, and send you forth quicker than you came in.

Luke Touch me, and I'll –

Wakefield Stand off, dame – Clara, be you quiet – let me come at him!

(*Wakefield seizes Luke, but is grappled in return by the throat. Luke dashes him to the ground, and rushes out of the cottage, with a loud laugh*)

Scene 3
An Apartment at the Squire's

Enter Bobby, cautiously, looking about him

Bobby Measter Luke, Measter Luke! I can't find him anywhere! I popped up-stairs so snug, when sarvants' back wur turned, because they do say he be often here wi' Squire; if I could but find him, I'd ax for t' letter job money, and go. Here be somebody coming! Dickens and daisies, it be Squire himself! He mustn't see me, by gum! Here be a cupboard-door open – I'll pop in here till he be gone. Gently, Bobby – gently. (*Conceals himself in closet*)

Enter Squire and Dick

Squire How far can we get on the road without changing horses?
Dick Why, your honour, we may run a matter o' twenty miles.
Squire That will do. Clap four of my best horses to the light chaise, and be at the Three Oaks by a quarter of nine, but make no noise in getting ready, and drive quietly to the place, without saying a word about it to anybody. Keep the steps down and the door open.
Dick I know, sir!
Squire And, understand – (*Gives him money*).
Dick Oh, sir, perfectly! Your honour intends to go to London, I suppose?
Squire Ask no questions, but obey me!
Dick It shall be done!

Exit

Squire It may be necessary to make these preparations, for have the girl I will!

Enter Luke

Squire Why, Luke, you appear ruffled! Nothing wrong, I hope?
Luke Who do you think be out o' gaol?
Squire Wakefield?
Luke Yes, sure! I know who's done it.
Squire Charles, I suppose?
Luke Ay, sure; but he ha' gone on his fool's errand. That be all correct.
Squire Then my rival has swallowed the bait?
Luke Oh, yes! and is now on the road to Ripley

Enter Servant

Servant Farmer Wakefield has sent to speak with you, sir.
Squire Sent! Whom?
Servant His daughter, sir.
Squire Desire her to come up

Exit Servant

Luke Hush, hush! It be all right yet. I know what she be come for.
Squire The puss breaks cover. Away, lad! Take the back stairs, and be at your station

Exit Luke

Enter Clara

Well, Clara, you come to your time, like a good woman of business. Sit down.
Clara I'd rather stand, if you please, sir.
Squire Well, as you please. Have you seen your father to-day?
Clara Yes, sir.
Squire And how is he?
Clara Better than he has been for many a day: he's at home, sir.
Squire At home!
Clara Yes, sir. A good friend has done what you were thinking about, sir.
Squire Well, I'm rejoiced to hear it. I hoped I should have had that pleasure.
Clara My father did not wish me to come, but I am disobedient for once; I should not have slept if I had not. That villain, Luke, sir, has insulted my father – shamefully insulted him!
Squire Indeed! Insulted him?
Clara Struck him, sir! and I come to you, Squire Chase, as lord of the manor, and a magistrate, instantly to secure the ruffian, for my father's life is in danger while he is at liberty.
Squire You have it in your power to place yourself and your family above insult from any one.
Clara I – I do not understand!
Squire There is one who takes more than common interest in your situation – one who has felt the expression of those eyes, and admired charms he is convinced were never intended to be obscured in a village.
Clara Sir, I – you amaze me – frighten me! What is it you mean?
Squire It is myself, Clara, that admires you, loves you!
Clara Do not forget yourself. Unhand me, sir, or I will call for help. Let me depart

(*A loud crash is heard in the closet. The Squire starts, amazed, and*

Clara rushes out. The Squire runs to the closet, and drags out Bobby, with a broken basin in his hand)

Squire Who are you, sirrah?
Bobby I be Bobby Trot, sir.
Squire How came you in that closet?
Bobby I wanted to speak to Measter Luke, zur, and I got in there, zur, and a great basin fell upon me, zur, without onybody touching it.
Squire Have you heard what has passed in this room?
Bobby He, he! You be going to Lunnun in a chay.
Squire That's quite enough. (*Holding him*) Here Thomas, John –

Enter Servants

Squire This fellow has been concealed in my closet, no doubt with an intention to rob the house. Take him to the constable, and lock him up in the cage till morning

Exit

Bobby I be innocent, indeed I be. Oh, dear, this be a stoppage! I shall never go to Lunnun

Exit, dragged by Servants

Scene 4
A cut wood

Low thunder – Enter Philip with a large bundle and a cudgel

Philip Holloa, anybody, ahoy! Nobody within hail? Let me see, here's a track of some sort. I'll follow it, must reach port at last. (*Lightning*) The clouds are preparing for action, splice my old shoes, but I must take care of my cargo. Steady she goes

Exit

Enter Luke, cautiously

Luke I thought I heard summut. No, it be all right. Dick ha' gotten the chay ready, and t'lass be coming across t'other meadow. Who's there?

Enter Squire

Squire Luke!

Luke All be ready, zur. Keep thee back

Enter Clara

Clara If I can but get home before the storm increases. That treacherous Squire – this is a sad world!

(*A clap of thunder. Luke rushes forward, and seizes her in his arms, she screams and struggles with him. The Squire is taking her from him, when Philip re-enters. – Lightning*)

Philip What ship ahoy! Sheer off, there! (*He knocks Luke down with his cudgel, who falls senseless, then grapples the Squire by the throat*) Slip your cable, my girl, and stand out to sea

Exit Clara – The Squire struggles with Philip, and runs off, pursued by him

Act 4

Scene 1
The interior of a village alehouse

Reapers discovered drinking

Enter Luke, with a handkerchief bound round his head

1st Reaper Fine morning, Master Luke
Luke Yes, I see it be.
1st Reaper Capital weather for the Squire to shoot.
Luke (*Half aside*) Yes, dom him. Thomas! I want a jug of ale

Enter Fillmug

Fillmug Jug of ale, Luke. What be the matter with your head?
Luke Doan't thee talk, Thomas, but bring th' ale

Exit Fillmug

1st Reaper You seem out of sorts, Master Luke.

Luke Be that ony affair o' yours?

1st Reaper I only made a civil remark.

Luke When I be ill, I'll let thee know.

Enter Fillmug with ale

Exit

Luke Just as it were all right – just as I were in the very nick o' the job, to be stunned to the ground by a blow that came from nobody knows where.

Philip (Without) Landlord, ahoy! Anybody aboard the 'King's Head?'

Luke (Starting up) That be the vary voice!

1st Reaper Master Luke, you have spilt t' ale, man

Enter Philip

Philip Ah, a messmate or two, I see! Holloa! What cheer, my hearties?

1st Reaper We be very well – hope you're the same.

Philip That's right, my boys – we shall soon know one another. Here, landlord!

Enter Fillmug

Bring a good allowance of grog alongside, and hand us something to stow in the bread-room

Exit Fillmug

I'm a stranger in this channel and want a little information. Is it the custom of the natives here to overhaul a young woman whether she will or no?

1st Reaper I don't know about that.

Philip Harkye, my lad! I was steering into port last night, and, while tacking about, I heard the cry of a ship in distress, bore up to the spot, and found a tight little brig grappled by a couple of Algerines. Saw how it was – bore slap upon the enemy – tipped him a broadside – boarded him on his lee quarter – drubbed him about his upper-works till his day-lights danced again – fell to work yard-arm and yard-arm with t' other – he lowered his top-sails, slipped under my stern, and got clear off – gave chase, but lost him in the dark – hailed the little brig, but found she had set all sheets to the wind, and put out to sea.

1st Reaper Beg pardon, master sailor, it is our time for work again. You have done yours, and have plenty of time to talk, but we have none to listen. (*Going across*)

Philip Avast, now! Don't sheer off till I've asked a question or two! Tip us a few of the farmers' names in this port.

1st Reaper Names? There be Farmer Jones, and Farmer Goslin, and Farmer Maydew, and Farmer Holly, and – there's no more.

Philip No more, you lubber? (*Laying hold of the 1st Reaper*).

1st Reaper Oh, yes, I'd forgot – one more – but he's no farmer now.

Philip His name, swab – his name!

1st Reaper His name is Wakefield.

2nd Reaper Come, lads – come! He be drunk!

Exeunt Reapers, Luke sits with his back towards Philip, but has taken the handkerchief from his head

Philip Service to you, mate! (*Drinking to Luke*)

Luke Same to you!

Philip Can you tell me of one Farmer Wakefield in these parts?

Luke Do you want to know about him?

Philip It's some time since I anchored in this channel, and then Farmer Wakefield was master of a tight bit of land or so – didn't spare grog and biscuits, and could keep up a Saturday night like an admiral; so, you see, I should like to learn how the good soul thrives in the sea of life.

Luke Very poorly, I can tell thee!

Philip Poor soul!

Luke He's been many a day growing poor, and now ha' gotten quite down – bad crops, bad debts, and rack and ruin more and more every day.

Philip Well, thank heaven, he's alive!

Luke Oh, yes, he do live.

Philip And his wife?

Luke Yes.

Philip And – and his children?

Luke Yes; that is, he had two, you see, but now he ha' gotten but one.

Philip That's a girl?

Luke Yes; t'other were a boy.

Philip He's dead, I suppose.

Luke Very like – very like.

Philip You don't know for certain?

Luke Why, you see, he were lost a long time ago – kidnapped away, it be thought, by gipsies.

Philip Holloa, brother, you've got a smart bump athwart your forecastle, there.

Luke (*Confused*) Have I? Oh, yes – I know.

Philip I think I know you.

Luke What, know me?

Philip Did you get that blow last night?

Luke No, no, not last night.

Philip You lie!

Luke What?

Philip (*Seizing him*) You were grappling with a young woman last night – you and another.

Luke If thee doesn't loose thy grip, I'll dash thy brains out.

Philip I see how the land lies. Here, landlord, you've got among the breakers. Landlord (*Calling*) – all hands ahoy!

Enter Fillmug and Charles

Fillmug What's the matter?

Charles Luke, what is the cause of this?

Philip Your honour, I saved a young woman from being ill-treated last night, and I could swear this is one of the crew that had his grappling-irons aboard of her.

Charles (*Aside*) It is as Clara suspected. (*Aloud*) You did save a young woman last night, my friend. Harkye, Luke, I have heard of your conduct, and be assured that proper authorities shall interfere.

Philip What, we've caught a mutineer, eh? Beg pardon, your honour, is the young woman your wife?

Charles No, no, not my wife. She is Farmer Wakefield's daughter.

Philip Shiver my topmast! but I'll know who you are (*Seizes Luke with both hands*) Harkye, I think I've seen your ugly mug before. If it's the same you'll go to the devil with a flowing sail, I can tell you. Noble captain, steer me to Farmer Wakefield's, and you shall swim in grog for a month.

Charles I am returning there this instant.

Philip Say you so? Not a word more on your life. Clap on all your canvas, leave this half-timbered pirate to founder as he will, and spank away to the Farmer's. Oh, you damned lubber!

Exit Philip, followed by Charles, Luke remains fixed with astonishment, mingled with fear

Luke Summut do pass to and fro upon my brain; but no, it cannot be – it cannot be! He were fair-haired, and, beside, it be twenty year ago, and nothing ever heard. I'll not think it. Landlord! Bring me a whole pint o' brandy; no water – not a drop! I'm stone cold; my finger-ends do feel like flakes of ice. Come, Thomas – come, the brandy!

Scene 2
Wakefield's cottage, as before

Enter Jenny and Clara

Clara He has something particular to tell me?
Jenny Very; and he won't say a word to anybody, while they do keep him locked up in the cage, not even to me.
Clara Mr Charles threatens to punish him severely for bringing a letter which stated his brother to be ill, and was the cause of keeping him from home all night.
Clara Don't they intend to take him before the Squire?
Jenny Yes, madam; for it be a hard thing, so it be, for a poor young man to lose his character because Squire do choose to say a thing that be false; but he does just as he likes.
Clara Good day, Jenny

As Jenny is going out, Farmer Wakefield enters

Wakefield Did Charles say he would be here again?
Clara Yes, father; perhaps in an hour.
Wakefield Where be your mother?
Clara Gone to market.
Wakefield Where do she get money to go to market? I have none.
Clara Has not Charles been our friend?
Wakefield True, I ha' borrowed a pound of him – I might as well say begged it; for I know not when I shall have another shilling to call my own

Enter Charles
Charles, be that you?
Charles I should not have come in so suddenly, but I have an impatient friend without, who has a desire to be introduced here.
Wakefield I don't want him; he can't come in, whoever he be. (*Pettishly*).
Charles This is a friend I know you will be glad to see.
Wakefield Where is he?
Charles You shall hear. (*Calling*) Neptune, ahoy!
Philip (*Without*) Hillioh! Is the captain aboard?
Clara Heavens! My preserver's voice!
Wakefield What, the man that fought for thee last night? Let him come in – let him come in

Enter Philip

Welcome, my friend – welcome. I'm glad to see thee, indeed I am; and thank thee for my poor girl's protection.

Philip What cheer, my old master? Glad to see you – I suppose that's the tight little vessel that fell in with the enemy last night? Split my binnacle, if she ain't as handsomely built, and prettily rigged, as e'er a frigate in the service.

Wakefield I'm very sorry, my good fellow, that it be not in my power to reward you as you deserve; but, if a father's hearty thanks –

Philip Now, no palaver. Only rate me on your good books, and I'm satisfied.

Wakefield Come, friend, sit you down. The dame will soon be home.

Philip The dame! Your wife, I suppose?

Wakefield She will make you as welcome as our means will allow. For I am but a poor man now, though I have known better days.

Philip Bless your old soul, don't mention it. (*Aside*) Pitch me overboard, if I can stand it much longer. And that's your daughter?

Wakefield Bring a chair, girl. (*To Clara*).

Philip Not for me, your honour. Avast, now, I've something to say, something to overhaul that concerns you.

Wakefield Concerns me?

Philip Bring up alongside, here. Ahem! Didn't you lose a son?

Wakefield What, what?

Clara Oh, sir, as you value my father's feelings, avoid that subject! He has forbidden it ever to be mentioned; my mother dare not name it.

Philip (*Aside*) I see how it is; my pumps will be at work in a minute. (*Aloud*) Lord love your heart, I can't help it. I've news of him!

Wakefield Of my boy! Speak – does he live?

Philip Tight and hearty.

Wakefield Thank heaven! Come hither, Clara. I be so agitated – let me hold thee. My boy, my poor boy – tell me – tell me –

Philip I was his messmate, you see –

Wakefield Well, go on; but don't thee hurry.

Philip (*Aside*) Strike my topmast, I shall run aground. (*Aloud*) He's anchored in foreign parts.

Clara Then he's not in England?

Wakefield But he's alive. Clara – Charles, run, look for the dame; this news must not be kept – fly! You'll find her on the road home from market; but, be careful, tell her slowly at first – and stop, Clara, tell her to bring home something good for the stranger; Mind that, now – mind that.

Clara Yes, father; and I'll tell her to hasten home.

Wakefield Do, girl, do. (*Exit Clara*) After her, Charles, after her; you'll manage better between you. (*Putting Charles out at the door*) My poor boy – how I should like to see him!

Philip Should you – should you? (*Aside*) No, I won't – not yet, not yet.

Wakefield How came he to turn sailor? Where did he go to? Who took him away from me?

Philip That is all duly entered in his log-book, and will be shipped home the first opportunity.

Wakefield If I could but see him once before I died. Do you know, when he were lost, I were next to a madman for a whole fortnight. I were then a prosperous man, with acres of land and full barns; but the loss of my boy made me neglect everything. Bad luck followed bad luck, and misfortunes did then begin which ended in my ruin.

Philip Very molloncholy. (*A loud shout without*) Hallo! is that your Yorkshire war-whoop?

Wakefield (*Going to the door*) As I live, the lads have gotten an old gipsy, and are ducking him in Prickle's pond.

Philip A gipsy! Stand aside – no – yes – start my timbers. I know him, Farmer – I know him. Belay, there, belay! Let me come alongside. Hilloah!

Exit

Scene 3
A view of the country. Nearly dark

Enter Villagers, dragging on Michael

Michael For the love of heaven, no more! You'll kill me, you'll kill me!

All The millstream – the millstream!

Enter Philip

Philip Hilloah! Avast, ye cannibals! Sea-room, sea-room, here. (*Philip drives them off with his cudgel*) Cheerly, old Triton, cheerly. How do you feel yourself?

Michael Blessings on you.

Philip What were they doing with your old hull?

Michael Another dip would have killed me! They wanted to drown me for only looking into a hen-roost. A murrain seize every mother's son of 'em!

Philip I understand. The old tricks, Michael.

Michael Who told you my name?

Philip I know the trim of your vessel well – but mum for the present. Bring a few of your lads to Farmer Wakefield's, in this port.

Michael What for?

Philip I want you to overhaul an affair of consequence.

Michael It must be after dark, then. I know Farmer Wakefield well enough by name. Perhaps I know a matter concerning him, too.

Philip I shall be on the look out for you. Don't let your memory start a timber.

Michael But, master sailor, tell me if –

Philip Obey orders, and I'll make you an admiral. Mutiny, and I'll blow you to the devil. (*Exit*)

Michael But, master sailor –

Philip (*Without*) I shall look out for you, old Mike.

Michael Old Mike! How should he know my name? Well, I must hear what the lads say to this business.

Enter Luke

Spare a halfpenny for the love of charity – poor old man – seventy odd – spare a halfpenny.

Luke Doan't thee bother.

Michael (*Aside*) Ah! Let me look at you, let me look at you. I know you – know you well. (*Aloud*) Come hither, let me whisper in your ear. (*Laying hold of his arm*) Don't thee flinch and shake at my cold hand, it is but chilly with the water. Bend down your ear, and I'll make you tremble from head to foot.

Luke Be you mad! Why dost thou grip me so hard? I doan't know thee.

Michael You don't? (*Michael whispers in Luke's ear*)

Luke (*Aside, in great terror*) Toads and serpents! (*Aloud*) Be it you? I thought you had been dead and buried. Here be money for you, so be quiet about that, not a word –

Michael Money! I won't touch it. When the poor old gipsy asked for charity, you had nothing about you; but, now he can tread you to dust, you can find silver in your pockets. I won't have it – not a halfpenny – not a farthing – not a mite

Exit

Luke Now I do know the worst. Ere this week be out the turf may be on my head. (*Bobby heard without, singing*) That be the lad's voice. Squire ha' let him out, I suppose. Now it be all over about the girl

Enter Bobby

Bobby I be out – I be out! Ah, Measter Luke, bean't you ashamed to look me in the feace? But it do sarve thee right, for I ha' lost my good character through being your postman, and I'm sure you can't help me to another; so the sooner I get to Lunnun, the better for I. (*Looking out*) Eh,

123

sure and sure, there be a chay going along the road like the wind!

Luke It be Squire's! Yes, it be, and there he sits inside, sure enough. Then he ha' run away, and left me to fight it out by myself. A chicken-hearted coward! He couldn't stay and face it out, as I do. A drop more brandy, a look at my wife's grave, a good think of what ha' passed, and then for the finish of my long, long day's journey

Exit Luke

Bobby What a cruel pity it be I hadn't my bundle! The chay must stop to change horses, so I'll run till I overtake it. Now for it – nothing shall stop me. Good bye, everybody, and now for Lunnun

As he is running off, two Villagers enter, and seize him

1st Villager So, we have caught you at last, my little tomtit.
Bobby What, be I stopped again?
1st Villager Farmer Charles has a word to say to you.
Bobby Oh, dear – oh, dear! Caged, horsewhipped, and killed! I shall never get to Lunnun

They drag him off

Scene 4
Interior of Wakefield's cottage

Philip, Wakefield, Mrs Wakefield, Charles and Clara, discovered

Mrs W. Don't thee say no, master sailor.
Philip No more, dame, I thank you. I've stowed away enough for the night. Come, Farmer, cheer up, don't be down-hearted. (*Aside*) Where's old Mike, I wonder? I suppose it must rest till the morning. (*Aloud*) Come, my lass, lord love you, I like to look at you. You do mount a smile and cheer us a bit. What say you to joining with me in a ditty? 'Poor Jack', 'Black-eyed Susan', or 'The Old Commodore?'
Wakefield No, no; no singing. I be tired, and –
Philip Belay, belay, don't run foul of my inclination. Come, come, pipe all hands for fun. Sew up old care in a blanket, and pitch him to Davy Jones.
Wakefield Well, well, do as you will. Come, girl, do thy best.
Philip That's your sort. That's tight and hearty. Splice me, what d'ye think o' that pipe, my commodore? Well, here's wishing you may be a captain's wife. No offence, I hope.

Mrs W. But I want you to talk about my poor boy.

Wakefield Silence, dame. Have I not told thee to speak no more on't at present? I'm thinking how the sailor may be accommodated here. Dame Hillock said you could sleep at her cottage? (*To Clara*).

Clara Yes, father.

Wakefield Hark ye, master sailor, you shall have my bed.

Philip Now, now, commodore –

Wakefield I insist upon it. 'Tis the best bed in my poor house, and you shall sleep in it.

Philip Huzza! (*Cuts a caper*) I could jump over the moon.

Wakefield Come, girl, get ready. Charles will go with you, but there be no fear of any more such work as happened last night.

Clara Good night, father.

Wakefield Kiss me, girl, and go – there, good night. Good night, Charles, and thank thee for your kindness.

Clara Good night, my friend.

Philip Good night, my lass. Lord love you. Heaven bless ye both

Exit Clara and Charles

(*Aside*) It's no use waiting for old Mike, he won't come to-night, so I'll surprise 'em all to-morrow.

Wakefield Dame, take a light, and show the sailor up-stairs.

Philip What, so soon? Well, just as you please – take care of my cargo though. (*Gives his bundle to Wakefield*) Pipe all hands at five o'clock, for I've a day's work to do. Heave a-head, dame. Good night, old commodore

Mrs Wakefield precedes Philip up the stairs with a light, and the scene shuts them in

Scene 5
The back part of Wakefield's cottage

Enter Luke, with a brace of pistols in his hand

Luke There be a light in the place where the Farmer sleeps. I'll watch here till it be out, and then he'll be in bed. I must get round the garden, climb up the gate at the side, and get in at the window. (*The light seen through the window goes out*) Ah, he ha' put out the candle! Now to make all ready for climbing. (*He places the pistols in a belt under his frock*) Now for it – gently, be quiet, don't thee be scared, or my hand will shake. Lay still, lay still. (*Striking his breast*) Now I be right again – 'twere but a little fit, and now I be firm as oak

Exit

(*Music*) – *Enter Michael followed by two Gipsies*

Michael There he goes. Hush, lad! I know he's after something; going to rob the house, maybe.
1st Gipsy He's climbing up the fence.
Michael Follow him, lads – follow him. See what he's about. Now, gently – no noise

Music and Exeunt

Scene 6
A Bedroom in the cottage

Philip is discovered lying asleep. Luke is at the window. He opens it gently, and advances

Luke He sleeps; and alone I think, Farmer, we shall be even

(*He cocks the pistol, and levels it at Philip. At that moment the 1st Gipsy appears at the window*)

My hand do shake so, I shall miss him.
1st Gipsy Aye, that thee shalt.

(*Music – The Gipsy throws him into the room – the pistol goes off in the air in the act. Philip springs from the bed, seizes Luke*)

Philip Holloa, farmer! Farmer Wakefield, we're boarded by pirates! I'll grapple you! What, Luke!

Mrs Wakefield enters followed by the Farmer, Clara, Charles, Michael, and the other Gipsy

Wakefield Luke, what be the meaning of this?
Michael Stop! Hear old Gipsy Mike. Master Luke stole away your boy, and sold him to me. I took care of him till one day –
Philip He ran away, and went to sea. I am that boy.
Michael, Wakefield, Mrs W., Clara, Charles You!
Wakefield You my boy Philip!

Philip Aye, old Mike will soon know me

(*Luke struggles with Philip, and succeeds in drawing another pistol from his belt, and is levelling it at the Farmer, when Philip thrusts back his arm, and Luke receiving the fire, falls dead*)

Wakefield My boy, my boy! Your old father's arms are open to receive you

(*Philip runs into Wakefield's arms; then Mrs Wakefield is warmly embraced by him. Wakefield kneels. Philip takes Clara round the waist, and occupies the centre of the stage, the Gipsies fill up one side, and Michael and Charles the other*)

Curtain

'*Holloa! Farmer, Farmer Wakefield, we're boarded by pirates – I'll grapple you –* '. A Cruikshank drawing of the incident in Scene 6.

THE PRESS

The News, October 22nd, 1826:

On Monday we witnessed the first representation at this house of a new 'domestic' burletta, called 'Luke, the Labourer; or, the Lost Son'. The characters are in humble life; the story is tragic enough, horribly so; and the moral is, to show the dreadful results attending the indulgence of a headstrong thirst for revenge. Without discussing the dramatic impropriety of its basis, in arousing feelings of horror *instead of those of* terror – *it must be admitted that Mr Terry drew an appallingly forcible picture in representing the chief character.*

[Here the plot is outlined]

The story it will be seen, is quite 'horrible' enough; but the harsh and inveterate passion, the unshrinking bloodthirstyness of Luke, *were portrayed with a force and truth that frequently made portions of the audience shudder with alarm and dismay. It is a repulsive character unquestionably – but it was sustained with amazing vigour. Mr T P Cooke's sailor was an excellent picture; had he been born in a ship's hold, bred on the decks, 'afloat' all his life, with ship-lingo for his mother-tongue, 'second nature' could not have been better personified. The other characters, especially Mr Salter's Yorkshire* Bobby, *and his lass, by Mr Hughes, with their well sung and acted duet, afforded much comic and acceptable relief. – Mr Terry's annunciation that the piece would be repeated every night of performance till further notice was received with rapturous applause by an exceedingly crowded house.*

The Atlas, October 22nd, 1826:

[This notice is interesting for its criticism of the technicalities of seamanship mentioned in the dialogue, and of the nautical expressions spoken by Philip. It commences with a description of the plot, and continues as follows]

Such is the main outline of the story, (a little insipid love affair, and some incidents, the mention of which is not material to the general sketch of the plot, we have passed over for the sake of brevity);

and these materials have been embodied with such effect, as to present one of the most interesting pieces that we have seen for some time. Terry's Luke is a performance of genius. There is a terrible truth in it. It is a Hogarth-like picture of the dissolute low ruffian. Every point in it tells. His very dress is one which we cannot but imagine no honest man could wear, or at least not wear as Terry wears it; and yet we look in vain for any principle of evil in the colour or set of his clothes, or style of his hat; but the effect of the whole is decidedly villanous, and the figure is one of that slouching and reckless air with which Hogarth draws the thoroughly-abandoned rogue, careless alike of himself and crime. The sentiments correspond with the promise of the outward man. The fiendish humour which Terry throws into a retort to the plea for pity on the score that the farmer was ruined – 'What of that ! we have all been ruinated one time or other', or words to that effect, accompanied with a chuckle of glee, is finely, but shockingly, expressive of character. His acting in the scene in which he finds Wakefield at liberty, and tells the history of his ill-will to him, is too just a representation of the workings of the worst passion. It almost shocks one to consider how natural is the malignity represented, and that such frightful enmity may be provoked by conduct in itself justifiable, nay unexceptionable. A bad servant is discharged, and thrown out of work; he is in want, begs to be reinstated in his place, is refused, sees his wife die of want because his late master will not relent, and he conceives a deadly enmity and turns all his thoughts and powers to vengeance. The reasoning is perverted, but too natural: the man does not trace his afflictions to the true cause, his own conduct, but to the fatal consequences of it on the resolution of another. A scene in an ale-house, in which Philip the sailor and Luke meet after the fray for the deliverance of Clara, is also to be noted among the striking situations. T P Cooke, the beau ideal of a tar, plays Philip; and the bull-dog-like tustle between him and the daring villain Luke, is excellent. One peculiarly relishes seeing the rogue under the gripe of a better man, as Luke in a former scene has savagely struck to the ground the old farmer; but Luke, though he has the worst of the struggle with the sailor, shows that dogged hardihood which is a common attribute of the cut-throat. Cowards are, we believe, commonly cruel, according to the old adage; but it does not thence follow that the cruel are cowards. The experience of the world shows the fallacy of the presumption. 'The bold bad man' is no rare monster.

The general scheme of Luke the Labourer is well conceived; it fails, however, in the writing, and in one or two of the characters. Much of the effect of Terry's fine bursts of nature is impaired by the injudicious use of expressions unfitted to the character. The labourer, in his agony of malignity, ought not to talk of burning brains, etc; this is a language proper only to play-wrights, novel-writers, and the despairing inditers of love-letters. The character of Farmer Wakefield is another objection-

able point. He is a person with whom it is difficult to sympathise: nothing short of his being knocked down can move us in his favour, seeing that he is particularly selfish and ungrateful. When contemplating the misery of his poverty in the hearing of his affectionate and devoted child, who has procured his release from a gaol, he dwells on the probability of his being borne to the grave without a passing bell to tell that Farmer Wakefield *was dead, as the greatest of all the calamitous anticipations that occurred to him. Whence we must infer, that leaving his child unprotected and destitute was an evil of secondary importance. Again, after* Philip *(who preserves, as the phrase goes, his* incog. *for a time – why, we do not exactly see, but for the sake of the surprise, we suppose), has announced the glad tidings that the lost son is well and prosperous in India, the party sit down to supper; and on the bearer of the good news asking for a song to cheer him, the ungracious old gentleman says, 'Oh no, let us have no singing here!' which shows a very inhospitable, and also ungrateful temper – not to mention the bad manners. In addition to his other unamiable qualities, he is insufferably maudlin in his conversation.*

The inferior characters were so filled as not to detract from the interest of the piece; with the single exception of that of the libertine Squire, who was represented by a corpulent gentleman, who talked of orses *and being* appy, *together with other such abominations, not to be named among Christians. A Squire may be made very boobyish and ignorant without any kind of violation of probability; but he should not be made Cockney, simply because he is a country gentleman. As we are finding fault, we must enter our protest, by the bye, against the nautical lingo of* Philip, *which is made up of technical terms, strung together without any shadow of meaning. He talks, among other nonsense, of the enemy* lowering his fore-top sail, and hoisting the peak of his mizen to get (or bear) away. *No such manoeuvre is known to the tars; it is purely of Adelphi origin. And here we may remark, that considering how nautical this amusing little theatre is, its tactics are strangely defective. It makes a better sea than any theatre in London, but it manoeuvres its schooner in a most Cockney style. The schooner appears clawing off the lee shore, with not an inch of after-canvas set – no sail on her main-mast; and it is a last resort and lucky thought to set the main-sail, which should have been set from the first to keep them to windward. This blunder arises, we concieve, from their confounding the manoeuvre of the frigate in the novel, with that of the schooner in the tale. The ship does not set her main-sail till the last pinch; but the main-sail of a ship is not essentially necessary to her when beating to windward, and that of a schooner is. When the Adelphi schooner does eventually set her main-sail, as a brilliant but late expedient, the sheet is not hauled aft, and the vessel claws off the shore with her sail set for going right before the wind! As we hear much of the nautical accuracy of this representation, these glaring blunders should be reformed.*

Fifteen Years
of a
Drunkard's Life

DOUGLAS JERROLD

Douglas Jerrold.
(*Enthoven Collection*)

DOUGLAS WILLIAM JERROLD (1803/57)

Douglas Jerrold earned his place in theatrical history as the author of *Black-Eye'd Susan** (Surrey, 1829), a nautical melodrama which was played for over 300 performances at its first appearance and was constantly revived until the end of the century, besides attracting numerous burlesques and imitations. With the exception of one or two of Boucicault's comedies it is perhaps the only play from the first three quarters of the nineteenth century still to be seen on our stages today.

Jerrold's father was an actor and an unsuccessful theatrical manager. Young Douglas was put on stage at an early age, but never cared for acting and much preferred the less exciting world of literature. At the age of ten he was placed on board the *Namur* as a midshipman in the Royal Navy; although he never saw actual combat he was serving on the brig *Ernest*

---

*The full text of *Black Eye'd Susan* is available in George Rowell's *Nineteenth Century Plays* (1953)

two years later which brought back wounded from the field of Waterloo, and his experience in the Navy was later to be used to advantage in his nautical pieces. On his discharge in 1815 he returned to his family then residing in Bow St, London, and was apprenticed to a printer. He continued to read and to study (he taught himself Latin, French and Italian) and began contributing poems and critical essays to journals of the day.

His first play, a low comedy called *The Duellists* was written in 1818 but did not receive a production until three years later at Sadler's Wells Theatre under the title of *More Frightened Than Hurt*. In 1825 he was engaged as resident dramatist at the Royal Coburg Theatre, where *Fifteen Years of A Drunkard's Life* was presented in 1828. However, the poor terms of his employment sent him to the Surrey Theatre in the following year with *Black-Eye'd Susan*; the success of this piece and his regular weekly stipend of £5 encouraged him to refuse to write adaptations – a stand which was taken by very few theatre-writers of the period. *Black-Eye'd Susan* was revived later that year for a further 100 nights; it made a star of T P Cooke as William who played it at Drury Lane in 1835 and made many fortunes for many people, although Jerrold himself is said to have made only £60 from the play.

He wrote over sixty pieces of all kinds, principally sparkling comedies and nautical dramas with such titles as *The Press Gang* (1830), *The Mutiny At The Nore* (1830), and the occasional domestic drama – *The Factory Girl* (1832) and *The Mother* (1838). An earlier curiosity was *Wives By Advertisement* (1828), a farce doubtless prompted by the trial of William Corder for the murder of Maria Marten (*qv*) – Corder had advertised for a wife in *The Sunday Times*.

The 1830's saw Douglas Jerrold gradually turning his energies more and more towards journalism; he contributed voluminously to magazines, newspapers and publications of all kinds, and also edited and founded several journals, sometimes disastrously. He is especially remembered for having revived the ailing *Lloyd's Weekly Register*, and for being a regular contributor to *Punch* from its second number in 1841 until his death sixteen years later.

Fifteen Years of A Drunkard's Life is the earliest of his domestic dramas, and is usually considered to be the first of the temperance dramas, giving rise to a vogue which lasted for some thirty years. The most famous example of the type was W H Smith's *The Drunkard* (1844), an American piece which survived until a few years ago in Los Angeles, and which ended its life as a musical.

Jerrold was a short, sturdy man who seems to have embodied many of the virtues and vices of his nautical heroes; he was vivacious and witty, impulsive and generous to a fault. In 1824 he married Mary Swann, and was survived by his son William Blanchard Jerrold, himself a writer of ability and a protégé of Dickens.

Fifteen Years of A Drunkard's Life. Frontispiece from Buncombe's
Edition. (*British Museum*)

FIFTEEN YEARS
OF A
DRUNKARD'S LIFE

Dramatis Personae

First performed at the Royal Coburg Theatre
November 24th, 1828

Vernon, a gentleman of rank and fortune, husband of Alicia, by
Mr Cobham
Glanville, a pretended friend of Vernon, by Mr Gann
Franklin, suitor to Miss Vernon, by Mr Wynne
Dogrose, servant to Vernon, by Mr Sloman
Copsewood, a young farmer, by Mr H Williams
Juniper, a rustic, by Mr Mortimer
Pounce, an emissary of Glanville's, by Mr Worrell
Wingbird by Mr E L Lewis
Butts, landlord, by Mr Porteus
Picklock by Mr Elsgood
Alicia, wife of Vernon, by Miss Watson
Miss Vernon by Mrs Lewis
Isabella by Mrs Congreve
Patty, sister of Copsewood, by Miss Tomlinson

Ladies and Gentlemen Visitors
Bailiffs
Robbers
Villagers
Etc

Time of Representation: Two and a Half Hours

Scene: England

Note: The Coburg playbill for the previous week announced this
play as *Thirty Years Of A Drunkard's Life*. This can scarcely have
been a printer's error; perhaps the piece was found to be too long,
and consequently shortened by the excision of an act. The last line of
this playbill is also interesting for its unspoken comment on the
all-pervasive Continental influence on British stages of the time:
'It is hoped that the Piece will not be less favorably [*sic*] received on
the score of its being no importation.' – *M.K.*

FIFTEEN YEARS OF A DRUNKARD'S LIFE

Act 1

Scene 1
An elegant apartment in Vernon's house

Dogrose lying asleep on a sofa. Time, morning

Enter Franklin

Franklin What! no one stirring yet, and broad day? (*Seeing Dogrose*) Why, the knave is fast asleep (*Shaking him*) Rouse, sirrah! rouse!

Dogrose (*Waking*) Yes, sir – yes, sir, coming! here's your slippers, sir – and here's your dressing-gown – and here's – la, bless me! I beg your pardon, sir – I thought it was my master.

Franklin Well for you it is not, I take it – He would scarcely be pleased to find his servants sleeping.

Dogrose Sleeping! ah, sir – I have watched all the night like a miser over his money-chest – my ears have been pricked up like a terrier's for the thunder of the knocker.

Franklin What! is Vernon out?

Dogrose The old trick, sir – the old game. The bottle, sir – the bottle –

Franklin Mad, infatuated young man! so faithfully as he promised. Some desperate effort must yet be made to save him.

Dogrose I know but one, sir – destroy all the vineyards – demolish all the distillers, and cry down the trade of brewer as wicked and unlawful.

Franklin Eh! who comes here – Vernon's attorney?

Dogrose The same, sir, master Pounce

Enter Pounce

Pounce Good morning, Mr Franklin. Dogrose, is your master stirring?

137

Franklin Mr Pounce – what business have you with Mr Vernon ?

Pounce Your pardon, sir. An attorney is a kind of conscience-keeper to his client.

Franklin Yes, and when men trust their consciences to such keepers, is it to be wondered at, if they are returned soiled ?

Pounce Sir, I've an idea that this is scandal – I've a witness – Dogrose – you've heard all this ?

Dogrose Not a syllable. When your character is the matter of conversation I always stop my ears.

Vernon (*Without*) What, house! Dogrose! William! Mary!

Dogrose There's my master!

Vernon rushes in labouring under the effects of intoxication

Vernon So – at home at last.

Pounce (*With the greatest servility*) Good morning, Mr Vernon.

Vernon Now I see your ink and parchment countenance, I remember I've some business with you – go into the library – don't think I'm drunk – no, no – I can sign my name with a flourish – sign my name with a flourish – F Vernon – F – F – (*Relapsing into insensibility, he stands listlessly*)

Pounce He's in an excellent condition – I have the papers already drawn up, and his signature will secure all

Exit

Dogrose Master!

Vernon Dogrose – eh! why havn't you caught her? – Oh, I'd forgot! – ha! ha! I hadn't told you – just as I got up to the door, I slid off the saddle, and the mare set away at full gallop. Take the whip and catch her

Exit Dogrose

Franklin Vernon!

Vernon Franklin! my old monitor – now no sermons – I know what you're going to say.

Franklin I fear me you are past the cure of lectures.

Vernon Lectures! Frank – you are a fellow of snow – a walking iceberg – a frog upon two legs. You've no heart for generous wine! now there was last night, Glanville, honest Tom Glanville, Brightly, Samford, and myself – how much do you think we murdered ? How much, now ? A cool two dozen – we four sat down to two dozen. But it's all over – I shall reform – I shall give it up – yes, it will never do – it will ruin my constitution – and my wife – Alicia too – yes, I must give it up – I said so at the conclusion of the fifth bottle – I shall give it – how my throat's parched – I must have one glass more.

Franklin. One more, when you have this instant forsworn wine ?

Vernon Yes, that is wine as wine – but this, this I take as medicine. One more glass to put me right for the morning. Go, go, Mr Franklin, get me one glass – only one glass. No wine – medicine – one glass of medicine – only one – only one !

(*Falls into a stupor on the sofa and the scene closes*)

Scene 2
View of the country – Copsewood's Farm at side

Enter Wingbird with a gun

Wingbird Well, here I am – my first appearance with a gun. I see no game yet. Eh! yes, there's something very like a partridge – no, it's a turkey. Ah! there's certainly a cock pheasant through the trees – no, it's the ribands in the hat of a recruiting sergeant. There's a black cat sleeping among that straw; nobody's near – for want of better sport I'll just see how a cat carries swan-shot. (*Presents his piece, and fires at a heap of straw at side – Copsewood jumps up from straw*).

Copsewood Eh! hallo!

Wingbird What, a man! Bless me, sir, you are not killed ?

Copsewood Killed! what by such a marksman as you; why, you wouldn't hit a goose at a yard distant.

Wingbird Excuse me, my friend, but there looks something like four in the morning written about your clothes; you don't look like one who put his night-cap on at nine o'clock last night.

Copsewood Night-cap! No, the truth is, I did take a little; I sold my corn well at the market, and so for luck's sake I – I – you understand. The night was confoundedly dark, and I thought I'd crawled into bed, but there, you see, was my sleeping-chamber (*Pointing to straw*).

Wingbird Yes, very pretty furnished lodgings for single gentlemen.

Copsewood You are come, sir, I presume, for the sporting season ?

Wingbird Yes, I've been taking lessons in town on purpose.

Copsewood A pretty amusement! Better imitate the example of Tom Copsewood and his companions, who never have but the distance of a well-filled table between them; and as for firing at one another, why so they do – but it's with bumpers, sparkling bumpers; and though half be killed and wounded at night, why they are hale and hearty in the morning – Eh! I feel a little staggered or so; but my morning's draught will set all right again. Will you step into the farm ?

Wingbird No, I am losing time; I must away, for I've not had a single shot. I'll just go over by yonder hill

Exit

Copsewood That's a good fellow – for I know he likes a glass – I can see three times three in his countenance

Enter Patty

Patty Where can my silly brother – Oh, there he stands – as usual. Thomas, Thomas!
Copsewood (*Seeing her*) Patty! Oh, what, it's you, sister, is it?
Patty Where have you been all night?
Copsewood What's that to you? Mind your churning and your poultry, and don't interfere with the affairs of men.
Patty Oh, Thomas! Thomas! this is a sad change.
Copsewood A change! why what's the girl whimpering at? There's nobody has any right to question; I have nobody –
Patty No one?
Copsewood No.
Patty And your mother, Thomas – your old time-worn father?
Copsewood (*Softened*) Well, what of them?
Patty They have waited your coming all night – many a weary turn has your father taken down yonder lane, the winds blowing his gray hairs about his cheeks; a hundred times your mother has crept on tiptoe to the casement, bending low her ear to catch your step; then sat down and wept.
Copsewood (*With emotion*) Well, I know it's wrong – I've been wild, but it's all over; kiss me, Patty – you are a good girl, and I'm reformed. Only, you see, I was a little joyful – I had got a good price for the grain – all ready money, all paid down.
Patty Where is it?
Copsewood Where – why in my pocket; here! (*Copsewood endeavours to put his hand into his pocket, and discovers that it is torn away*) Oh! heaven, it's lost! I am a wretch indeed!
Patty Compose yourself, dear brother.
Copsewood Compose! what – and father, mother, you, beggars? and I – Oh! fool! beast! drunkard!
Patty Dear Thomas, come into the farm.
Copsewood What! to look on outcasts? and I that have made them so; never will I cross its threshold again unless to bring them comfort. Farewell, Patty, and for ever!

Rushes off – Patty falls upon her knees in the attitude of prayer

Scene 3

An apartment in Vernon's house

Enter Glanville and Alicia

Alicia Alas! sir, I fear to flatter myself with the hope.

Glanville Trust me, you look too gloomily upon the matter; Vernon will, doubtless, speedily be awakened to his error. Is he at present engaged?

Alicia I believe with Mr Franklin; he is a worthy man.

Glanville (*Sarcastically*) He is blessed with your good opinion, madame. And your sister-in-law's

Enter Vernon

Vernon Alicia, I have been a truant – I come in penitence to ask forgiveness. Come, Glanville, join with me. From this day I am an altered man. By heaven! I now look with astonishment and disgust at the scenes which have of late engaged me. A tavern life! Oh! let it pass away as a hideous dream, and be no more remembered.

Alicia Oh! happy, happy Alicia!

Vernon No – now I am quite reformed – ne'er again will I leave my happy home – but with thee, and our best friend, Alicia, wear out a long and stainless life of –

Enter Servant

Servant Sir John Gayly has left his card, and hopes, sir, that you will remember the appointment this evening at the George. (*Exit*)

Vernon Sir John Gayly! I had forgotten –

Alicia You will not go?

Vernon No, certainly! – and yet, as I promised, it might appear disrespectful to the Baronet – so I must go – but this is the last time – and mind, I'll take no wine – not a drop of wine – not –

Enter Servant with salver and decanter, and one wine glass

Eh! what's this? Oh! I had forgotten – my usual morning's draught.

Alicia You may take it away, your master will not partake of any this morning.

Vernon No, no – never bring it to me again. But stop as it is here now, I may as well take one glass! (*Drinks*) My love, this is the first of the last supply, is it not? It tastes well, and yet – (*Drinks*) – Very well – very well – give me another! (*Drinks it off*).

Alicia Is this your promise?

Vernon 'Tis my last sin, believe me. I am now wholly, unalterably

141

reformed. (*Leads Alicia off*) Well, Glanville, you will join us to-night?

Glanville Well, on one proviso – that you make no such bets as you were guilty of last night.

Vernon Bets! last night! My dear fellow, I remember no bets.

Glanville What, do you not remember how I advised, nay, implored you, to break off the wager with the French Count?

Vernon The French Count! I remember that our host's wine was excellent – but for the bet –

Enter Servant, shewing in Clerk

Servant A gentleman, sir, from Mr Bullion, your banker's

Exit

Clerk I wait, sir, from our house, to enquire whether you intend to wholly withdraw yourself from our books?

Vernon Certainly not. Why this question?

Clerk Your check, sir, was presented this morning for the whole amount of the cash banked with us.

Vernon My check! impossible!

Clerk Here, sir. (*Shews the check*).

Vernon Some fiend – some devil has been at work –

Glanville Be composed – 'tis the check you gave the Count.

Vernon Impossible! some damned cheat – some trick! – Let me remember – last night – No, no, no! all is a hideous mass of violence and disorder – I cannot grasp a single circumstance.

Clerk What answer, sir, shall I give to my employer?

Vernon Say! that I am a wretch – a beggar – no, no – I will wait on Mr Bullion – will explain all – there is an error – 'tis but a trifle – a – Oh! I shall go mad! –

Exit Clerk

Glanville! I'll have revenge; where is this Count? – where is the villain who has practised on my indiscretions?

Glanville Know you not that he was to leave England this morning; the vessel was in the harbour – and see – (*Goes towards window*) – see where she sails.

Vernon My curses sink her!

Glanville This is weakness; what, to rave thus for a few thousands!

Vernon Thousands! Do not my creditors get every day more clamorous? Am I not dunned, hunted? And all thro' this infernal vice. Glanville, what's to be done? Some bold stroke, or my credit's gone.

Glanville You have yet your wife's estate: this house –

Vernon This house! it was my ancestors'–my noble ancestors'–part with it–impossible!

Glanville I said not part with it – yet money may be raised. Is not Pounce here? He is secret and persevering – why not trust him?

Vernon I will; all may yet be regained. Glanville, excuse me to the Baronet: to-night I'll stay at home.

Glanville Why not have the party here?

Vernon Here!

Glanville Aye – the affair at your banker's may be whispered – a little fête now, would give the falsehood to any ugly rumour. You understand?

Vernon It would be so; but there is no time.

Glanville I have it; Mrs Loverout gives a masquerade tonight. I know she will, at my solicitations, bring the maskers here; and then –

Vernon As you will! I feel a burning thirst.

Glanville Come, shall I prescribe for you. Wine!

Vernon Aye – wine, wine! There is some demon in my heart that leaps at the sound; the monster's up – and wine, wine alone can satisfy it

Exeunt

Scene 4
A front wood

Enter Franklin and Miss Vernon

Franklin The infatuation every day grows stronger on him.

Miss Vernon Be assured, Franklin, that in remaining with my brother I have no other view than a hope of re-awakening him to a sense of his indiscretions. Grant me a short time longer, and then whatever may be the result of my endeavours, I am yours.

Franklin For me, content with such a promise, be mistress of your time. Come, I will see you to the house.

Miss Vernon I will not detain you, 'tis but a short way – in one hour I shall expect you

Exit

Enter Copsewood, singing

Franklin What, Master Copsewood, are you not ashamed of yourself?

Copsewood Ashamed! what for? hav'n't I been drinking? isn't that all correct, eh? (*Sings*) 'If you doubt what I say, take a bumper and try'.

Franklin An honest, industrious fellow like you to make yourself a mere receptacle for drink.

Copsewood Receptacle! (*Sings*) 'And so out of Toby they made this brown jug'. Oh, I've been getting tipsy like a gentleman: what do you think I've been drinking?

Franklin What! why, if you must drink, what an honest yeoman like yourself ought to partake of – good Sir John Barleycorn.

Copsewood Beer! once it was delightful, but now, my genteel company forbids it.

Franklin Indeed! Well, now let me advise you to go home.

Copsewood I will, because I know sister expects me.

Franklin Ah, the pretty Patty; she's a charming girl – good-natured lively, innocent, and unaffected.

Copsewood Ah, that's all true; but bless you, you've left out the first and best of all her virtues.

Franklin And what's that?

Copsewood She makes punch like an angel.

Franklin Well, farewell, friend; and take this brief but sincere warning – reform, reform and live soberly

Exit

Copsewood So I will – that I'm determined. (*Takes flask out of his pocket, and drinks*) So I will! sobriety is good in its way, and I'm determined to patronise it

Enter Bailiff

Bailiff What, Master Copsewood, and tipsy!

Copsewood Well, what's that to you?

Bailiff Oh, nothing! only I hope you are ready for to-morrow; you know the day of the month, I suppose – not an hour will be given you, and this I tell you in friendship

Exit

Copsewood To-morrow! Oh, the thoughts are coming upon me like flashes of fire! To-morrow the rent's due – that money – lost – Father, mother, sister, all turned out, houseless beggars – and I – I the cause – Eh! who's that in yonder lane? 'tis Squire Bullion's clerk – and what – he's counting notes – and now he takes out a bag – gold – bright, glittering gold! My father, mother – are you to starve – to – no – this, this will arm me for anything; (*Takes out flask, and drinks off contents*) Now, now I feel the robber strong within me, and come what will, the gold is mine

Exit

Scene 5

An Elegant apartment, fitted up as for a gala

Vernon, Glanville, and company sitting (all in dominos) drinking

All Ha, ha, ha! Excellent! a wit – a wit!

Vernon (*Greatly exhilarated*) No, no, gentlemen, you flatter; I'm naturally a dull fellow, but wine, glorious wine will act as the steel to my flinty sense, and sometimes strike out a bright spark or so. (*Music strikes up without*) Our visitors! Come, gentlemen, mask – mask.

(*They mask themselves – the doors are thrown open, and Masqueraders enter – A dance – after the dance, Alicia and Miss Vernon, who are in character dresses, single out Vernon*)

Vernon (*Between them*) Well, ladies, what would you with a poor unknown? Your name?

Miss Vernon Prudence.

Vernon A pretty name for a masquerade. And yours?

Alicia Temperance.

Vernon Oh, sisters! Prudence and Temperance – well, my fair ladies, Adieu!

(*Vernon is retiring, when half-a-dozen masks, dressed as bravoes, surround him*)

Vernon Eh! what, between robbery and peace-making. Well, gentlemen, which side is to have me?

All Both! (*They throw off their masks*)

Vernon Bailiffs!

Alicia Husband!

Miss Vernon Brother!

Vernon Villains, let me pass!

(*He runs when two more bailiffs present themselves, with pistols. A shout of 'Stop thief!' is set up – Copsewood rushes down, pursued by Rustics and Clerk*)

Copsewood Save me! save me! – (*He throws the bag of gold to the Clerk, falls at his feet, in attitude of entreaty – Picture*).

Act 2

FIVE YEARS HAVE ELAPSED

Scene 1
A Chamber

Enter Dogrose

Dogrose Well, I've bad news for my poor mistress – poor lady – here she sits, day after day, painting and painting, whilst her husband, the lost Mr Vernon, squanders the little gathered from the wreck of his late fortune, in riot and intoxication

Enter Alicia

Alicia Now, my kind friend – servant no longer – have you brought back any orders ?
Dogrose Alas! madam – I took home the drawings – and here, here is the payment – (*Gives purse*) but, I can hardly find courage to tell you, they desired me to inform you, that –
Alicia Speak!
Dogrose That no more will be wanted for some time.
Alicia Then are we desolate indeed! Oh, Vernon –
Dogrose Ah! lady, a foolish, indolent, profligate –

(*Knocking without*).

Alicia Hush! 'tis he –

Enter Vernon, his appearance is gloomy and haggard, he looks sullenly at Dogrose, who goes off

Vernon So! what does that menial here ? – why am I to be continually reminded by his presence of the fortune lost –
Alicia By your own intemperance.
Vernon Still, more complaints. For these five years past, I have borne –
Alicia *You* have borne! ungrateful man.
Vernon What!

146

Alicia Nay, I will give utterance to my anguish, *You* have borne – and what have I endured? Have I not seen our domains, your ancestral halls, melt and fade away like a vain pageant of ice? Have I not seen you sink, day by day, from the most exalted station, almost to the wretched footing of the outcast? Have I not seen your intellect obscured, your temper broken, by that base infatuation which my heart sickens to think upon, and my lips refuse to name? Know you how yesterday's dinner was procured – by what witchery the money was obtained? for 'tis long since you have given me any.

Vernon How it was procured! – how? –

(*Alicia holds her hand to him*)

Vernon Ha! your ring! –

Alicia You see, 'tis gone. It bought *your* dinner – it bought *your* wine – that ring, which, in the sweet promise of youth, in the day-spring of our mutual love – was fixed upon my hand by the noble, generous, Vernon.

Vernon Oh, this sacrifice is too much. Alicia – dear Alicia – yes! I see it in your pale cheek, and drooping lip – your eyes! – those eyes which I have worshipped as the glorious sun – all reveal your constancy and my disgrace. Stay – here let me be fixed the statue of remorse (*Is about to kneel*).

Alicia Ah – all – all is pardoned – all forgotten – (*They embrace, the purse falls from Alicia's dress*)

Vernon (*Taking it up*) – Ha! – (*With a mingled feeling of sorrow and contempt*) Oh – Alicia – is it so?

Alicia Stay, I can explain all.

Vernon Not a word – 'tis all explained. The wife would reclaim the truant husband; and with a subtle story lure him back again to home and obedience. You had no money?

Alicia On my soul, Vernon –

Vernon Be dumb. This – this – is all eloquent. Farewell.

Alicia Vernon! in mercy, stay! – where would you – answer – oh, I see – the tavern, the tavern.

Vernon No matter! be silent. What, tears! – 'tis well – you are proficient in your craft.

Alicia On my knees! – Vernon! –

Vernon Hence, hypocrite!

(*Vernon throws her from him, she falls, and scene closes*)

147

Scene 2

Enter Copsewood and Glanville

Glanville Have you any recommendation as to character?

Copsewood Why, sir, I don't know; when I was a youngster, the whole village would have put their hands to a recommendation; but somehow or other, the older I grow, the more folks think I can recommend myself.

Glanville Have you been brought up to service?

Copsewood No; I had once a farm of my own: that is, I managed it for father and mother; but they are dead, and then my sister –

Glanville Is she dead too?

Copsewood Aye. Every thing went wrong – I went wrong too; and there was a fine gentleman – a villain! – he professed to serve us, and, in short, he poisoned the mind of Patty.

Glanville What! Copsewood!

Copsewood Aye – why, you know the – what – thou art the villain –

Glanville No!

Copsewood Thou liest! the blood runs from thy cheeks, and thy lips quivers! – now feel a brother's vengeance! –

He grapples with Glanville, throws him down, and is about to strike him with his cudgel, when Franklin comes on and goes between them

Franklin Rise, sir – (*Recognizing him*) Glanville!

Glanville Franklin! I thank you sir, for this courtesy – for yonder ruffian, the law shall find security

Exit

Franklin Is it not Copsewood?

Copsewood (*Abashed*) Sir –

Franklin You have I hope, reformed.

Copsewood I try, sir; but if the truth must be told I make but slow progress.

Franklin But why thus assault Mr Glanville?

Copsewood I'll tell you sir, if I can, though to my own shame. When I took to visit inns, and such places, the farm went to wreck – father and mother died – sister Patty was lured away – my good name was gone. I tried at every place to get work, but couldn't – I was a beggar and a vagrant for four long years. I went to London, and there, for want of better employment, I worked at – it is an ugly word – an undertaker's. Well, sir, one night the churchwardens came and told me to follow them. I did so. They said a poor girl, unknown and unattended, had just gone from this world We came to the place – I entered a loathsome hut – a den

of dirt and misery – and in one corner, thrown aside, as in the very cold-
ness of contempt, lay the body, I took a light and bent myself towards the
corpse – I snatched the coverlet aside, and there – oh, my bursting heart!
lay my sister! my poor sister! ah! how changed – in every feature, in every
line, was writ the story of a broken heart; her very locks – sir, she was not
seventeen, yet there were gray hairs upon her!

Franklin Unhappy girl!

Copsewood I swore, silently, yet deeply, an oath of vengeance on her
destroyer – you, sir, saw Glanville in the dust. Now wonder you that his
blood is not trickling at my feet?

Franklin How did you first encounter him? he has not long
arrived here.

Copsewood So I heard, though I was not told his name; I applied to
him – for employment, as his servant.

Franklin Come with me – be trusty, and you shall not need a friend.
But mind, you must observe sobriety – do you hear, you must observe –

Copsewood Yes, sir – yes – *I'll try, sir*

Exeunt

Scene 3
The interior of Franklin's house

Enter Dogrose

Dogrose Well, it's lucky that Mr Franklin having married Mr
Vernon's sister, I was promoted to be his butler, and thus am enabled to
assist poor Madam Alicia – for her husband and Mr Franklin must ever, I
fear, be foes

Enter Juniper

Well, master Juniper, I suppose having recruited yourself in the pantry,
you are now ready to travel?

Juniper Why, only another glass.

Dogrose Well, you shall have it, and then you must away – for the
truth is, my master has no relish for visitors of your order.

Juniper Of my order?

Dogrose Yes; you know there were some odd tales about you in the
village –

Juniper Aye, that's years ago (*Aside*) for further particulars, see the
Newgate Calendar! – never mind all that – it was in my tender years, you
know.

Dogrose Eh, who's this? step aside.

Juniper I'm off

Exit

Enter Franklin and Copsewood

Franklin Here, Dogrose, is an old acquaintance – make him welcome. To-morrow, Copsewood, let me see you early

Exit

Dogrose Well, master Copsewood, and how has the world slid ?

Copsewood Ill enough. But why keep such a distance ? – are we not friends ?

Dogrose Why –

Copsewood Aye, I see your thoughts, man! that bag of gold, eh – (*Dogrose nods*) ah – well, it was a foolish affair; but I paid for it – deeply, character lost – father, mother –

Dogrose Well, I'm not one of those squeamish people, who having but little honesty themselves, make up for the want by their uncharitable suspicions of others; and so, master Copsewood, here's my hand.

Copsewood Thou art a worthy fellow – a worthy fellow. Come, hast thou not a glass ? One glass – as I'm an honest man, I have had but four to-day –

Dogrose Well, we'll have a glass.

Juniper (*Entering*) And here's one that will join you – who'd have thought of seeing you master Copsewood – come, we can make a night of it

(*Dogrose goes off and brings on stone bottle*)

Dogrose But one word, my gentle visitors, this must be what we call in genteel society – a select party.

Juniper Oh, of course.

Dogrose No intemperance.

Copsewood Oh, no, no. 'Twould be a breach of hospitality. I'd thank you for the spirits. The man in the moon, if he tipples, need not drink better brandy than this. (*During the foregoing, Copsewood and Juniper have been helping themselves most profusely*).

Juniper Come – let's have a song – and I'll sing it. (*Begins to sing*).

Copsewood No, no – I'll sing the song (*Begins to sing*).

Dogrose Neither of you shall sing – I am master here, and I'll sing. (*Begins to sing*).

Copsewood Come, no quarrelling, no quarrelling – now, I've hit upon such a plan – such a scheme – ha! ha – egod, I'm the boy! We'll all sing together!

(*They sing, and at length each sinks into a state of stupefaction, and scene closes in*)

Scene 4

A room in an inn

Enter Glanville and Pounce

Pounce How strange! I thought he had been abroad.

Glanville Aye, and so 'tis said he was. He is now, however, in this house.

Pounce Has he seen you?

Glanville Yes.

Pounce And did he not spurn you, for your desertion of him, after the destruction of his property?

Glanville Spurn me! I tell you the devil, drink, never worked so great a change in the nature of any man, as in this Vernon – all his thoughts, feelings, actions, begin and end in a bottle.

Pounce You may mistake him.

Glanville I have proof. At our first meeting he swelled a little and glared sullenly. I mentioned wine – and at the very sound, his mounting spirit dropped – and now look! – see where 'tis drugged within him! – (*Throws open door in flat, and discovers Vernon on the floor*) – See, where the image of noble, ambitious, god-like man – the master of the earth, and all its beings – the creature that binds the elements to his will – that tempts the billows in their wrath, and blunts the lightning – the gifted soul that would read the will of fate within the star-lettered front of heaven – see where he lies, gorged to the throat with wine! The mockery of life, the antipodes of reason. Enough of this – Vernon must be disposed of.

Pounce Disposed of!

Glanville Aye, 'tis necessary for our safety. I am told that Franklin, his brother-in-law, though despising Vernon, yet for the sake of his wife and child, is striving to find out that French Count.

Pounce Well!

Glanville Well! are you a born idiot, or just moon-struck? – know you not, that if Franklin prove successful, the draft, which in Vernon's name I forged, making him, poor fool, believe it his own act – and which you caused to be presented – must come against us? Now you see the necessity?

Pounce I will undertake – I have, as you know, undertaken desperate things during our partnership of crime, but this –

Glanville No matter – my own hand shall stead me.

Pounce Consider, ere 'tis too late.

Glanville 'Tis too late to consider. Will it not, after what I have done, be an act of charity to put that piece of scarcely-breathing lumber (*Points to Vernon*) into a quiet grave! – By heaven! I would rather be the villain that I am, with all my faculties strong and active in crime, than that poor dull piece of saturated clay. Do you retire, and watch my steps when

I leave this place with Vernon

Exit Pounce

So! now for my victim! (*Approaches Vernon, and after some difficulty rouses him*) – Come, how now! what, Fred! cast down, and with only four bottles!

Vernon Where am I! – what has – Glanville! or it is some ghastly dream?

Glanville (*Who pours out more spirits*) Here! here! this will awaken you.

Vernon (*Swallows it*) – 'Tis of the right kind 'ifaith! Another, another! (*Drinks*).

Glanville Ah! now you look like yourself!

Vernon Myself! – who is that? Ha! I remember, it was Vernon – Frederick Vernon – the happy, rich, respected – that was Fred Vernon – Where, where is he? (*Vernon seizes the decanter – drinking*) So! now I have found him – now I am fit for any thing. Come, where will you go, Glanville? – will you go to my house? – we'll have a splendid feast – a supper for Lucullus – Come! But you don't drink! no man sups with me who don't drink.

Glanville (*Affecting intoxication*) Don't drink! why I have drunk like an emperor – like an emperor!

Vernon This way, then – this way, then

Both Exeunt

Scene 5
A street – Franklin's house – night

Enter Alicia

Alicia My search is in vain – he's no where to be found. Perhaps – I shudder to think on it – my husband lies in the cold air, at the mercy of the elements! Oh, Vernon, if not for my sake, at least for your poor child's – for your sweet, innocent boy, the unconscious witness of his mother's agonies – return! return to your desolated home! In yonder house, the abode of virtuous love, live Franklin and his happy wife, the wretched Vernon's sister. Oh! I can picture the scene within that house! – domestic joy, with every grace of life, has sanctified its hearth-stone – Perhaps Louisa, now happy in her love, is sitting with her husband; or, with him, silently blessing, with that devoted fondness which only those who have a child can know, their little infant, as her sweet eyelids close in slumber –

152

whilst at my home, desolation frowns from the bare walls! – my child, sunk to sleep in its wild cries for bread – and my husband! – oh! 'tis a contrast to strike the brain with madness! Ha! some one approaches! and with strange precaution! – Let me a moment observe! – (*Retires*).

Enter Picklock and Two Thieves

1st Thief   Depend upon it, Picklock, you may trust Juniper.
Picklock   Oh, I never doubted him. But whereabouts are we ?
1st Thief   This is the spot – and that the house.
Picklock   Hark! the chimes! – (*Strikes twelve*).
1st Thief   It is the hour – now for the signal!

(*Picklock whistles, and is answered from the house*)

Picklock   Now, comrades; here is a booty! – stand firm, and we may make our fortunes. (*The door is opened by Juniper*) – Ha! come! (*Thieves enter Franklin's house*).

Alicia comes forward

Alicia   Eternal heavens! they will be murdered! – how shall I act ? – shall I cry aloud for help ? – no, no – they may be sacrificed in the tumult! Let me seek effectual assistance. Louisa! Franklin! I fly to save you

Exit

Enter Vernon and Glanville

Vernon   No, no – I say it was not sherry, it was brandy; good, glorious brandy! my heart is like a volcano with it now.
Glanville   I say it was sherry.
Vernon   And I say it was not.
Glanville   Would you quarrel with me ?
Vernon   Quarrel! why not! – I'm a man, I hope!
Glanville   No matter – you are wrong.
Vernon   Say that again! – and if you do –
Glanville   What, am I threatened ? – let this end it, then!

(*Draws his sword and stabs Vernon – who draws a pistol from his breast, fires it at Glanville, who falls. At this instant, the inmates of Franklin's house are alarmed – The Thieves rush out, thinking themselves betrayed. Alicia runs on with Neighbours, etc, who overcome the Thieves, and Juniper and Copsewood, who are identified with them. Alicia supports her wounded husband – Picture*)

153

Act 3

TEN YEARS HAVE ELAPSED

Scene 1
A rustic view, with house at side

Enter Wingbird and Dogrose

Wingbird What, honest Dogrose! why this is a busy day for you, eh?

Dogrose Yes, sir; and all I hope is, that Miss Isabella will be happier than poor Madame Vernon, her aunt.

Wingbird Well, I wish her joy with all my soul.

Dogrose And so do I sir.

Wingbird I have heard that Vernon is dead – is it so?

Dogrose Why, so we believe, sir; 'tis now ten years since he was heard of; he had an affray with that Glanville you have heard me speak about, and after that he went abroad, and no tidings have since reached us; his wife and son have since that time been protected by Mr Franklin. But, bless me! I've so much to do, that I can't waste another moment in talk – not a moment – a good morning, sir – good morning

Exit

Wingbird Good day, friend. Ah, yonder I see the villagers assembling – I'll e'en mingle with them until the party joins us

Exit

Enter Alicia and Isabella

Isabella My dearest madam, why should you on this day cherish such gloomy thoughts?

Alicia Bless you, my child – bless you! Oh, Vernon!

Isabella Tears again! Dear madam, the grave has closed o'er my uncle this many a year – why revert to this?

Alicia 'Tis rumoured so; but how or where he died we have no direct proof. Heaven pardon me, but I almost fear he lives.

Isabella Fear, dearest madam! fear!

Alicia Aye – death must have been terrible to him, come when it would; but life! if he still lives, and with that frightful vice craving within him – oh! what a spectacle of crime and horror. But 'tis unjust towards you my child, to indulge these thoughts.

Isabella Here comes my father

Enter Franklin

Franklin My dearest Isabella, your mother should have lived to see this day, your birthday

Enter Dogrose

Dogrose Oh, sir, sir – here are all the good neighbours in attendance.
Franklin We attend; come, Isabella

Exeunt Isabella, Franklin and Alicia

Dogrose There they go, happy as larks. Ah, that I was young again – the sweet golden age from eighteen to thirty

Enter Glanville, carrying a pack

No light companion that for a hot day's march – eh, friend ?
Glanville You speak truly – If you have the charity of a man, give me a cup of water.
Dogrose Water – that's a bad commodity to travel with; perhaps I may find a better; stay here till I return

Exit

Glanville So, Glanville, after ten years wandering, after all your villanies, what are you ? A mendicant, or little better. Hunted by the unceasing persecution of Franklin, who detected the forgery, I have lived an exile from my country. Why do I return ? Perhaps death has laid my enemy in his grave, and then –

Re-enter Dogrose, with a flask – At this moment Vernon, grey-headed, and in tatters, is seen to look in from wing

Dogrose Here, friend, this I take it will put new life into your feet. Farewell, and a good journey to you

Exit

(*As Glanville puts the flask to his lips, Vernon hurries down beside him and lays his hand on his shoulder*)

Vernon A drop! but one drop for the love of heaven –
Glanville No, beg it as I have done

Glanville looks sullenly at Vernon, and goes off

Vernon He's gone; my limbs can scarcely support me. 'Tis over –
death creeps upon me

Re-enter Isabella

Isabella Ah, yonder wretched man – some poor traveller o'erwearied
in his journey – I'll in and bring some aid

Exit Isabella, who returns with wine

Come, cheerly, good man! (*Vernon revives*)
Vernon I thank you – you have a gentle heart.
Isabella Here is wine.
Vernon Wine! (*with an effort he empties the flask*) There is life in
every drop; 'tis long since I have tasted it.
Isabella Whither are you journeying?
Vernon No where; the whole world presents an equal path to me.
Isabella Have you no kindred?
Vernon 'Tis a question I dare not ask myself.
Isabella Here, my good man, is money – take it, and heaven bless
you

Exit

Vernon Oh! that I had ne'er been born – ne'er had life to crawl a
wretched outcast, hateful to the world, loathsome to myself. Here is
money – 'twill buy me – what? – Ah! there is an inn – my heart is bursting
– my throat's on fire – let me, though in frenzy, strive to quench it

Rushes off

Scene 2
The inside of a country inn

Landlord discovered

Enter Copsewood, his appearance that of extreme misery

Copsewood Bring me some ale. Well, what do you look at?
Landlord You've money in your purse, I hope.
Copsewood There! (*Gives money*) 'tis my last.
Landlord Sorry for it.

Copsewood Indeed.

Landlord Yes; for both our sakes

Exit

Copsewood And is there never a true fellow among you to ask a stranger to wet his lips? What, all silent? Well, no matter (*The Rustics, having finished drinking, go off one by one*) Well, Tom Copsewood, and here you are after fifteen years madness, for I can find no better word, an old, decrepit pauper – name and health lost – and for what? – for what –

Re-enter Landlord

Oh! the ale – the ale! (*Takes ale and greedily swallows it*).

Landlord You are a stranger about these parts?

Copsewood Aye, just put a-shore.

Landlord Just put on shore. Why, there has been no vessel near here this week past but the convict-ship. And what's your business in this part of the country?

Copsewood To get work, if I can find any one charitable enough to employ me; but I fear the sick and the old can obtain but few masters.

Landlord Work! what can you do?

Copsewood Anything. At least, I am willing to try.

Landlord I'm afraid you will stand a bad chance, friend. There is something suspicious about you, that would prevent a respectable –

Copsewood Yes, there it is. If a man once fall, no matter when – no matter how he may have suffered – repented of the rashness – the good, respectable people of this world, raise their hands, set up the long loud cry.

Landlord You may have done wrong once. Well, shew me the man that has not, and let him tell you to starve on the highway – I have committed many an error and have no right to say so, nor will I.

Copsewood Bless you! I thought you one of those hard faced men, whose looks –

Landlord Why, as for looks, friend, I fear if either of us were to be recommended by looks, neither would stand great chance of preferment. But come with me.

Copsewood To the world's end. You have poured oil upon my bruised heart – you have taken a load from my brain. Drink! no, never again – never!

Landlord To-day my servant quitted me, you shall supply his place. There is a hamper of wine and brandy to take up to the manor-house – mind, be worthy of my trust.

Copsewood Worthy! may heaven strike me from the earth when I disgrace it

Exeunt

Scene 3
A grove

Enter Franklin and Wingbird

Wingbird This, neighbour Franklin, must be a happy day for you.

Franklin It is; and yet its brightness is at intervals shadowed by gloomy thoughts. Poor Vernon! I cannot think of him even now without emotion.

Wingbird Nor without feeling, I should imagine; how nobly you have acted towards him by protecting his wife and child.

Franklin It was my duty. Yet could I bring that villain Glanville to his earthly compt – I had then no wish, no hope, ungratified.

Wingbird But the forgery, of which Glanville was guilty, has been made manifest to the whole world.

Franklin Yes; yet the culprit has, hitherto, escaped. Had Vernon's pistol been true, he had long since been numbered with the dead. However, my wretched friend, though severely wounded by the hand of the assassin, was compelled to seek in a foreign land an asylum safe from the outraged law

Enter Dogrose

Dogrose Sir, the guests are all waiting for you – the servants have been searching for you – Miss Isabella has almost been crying for you – and here I'm come –

Franklin Well, well, I attend you. Mind, Wingbird, you are expected.

Wingbird I will not fail

Exit Franklin

Dogrose Be sure, sir, you don't, for I can tell you there'll be rare sport. There's the musicians invited, half the villagers too – and more than that, there is to be a little fête in the servant's hall

Exeunt severally

Enter Glanville

Glanville The whole village seem keeping holiday. All flock to the manor-house. I see no place where I may find shelter for the night. Eh, who comes here ? (*Retires*)

Enter Copsewood

Copsewood I am a new man – I feel as I have not felt these ten years: I seem to have shaken off the infirmities of time and dissipation, and to have become young and vigorous again. I am to take this wine and brandy to the manor house – aye and I will – every drop of it – every drop. (*Puts down basket and takes bottles out as if counting them*) How they sparkle! Ha! But what's that to me? – it's not mine – not mine

Enter Vernon

Vernon (*Seeing bottles*) How now, comrade?

Copsewood Well, what are you looking at? It's not mine – not mine – or you should be welcome, heartily welcome. How they sparkle. I wonder if all the corks are in tight? (*Trying them*) – Yes – yes.

Vernon Well, comrade I see you are one of the fine old school. Here – here's a draught for you – it's brandy real brandy. (*Giving bottle*).

Copsewood Brandy! No, I mus'n't – I mus'n't touch it.

Vernon You won't? well, then –

Copsewood No, no – I won't offend you by refusing – I'll just wet my lips – but I don't want it – (*Drinks heartily*) I don't want it – (*Drinks again*) – Oh, there's nothing like it! Oh, what a world would this be if all the rivers were brandy, and the green fields tobacco.

Vernon You say rightly – rightly. But, hallo! friend, you have emptied the bottle.

Copsewood It can't be!

Vernon No matter; now you know it's your turn.

Copsewood What, you mean – no, I can't – it's not mine – they are all counted, and the corks are all in so damnably tight.

Vernon And don't you yet know how to empty a bottle without drawing a cork? (*Vernon looks about, and picks up a straw*) Now then – stay, here's a gimlet. (*Bores a hole in cork, through which he puts the straw*) There, now – there's a touch of practical philosophy for you.

Copsewood You're a clever fellow – give us your hand – come with me – here we shall be seen; we'll go down yonder lane, and make a hole in the cork of every one of them – what's half a pint out of each of them? Come along, you're a boy of my own heart – Come

Exeunt

Scene 4

A garden

Enter Alicia, Isabella and Franklin

Alicia Do not, my dearest child, misconstrue my motives, whilst I withdraw myself thus early from the festivities that await you. I am not well, and should but cast a shadow o'er your mirth.

Isabella Nay, dear madam, but for another hour.

Alicia Bless you, my child, bless you. Return to your friends, whilst I, within my silent chamber, call on heaven to shed around you its choicest blessings, peace and innocence

Exit

Enter Dogrose

Dogrose Come, sir, now the grand affair will commence; all the actors are in readiness, and all they want is an audience.

Franklin As master of the ceremonies, lead on, we attend with due submission

Exeunt

Enter Copsewood and Vernon, each carrying a bottle

Vernon Well, here's to our better acquaintance, brother.

Copsewood Better acquaintance! we'll never leave one another again; – no, no, we are made for bosom friends – how stands your bottle?

Vernon Why, how do you think it should? I have had it twice to my mouth; you wouldn't be so unconscionable as to expect any in it, would you?

Copsewood No, for look at mine – I have only taken one draught and a half – and see what mischief I've done.

Vernon Well, is no more to be had?

Copsewood I can't say – what do you think?

Vernon Suppose I try that room?

Copsewood No, no – if you are detected!

Vernon I am armed.

Copsewood But you would not use violence?

Vernon No – except for self-preservation. I know 'tis wrong, but the devil, drunkenness, urges me on – stay here and watch.

Copsewood Be cautious, then

Vernon goes into Alicia's chamber, and Copsewood goes slowly off – watching

Enter Glanville

Glanville All is discovered! I am in the very house of my oppressor. What's to be done? – could I but strike Franklin, and fix the deed on them – ah! it shall be so! (*Takes out pistol*) at the alarm, Franklin will doubtless appear – in the confusion he will prove an easy prey (*Calls out*) What! house! within there – thieves! thieves!

(*Alicia screams within – she runs from the chamber wounded, exclaiming,* 'Murder! murder!' *followed by Vernon, holding a dagger – Franklin, Isabella, and others, run in – As Franklin appears, Glanville discharges his pistol – the ball strikes Vernon*)

Glanville Ah, foiled!
Franklin That voice! Glanville!
Copsewood Glanville! – where! – ah! – there stands the villain! – die!

(*Copsewood stabs Glanville, who falls; he is about to stab himself, when he is restrained by Rustics*)

Vernon (*Who is raised up*) Oh! wretched Vernon.
All Vernon!
Alicia Vernon! – Almighty powers! – Vernon! – my husband! my –
Vernon Thy husband? (*Recognizing her*) Alicia! – it is, it is. Hell roars beneath me – I am thy murderer! (*Falls*).

(*Alicia makes an effort to embrace him as he is falling, when she sinks in Franklin's arms*) Picture and Curtain

THE PRESS

The Stage, or Theatrical Inquisitor, December, 1828:

Coburg Theatre, *November 24th*. Fifteen years of a Drunkard's Life [*1st time*].

A highly interesting and well written production from the pen of the author of Ambrose Gwinnett – *was produced this evening under the above title, with very great success. The author must indeed be possessed of the pen of a ready writer – for he not only produces a new melo drama, or burletta, at this house, almost every other week, and has also, we understand, been engaged at Sadler's Wells on the same terms, but he is editor of a Sunday newspaper (the* Weekly Times) *besides. One would almost think the compilation of the latter was fully sufficient to employ every moment of his time – for the labour required in the editing of a newspaper, is by no means of a trifling nature. His indefatigability well deserves the reward it meets with – for his dramatic pieces are generally allowed to be the best of their kind – and his Sunday paper for amusement, entertainment, and sound observation, is not to be equalled by any one of the like class.*

From the title of the present piece, our readers will at once perceive, that the idea is founded on the celebrated drama of The Gambler's Fate; *and if those who witnessed the representation of the latter, felt an interest in its progress, from the domestic events and scenes which its representation was calculated to call to their remembrance – how much more, will they be interested in that of the present piece, which is of a still more domestic nature, and which shadows forth incidents and casualties of common every day occurrence in almost every family; the attendant evils, and consequent remorse inseparable from a continued round of drunkenness, the gradual decline and fall from a state of affluence and comfort, to one of degradation, wretchedness, and misery, and the commission of aggravated crime, are excellently, inimitably portrayed. Representations of this description, may indeed be said*
'– To point a moral, And adorn a tale –.'
For what can tend to the prevention of an indulgence in a gross and bestial vice, more than a display of the follies, wickedness, and crimes by which such an indulgence is attended.

162

The plot of this piece is twofold; – but it is woven together with so much dramatic skill, that throughout the whole, each of the two principal characters depends upon the other, and although both pursue different roads, and have different manners and habits, yet their indulgence in the one dreadful vice of drunkenness, which overclouds their better reason, and renders them worse than beasts, at last involves them in one common ruin.

As the bills themselves state, 'the piece contains scenes of the most highly wrought character; a development of circumstances which may fairly be inferred, as the natural results of proneness to inebriety, a frightful series of horrors, arising from the seductive, but destructive cup of the Bachanal; the dissipated life of the infatuated man of rank and education, is contrasted with the interference of the mere uncultivated rustic; the really excellent qualities of either individual, are shewn as availing nothing against the poisonous blandishments of drink; both parties are led on from ill to ill, until at length they are plunged into an overwhelming sea of guilt and horror, and leave behind them a memory of the blackest infamy'. In order to produce the desired effect, the dramatist has availed himself of a licence, lately become common, that of spreading his work over a long term of years, by which plan the degraded state of each victim is shewn with a more touching force, and all the sad varieties of the vice brought into one focus.

[There then follows a scene by scene outline of the plot]

H Williams (from Drury Lane theatre), a very clever and able actor, sustained the part of Copsewood, *with great judgment and effect – his love of drink, his horror on discovering the loss of his money, and his tale of woe, when recounting the death of his parents and the seduction and miserable end of his sister, were given with much force, power, and feeling. His acting was highly meritorious, and loudly applauded. Cobham's delineation of the habitual drunkard was the truest natural representation we have for some time witnessed. Altogether the piece is cleverly written, and was as cleverly acted.*

Morning Advertiser, November 25th, 1828:

Coburg Theatre: – The Manager of this very amusing Theatre seems to take for his motto:

> 'Eye nature's walks, shoot folly as it flies,
> And catch the manners, living as they rise.'

A new Melodrama, called 'Fifteen Years Of A Drunkard's Life', was brought out on Monday. The incidents are well calculated to show the

163

baneful effect of that vice which turned the companions of Ulysses to swine. Vernon, *the man of dissipation, is led by his inordinate desire for drink into the most distressing degradation; and, finally, in a state of intoxication, he commits murder. The other characters excite a strong interest:* Cobham, Miss Watson, Gann, Wynn, *and, in short, all the performers sustain their parts with great talent.*

The piece went off well, and was given out for further representation amidst loud applause.

The Ocean of Life

J T HAINES

JOHN THOMAS HAINES (1799/1843)

J T Haines wrote some 50 pieces for the minor London theatres, and was extremely successful in his day, although the lack of copyright protection for stage plays at the time precluded him from making any fortune. Most of his plays were of the blood-and-thunder variety, and he was especially known for his nautical melodramas – *My Poll And My Partner Joe** (1835) made a profit of £4,000 for the Surrey Theatre where he was resident dramatist.

His first play was a version of *Quentin Durward* for the Coburg in 1823 and attracted no particular attention, but *The Idiot Witness; or A Tale of Blood* for the same theatre later that year made his reputation. Naval pageants and masques had been popular since the last quarter of the eighteenth century, and Nelson's victories were responsible for an upsurge of patriotic feeling which naturally found expression on the boards of the minor and major theatres. One of the first was Moncrieff's *Shipwreck Of The Medusa* (Surrey, 1820) which featured a shipwreck on stage, and which firmly established the nautical hero as an honest, bluff but courteous able-bodied seaman whose speech was peppered with nautical metaphor.

The most celebrated impersonator of the Jolly Jack Tar, with his manly sentiments, excessive displays of courage and exorbitant patriotism, was T P Cooke – Mat Merriton in *The Ocean Of Life* – whose cutlass-wielding abilities and masterly execution of the hornpipe were unrivalled. Cooke portrayed to perfection all the requisite qualities of the nautical hero, which included devotion to the sea, cheerfulness in adversity and fidelity to the little woman waiting on the quayside; after his performance as William in Jerrold's *Black-Eye'd Susan* he was never accepted in any other kind of role. In *Noctes Ambrosianae* Christopher North, who saw Cooke perform in Edinburgh in 1827, described him as 'the best sailor out of all sight and hearing that ever trod the stage'. This type-casting was unfortunate for Cooke, who at the start of his career at the Lyceum (later the English Opera House, and later still the Lyceum again) in 1804 had shown considerable promise as a versatile and power-ful actor. Like Douglas Jerrold, he had also served in the Royal Navy, and had been present at the seige of Toulon in 1796, at the Battle of Cape

---

* The full text is available in Michael Booth's *Hiss The Villain* (1964)

St Vincent the following year, and at the blockade of Brest. He was born in 1786 and died at the age of 78 at his son-in-law's house at 37, Thurloe Square, London, having played in *Black-Eye'd Susan* until the age of 70.

J T Haines also wrote an early social problem play *The Factory Boy* (Surrey, 1840) in which the villain is a tyrannical mill-owner instead of the usual rascally ship's captain or French spy. He occasionally acted in his own pieces, and at the time of his death was the stage-manager at the English Opera House.

The Ocean Life. Frontispiece from Cumberland's Edition.
(*British Museum*)

THE OCEAN
OF LIFE

Dramatis Personae

As originally performed at the Royal Surrey Theatre
April 4th, 1836

Sir Timothy Tadpole by Mr C Pitt
*Captain Blundell, of the Ariadne – afterwards Lord Blaydon,
by* Mr Maitland
Honourable Mr Morville by Mr Goldsmith
James Westfield, a Missionary, by Mr Young
Mr Allensby, uncle to Isabella, by Mr Cullen
Hal Horsfield, skipper of the Rapid Trader, by Mr Dillon
Mat Merriton, Boatswain's Mate of the Ariadne, by Mr T P Cooke
Jemmy Jumble, a tailor in search of a lost estate, by Mr W Smith
Tome Toprail, seaman of the Rapid, by Mr Dunn
Giles Gratings, seaman of the Rapid, by Mr C Dillon
Skinrat, a trader in furs, by Mr Asbury
Clipcoin, a trader in gold dust, by Mr Dixie
Jack Peters, a negro servant to Sir Timothy, by Mr Morelli
Black George, keeper of a Drinking Cabouse, by Mr Wilson
The Honourable Isabella Morville by Miss Macarthy
Mrs Morville by Mrs W Daly
Mrs Skinrat by Mrs Stanley
Miss Jemima Jenkinson, afterwards Mrs Tadpole, by Miss Martin
Miss Fanny Fubbs by Mrs Lewis
Traders
Seamen
Boatmen
Indians
Lasses
Etc

THE OCEAN OF LIFE

Act 1

Scene 1
An apartment and gallery in the house of Sir Timothy Tadpole, at Buenos Ayres

Company discovered, extravagantly dressed – Miss Jemima Jenkinson – Sir Timothy Tadpole, followed by a Black Servant carrying refreshments, Captain Blundell and Mr Allensby come forward

Blundell Where is your lovely niece, Mr Allensby?
Allensby She quitted the room just now with her aunt.
Blundell Oh, sir! dared I hope ever to call her mine, I should look forward to my cruize on this confounded station with comparative rapture; but I fear her heart is pre-engaged.
Allensby I have heard her express herself in the highest terms when speaking of Captain Blundell.
Blundell Oh, sir! do not raise a hope which may never be realized: she sails this evening for old England.
Allensby Having finished the business which brought me here, I have secured a passage in the Rapid; our property is already on board.

Sir Timothy Tadpole and Miss Jemima Jenkinson advance

Miss J. I declare, now, Sir Timothy Tadpole, you are monstrously provoking! I appeal to Captain Blundell, whether we of the *bong-tong* ought to touch anything from that nasty black nigger fellow.
Sir T. Most divine Miss Jemima, as the immortal Shakespeare said, 'a man's a man, for aw' that'.
Miss J. The filthy creatures! I can't abide them!
Blundell (*Aside*) Vulgar impudence! – How unlike Isabella!

Retires with Allensby

Miss J. (*Aside*) Them fish is werry hard to hook; but I'll be Lady

Tadpole yet.

Sir T. (*Bringing forward a negro*) Jack Peters! You remember my directions?

Peters Iss, massa.

Sir T. You will take Lilly-Finger, and two or three more of my rascals; and –

Peters – seize the Missee Isabel?

Sir T. Know, also, where to convey her?

Peters Him cabouse – Spanish Town.

Sir T. Right. Your skin ought to have been white.

Peters Wish him had, massa: black not fashionable, only when people die.

Sir T. Hush! she comes

Exit Peters

Enter the Honourable Isabella Morville

Isabella Oh, the time approaches! – A few hours more, and we shall be on our way to dear old England! – The thought makes my heart leap with pleasure.

Blundell A certain proof, Miss Isabella, that Buenos Ayres contains no one you regret parting from.

Isabella I shall lose a friend in Captain Blundell; but in England I have a father and mother anxiously waiting to fold me to their bosoms.

Miss J. Surely it's unpossible that we are so soon to regret the departure of the Honourable Miss Isabella.

Allensby Our luggage is on board; we shall sail in the evening.

Miss J. (*Aside*) I'm very glad of it. I'll be Lady Tadpole yet. (*Exit*).

Re-enter Jack Peters

Peters Massa Sir Timmy, gennelman want see you.

Sir T. What's his name?

Peters Him neber ask – fear him forget.

Sir T. Fool! what kind of man is he?

Peters Oh, werry nice man; call me gennelman.

Sir T. Show him in

Exit Peters

Jemmy (*Without*) Oh, I'm to walk up, am I? Very well – very well.

Sir T. Who have we here?

Enter Jemmy Jumble, – his dress the extreme of ragged wretchedness, his face excessively pale and thin, and his feet peeping through his boots

Jemmy Ha! Timmy Tadpole! my buck, how are you? I thought it was you. How do you do, ladies? Servant, gentlemen!

Sir T. And pray, sir, who are you?

Jemmy Me? – Come, that's a good one!

Sir T. Who the devil are you?

Jemmy I am Jemmy Jumble.

Sit T. And who's Jemmy Jumble?

Jemmy Why, your old schoolfellow – haven't I been to your old father's chandler's shop to show my black eye ever so many times.

Omnes Chandler's shop!

(*Sir Timothy retires up, and sits down thoughtfully*)

Blundell But what has brought you here?

Jemmy I came to take possession of an estate – a large plantation.

Blundell Well, but where is it?

Jemmy I don't know. When I came here, they told me a hurricane had swept it away: although I've been hunting these last six months, I can't find a bit of it.

Allensby (*Apart to Blundell*) My niece is anxious to take her departure without the ceremony of a farewell. Will you accompany us?

Blundell I will

They all Exeunt except Sir Timothy and Jemmy

Sir T. What brought you here, fool?

Jemmy I was hungry; I've had nothing to eat for the last three days but what a brave sailor, Mat Merriton, as he calls himself, gave me.

Sir T. How did you find me out?

Jemmy I heard your name from Mat; though there was a Sir tacked to it. You called yourself My Lord at school.

Sir T. I will do something for you if you hold your tongue about the shop.

Mat (*Without*) Now, my lads, keep a look-out for his honour – do ye hear?

Voices (*Without*) Aye, aye

Enter Mat Merriton

Mat Servant, sir! Is Captain Blundell – (*Seeing Jemmy Jumble*) Eh! what! my ragged friend, the plantation-hunter! Come, tip us your flipper. If you haven't found an estate, you seem to have grounded on a pretty smooth bottom here.

Jemmy Oh, yes, I'm quite at home; take a chair – My friend, Sir Timothy Tadpole – my friend, Mat Merriton, of the Ariadne! Will you take anything, eh? Ring the bell, Tim.

Sir T. (*Aside*) Curse the fellow!

Mat And so you are anchored here? Now, I suppose, you'll sport

173

some new canvas, and new paint and pitch your starn.

Jemmy Pitch my starn!

Mat But mayhap your honour will tell me if the skipper's aboard. I want to report to him, that the Rapid is getting under weigh, to drop down the river before the evening.

Sir T. Ah! so soon? (*Aside*) I must urge them, then, or she may escape. (*Aloud*) I will soon return

Exit

Mat His honour's steering right head on to find the skipper, I fancy. My old trousers! but you've a snug berth here – finer than an admiral's cabin.

Jemmy And so you are going to England in the Rapid?

Mat I going to England in a trading craft! Not I: I'm a regular-built man-of-war's man

Re-enter Captain Blundell

Blundell Merriton!

Mat Here, your honour.

Blundell Get a boat's crew to carry some despatches for England to the Rapid.

Mat Aye, aye. But, your honour, I have a favour to beg.

Blundell What is it, Merriton? You are a good seaman; and an officer should never refuse a favour to the man that does his duty.

Mat I merely wished to ask your honour to let me be one of the crew to take the despatches aboard the Rapid.

Blundell A sweetheart there – eh, Merriton?

Mat No, your honour; I never had a matter of that sort athwart my heart in all my life time; – but I've an old father and mother, and a little blue-eyed sister, at home: I know they've been fretting and fretting, and I've been saving and saving, ever since I've been at sea; let me ship off my small stock of yellow boys in the Rapid for the old couple and sister, sir.

Blundell Take charge of the boat yourself, Merriton.

Mat Thank your honour. Shall I tack a bit, and stand in here presently for the despatches?

Blundell Do so; I will go and prepare them

Exit

Mat (*To Jemmy*) And haven't you got a letter to send?

Jemmy (*Tipsy*) No: I never had but one sweetheart; her mother kept a tripe shop at the end of Barbican. She had a hundred and fifty pounds left her; and then her nose took a turn up whenever she saw me,

174

and she told me to box my trotters, for I was no better than cat's meat in her eyes. I hadn't the estate then, which – I haven't got now. But I must just speak to my friend, Sir Tim. (*Staggers off*)

Mat Well, as ye please. My eye! I fancy I see old father, when the shiners are stowed in his hand. There he stands, smoothing his thin gray hairs down; and the old mother looking over his shoulder, with her clean white cap on, and her dear old eyes dim with tears; and little sister, in her red shoes that I bought for her, is clapping her hands, and jumping about the – But, lord love my heart! sister's a woman now; Bless 'em – bless 'em!

Exit

Scene 2
Another apartment in the house of Sir Timothy Tadpole

Enter Miss Jemima Jenkinson, Miss Fanny Fubbs, and Skinrat

Miss J. La! my love, what made you think of seeking for me here?

Miss F. Oh, I knew you were always acquainted with great people, and hearing that there was a party here tonight, says I to uncle Skinrat, says I, 'Ten to one but Miss Jemima Jenkinson is at Sir Timothy Tadpole's'.

Miss J. You were right: my acquaintances are all aristocracktic. Well, Miss Fubbs, my love, and what does your uncle want?

Miss F. Uncle Skinrat will tell you; we know you are a capitalist.

Miss J. I hope nobody else thinks so, or I shall be pestered by suitors more than I am already.

Skinrat I'll come to the point at once.

Miss J. Do; you keep me from my titled friends.

Skinrat There's an Indian village on the coast, where old Clipcoin and I keep agents; he to buy gold dust – I to buy furs; and –

Miss J. (*Pettishly*) What has a person of my high connections to do with trade?

Miss F. Uncle's coming to it now.

Skinrat My agent writes me word that he has a splendid cargo of commodities, and that I must bring so much money. Now I haven't quite enough; but if you'll lend me a little to make it up you shall share in the profit.

Miss J. I have anything to do with your paltry trade! Insolent! – Leave me, base people! Miss Fanny Fubbs, you and I is no longer acquaintances!

Enter Jemmy Jumble

Miss J. Oh! (*Aside*) He here! – I'm ruined! – I shall never be Lady Tadpole!

175

Jemmy Well, my pretty Jemima, how are trotters?

Miss J. (*Recovering herself*) Ah! my dear James! – To see you thus! – You have been shipwrecked.

Jemmy (*Astonished*) The devil I have!

Miss J. (*Embracing him*) Oh, my dear James! (*Apart to him*) Say as I say, and I'll make your fortune.

Jemmy (*Embracing her*) My dear Jemima!

Miss J. (*Introducing him*) My friends, this is my cousin, the Marquis of Barbican.

Miss F. Happy to see your lordship escaped from such a dreadful shipwreck.

Skinrat It must have been dreadful, indeed: it has almost skinned your lordship.

Jemmy That's soon repaired. (*To Skinrat*) What are you, my good man? – A tailor, eh? (*Aside*) Perhaps he'll stand tick. (*Aloud*) Are you a tailor, my old cock?

Miss J. No; he's a most respectable dealer in furs; he wants to borrow a small sum, and as you, cousin, always loved honest tradespeople.

Jemmy How much – how much, my good man?

Skinrat Fifty pounds will be enough; and I shall be back in a few weeks.

Jemmy (*Loftily*) You are sure fifty will be enough? You can have a hundred from me quite as easily. But where are you going?

Skinrat Over land to an Indian village.

Jemmy I'll go with you; perhaps I may find my lost estate.

Miss J. (*Apart to Skinrat*) You shall have the money. (*Aside*) I shall get rid of him.

Jemmy Wait upon me in the evening; we can arrange.

Miss F. Oh, bless you, my lord! – Bless you, Miss Jemima!

Skinrat (*Crossing*) I'm an honest man; I wouldn't injure anything! Come, Fanny. I must arrest old Cowhide, the tanner, and then we'll go to prayers!

Exeunt

Miss J. What demon brought you here?

Jemmy What the devil put it into your head to make me Marquis of Barbican?

Miss J. Do you know any one here?

Jemmy Only Sir Timothy Tadpole and Mat Merriton.

Miss J. Sir Timothy Tadpole! – Oh! I'm ruined!

Jemmy You're ruined! – What, is the trotter-market done up? –

Miss J. (*Aside*) I must make friends with him, or I shall never be Lady Tadpole. (*Coaxing him*) Jemmy, you and I are old friends, you must see me home; I have something particular to say to you.

Jemmy See you home! – Have you a carriage? – Or shall I order the

Marquis of Barbican's ? (*Laughing*).

    Miss J. (*Taking his arm*) This way.

    Jemmy (*Laughing*) Countess of Cats'-meat! – Ha! ha!

Exeunt

Scene 3

A drinking Cabouse in Spanish town

Hal Horsfield, Tom Toprail, Giles Gratings, Black George, and a number of rough sailors, discovered drinking

Hal Here's a safe voyage to the Rapid, and may none of her passengers die of sea-sickness!

    Omnes Ha! ha! – Success to the Rapid!

    Toprail We have lady-passengers – eh, skipper?

    Gratings Ay, and an old man, with lots of rhino in their luggage.

    Hal And if people do slip overboard, one can't help it, in a small craft like ours.

    (*A scream, a noise of voices, and a clash of swords, without – they all start up*)

Enter Jemmy Jumble, hastily

Jemmy Oh, lord! Such a fight! – That Mat's the very devil! We saw some nigger fellows dragging a girl along; in he darted upon them, and, lord! how he did lay about him!

    George Was any one near?

    Jemmy I saw some soldiers.

    George Soldiers! – I have customers who must not be found here.

    (*He blows out the lantern-light – room dark*)

    Jemmy Oh, lord! I've run out of the frying-pan into the fire!

    (*Creeps under the table*)

    George Horsfield!

    Hal 'Tis but a false alarm.

    George It might lead to the house being searched; and then, you know, you have something at stake. This way

Exeunt all but Jemmy

Mat (*Without*) Ho! house, ahoy! – Show a light to a ship foundering!

Enter Mat Merriton, bearing Isabella Morville, insensible, on his shoulder

177

Mat How! all dark! – Take care – no foul play; for here's a king's cutlass in a good hand. Not a word ? So, all's right; and now, my gentle craft, though I haven't a light to take your number, or see whether you are pretty or ugly, white or black, yet you're a woman; and that's enough for a true man's heart to know, be he sailor or land-going lubber.

Jemmy (Peeping out) Is that you, Mr Merriton ?

Mat Where are you ?

Jemmy Here – under the table.

Mat And where the devil's the table ?

Jemmy Over me.

Mat Psha! come out.

Jemmy (Creeping out) It's I, Jemmy Jumble.

Mat What, Jemmy! – Heave to, my lad, will you, and take charge of this craft, while I try the soundings for a light.

Jemmy It's of no use – they've put it out.

Mat Avast! the little pinnace is bearing up. (*Isabella slowly revives*) There, my lass. There – there!

Isabella (Faintly) Now I remember; yes, yes – I was rescued. Are you the generous man that saved me ?

Mat Don't talk of that, my lass: when I'm in the same mess, you'll save me, and that will square all scores.

Isabella Oh, take me to my friends!

Mat So I will, when I know 'em. Harkye, Jemmy, bear a hand, and hoist a signal-light.

Jemmy I daren't stir, bless you!

Mat Then, d'ye hear, take charge of the little lass, and I'll be back in the shipping of a handspike.

Isabella Nay, do not leave me!

Mat (Aside) How queer it makes a man's heart feel to hear a pretty speaking-trumpet like that passing – 'do not leave me!' I don't wonder at the shore-going lubbers getting married. (*To Isabella*) I'll be back in a twinkling, my pretty lass

Exit

Isabella He is gone! What will be the terrors of my aunt and uncle ? The vessel will put to sea, and I shall be left surrounded by enemies!

Re-enter Black George, listening

Jemmy I hope Mat won't be long, ma'am: it's a hawful situation to leave two innocent people in, all alone in the dark!

George (Seizing Isabella by the arm) This way, miss. I'll lead you to your friends.

Isabella 'Tis not the same voice! – Who are you ?

George The sailor, miss, who rescued you.

Jemmy (*Aside*) That's a lie! – There'll be another fight!
(*He creeps under the table*)
Isabella Oh! I cannot be deceived! – Unhand me!
George (*Dragging her off*) This way – this way!
Isabella Help! help! oh!
Blundell (*Without*) 'Tis her voice – follow me!

George looses his hold, and hurries off

Enter Captain Blundell, Mr Allensby, and two Sailors, with torches

Blundell Ah, Miss Morville! – Thank Heaven! we have found you.
Allensby We have sought through the whole city for you.
Blundell What villain has done this?
Isabella Question me not now; I am sick with terror! But for a brave sailor, I – Oh! uncle, for mercy's sake, lead me hence!
Allensby The ship has already dropped down the river, and we must hasten on board.
Isabella Anywhere, so I escape from this place.
Blundell Lead her into the air; it will revive her.
Allensby This way – this way!

Exeunt, conducting Isabella off

Jemmy (*Crawling from under the table*) Now how shall I find my way out? – What shall I do if I run over any more of 'em? There isn't always a table to fly to.
Mat (*Without*) Yo ho, there, in the hold!

Re-enter Mat Merriton, with a torch

Mat (*Looking about*) Where's the young thing that –
Jemmy She's gone.
Mat Gone! Where is she, eh?
Jemmy We were in the dark; somebody came and took hold of her; he said he was you.
Mat A pirate, under false colours!
Jemmy Then another somebody came in, and the first somebody ran away.
Mat Which way did they take the girl? (*Seizing him*) You lubberly swab! pilot me in her wake, or, d – me! I'll throttle you!

Exit, shaking Jemmy, and shoving him out

Scene 4

Between decks of the Rapid

Enter Hal Horsfield and Tom Toprail

Toprail There's a gun fired from the frigate for the Rapid to heave to.

Hal Curse the frigate! – Bend on, I say: we've a stiff breeze, and we shall hear no more of the Ariadne.

Toprail Belay there, Master Skipper: she's the swiftest sailor in the navy; she'd pounce on the Rapid like a hawk.

Hal The devil seize her sailors, and may the sharks have her captain! (*A gun heard*) There! she's talking again. Pass the word to heave to. (*Exit Toprail*) The lady-birds are on board, and the gray-head –

Re-enter Toprail, hastily

Toprail A boat has pulled out from the Ariadne.

Hal A love message from one of the officers, or some such boys' play, I suppose. Where's the young petticoat?

Toprail Looking over the taffrail.

Hal A neat craft, that!

Toprail You're right, skipper; I shouldn't care if she was all my own.

Hal (*Looking off*) But here she comes; top your boom, Tom, and see the ship put right before the wind the moment the despatches are on board.

Toprail Aye, aye

Exit

Enter Mr Allensby and Isabella

Allensby I perceive a boat approaching; comes she not from the Ariadne, captain?

Hal She does, sir.

Allensby Some message, no doubt, from Captain Blundell. You will convey our compliments to the captain, and tell him we are all safe on board.

Hal I will, sir.

Isabella And say, that I shall ever remember his services.

Hal Yes, miss. (*Aside*) Poor thing! 'tis a pity she'll never see him again! (*Exit*).

Isabella I know not why, uncle, but I do not like that man.

Allensby 'Tis his rough habit, my love: the sons of the sea are rude, but honest.

Isabella I love a sailor from my heart; their very harshness has a genuine warmth in it, dear to every woman; but that man –

Allensby Come, let me conduct you to your cabin.

Exeunt

Enter Mat Merriton and Hal Horsfield

Mat So, you are the skipper of this craft, are you? – A taut little thing, fit for something better than carrying sugar and cockroaches; so I've got a little stock of money, which I want you to convoy to my old father – will you? You're bound for Plymouth; he anchors at Cawsand Bay; so it's not much out of your course.

Hal What's the amount?

Mat A matter of fifty pounds. 'Tis not much, but it's my all. Will you take it to him, Master Skipper?

Hal To be sure I will; I'd do anything for a good son, who wishes to serve an old worn-out father.

Mat Tip us your flipper! – My old trousers! you're one after my own heart! You'll soon know him; he's a fine old chap – stands six feet high without his shoes, and is a better man than ever his son will be. (*Giving a purse*). There's the money.

Hal (*Aside*) An infernal milksop! (*Aloud*) They shall have the money.

Mat Thank ye – thank ye! – They tell me your name's Horsfield: that's enough. I know you're an honest man, and I shall be happy. But, avast! avast! – I'm forgetting that I've a despatch from Captain Blundell for one of your passengers – Mr Allensby. (*Giving a packet*) There it is. I say, Master Skipper, take a tar's advice, and don't hug the land: you'll have a squally night, and a squall comes on in these latitudes sometimes before you can take in a reef.

Hal Aye, aye; I know them

(*Music*) – *Re-enter Toprail, hastily*

Toprail (*To Horsfield*) There's a white squall right ahead; – you are wanted on deck.

Mat The devil there is! – It may overtake us before we reach the harbour

Shouts and noise as they rush off

181

Scene 5

The open sea, nearly dark. – The Rapid discovered beating about in a squall – thunder and lightning – Sailors seen on deck, endeavouring to work the vessel – the mast breaks with a terrific crash, and all is confusion on board – the Rapid sinks – the sea covers the wreck – the moon emerges from the heavy clouds – green fire is lighted up, and as a raft, on which Isabella and Mat Merriton are seen floating, reaches the centre, the scene closes

End of Act 1

Act 2

Scene 1
Break of day – A desolate and rocky coast

Hal Horsfield and Toprail discovered, each with a small keg slung under his arm – Gratings, with a box of biscuits – Mat Merriton sitting on a trunk – and Isabella Morville, laying apparently lifeless on the beach – her head resting on Mat's knee

Hal So, at last, Davy Jones has got the good ship Rapid.

Toprail Aye, and some bold hearts with her, Master Horsfield.

Gratings And a good store of rhino in the old man's luggage.

Hal If the sea would but turn us up that trunk! –

Mat Hark ye, my lads – pass us a little of that rum, just to wet the young thing's lips.

Hal Oh, the young thing's lips are wet enough with salt water; she'll never open them again.

Mat You growling grampus! Pass the rum, I say!

Hal, Toprail and Gratings Not a drop! not a drop!

Hal Come, let us look what the sea has washed up

Exeunt Horsfield, Toprail, and Gratings

Mat Oh! may it choke you! Ha! life's hoisting the red flag in her pretty face! There – that's right; open your pretty head-lights; and thank Heaven's mercy.

Isabella (*Recovering*) Where – where am I?

Mat That's more than I can tell you, my pretty lass.

Isabella Are they all gone? – Who are you? –

Mat You mustn't mind that now, my pretty one – but I'm Mat Merriton, of the Ariadne.

Isabella (*As if recollecting*) The Ariadne!

Mat Aye, and a more unlucky dog-fish never swam the ocean of life; but, if you'll take my word for it, my girl, I'm an honest fellow, and will never do you harm.

Isabella What is to become of me? Alone, here – none to care for me, and –

Mat Come, come – you mustn't whimper – this is a savage coast, and if you cry and tremble thus, you'll lose all your strength.

Isabella You say truly; Providence has saved me for its own wise purposes, while it destroyed my relatives; I will endeavour to sustain myself, that I may be worthy of its holy aid.

Mat That's a brave lass, eat a bit of biscuit. (*He raises her tenderly*)

Re-enter Hal Horsfield, Toprail and Gratings

Hal How's this ? – A skulker added to our mess!

(*Isabella alarmed, clings to Mat for protection*)

Mat Cheerly, don't be afraid. You see, shipmates, I have contrived to cheer up the pretty pinnace. I told her she was among men – sailors every inch – and that she needn't be afraid of us.

Hal Why, you're not going to carry that ballast with you, are you ?

Toprail and Gratings No – no!

Mat Why, you skulking swabs – mind, I wish to be civil – you rascals, this is a woman – a woman in a wild desert, with only you to aid her; and would you leave her to perish ? Is this your gratitude to heaven for saving you from the wreck ? Hark ye: if Providence don't repent of its mercy, it is because we have this good girl along with us; and while I have an arm to hold her up, she shall never drop

Exeunt Horsfield, Toprail and Gratings, grumbling, Mat following, with Isabella

Scene 2
A thick forest

Enter Hal Horsfield, Toprail and Gratings

Hal I tell you, we must be on the main land, we shall drop upon some Indian village or other; but, if that lubber astern is going to tow the woman in his wake, we shall be on short allowance long before the end of our trip.

Mat (*Without*) Hollo, there! back water, my lads! The poor girl is tired, and nearly exhausted

Enter Mat Merriton, supporting Isabella

Mat There, cheerly, lass – let us stick by one another in our trouble. I have taken you in tow, and will bear you safe into port, unless I founder myself.

Isabella Providence, indeed, seems to have made you my guardian angel.

Toprail Guardian angel! Rather rough in the feathers for one of that craft.

Hal I'm apt to think the lass likes him best as a man; she's no bad judge, either. (*The sailors all laugh*).

Mat Avast, you lubbers! is this a time for your rascally jokes, when death is this moment at your heels? Let the young woman alone – she's safe enough in my company, but curse me if I think she would be so in either of yours.

(*The Sailors all laugh*)

Isabella (*Shuddering*) Wretches!

Mat Hush! don't be afraid; but lie down, and I'll watch by you.

Isabella I will do as you wish (*Reclining on the bank*) but I dare not sleep.

Mat Well, well – tired nature, my lass, will take the watch in her own hands. (*Spreading his jacket*) There, there – I wish I had another jacket to put over your pretty head. Spite of herself, my lads, the girl will sleep.

Hal And when she does, eh, shipmate! a little kiss might –

Mat No, no – you only joke – you are men, not devils; you are joking, to be sure.

Hal Aye, aye! Come, take a pull at the rum.

(*Mat drinks, and then crosses softly to Isabella*)

Mat She sleeps, so make no noise; and I'll mount one of the trees there-away, and look out for some land-mark.

Sailors Aye, aye!

Mat Merriton surveys them cautiously, and exits.

(*Horsfield makes a sign to Toprail and Gratings – they all rise*)

Hal (*Crossing to Isabella*) She's a pretty flower to find in a desert; 'twould be wrong to pass by without tasting its sweetness.

(*He stoops to kiss her; she wakes*)

Isabella (*Shrieking*) Oh, mercy! – Merriton! Merriton!

Hal (*Seizing her*) It's of no use piping all hands, my lass. Merriton isn't here; and if he were, we are three to one.

Isabella (*Struggling*) Villain! Is there no help! God! am I reserved for this – off – off! (*Shrieks*).

Hal You are mine! – I only can save you

Re-enter Mat Merriton, hastily – he seizes Hal Horsfield, hurls him round, and with a terrific blow strikes him to the ground – a pause – Hal Horsfield, Toprail, and Gratings, rush on him with their knives – Mat draws his cutlass, passes his arm round Isabella, and the Sailors draw back

185

Hal Fool! – What can you do against three ?

Mat Three! – You bull-headed dog! there's three to three: here's my good arm, this good cutlass, and this good girl – strong in her innocence.

(*They rush on Mat – he cuts down Horsfield, who drops his knife, and falls – Toprail and Gratings close with Mat – Isabella, snatching up Horsfield's knife, stabs Toprail, and he falls – Mat throws Gratings over his shoulder*)

Mat Bravely done! Well, my blackbirds, how do you like yourselves ?

Hal (*Binding up his arm*) Hark ye, Mat Merriton! Hal Horsfield tells you, that if famine spares you, you shall one day bitterly repent this. (*To Toprail and Gratings, rising, and pointing to the provisions*). Away, lads; and leave them to perish in the wilderness

Gratings seizes the bag of biscuits, and Toprail, though suffering from his wound, seizes the keg of rum – they laugh, tauntingly, and exeunt

Isabella (*Dropping on her knees*) Thank heaven they have gone! – Oh! I do indeed thank God.

Mat If they had left us a morsel to eat –

Isabella Better to starve alone, than to live with them.

Mat (*Aside*) Bless her heart, she an't afraid of me. What brought you all the way to Buenos Ayres, eh ?

Isabella (*Aside*) Did he know my rank, I might lose his aid. (*Aloud*) I came out as attendant to Mrs Allensby. But I feel faint.

Mat When I mounted a tree thereaway, things looked greener a little to starboard; some river, I guess. Come, I'll carry you to it; but by what name shall I drink to you ?

Isabella They call me Isabella –

Mat I'll call you pretty Bella; and may every heart wish you as well as I do! Come. (*He lifts her on his left arm, but staggers back*).

Isabella What is the matter ?

Mat Nothing, my sweet Bella; I bruised my arm a little in the wreck, and those infernal sharks have given it a bit of a slew.

Isabella (*Tenderly*) You will die here alone.

Mat Don't let your tears fall like sharp shot into my heart – dry your eyes; let me wipe them off, my sweet Bella.

(*He approaches, as if to kiss her – her look and action arrest him – he starts with self-reproach*)

Mat (*Confused*) I ax pardon, lady – that is, my pretty Bella; forgive me; take my hand – and – and Mat Merriton will be a brother to you.

Isabella I believe you, Merriton – I trust myself to you, without fear; there is my hand.

Mat And when I betray my trust, may I founder in the black gulf of the world's hate! Come, lean on me – I meant no harm, pretty Bella –

none, as I am a sailor

Exeunt

Scene 3
An Indian village, and picturesque country

Indians and Traders, discovered – Skinrat and Clipcoin – Hal Hors-field, Toprail, and Gratings – Jemmy Jumble, Mrs Skinrat and Miss Fanny Fubbs

Jemmy Egad! this is comfortable – this must be the estate I'm in search of. I wouldn't mind settling here: how many wives do they allow a man in these parts – eh, Mrs Skinrat?

Mrs S. How many! – Oh, horrible. Mr S. shall never come again, if they allow more than one.

Jemmy Don't be afraid; bless you, I've heard him say that he found one too much.

Mrs S. Eh! what, he said so? (*Calling*) Skinrat!

Skinrat I've made a good bargain; we shall clear one hundred and fifty per cent: these poor savages, I pity them; they know nothing of religion – they're easily cheated.

Jemmy Miss Fubbs, my love, suppose we stay and enlighten the natives; let you and I remain, and live in a state of nature.

Miss F. Oh, horrible! – Oh, my lord!

Mat (*Without*) Help! help!

Enter Mat Merriton, with Isabella, insensible, on his shoulder

Mat If there be Christian souls here, help two ship-wrecked sufferers. (*He places Isabella on the ground*).

Hal He here! – Confusion!

Jemmy (*Running to him*) Mr Merriton, is that you? – Yes; and I know the poor girl, too, though I don't know who she is.

Mat Lift her pretty head from the hard earth, will you, lad; softly, softly, I fear she's dead. But – are you women, or are you fiends? – There's the loveliest little craft that ever – (*Seeing Horsfield*) Oh! Come here, lass, I am strong yet, and I'll stand by you – I'll –

(*He fixes his eye on Hal Horsfield, and, while attempting to draw his sword, falls by the side of Isabella – the females are going to assist her*)
God bless you! and may you all be rated in the log-book aloft for your kindness to this frail bark! Jemmy, my boy, what are you about?

Jemmy Blubbering like a baby.

Mat And well you may, to see such a pretty flower as this under the

187

heel of those who have not the heart to love it in its bloom. Is there no Christian here to aid us.

Westfield Yes, my son, here is one, with Heaven's help, will aid you. I am a servant of that Providence which has watched you through the desert. Come to my cottage, and all that I can do to assist you shall be done.

Mat Do you hear, my pretty Bella? – Come. (*Attempting to carry her*) Lord love me! I never felt so like a child! – But her hand is getting warmer. Oh, dear! I could cry with gratitude!

Westfield and the Indian Girls assist Isabella – Jemmy Jumble supports Mat

Scene 4
The Interior of Westfield's hut

Enter Westfield and two Indian Girls, supporting Isabella, partially recovered, followed by Mat Merriton

Mat So, we are in some sort of a port at last, my lass.
Isabella Where? where?
Westfield Among friends, my poor girl.
Isabella Ha! I remember – the wreck – the desert – those wretches! (*Starting up, and gazing wildly*) Ah! my friend – my saviour – my deliverer! you are here, and I am safe!

She rushes to Mat, he takes her in his arms – she starts away, but returns and gives her hand

Enter Jemmy Jumble, in alarm

Jemmy They're going – they're going! Oh, Mr Parson! go and preach to them! – Mr Sailor, go and fight with them! Those rascally sailors have been giving you and miss a pretty character.
Mat Have they dared to say anything against Bella?
Jemmy Have they! – Lord bless you! such things, that the traders' wives turned up their eyes, and grunted like pigs at a methodist.
Mat Do you take charge of the convoy for two minutes. (*To Isabella, who clings to him*) I won't quarrel, my pretty one; I'll just give one or two of the lubbers a salt eel

Exit

Jemmy Sha'n't I be in for it, if Mat says I told him! Like a good

188

general, I'll fortify. (*Going to the door*) Not a bolt on the door! – Lord bless me! (*Driving a fork into the latch*) There, they can't lift it now.

(*Jemmy places his back, against the door – a loud knocking heard – Isabella rises in alarm*)

Jemmy Who's there?

Hal (*Without*) Open the door, Mat Merriton! – 'Tis I, Hal Horsfield.

Isabella (*Clinging to Jemmy*) For Heaven's sake, no!

Jemmy Not exactly. I'm one of those kind of soldiers who are very brave, but who fight best in ambush.

Isabella Do not desert me!

Jemmy I can't; there's no back way out.

Voices (*Without*) Force the door! force the door!

Jemmy (*Observing the poker in the fire red hot*) Ha!

(*A hand is put through to lift the latch – Jemmy places the poker on it, and it is instantly withdrawn*)

Jemmy (*Capering about delighted*) Who's next? – Who's next?

(*Toprail puts his head in at the small window – Jemmy instantly claps the poker on his cheek – a loud crash is heard, and the door is burst open*)

Enter Hal Horsfield, Toprail and Gratings – Jemmy keeps them at bay with the poker. Toprail and Gratings chase him round – Hal Horsfield seizes Isabella, who screams – exeunt

Scene 5
The Indian village

Enter Westfield, Skinrat and Traders

Enter Hal Horsfield, dragging in Isabella, followed by Jemmy Jumble, Gratings, and Toprail – Jemmy still annoying them with the poker

Westfield Nay, nay! – When man should aid his fellow-man, the attempt to do him harm is doubly sinful. How have these sufferers injured you?

Hal 'Tis not a very pleasant thing for a man to see his wife taken from him.

Omnes His wife!

Jemmy Your wife! – What a thumping lie!

Hal How do you know?

Enter Mat Merriton, hastily

189

Mat But I do, you cowardly pirate! you devil's own bird! – and there's One aloft knows it also. Why, the angels and old Beelzebub would as soon serve together on the yards, as this pretty little pinnace sail in your company.

Hal She's my wife, I say.

Isabella Oh, no! – believe him not! If you are women, you will pity me; if you are men, you will protect me! But for this brave sailor, I must have perished in the storm – I must have fallen in the desert, beneath a fate more dreadful. Save me – shield me from his power!

Westfield This is the voice of truth. (*To Horsfield*) Man, she is not wed to you.

Mrs S. She shall not travel in my company with out I know she's the wife of somebody.

Skinrat Yes, we've a reputation to lose.

Westfield And if she do not travel with you, she is lost: she cannot live for twelve months in the desert.

Hal (*Pointing to Mat*) You are not his, are you?

Isabella Oh, no! no!

Hal (*Appealing to the Traders*) You hear?

Mrs S. (*To Isabella*) Then more shame for you!

Miss F. Oh, horrible! dreadful! I wouldn't enter a conveyance with one of your stamp for worlds!

Isabella (*Aside*) What can they mean?

Westfield It is plain, my child, the wicked sometimes prevail: 'tis hard your fellow-creatures should prove more cruel to you than the raging elements. One way of escape alone remains. This brave man is every way worthy of you: become his wife.

Isabella (*Starting*) His wife!

Westfield Ay; – thus you will prove the falsehood of this ruffian, and give the generous sailor a right and title to defend you.

Mrs S. And on that condition alone shall she ride with us. I'm a woman of virtue.

Mat Don't fear, my pretty Bella; I'll love you better than all the world.

Isabella Love!

Mat Aye; better than I love ship, mess, or messmate. You shall be my life – I'll be a husband –

Isabella (*Recoiling*) Husband!

Hal You see she dare not; she is mine already.

Isabella Not thine! – Anything but that! (*Rushing into the arms of Mat*) I am thine!

End of Act 2

A period of two years is supposed to have elapsed between the second and third acts

The young T P Cooke. Engraving from a portrait by S W Reynolds, Jnr.
(*Enthoven Collection*)

T P Cooke as an old man, showing the naval medal he always wore on stage. Engraving from a photograph.
(*Enthoven Collection*)

Act 3

Plymouth Harbour

Music – Jemmy Jumble, Sailors, Boatmen, Girls, etc, discovered

A Triple Hornpipe

Jemmy You seem to be all right there, my hearties – Haven't you a drop for poor Jemmy?

Boatman Ay, ay; drink to the Ariadne. My eyes! how proudly she came into harbour, towing the Frenchman in her wake! (*They rise and come forward*).

Boatman No more work to-day. A lot of the brave boys of the frigate are coming ashore; we'll give them just such another salute as they gave the enemy.

Jemmy I tell you, I must work, or my child will be wanting its dinner.

Girl Why, you haven't got a child, or a wife either – I intend to stick up to you myself. (*They all laugh*)

Enter Mrs Tadpole, formerly Miss Jemima Jenkinson, with a wash-tub

Mrs T. (*Crossing to Jemmy*) Is that job done, Mr Jumble?

Jemmy Only wants pressing, Mrs Tadpole.

Mrs T. Then make haste, and press them, will you, Jemmy? and I'll step in and second those shirts for the gentlemen in prison

Exit into house

Jemmy Did you see that woman, my lads? She was once a lady of title, and rode in a carriage.

Sailors No!

Jemmy And I was a marquis – of her making, mind you; Marquis of Barbican.

Sailors (*Laughing*) Oh! – Ha! ha! ha!

Boatman Spinning a yarn again, Jemmy, eh! I'm blessed if you don't patch up a story better than a pair of breeches.

(*A gun fired – loud and distant shouts heard*)

Boatman There! the brave fellows are landing now. – They've made the captain a lord, and he deserved it, too; for this is the third prize he has sent into English ports within the year. Here they come

Enter several Sailors, joyously – they are cordially welcomed by the others – Mat Merriton follows, melancholy and thoughtful, in a warrant-officer's uniform

Mat (*Starting from his abstraction*) Welcome, shipmates, to old England's shores once more. Many of you have fathers, mothers, and sweethearts – some have a wife; but I have nothing – not one left – not a soul to welcome me!

Sailor You will drink with us, Master Merriton?

Boatman Do, sir; your whole country welcomes you. Come, drink the health of your noble captain, whose life you saved.

Mat Thank ye, lads, thank ye; Come, here's the health of Lord Blaydon; a better or braver officer never trod the planks of a British quarter-deck. God bless him! (*Drinks*).

Omnes Hurra! hurra! hurra!

Jemmy (*Seeing Mat's face*) Hurra! – 'Tis he! – Hurra! hurra!

Mat (*Recognising him*) What, my ragged plantation hunter! – Give us your flipper. (*Squeezing his hand violently*) How are you? – Where have you been? What rigging's this? Up with your answering pendant. Lord love you!

Jemmy (*Shaking his hand in pain*) Oh, my finger! – I shan't be able to feel a needle for the next month! And how's my old friend, Isabella? Is your wife here, eh?

Mat (*Agitated*) Don't ask me, lad; I haven't my pretty Bella now.

Jemmy How! – Dead?

Mat No, no; but she left poor Mat in his distress the moment we got to Buenos Ayres. I did but leave her at the inn to procure refreshment; when I cam back, she had cut her cable, and I've never seen her since.

Jemmy Perhaps those sailors –

Mat No: to give the devil his due, they had no hand in it. I went every day in search of her, and half the dollars the captain gave me to new rig with, I left at the inn for her; because I thought she might come back, and there would be no Mat near to help her. With the dollars I left her my blessing; we put to sea, and never returned.

(*A Sailor, after reading a newspaper, shows it round to the others, and they all shout* 'Hurra!')

Mat Belay there, shipmates! – What's the signal?

Sailor The paper here says, the captain's going to be married.

Mat Let's overhaul the log, will you? (*Mat takes the paper and reads*) 'Marriage in High Life – To-morrow will be married, at St George's, Hanover Square, Sir Richard' – Lord! what a long name! –

'son of' – Um! – 'to the Honourable Miss Mary Allensby, daughter of –'
Allensby! – Why, that was the name of the family that sailed in the
Rapid. 'And it is confidently reported, that the gallant captain, Lord
Blaydon ' – that's the captain's name – 'will, at the same time, lead to the
altar the cousin of the bride, the Honourable –' I see! (*Dashing down the
paper*) The fog's clearing away. The captain may be able to throw a light
upon my poor brain about Bella. I shall find her yet. Bear a hand, Jemmy;
keep the can afloat, my boy; crowd all sail for London and my pretty
Bella! You'd know her again, Jemmy ?

Jemmy   To be sure I should.

Mat   My old trousers! I'm so rejoiced already – my heart's up in my
mouth! (*Throwing dollars to the Sailors*) There's money for you, shipmates – keep it up! –

(*The fiddle strikes up, and the Lasses and Sailors dance*)
Hurra! my lads – heave a head! bear a hand! hurra! – Bella! Bella!

*Exit, hastily, dragging off Jemmy, waving his hat, and hurrying. The
scene closes amidst fiddling, dancing, and cheering*

Scene 2
London – A splendid apartment in the house of Mr Morville

*Enter the Honourable Mr Morville, with a letter in his hand, followed
by Mrs Morville*

Mrs M.   And so Captain Blundell is created a lord ?

Morville   Yes, in reward for his services. But that is not all: he writes
that his love for Isabella is more ardent than ever, and once more makes
her an offer of his hand.

Mrs M.   What can be the cause of her melancholy ? – For nearly two
years, from the moment the first joy of meeting her parents was over, I
have observed it.

Enter Fanny Fubbs, hastily, habited as a waiting-maid

Mrs M.   Stay, Fanny; where are you going ?

Miss F.   Miss Isabella has just come in, ma'am; I don't know what's
the matter with her.

Mrs M.   Is she ill ?

Miss F.   She nearly fainted in the carriage, ma'am, because some
men were crying papers in the street about the victory of the Ariadne.

Morville   That is Blundell's ship. (*To Fanny*) You have lived with
my daughter nearly a year now.

Miss F.   Yes, sir.

Morville She engaged you, because she knew you in Buenos Ayres. Do you know the cause of her melancholy?

Miss F. (*Going*) La! sir, how should I?

Morville Stay, Fanny, I command you, girl.

Miss F. What, and leave miss to faint? She is my mistress, and nobody else

Exit

Mrs M. The impertinence of that girl is unbearable.

Morville And her power over Isabella inconceivable

Enter a Servant

Servant Lord Blaydon. (*Bows and Exits*)

Enter Lord Blaydon, in the uniform of a post-captain

Morville Welcome, my lord, and right glad I am to call you so! – Welcome from the storm and the battle once more, crowned with victory!

Mrs M. I need not say, that every woman's heart cries welcome!

Blaydon (*Shaking hands with them*) Thank ye! – We have indeed achieved a daring conquest; but you say, madam, every woman's heart bids us welcome: where is the charming Isabella? – Does hers respond to that sweet cry?

Re-enter Fanny, ushering in Isabella, elegantly attired, and wearing a gold chain round her neck

Isabella Mother – (*Seeing Blaydon, her countenance is lighted up with a momentary expression of pleasure*) Welcome to the brave! (*Giving her hand*) And you have again shown the flag of victory at the mast-head of the dear Ariadne!

Blaydon (*Joyfully*) The dear Ariadne!

Isabella (*Confused*) Yes – I had a friend once – who –

Mrs M. Isabella!

Isabella (*Weeping*) Mother – I – pardon me; I am very happy to see Captain Blundell – I mean, Lord Blaydon – (*To him*) But I am not well; your goodness will excuse me.

Morville My lord, you are doubly welcome just now: to-morrow a ward of mine, a cousin of Isabella's, is to be married. Stay with us, my lord; and, if you can prevail on Isabella, give us a repetition of the same trouble

Exeunt Mr and Mrs Morville

(*Isabella stands immersed in a reverie, examining something attached to her neck-chain*)

Blaydon Isabella!

Isabella (*Absorbed in thought*) And I fled! (*Bitterly*) Oh, pride! pride!

Blaydon (*Aside*) There is some secret here; it were unmanly not to rouse her. (*Taking her hand*) Miss Morville!

Isabella (*Starting*) Yes, you have had a victory; I heard them in the street boasting of it. You must feel a pride in the approbation of a whole nation. (*Fervently*) I love a sailor! (*Checking herself*) I – pardon – I –

Blaydon Miss Morville, there is something in your bosom which must for ever destroy my hopes. Although I must lose all hope of ever becoming your husband, I proffer, on the honest word of a seaman, that I will be a brother to you.

Isabella (*Screaming*) Oh, agony! – That proffer has been made – the pledge has been fulfilled – and I have been unworthy!

Blaydon (*Tenderly*) Miss Morville, you alarm me; suffer me to conduct you to your room.

Isabella (*Firmly, recovering herself*) Blundell – my friend, I trust to your honour – you will not betray me! Leave me till I have mastered my misery! – Go! go! (*Wildly hurrying off Blundell*) My brain is bursting!

(*A pause – she remains for a moment as if in prayer*)

Re-enter Fanny

Miss F. Why, that's your old lover, Captain Blundell.

Isabella Leave me!

Miss F. I remember him at Buenos Ayres. How surprised he'd be if he knew of your marriage in the –

Isabella (*Starting, and looking fearfully around*) Hush!

Miss F. Oh, there's nobody here but me, and you know I was present.

Isabella But you promised–

Miss F. To be sure I did; but I want some new things for the wedding to-morrow.

Isabella Take the money from my desk; begone, and be silent!

Miss F. (*Aside, going*) This secret's a fortune to me –

Exit

Isabella What am I to do? This fatal secret renders me the slave of yon mercenary creature. Oh, pride! how art thou punished! – base ingratitude! how art thou rewarded!

Enter a Servant

Servant A stranger, madam, wishes to see you. A sailor.

Isabella A sailor! – Should it be – Admit him. (*Exit Servant*) Does he live ? – Has he found – Has the brave – the generous Merriton come to claim his ungrateful, but still loving wife ? Ha! he is here. My eyes grow dim; I dare not –

Enter Hal Horsfield, raggedly attired

Isabella Ah! that ruffian!

Hal (*Surveying her insolently*) You were a pretty craft in the desert, but now you are a first-rater. Your trim is altered since we first met. (*Looking round*) You have parted convoy, too. Where's Mat Merriton ? A wife's house should be her husband's; but you gave him the slip at Buenos Ayres; you are of the lady breed. I couldn't wish him worse fare than he has got from you.

Isabella (*Aside*) True – true! (*Recovering herself*) Begone! – Is your insolence madness, that you dare thus insult me ? – I who know you to be the basest of mankind!

Hal Good words, mistress, if you please. I can keep a secret for a pretty girl.

Isabella What would you have me – Ha! my father!

Re-enter Mr and Mrs Morville

Morville Who is this stranger, Isabella ?

Isabella One of the sailors who escaped the wreck, and passed through the desert with me.

Hal Yes, your honour, I was cast away with miss; and I'm glad to find her so snugly anchored.

Morville And I rejoice to see the brave sailor whom Providence so graciously sent to her in her distress. You shall not go unrewarded. Here, my good fellow, here is a ten-pound note for you; call in a few days, and I will provide for you permanently.

Isabella (*Crossing rapidly to him, and giving her purse unseen*) Yes, call in a few days, and then see me. Go – go! not a word! (*Hurrying him off, and bursting into an hysterical laugh*) Saved! saved! – Ha! ha! ha!

(*She falls insensible, and the scene closes*)

Scene 3

A splendidly illuminated ball-room, sumptuously furnished

Enter Isabella, elegantly dressed, and holding in her hand a dollar attached to her neck-chain

Isabella Oh! fatal falsehood! to what have ye reduced my life ? Look around you, Pride, and feast your gloating eyes on splendour – look within, and sicken at despair! The saviour of my life – the guardian of my honour – the husband of my love, as two long years of misery have shown –
(*Kissing the dollar, and folding it to her bosom*)

Enter Mrs Morville, Mr Morville and Lord Blaydon

Mrs M. (*Anxiously*) Isabella, what is that dollar ? – What memorial is it ?
Isabella It is my all: do not – do not ask me further! If you knew, you would hate – despise – loathe me! Leave me to my misery; I am unworthy of you!
Mrs M. Calm yourself; the party are assembling for your cousin's wedding; the bride expects her bridesmaid.
Isabella I will not go; my presence would bring a curse upon her!

Enter a Servant

Servant A sea-faring man, Miss Isabella, entreats to see you.
Isabella (*Alarmed*) Tell him to begone – bid him begone!
Morville Not so; admit him; I will sift this mystery. – Send him up instantly

Exit Servant

Isabella (*Faintly*) No! oh! no!
Morville I will know the meaning of all this.
Blaydon It were best that I retire; Miss Morville will pardon me.
Isabella (*Firmly*) No, my lord; you are an honourable man, and shall know the worst: Father, the man you are about to behold is a ruffian: listen not to him, and you shall know all!

Enter Mat Merriton, he humbly bows around

Morville What do you want with my daughter ?
Mat If her name is Isabella, your honour, I wish to know if she is the Isabella I once knew.
(*Isabella, hearing his voice, starts*)
Isabella (*Joyfully*) Merriton! it is Merriton!
Mat (*Much affected*) Bella! my pretty Bella!
(*She throws herself into his arms – he kisses her forehead, and presses her, quite overcome with joy, to his heart*)
Morville (*Enraged*) What means this frantic conduct ? – Release her from your grasp!
Mat (*Staggering*) No, no!

Blaydon Merriton, by what right dare you thus –

Mat Avast, your honour: she's my wife.

Omnes (*In astonishment*) Wife!

Morville Fellow, are you mad? Isabella – wretched girl! have you nothing to say against this degrading falsehood?

Mat (*Indignantly*) Falsehood! She's mine: we were forced to get spliced to save her life; 'twas among the savages, warn't it, my sweet lass? – But Master Parson made you mine – eh, my pretty one?

Mrs M. Are you so lost, Isabella? – Do you not deny it?

Isabella I am his wife; but for him you would have cursed the sea that did not swallow me. We were in the desert with three ruffians; I had no friend but him; he was my saviour there – my faithful brother, while I remained near him. A fearful necessity united us.

Morville My lord, what am I to think of this?

Blaydon Believe every word you have heard spoken, true; for I well know the wild valour and open-hearted generosity of that noble-minded seaman; and 'tis to him that I owe the preservation of my life.

Morville Merriton, I am bound to be as grateful as a father should be; but she can never be your wife.

Mat But she *is* my wife, your honour – she is!

Morville Are you aware that, from the circumstances attending the marriage – from Isabella's being under age at the time, the law can invalidate your union?

Mat Oh! no, no! – Can it?

Morville It can.

Isabella (*Fervently*) Thank God it can! – for Merriton will now be convinced that affection, not necessity, is the bond of his claim over me. Merriton, if you can forgive me, take me; there is my hand.

Morville All opposition is useless. Heaven has strangely united you: may it continue to bless and protect you!

Mat (*Much affected*) Oh! madam – sir – your honour –

Blaydon Your fair bride shall not receive from me a husband unentitled to the rank she moves in. I therefore present to you, Merriton, the command of the Thetis privateer, now fitting for sea; and there, sir, is your appointment (*Giving a paper*) entitling you to walk the quarterdeck in his majesty's navy; – time, and your own courage, must do the rest.

Mat Oh! your honour, time shall do the rest!

Mrs M. A mother's blessing light upon your union!

(*A distant chime of bells heard*)

Enter Male and Female Visitors

Mat Hark! there's the wedding peal. No time for spinning long yarns now; but I must make bold to ask one question: is there lady or lowly lass, seaman or landsman, alow or aloft, here, that can blame my

pretty Bella for marrying one, whose only boast is, that his commander is
pleased to think him –

    Blaydon (*Advancing to the front*) Every inch a Sailor!

(*The bells strike a merry peal – Isabella rushes into Mat's arms, and the
curtain descends.*)

THE PRESS

The Times, April 5th, 1836:

Surrey Theatre
This theatre, which has recently been painted and decorated with very considerable taste, commenced what the bills call its summer campaign last night. The performances selected for the entertainment of the holyday folks were 'a new nautical drama', called The Ocean of Life; or every inch a Sailor; *to which was added the popular drama of* My Poll and my Partner Joe; *the whole concluding with a new burletta called* Major Linkey; or the Affair of Honour. *Of the second performance it is only necessary to say that it was acted last night for the 99th or 100th time. Of the first we can speak only from the 'action' (for hearing was last night wholly out of the question). The action, however, was very good, and from the variety and stirring character of the incidents, bids fair to be as popular as any of its predecessors in the same line. T P Cooke, as* Mat Merriton, *was the hero of the piece, and it is only necessary to say of his performance that he fully sustained his character in the unrivalled personification of the British sailor. Miss Macarthy, as the* Hon Isabella Morville (*the bride of Mat Merriton*), *played with her usual good taste and feeling. This young lady is a most promising actress, and will become – or we should rather say, has already become – a very valuable acquisition to the stage. Without any effort at imitation, her acting reminds us more of the simple and natural manner of Miss Kelly than that of any other lady at present on the stage (Mrs Fitzwilliam and Mrs Yates excepted). W Smith, as* Jemmy Jumble, *was in his usual merry vein, and kept the house in a roar as long as he was on the boards. The other characters in the piece were well filled. The performance of* Major Linkey *was so late that we must receive our notice of it to another occasion. The house was crowded in every part.*

The Morning Chronicle, April 5th, 1836:

The Surrey
A new nautical drama was produced here last night, entitled 'The Ocean of Life; or Every Inch a Sailor', in which Mr T P Cooke made his first appearance, after his provincial engagements, before one of the most crowded and boisterous audiences which perhaps ever congregated,

even within the walls of the Surrey Theatre on a holiday night. To give any account of the plot of the new piece would be an impossibility, as such was the constant uproar which prevailed in the house throughout the evening, that not ten consecutive words of the dialogue were heard by the audience, if the term be not a misnomer under such circumstances. It appeared, however, to comprise an abundant stock of the usual materials of melodramatic interest. Of course there is a 'female in distress', enacted by Miss Macarthy, who is persecuted through three long acts, to the great delight of the hard-hearted spectators, and in the end is bedecked in white satin, to repay her for her troubles past, and receives the congratulations of the lovers of poetical justice in the arms of her gallant protector Mat Merriton (Mr T P Cooke), a character which, in such hands, we need scarcely add, is 'every inch a sailor'. The most striking incidents (including of course the combats) were must vociferously applauded, and the whole performance seemed to go off with unqualified success. It was followed by My Poll and my Partner Joe, and a new farcical burletta, entitled Major Linkey, which kept some three thousand pairs of aching sides in perfect good humour till a late hour.

Maria
Martin
or
The Murder
in the
Red Barn

ANONYMOUS

Maria Marten. (*Radio Times Hulton Picture Library*)

MARIA MARTEN (1801/27)

One of the not least remarkable observations to be made about the Maria Marten case is that despite her fame as the progenitrix of one of the most celebrated melodrama figures of all time, only one stage version of Maria's unhappy fate appears to have been published in the nineteenth century: this is the version I have used herein which consistently misspells her name – an error perpetrated even in *The Times*. My author is not named – probably he was the resident writer for the Star Theatre, Swansea; the date of the first performance is lost, although the date of

Wiliam Corder. "A correct likeness of William Corder, taken in Bury Gaol, previous to his trial for the murder of Maria Marten, in the Red Barn." (*Radio Times Hulton Picture Library*)

publication seems to have been as late as 1877, by which time it must have seemed very old-fashioned.

One possible reason for the lack of enthusiasm on the part of nineteenth century publishing houses might have been that the facts of the case were very sordid indeed, besides being too well-known through newspaper accounts and ballad sheets for any wholesale whitewashing to be credible. Perhaps this also accounts for the reluctance of the more reputable playwrights of the time to sully their reputations by chronicling Maria's misdeeds – although some may have done so anonymously. So we have the odd situation that the most famous wronged girl of them all was proscribed by 'respectable' melodrama; but time has been kind to Maria, and she is now regarded as a kind of Ur-heroine. The reality was much less glamorous.

But once Maria's stage career had started in the booths, the fit-ups and the gaffs (plays based on her story were being performed even before Corder's execution) there was no stopping her. Her mother's dreams on three successive nights that her body was buried beneath the floor of the Red Barn at a time when it was not even known that Maria was dead; Corder's ultra-respectable life and no less respectable wife in Ealing for whom he had advertised in the *Sunday Times* and the *Morning Herald* after killing Maria; Maria's disguise in male clothing on the night of her death on May 18th, 1827; the mysterious death of her's and Corder's child – all these aspects of the case represent pure melodrama, which makes it all the more surprising that the first recorded stage version to appear in London was not until 1840, at the Marylebone Theatre, under the title of *The Red Barn.**

But before this date and for long after, there were dramatisations by the tens of dozens being performed all over the British Isles,† and indeed poor Maria's fate is still being re-enacted regularly to this day in Montague

Corder's advertisement in the *Sunday Times* of November 25th, 1827 ran as follows:

'*MATRIMONY – A Private Gentleman, aged 24, entirely independent, whose disposition is not to be exceeded has lately lost chief of his family by the hand of Providence, which has occasioned discord amongst the remainder, under circumstances most disagreeable to relate. To any female of respectability, who would study for domestic comforts, and willing to confide her future happiness to one in every way qualified to render the marriage state desirable, as the advertiser is in affluence. Many very happy marriages have taken place through means similar to this now resorted to, and it is hoped no one will answer this through impertient (sic) curiosity, but should this meet the eye of any agreeable lady who feels desirous of meeting with a sociable, tender, kind, and sympathising companion, they will find this advertisement worthy of notice. Honor and secresy (sic) may be relied on. As some little security against idle applications, it is requisite that letters may be addressed (post paid) AZ, care of Mr Foster, stationer, 68, Leadenhall-street, with real name and address, which will meet with most respectful attention*'

*The Royal Pavilion, Mile End, had staged *The Murder In The Red Barn* in 1828, but Mile End in those days was well outside London

†Even Irving had to appear in one at the Prince Of Wales, Liverpool, in 1865

MARYLEBONE THEATRE,
LICENSED PURSUANT TO ACT OF PARLIAMENT.

On Monday, April 6th, 1840,

The Performance to Commence with a Drama, in Two Acts, entitled

THE RED BARN,

William Corder..Mr. Pennett,   Farmer Martin..Mr. Robotham,
George, (his Son) Miss Robotham,   Timothy Bobbin..Mr. J. Douglass,
Johnny Rawbold..Mr. Mellon,   Mr. Lee. (the Officer) Mr. Robberts,   Mr. Moor...Mr. Curling
Waiter, Mr. Lewis,   John..Mr. Cave,
Maria..Mrs. Douglass,   Dame Martin..Mrs. Robotham,   Sally..Mrs. Robberts.

SONG.   " The Charity Girl,"   by   Master MARS.

NEAPOLITAN HORNPIPE.   -   **BY**   -   **MISS WHITE.**

After which the Laughable Farce of

MATRIMONY.

In which Mr. H. WIDDICOMB,   Mr. ATTWOOD,   and Mrs. FREWIN will appear.

A COMIC FANDANGO, BY MASTER MARS.

Mr. COLLINS, the ENGLISH PAGANINI.

Will Play a Solo on One String,   *Concerto, Master L.Collins, Violoncello,*
Concerto. Master V. COLLINS, Violin.   Grand Concerto & Thema with Variation, (De Beriot)

The Performance to conclude with

KORAC,

Zembuca..Mr. Robberts.   Korac..Mr. Pennett,   Frederico..Miss Robotham,
Selim..Mr. Reeves,   Anselimo..Mr. Lewis,   Mirza..Mr. Douglass
Rosombiro..Mr. Robotham,   Popo..Mr. H. Widdicomb,   Ina..Mrs. Robberts,
Immalee..Mrs. Kemp.   Statta..Mrs Robotham.

On Tuesday, Friday, and Saturday, the Performance to Commence with

ZEMBUCA.

Principal Characters by Messrs Robberts, Robotham, Douglass, Pennett, Lewis, Wilson, &c.
Mesdames Wilmot, Robberts, and Robotham.

DANCE   -   *by*   -   *Miss WHITE.*

After which the Farce of

MARRIED LIFE!!!

Characters by Messrs. Attwood, H, Widdicomb, and Mrs. Robberts.

To Conclude with the Drama, entitled

THE LAST STRUGGLE!!!

Supported by Messrs. Pennett, James, Robberts, Widdicomb, Attwood, Douglass, Lewis, &c.
Mesdames Douglass, Robberts, and Robotham.

BOXES, 2s.   PIT, 1s.   GALLERY, 6d.
NOTICE!   **No Bonnets admitted in the Dress Circle.**
Half-price to Boxes half-past 8, to Pit a Quarter before 9 o'clock.

MORGAN, Printer 39, New Church Street adjoining the Marylebone Theatre.

The Red Barn. Poster of Marylebone Theatre, 1840.
(Enthoven Collection)

207

Slater's very poor 1928 version,* in Constance Cox's 1969 one-acter, and in Brian J Burton's full-length 1964 version which is taken from various sources, including a novel on the subject.

Corder's captor, Pharos Lee (or Lea) is said to have started the vogue for murder mystery plays, with clues, sleuths and the deductive process, of which Hawkshaw (the 'Nailer') in Tom Taylor's *Ticket-of-Leave Man* (1863) is the archetype.

The first of the Genre was probably Jerrold's *Vidocq!; or The French Police Spy* (1829), based on Vidocq's memoirs; Jerrold also wrote *Wives By Advertisement*, a farce, in the previous year, which was also obviously prompted by the Maria Marten case.

Maria was born in 1801, the daughter of a mole-catcher, in Polstead, Suffolk. Corder was three years *younger*, the younger son of the local squire; he was only five feet five inches tall (the same height as Edmund Kean). The following extract is from H G Hibbert's *A Playgoer's Memories*†:

> *Few trials for murder have so stirred the country as did that of William Corder, who shot and stabbed his paramour, Maria Marten.* The Times *reported the proceedings verbatim. And yet it was a squalid business – impossible to give it a glamour of romance, or the quality of mystery. Maria was nearly twenty-six, good-looking, we are told, the daughter of a farm labourer living at Polstead in Kent (sic). She had three illegitimate children, by various fathers, and when with the support of her step-mother she began to exert pressure on the father of the third, William Corder, he murdered her and concealed his crime with so much skill that it was not revealed until Maria's mother spoke of dreams, which led to the discovery of the body, and to the arrest and conviction of William. The dreams gave a supernatural interest to the story – but village scandal said that Mrs Marten did not recall her dream till Corder grew lax in his remittances!*
>
> *Maria's first lover was Thomas Corder, an elder brother of William. He was drowned, and their child died. Her second lover was an 'independent gentleman of Woking' whose name was sedulously guarded by the reporters of the trial. He made penitent payments to Maria, which William Corder intercepted. The offspring of this second union lived many years, in Colchester, and would threaten to invoke the magistrates to prevent performances of* Maria Marten *by strollers unless he were*

---

*Taken from a tattered old manuscript by John Latimer, resident writer at the Queen's Theatre, Battersea, around the middle of the nineteenth-century

†Published in 1920, pp 83–85

mollified – surely the most curious collection of a royalty ever known! William Corder's child died; but there is not the least evidence in support of the allegation that he did away with it.

William Corder was a short, weak-legged, weak-eyed creature, who came into a thousand or so as the older members of his family, well-to-do farmers, died. He was living in London when Maria and her people, her second lover, the Woking gentleman, acting in concert, became importunate. He agreed to marry Maria, making the stipulation that she should leave home secretly, disguised in a man's clothes which he provided, to join him. Maria was never seen again alive. Corder wrote regularly, saying that she was well and happy, acting as companion to a lady, having deferred their marriage. Months passed, till Mrs Marten's disturbed slumber induced a search-party to the Red Barn on the Corders' farm. Her the body was found, lightly covered with earth, over which the fruits of the corn harvest had been piled. Corder proved to have been long married, at Ealing, to an amiable schoolmistress, who had answered an advertisement in The Sunday Times, *and who was loyal and tender till his last breath. After his execution an accumulation of letters addressed to an agency in response to a matrimonial advertisement was earmarked to Corder, and published.*

Corder defended himself obstinately. His last story was that after a bitter quarrel Maria shot herself and that in terror of suspicion he hid the body. But his case was hopeless, and ere his execution he confessed, though he persisted that he never used a knife. Justice was carried out with almost Scriptural savagery. The body, half naked and half dissected, was exposed to public view, and the skeleton of the wretched creature was made a permanent exhibit. In the Free Library at Bury was deposited a verbatim report of the trial, bound in Corder's skin.

Many thousand people witnessed the execution, and it is said that a man who returned to Bury from the ghastly entertainment was so wearied by inquiries as to whether or no Corder was really dead that he took refuge in the local theatre, where a performance of Macbeth was in progress. 'Is justice done on Cawdor?' were the first words he heard. 'Yes' he cried, 'I saw him hanged at Norwich this morning; and I'll answer no more questions'.

This barbaric execution took place before ten thousand ghouls on Sunday, August 17th, 1828. Hibbert's summary (largely taken from the DNB) seems to be substantially accurate – especially with regard to the interest aroused. The following is from the New Newgate Calendar of 1886:

'*When his lordship had taken his seat on the bench, the names of the jury who had been summoned to try the prisoner were called over; but the*

Execution of William Corder outside Norwich Gaol, August 11th, 1828. (*Radio Times Hulton Picture Library*)

crowd was so great, and the sheriff's force so ineffective, that it was almost impossible to make way for them into the court. After the lapse of nearly an hour they were brought over the heads of the crowd to the passage leading into the hall, some with their coats torn, their shoes off and nearly fainting'. *

However, the famous report (which sold over a million copies) bound in Corder's skin was not deposited at the Free Library; it can today be viewed with other relics of the case at the Moyse's Hall Museum, Bury St Edmunds. Corder's skeleton (minus skull, which was placed on public exhibition in London) is still in use by medical students at the West Suffolk Hospital; in Ipswich there is to this day a department store called Frederic Corder & Son Ltd, although the management, perhaps under-

---

*Reprinted in 1960 by the Folio Society, edited by Lord Birkett

standably, are reluctant to admit any connection with the eminent murderer. The ancient crime was once again brought to public attention as recently as 1971, when the old Corder home, the grounds of which still include the notorious Red Barn, were put up for auction with a £30,000 reserve price. There were no takers.

But let young Squire Corder have the last word:*

After Mrs Corder had retired, Mr Orridge, the worthy governor of the jail, made the strongest efforts to induce the unhappy prisoner to confess, pointing out to him how greatly he would add to his crime, should he quit the world still denying his guilt. Corder then exclaimed, 'O, sir, I wish I had made a confidant of you before. I often wished to have done it, but you know, sir, it was of no use to employ a legal adviser and then not

---

*Ibid

211

to follow his advice'. Mr Orridge said that there was no doubt that was very proper, up to the time at which he was convicted, but that now all earthly considerations must cease. The wretched prisoner then exclaimed, 'I am a guilty man', and immediately afterwards made the following confession:

*'Bury Jail, August 10, 1828 – Condemned Cell,
Sunday Evening, Half-past Eleven*

*I acknowledge being guilty of the death of poor Maria Marten, by shooting her with a pistol. The particulars are as follows. When we left her father's house we began quarrelling about the burial of the child, she apprehending that the place wherein it was deposited would be found out. The quarrel continued for about three quarters of an hour upon this and about other subjects. A scuffle ensued, and during the scuffle, and at the time I think that she had hold of me, I took the pistol from the side-pocket of my velveteen jacket and fired. She fell, and died in an instant. I never saw even a struggle. I was overwhelmed with agitation and dismay – the body fell near the front doors on the floor of the barn. A vast quantity of blood issued from the wound and ran on to the floor and through the crevices. Having determined to bury the body in the barn (about two hours after she was dead), I went and borrowed the spade of Mrs Stowe; but before I went there, I dragged the body from the barn into the chaff-house, and locked up the barn. I returned again to the barn, and began to dig the hole, but the spade being a bad one, and the earth firm and hard, I was obliged to go home for a pick-axe and a better spade, with which I dug the hole, and then buried the body. I think I dragged the body by the handkerchief that was tied round her neck. It was dark when I finished covering up the body. I went the next day and washed the blood from off the barn floor. I declare to Almighty God I had no sharp instrument about me, and that no other wound but the one made by the pistol was inflicted by me. I have been guilty of great idleness, and at times led a dissolute life, but I hope through the mercy of God to be forgiven.
W Corder
Witness to the signing by the said William Corder,
John Orridge'*

MARIA MARTIN
OR
THE MURDER
IN THE RED BARN

Dramatis Personae

As performed at the Star Theatre, Swansea

William Corder by Mr C Henry
Farmer Martin by Mr H Macfarren
George Martin, his son, by Mr J Pearce
Timothy Bobbin, an 'original', by Mr A Emm
Johnny Raw, his friend, by Mr H Rignold
Mr Lee, an officer, by Mr J K Murray
Sheriff by Mr Norton Wilson
Locker by Mr Frank Millard
Maria Martin by Miss E Temple
Anne Martin, sister to Maria, by Miss N Stanley
Mrs Martin by Miss L Ramond
Villagers
Etc

NB: Since this version of *Maria Marten* is extremely short I have
not abridged it – the text is given in full, exactly as published in 1877
—*M.K.*

MARIA MARTIN;
or
THE MURDER IN THE RED BARN

Act 1

Scene 1
Interior of Martin's cottage

Maria discovered

Maria What can be the cause of my dear William's absence? He promised to be here by breakfast time, and now the day is nearly past. My heart forbodes some evil. Heaven grant that nothing serious has happened to occasion this delay.

Enter George Martin at door

Well, George, have you seen him?
George No, Maria, he has not been at home since morning. I should like to know what you are always fidgeting about so when he's not here, as if there wasn't another lover to be had?
Maria Hush, George; speak not thus; William is dear to my happiness. My every hope of life, of future joys, is centred in him.
George Well, there's no accounting for taste; for my part I think him a nasty, mean, ugly, sulky fellow.
Maria Nay, George; do not be so severe.
George Well, I can't help it, sister; I must speak my mind. I don't like the look of him.
Maria That may be; but were you a young woman, my dear little brother, I think you'd just feel towards him as I do.
George Perhaps I should, and perhaps I shouldn't; but there I'll cross the fields again and see if I can meet him.
Maria Do so; and should you see him, say how anxiously his poor Maria awaits his coming.

George I will, Maria. (*Going, but returns*) Egad, I nearly forgot. Do you know I saw him in the meadow yesterday evening kissing Susan the milkmaid.

Maria Oh, fie upon you, George! you are telling stories. What! William Corder?

George Yes, William Corder, with his own ugly mug. But never mind, Maria, I'll try and find him for all that; and the very first time I clap eyes on him, in spite of all, I'll tell him –

Maria What, George?

George How deeply and fondly my silly sister loves him. Ha! ha! ha! (*Exit door in flat*)

Maria Happy, happy, boy! He knows not yet the miseries life is subject to. His young heart is free to speak his mind without restraint. But William – William's here

Enter William Corder

Dear William, what was it delayed your coming? Have you any news about the child?

Corder No, none of any consequence, Maria. Has Mathews been here?

Maria Not yet; but tell me, William, when will you fix the day?

Corder Shortly, shortly, my dear Maria. The magistrates have promised to assist me, and the licence soon shall be obtained. Where is your mother?

Maria Without. I'll fetch her, shall I?

Corder Do

Exit Maria at door

How well this pent-up soul assumes the garb of smiling love to give my fiend-like thoughts the prospect of success! In vain does nature, reason, conscience, all oppose it. The thought has got such firm possession of my heart, such despotic sway, that nought can turn me from my fixed resolve; and conscience, feeble guide to virtue, only shows us when we go astray, but wants the power to stop us in our course. The deed were bloody, sure; but I will do it, and rid me of this hated plague. Her very shadow moves a scorpion in my path. I loathe the banquet I have fed upon. By heaven! be still, my heart

Enter Dame Martin at door, followed by Maria

Ha, mother, I wished to speak with you!

Mrs Martin Well, William, have you been successful? think you the licence can be got?

Corder Doubtless, mother; to-morrow Maria must accompany me.

In the meantime, be careful. There is a warrant issued for her apprehension, relating to the child. Don't be alarmed, my love, for when the marriage rites are performed, I'll claim thee as my lawful wife, and Heaven will bless our union.

Maria But say, dear William, where shall I remain?

Corder Here, with your mother.

Mrs Martin Yes, Maria, there is less danger here; and besides, William will provide against every ill, for sure he knows the proper steps to take.

Corder (*Aside, meaningly*) Ay, that I do.

Mrs Martin What is it, William, that disturbs you?

Corder Mother, I cannot bear to see my own Maria thus. 'Tis that which preys upon my thoughts, and makes me feel her sorrows tenfold. We cannot change the softness of our natures, or steel the heart against injured worth, nor call such passion weakness. (*Crosses to her*) No, mother, no. Farewell, Maria love, farewell! I shall return within an hour, and bring thee news that will cheer thee, though life were on the issue

Exit at door

Maria Hear'st thou, mother, how deeply he laments the sorrows he would fain compress. I know his nature – open as his heart – will never rest till he secures that peace he has destroyed.

Mrs Martin Poor fellow! Pray Heaven his success may equal his exertions, and all may yet go well. Come, child, the day is waning fast. Your father will soon return; let us forth and meet him on his way.

Maria Yes, dear mother, and greet him with smiling faces, and thus make glad a father's heart with news of his daughter's happiness. May Heaven, in its mercy, look down on our humble roof, and shower blessings on the whitening heads of my aged parents

Music – Picture – Close in

Scene 2
A country lane

Enter Anne Martin followed by Timothy Bobbin

Timothy Well, now, Anne, that we are here alone, I'll tell thee a bit of my mind. In the first place, I love thee most confoundedly, and in the next, I'll run away with thee directly.

Anne What, Timothy, whether I will or no?

Timothy Sure a little thing like you should have no will of your own, but do whatever thee's bid.

Anne Why, what an impudent fellow you are; but I'll let you know that I *have* a will of my own, and I'll like to see the woman that has not.

Timothy Hush! not so loud; depend on't, I'll make thee do everything of thy own free will; but tell me, you little dev – dear, do you see anybody coming up the lane ?

Anne What do you ask for ?

Timothy Nothing, only you see I might be taken by surprise, and so –

Anne And so you're afraid to be seen in my company. Is that it ?

Timothy You never was more out in your life. I only thought while I was making love somebody might surprise us.

Anne Upon my word, Mr Timothy, you should never have thought of coming to me to make love if you're not able to stand your ground.

Timothy Ay, that I will, for the devil himself couldn't resist you. (*Attempts to kiss her*).

Anne Stand off, if you please; learn how to make love in a quiet, peaceable way if you can, and don't be so rumbustical when there's no occasion.

Timothy No occasion, how can you say that now ? Only dart those little rogish eyes at me, you jade, and you set I all of a blaze, that'ee do.

Anne Then since you can't be quiet I think I'd better extinguish that blaze before it goes any further.

Timothy Ha' done wi' thee joking, and come to the point at once. You say you will marry me ?

Anne Well, and what then ?

Timothy What then, why, you know, it would very soon be all over.

Anne All over, would it ?

Timothy Yes; all.

Anne What all ?

Timothy Yes all; don't you think it would be quite enough ?

Anne Enough! no, nor half enough.

Timothy The devil it wouldn't.

Anne No, Timothy; I should like whoever marries me, that he love me for ever and ever, and a day after that.

Timothy Oh! I vow you are too unconsciousable in your demands. What in the vassal world shall I do ? Tell me what mun I do ?

Anne Why, Timothy, I say the man that marries me, must love and cherish me for ever and a day, and you say when we're married it will all be over.

Timothy Very well, if you'll agree to be married, I'll love 'ee every day for ever; but I dunna about the *cherish*.

Anne If you love me, Timothy, you'll be sure to cherish me.

Timothy Oh, be I – very well; and now, my little dear, shall I buy the wedding ring ?

Anne With all my heart, Timothy.

Timothy Then we'll retire to a snug little cottage of our own, get plenty of sheep but no horned cattle; then how happy we shall be with a little chubby babe dandling on the knee – what a comfortable farm we'll keep

Duet, and exit

Enter William Corder

Corder Am I turned coward, or what is it makes me tremble thus? Have I not heart sufficient for the deed? or do I falter with remorse of conscience? No, by heaven and hell 'tis false! a moment, and I launch her soul into eternity's wide gulph, the fiends of hell work strong within me. 'Tis done! I'll drown my fears and slake my thirst for vengeance in her blood. Who's there! – Hah! 'tis no one; – and yet methought I heard a footstep: how foolish are those startling fears. Come, shroud me demons! Hide, hide my thoughts within your black abyss! The Red Barn is the spot I've fixed on to complete my purpose! everything is ready to inhume the body, that disposed of, I defy detection! (*Chord*)

Enter George Martin

Ha! hell fiends! (*Recognises him*) Is that you, George? Have you been long here?
George Scarcely a moment. I came by the desire of Maria to search for you. She seemed uneasy on account of your absence. I love my sister and cannot bear to see her suffer.
Corder 'Tis well. Did you observe anyone, George, as you came.
George Not a living soul, William.
Corder (*Half aside*) By heaven! if I thought he overheard me, I'd strangle him.
George Are you speaking to me, William?
Corder No, no, child, come let's seek Maria

Exit hurriedly

George I can't for my life find out the reason why Maria is so fond of him; to be sure he says he loves her, but if he does I think he has a very peculiar way of showing it, and to my mind he looks and acts more like a great rascal than an honest, straightforward man

Exit after Corder

Scene 3

Martin's cottage as Scene 1

Farmer Martin, Mrs Martin, and Maria discovered

Martin And so, my child, Corder has promised to make good his word?

Maria He has, father, I expect him every minute; you know how sure he is to execute whatever he resolves upon, 'twas seeing me unhappy alone determined him.

Martin 'Tis a generous, noble act; Heaven will reward him for it.

Mrs Martin Poor William, his heart was nigh to bursting when he left us.

Maria The world has treated him unkind, and Fortune's frowns have soured a generous heart; but I shall prove the means whereby that heart shall be restored to all it once possessed, and life's dark path to him again be sunshine.

Martin What says Mathews; does he know of it?

Mrs Martin He does, and promises by every means within his power to advance their prospects.

Martin See; here comes William

Enter William Corder

William, I thank thee; give me thy hand. The poor old father's tears will cease to flow when gazing on his children and his household happy all around him. To you I'll owe it, take with thee, then, a father's blessing.

Corder Thank thee, thank thee, father. Maria, I'm true to my appointment, everything is settled, let us not delay time.

Maria I shall soon be ready, William.

Corder Quick! make haste. Here is the dress which I have procured for you, your mother can assist in disposing it.

Maria But how am I to pass this time of day? Shall I not be observed?

Corder Do not be afraid of that; all is right; you have been disappointed many times and shall not be again.

Maria Where am I to go?

Corder On to the Red Barn, and stop there till I join you with my horse and gig.

Maria How am I to convey my things?

Corder I'll take them to the barn myself.

Maria Think you I shall be able to reach the appointed spot unperceived?

Corder Fear not, there's none of my workmen in the field near the Barn, and I'm sure the coast is clear.

Maria Come then, mother; William, you'll not be long?

Corder No, dearest. (*Aside*) I'll be there *too soon for you*

Exit Maria and Mrs Martin

Martin Will you take any refreshment, William, before you go ?
Corder No farmer, the night is far advancing, and the sooner we are
off the better. The magistrates, they say, are on the watch – we must be
careful to elude them

Enter Mrs Martin with Maria's bag

Mrs Martin Here, William, is Maria's bag. She'll soon be ready.
Corder Mother, I'll on before and make the necessary preparations

Exit Mrs Martin

Good day, father; tell Mathews, should he call, we're gone to Ipswich
and from thence to proceed to London.
Martin 'Tis well. I'll see to that. Bless you, William, bless you, and
may heaven prosper you, in everything

Exit Martin

Corder No; 'tis hell must guard me now

Music – Closed in

Scene 4
Front wood

Enter Timothy Bobbin

Timothy Well, here I be. I a gotten the ring, and a nice bright
yellow one it is, too, when I rubs it on my breeches, but I munna dirt un,
'cause I bought un to get married in, now I'll just go and show her the
ring. Eh! why, as I live if there be'ant a dandy young fellow kissing my
Anne; I say, Measter (*Calling off*), I do'int like to holler too loud 'cause
she'll think I be jealous. Oh! ay – here comes dandy chap, won't I give
him a warning. I'll just step aside and watch un

Enter Maria disguised

Maria Now, then, all is ready, and I shall no doubt get off undiscovered.
Timothy (*Behind*) Undiscovered! Dang me if he be'ant a-going to

221

run away with her.

Maria 'Tis a wild romantic project, but away with the thought, the sooner 'tis over the better; poor Anne is quite uneasy at my going, and says –

Timothy (*Comes forward*) Dang me if I can stand it any longer.

Maria Ah! a man?

Timothy Yes, and as good a man as you be.

Maria What will become of me? am I discovered?

Timothy To be sure you are; didn't I overhear you talking to that young woman just now?

Maria Well, but I couldn't imagine –

Timothy Noa! you couldn't imagine that I was so near, I dare say; but pray what call have you to that young woman I saw you kissing?

Maria (*Aside*) Oho! a lover of Anne's, I suppose.

Timothy I tell 'ee what, sir, I maun have satisfaction.

Maria You shall have it, sir, and that instantly.

Timothy Dang'd if he aint a regular bantrin cock, he'll shoot un if un say much to un.

Maria As I live here comes Anne. Now, sir, prepare yourself

Enter Anne Martin

Come here, my dear little angel. (*Aside*) Not a word, he don't know me. Now sir, what are you pretensions to this young woman?

Timothy What's that to you? I never pretends to anything I can't perform.

Anne Well but, Timothy, you've not performed anything yet; to be sure you've promised, that's all.

Timothy Yeas; I promised to make thee an honest man's wife, and that's more than a great many will do, that wears a better coat un I.

Maria (*Blustering*) Sir, do you mean to insinuate?

Timothy Noa, I don't, but if the cap fits, you can take off your dandy hat and put un on.

Anne Timothy Bobbin, you're a great fool, and ought to be ashamed of yourself!

Timothy Ought I? What cause? I sticks up for my rights, this sort of thing might do for fine folks in Lunnon, but if I has a wife I wants all the kissing to myself.

Anne But I am not your wife yet.

Timothy Noa! Thee be'ant, but thee promised 'ee would be, and aint I bought the ring, and now when I comes here, I catch you kissing and romping wi' other chap; but I mun tell thee, miss, that kissing sometimes, you know, comes to sommat else – mind that now.

Anne I know it, Timothy, and therefore we'll kiss again. (*Kisses her, and embrace*).

Maria Ay, that we will, and never have I imprinted on the lips of

222

woman a dearer pledge than this – and this – and –

Anne Nor I on yours, dearest – you, whose fate is so linked with mine.

Maria Lovely Anne, come once more to my arms, and when I cease to love thee – (*They embrace*).

Timothy It be a pity you bean't chained together.

Maria How dare you interrupt me ? Yes, charming angel, when I cease to love that heart which beats so fervently in union with mine, may every hope on earth desert me, and fortune's purest, brightest, smile beam unpropitious.

Timothy Oh, brimstone and treacle!

Maria Adieu, then, dearest. May every bliss be thine till next we meet. One last embrace. (*Aside*) And now for the Red Barn, and my dear, dear William

Exit

Anne (*Going to him*) Timothy, do you love me ?

Timothy Go away, you false-hearted creetur, I wunna listen to 'ee.

Anne (*Feigning surprise*) Why, I declare he's jealous!

Timothy Jealous! dom'd if I bean't. You're a false, deluding, wench, and I'll never speak to 'ee again.

Anne Yes, you will, Timothy; and what's more, you'll kiss me, too.

Timothy Shall I. When ?

Anne When you catch me

Runs off

Timothy Dang'd if I doan't try!

Runs after her

Scene 5
The Red Barn

William Corder discovered

Corder How dreadful the suspense each moment brings! Would it were over. There's not a soul abroad – everything favours my design. This knocking at the heart doth augur fear. 'Tis a faint, foolish, fear that must not be. Suspicious self will sleep, ay, sleep for ever. Yet, 'twixt thought and action, how harrowed is the brain with wild conjecture. The burning fever round my temples gives to this livid cheek a pallid hue. Hark! By heavens she comes! Now all ye fiends of hell, spur me to the deed – teach me not to feel pity nor remorse; let me but show the cause of quarrel for the act.

Hand, heart, be firm, my reputation save,
And hurl my victim to an early grave. (*Retires*)

Enter Maria Martin

Maria How silent is all around. A fearful gloom seems to hang about this place. The night is dark and drear. A funeral darkness falls from the skies, and envelopes the earth. A chill is on my heart, and horrible imaginings crowd upon my brain, foreboding terror to my soul. Oh, William, William, to thee I trust for future happiness! In sweet companionship with thee to sail smoothly on down life's rough stream, till death our fond hearts sever. Here will I await his coming – think of the happy days in store for me; such sweet thoughts will surely dispel the sorrows which now fill my troubled heart

Re-enter Corder (Chord)

Corder Oh, you're here at last? I thought something had happened to prevent you keeping your appointment. I fear the magistrates are on the watch. Were you observed on the way?

Maria No, dearest William.

Corder Are you quite sure you passed unobserved?

Maria Quite. Now, dear William, let us leave this place, lest we should be seen and recognised by anyone.

Corder Stay! Ere we leave this place we must understand one another.

Maria What mean you, William? Why grasp me thus? You hurt my arm. William, dear William, you are agitated – ill. Your lips quiver, your limbs tremble, there is a wild look in your eyes that appals me. Speak! speak! and ease my tortured breast.

Corder Maria, listen to me, and let my words sink deep into your heart. There is a bond of crime between us; we are linked together by blood.

Maria Oh, William, do not speak of that at such a time as this and in such a dismal place. Let us leave at once. I am shivering with cold, my blood is frozen in my veins, and I am faint with terror.

Corder Maria, you threatened me a short time ago, should aught occur touching our child, I should go with you to prison.

Maria William, heed not that; 'twas said in the heat of passion, as who can guard their tongue when anger sways the heart? 'Twas spoken, and forgotten as soon as spoken. Have I not proved a thousand times since how much I love you? So think no more of that.

Corder Would it had never been spoken, for it hath roused a scorpion here, that doth gnaw and lash me on to vengeance! Hast thou not threatened me ? And am I not in thy power ? No – (*Pause*) – thou art in *mine*, and by Heaven I will keep thee so; ay, and for ever.

Maria Do I hear aright? My ears must mock me. Oh, William, how have I lost thy love – how become the object of your scorn ?

Corder Ask thy own false heart, and it will tell thee. All thy love was lavished on the hated Mathews, but he shall feel my vengeance.

Maria No, no; as there is truth in Heaven, I have never wronged thy love.

Corder Nay, did you love me you would secure my fame.

Maria Oh, William, thy fame is dear to me as my blood. What have I not sacrificed for thy love ? Am I not a creature lost in shame, for men to point at and women to mock ? Am I not a poor, forlorn, frail thing, whose heart is bruised and bleeding with excess of agony – whose form is bowed with suffering miseries.

Corder I'll hear no more.

Maria Oh, William, behold me on my knees. For my aged parents' sake, I ask thee, I pray of thee to keep thy promise and make me thy lawful wife. Let me once more walk erect, and look my fellow-creatures in the face, without the blush of shame mantling my cheeks.

Corder Marry thee! You cannot think me so lost. 'Tis time the mask should fall, and you know me as I really am. Mark me, Maria, I brought you here not to marry you, but to let you know my resolution. Instantly swear to keep the murder of our child a secret, and renounce all pretensions of becoming my wife, or, by Heaven, you never quit this spot alive.

Maria Oh, wretch, wretch! And have I trusted in such a fiend ? But no; it cannot be! Oh, William, William, tell me but that you have sported with me, and I will bless you.

Corder Will you take the oath ?

Maria Never, villain! traitor! I will die first!

Corder Your blood be upon your own head

(*Music. She tries to escape. He seizes her – throws her round. She falls on her knees*).

Maria Oh, mercy, mercy, William! Do not harm me! Spare me – for my child's sake – spare me!

Corder That word has fixed your doom. What is Mathews' brat to me ? Will you take the oath ? Nay, shrink not, 'tis in vain, for I am desperate in my thoughts, and thirst for blood.

Maria Ah, do not kill me. As you hope for mercy, spare – oh, spare – my life.

Corder It is in vain. You know my purpose. Prepare!

(*Music till end of Act*). *She shrieks as he attempts to stab her*

225

Corder By Heavens, I cannot. Yet I must not falter lest that her cries bring aid.

Maria Spare me! Mercy!

Corder I have none. Thou diest! No struggling.

He again attempts to stab her. She clings round his neck. He dashes her to the earth, and stabs her. She shrieks and falls. He stands motionless till the curtain falls

Act 2

Scene 1
Martin's cottage

Farmer and Mrs Martin discovered

Martin 'Tis strange! no tidings yet of Maria.

Mrs Martin It is indeed surprising, and William too, he promised to write as soon as the ceremony had taken place.

Martin You look ill, Dame, the events of the last four weeks have robbed you of repose and broken your rest, and remember, Dame, we are getting aged now.

Mrs Martin Yes, Thomas, we are fast declining in the vale of life and soon must be overtaken by death, who hovers o'er our heads ever ready to place his icy fingers on our hearts.

Martin Yes, Dame, and the prayer of the aged parents shall be as they šink into the silent grave 'May their last moments on earth be blessed with the tears of their beloved children'.

Mrs Martin Amen.

Martin And now, Dame, you need repose, go sleep for awhile, 'twill drive these sad thoughts from your breast and recruit your strength; in the meantime I will once more make inquiries concerning our dear Maria.

Mrs Martin I will do as you advise me, and may Heaven bless and comfort us with news of our darling child.

Martin We will hope for the best. I'll go to the Post Office and see if there is a letter. Cheer up, Dame, rest awhile, I'll not be absent long.

Exit

Mrs Martin A strange drowsiness comes o'er me – a feeling I cannot shake off, it steals upon me and wraps me in a shroud, and were I super-stitious I should fear some dire calamity lurked unseen, or death were nigh. Oh, Maria, my thoughts are of thee – Maria, my beloved child – I – I – (*Sleeps*)

Scene opens and discovers visions, at the end of which Mrs Martin shrieks and starts up

227

Oh, mercy! Maria, my poor, dear child, is murdered! Help! help! (*Falls senseless*)

Enter Farmer, Anne, George, Villagers, etc. Farmer rushes to Mrs Martin and raises her

Martin Dame, dame, what has happened?
Anne Oh, mother, dear mother, speak, oh, my poor, dear mother.
Mrs Martin (*Looking eagerly around*) Where, where am I?
Martin What's the matter, Dame, what has occasioned this?
Mrs Martin Maria! My poor child is murdered! (*Chord*).
All Murdered!
Mrs Martin Yes, foully murdered at the Red Barn!
Martin How know you this?
Mrs Martin My dream! my dream!
Martin Alas! She raves. The continued silence of Maria has preyed upon her mind. Come, cheer thee, Dame; cheer thee.
Mrs Martin No, no; I saw the villain strike her down as plainly as I now see these anxious faces around me.
Martin Compose thyself; can a mere dream disturb thee thus?
Mrs Martin Oh, husband, it was no dream, but the voice of Heaven conveying to a mother's heart the murder of her darling child. Oh, Thomas, husband, our child lies buried in the Red Barn.
Martin Well, Dame, the Red Barn shall be searched at once.
Mrs Martin Oh, Maria, my darling child.
Martin Friends, neighbours, you all knew my child. Will you assist a heart-broken father to search for her?
All Ay, we will – to the Red Barn – to the Red Barn

Picture – Closed in

Scene 2
Front wood

Enter Timothy Bobbin, tipsy

Timothy I wonder where my sweetheart is? She promised to meet me by the blackberry bush, and she did not come; so I waited and waited till I couldna wait any longer. I shouldn't wonder if she ain't gone out wi' t'other chap, and left I to die an old maid. Never mind; I ha' gotten t'ring, so I'll get married to the first I meet. I've been down to the 'Cat and Fiddle' and had some yale, and then I met the parish pump – no, I mean the beadle – and he threatened to put I in the stocks for being drunk and disorderly; so I comed downt' lane to find the blackberry bush, so here I stops till my Anne comes. (*Lies down*)

Enter Johnny Raw

Johnny Vell I'm blest if I ain't lost my way. My ma sent me down to these 'ere parts for the benefit of my health; and I come out to take a walk, and blest if I can find my way back again.

Timothy (*Singing*) 'Meet me by moonlight alone – al – o – ne.'

Johnny 'Ullo! There's somebody laying in the road. Blest if it ain't one of the natives. I say, Mr Clodhopper, do you live about here?

Timothy Yes, in the blackberry bush. (*Sings as before*).

Johnny Vot rum places these 'ere yokels live in. I'll pick 'im hup and hask 'im to show me the vay home

(*Goes to lift him up. Falls on the top of him. Tim catches hold of him, and they roll over*).

Timothy I thought un ud' come to gi' I a buss, lass.

Johnny Let me go! Let me go! I'll tell my ma. I ain't a gal.

Timothy What! bean't thee my sweetheart?

Johnny No, I'm Johnny Raw; and I want to go home to my ma.

Timothy Where be thy home? I'll take 'ee to it. Get on my back, and I'll gi' 'ee cockhorse.

Johnny Vy, blest if you can carry yourself, let alone me!

Timothy Get on my back, Mr Johnny Raw, or I'll gi' thee a punch o' the yead.

Johnny If you hit me, I'll tell my ma.

Timothy Won't 'ee get on my back? Won't 'ee? (*Squares at him*).

Johnny Yes, yes. Don't hit one of your own size. (*Johnny gets on Tim's back, and they both roll*). There, I told you so. You've made my nose bleed. I'll tell my ma.

Timothy Don't 'ee mind, get up again.

Johnny No, I won't; I'll tell my ma.

Timothy If thee doan't get on my back, dang me if I doan't get on thine, and thee shall cockhorse me. So gee up, gee up!

Tim, after several efforts, gets on Johnny's back, who exits with him, Tim, crying 'Gee up;' and Johnny, 'I want my ma'

Change scene

229

Scene 3

Front chamber in Martin's cottage

Enter Martin and Anne, leading Mrs Martin

Martin Speak no more. Leave me to myself. 'Tis over, past; and I am a broken-hearted man.

Anne But, father, dear father, where's that fortitude you used to boast so much of?

Martin Fortitude! Who? Where? Show me the father that can behold his murdered child and not betray his feelings! My poor Maria! and has the old man lived to see it?

Mrs Martin Try, Anne, try – see if you can yield him any comfort; for me to attempt, alas! it is in vain.

Martin The child of all I loved the most was torn for ever from these arms.

Anne Dear father, you have a daughter yet who will strive to make you happy.

Martin Never! Never! I loved you all; but she was the darling, the pride of my heart, the hope, the sunlight of my life. Oh, I was happy once. My honest English fireside, circled with my little family, all joyous, all content. But a villain – a damned treacherous villain – has blasted all my hopes, robbed me of my child, and savagely murdered her!

Mrs Martin Oh, Heaven, support me! (*Falls on Anne's neck*).

Anne Mother, dear mother! Alas! alas!

Martin Oh, Heaven deliver the murderer into the hands of justice – show no mercy for the bloody deed: let not those glorious laws – the brightest pearls which gem our monarch's throne and dear to every Briton's heart – be thus outraged and basely violated!

Anne Father! Father!

Martin I took him to my arms, fostered him called him my son; and as he led my poor Maria from this humble roof, I cried 'Heaven bless thee'. Yes, I gave the murderer of my child a blessing – a poor old father's blessing! Oh, Heaven shield me, or I shall go mad! (*Crosses*).

Anne Your poor Anne will comfort you – do all she can to make you happy.

Martin I know it, my child, I know it; but my poor Maria, I see her now before my eyes, mangled and bleeding, pointing to her gory wounds. Oh, what a sight for a poor broken-hearted father! She beckons me! My child! Maria! Thy father's coming; he will revenge thee, child! He will revenge thee!

Rushes off

Mrs Martin Come, Anne, let us follow him, lest in his frenzy he may commit some rash act that will add to our sorrows.

Exeunt – End of scene

Scene 4
Interior of Corder's house

William Corder discovered at breakfast

Corder How strange is every action of my life. I met by chance a lady some time ago at Seaford, where I had been for the recovery of my health. From thence I came to London. Some time elapsed, when passing on through Fleet Street, again did I accost her. We parted, and wonderful to say, this is the very woman who has answered my advertisement, and whom I have selected as the future partner of my life. Last night my rest was disturbed by a distressful, horrid dream, the thought of which I cannot banish from my remembrance. Methought I saw Maria Martin's form arrayed in white wandering along the fields by her mother's cottage. Twice she seemed to pause and cast her eyes towards the Red Barn. I saw no more. Dreams oft denote some hidden truth; and I am given to credit them. Were it not that all is so secure and rank suspicion lull'd into a deep repose, by heaven! this soul might take the alarm. But no; she sleeps for ever; and dreams are but the fleeting visions of a troubled mind – no more. (*Knock*) Who's there?

Enter Servant

Servant A stranger, sir, is coming up the garden, who has been enquiring for you.
Corder (*Uneasy*) A stranger enquiring for me? Who? When? Where? Ha! (*Looking out of window*) I'll retire – say I'm not at home nor know you when I will

As he is going off, enter Lee, the officer, who stops him. Exit Servant

Corder (*Agitated*) Were you enquiring for me, sir?
Mr Lee (*First looking at him steadfastly in the face*) Is your name William Corder?
Corder My name is Corder, sir, what, what pray is your business with me?
Mr Lee (*Slowly and distinctly*) Of a very serious nature, Mr Corder.
Corder (*Expressing great uneasiness*) Serious?
Mr Lee Have you ever known a young woman named Maria Martin?

Corder Never, never; you must be mistaken, certainly you must. I am not the person you are seeking for.

Mr Lee I do not think I am mistaken. You surely must recollect a young woman of that name.

Corder No, no; I never knew a person of that name; you are certainly mistaken.

Mr Lee Pray, have you ever known a man the name of Martin?

Corder No.

Mr Lee Are you sure, come – come, take your time – reflect a little.

Corder Why, yes, I think I do recollect something of a person of that name.

Mr Lee Now, William Corder, I have asked you twice, I shall ask you a third time. Did you ever know a young woman of the name of Maria Martin? Softly now, recollect yourself.

Corder No, never; it certainly must be some other person.

Mr Lee Then, William Corder, it becomes my painful duty to tell you that I arrest you on a charge of murder

Corder starts. Chord. Lee places his hand on Corder's shoulder and shows handcuffs.

The murder of Maria Martin!

Corder Murder! me! Oh, impossible – I – not me, it cannot be.

Mr Lee Her body has been found in your barn.

Corder And does it follow that because her body has been found in an old barn belonging to me that I am to be accused of murder?

Mr Lee No, *because* she was last *known* to be in *your* company, and *you* being the only person who had a *motive* in her death!

Corder (*Anxiously*) When, when was the body found?

Mr Lee Last Saturday morning.

Corder (*Aside*) Great heaven, the morning of my dream.

Mr Lee It is necessary, Mr Corder, that you accompany me.

Corder I fear this will alarm my family.

Mr Lee If it is your wish, I will say I have arrested you for debt.

Corder Do so, I shall feel obliged. (*Walks across the stage several times as if lost in thought*) May I have five minutes conversation with my wife alone?

Mr Lee Alone! Impossible; I cannot suffer it.

Corder Then I will step into the next room, change my coat, and go with you.

Mr Lee Pardon me, sir; I must not lose sight of you a single moment.

Corder Implacable.

Mr Lee Mr Corder, I am ready to attend you.

Corder Whither would you take me?

Mr Lee To Lambeth street Police Office, in order to answer the complaint preferred against you before the magistrates assembled there.

Corder Sir, I am ready. Fate – fate thou hast indeed caught me!

Chord. Lee places handcuffs on Corder

Picture – Closed in

Scene 5
Front street

Enter Timothy Bobbin

Timothy Well, here I be up in Lunnon, to see all the foine sights. I come up along o' my sweetheart and her mother and father; what a queer place this Lunnon is; everybody seems to be knocking agin everbody else, and nobody don't take any notice on it. Somebody knocked up again I just now, and when I turned round again to punch his yead, dang me, if somebody else didn't knock my hat over my eyes, and when I put my hand in my pocket to pull out my hankercher to wipe un, curse me, if it hadna' gone, and everybody was a-laughing at me. I wonder where I be ? I come to see t' hanging and I canna find out t' place. (*Looks about*)

Enter Johnny Raw

Johnny Veire's my ma ? I've lost her in the crowd, and blest if I can fine her. Ullo, 'ere's a chap. I'll ask him. I say, sir, have you seen my ma ?

Timothy Dang'd if I dunna know that chap. Be'ant thee t' lad that gi' I t' cock horse down in our parts.

Johnny (*Aside*) Blest if that aint the yokel what made my nose bleed. In course it is, and now I got yer here, you just come down our street and see what me and my pals will give yer.

Timothy I dunna want nothing o' your pals. I be mortal glad to see thee. Be'ant thee glad to see I – gi' us thee hand.

Johnny Vell I'm blest! after making my nose bleed! I tell yer vot it is, you shall have a jolly volloping ven I finds my ma.

Timothy What dost 'ee mean ?

Johnny I s'pose yer think we couldn't do it, don't yer ? Ve knowe a thing or two down our street. Vy it vos only the other day that me and my ma, the butcher next door, two policeman and some of my pals, pitched a beggar off our steps into the road, and although he had been ill for two years and walked with a crutch, ve managed him between us.

Timothy Lor', thee doan't say so. But I say, Johnny Raw, where be'est going this morning ?

Johnny Vot's that to you ? I want my ma.

Timothy There, doan't 'ee be rumbustical, or dang me, I'll bung your eye up.

Johnny Vill yer? If yer do I'll break a vinder, and ven the policeman comes I'll give you in charge.

Timothy Will 'ee? then dang it, here goes! (*Squares at Johnny*).

Johnny I want my ma

Enter a Mob (ad lib) who insist on them having a pitched battle. They are persuaded to take off their coats and hats. During the fight they are stolen. Officer enters, takes charge of both, and drags them off – Mob shouting, etc

Change of scene

Scene 6
The condemned cell (Slow music to open)

William Corder discovered in chains. A small lamp burning on the table, with pen, ink, and paper

Corder Life's fleeting dream is closing fast, and the great conflict 'gainst which I warr'd with Heaven and man is now upon the wane. All earthly hopes are gone; this bosom is a waste, a wilderness, a blank in the creation. Sin hath blighted all, and left me desolate – a very wretch – fit prey to the unlettered hangman. A short – short – hour, and oh, the great account I have to render freezes up my soul, so that I grow sick and pant to taste oblivion's cup though poison'd with my crime! I'll try and sleep; perhaps her potent spell may lull me to a sweet forgetfulness – a calm repose. (*Lies down and sleeps*)

Ghost music. Blue fire. The spirit of Maria Marten appears

Spirit Can'st thou, murderer, hope that sleep – soft, balmy sleep – can e'er be thine? Look on thy sinless victim, who in life adored thee, now wandering here unearthly, pale, and cold. See! see! from whence her life-blood gushed. William! William! thy poor Maria pities and forgives thee – thee, her murderer

Blue fire. She goes to William, shrouds him with her garment three times, and vanishes. Bell tolls. Corder wakes and starts up.

Corder I come! Mercy – pardon – pity – spare me! Hence! Avaunt! thou are not of this earth! Ah, what – gone – vanished – shade – vision – Maria, I'd speak with thee – gone – no sound – all quiet! Oh, where –

where! I – oh, Heaven, 'tis but the darkness of my soul doth haunt me thus! All – all – is but a dream! Guilt – guilt – I cannot hide thee!

Enter Sheriff, Gaoler, Hangman, with rope and attendants. Corder goes to table, and takes from off it a written document, which he hands to Sheriff

Corder There is my confession. I am – I am her murderer.
Sheriff Then Justice has fulfilled her sacred office to the bent.
Corder She hath! she hath! Guilt – sin – crime – horror – all is there!

(*Bell at intervals*).

Sheriff The world shall hear of this.
Corder I am guilty of the crime. May Heaven have mercy on my soul!
Sheriff Lead him forth to execution. (*Ghost music*).
Corder I am ready; my course is finished. May innocence and virtue pray for the peace of my departing soul! My span of life is short, and few my days; yet count my crimes for years, and I have lived whole ages. Thus Justice, in compassion to mankind, cuts off a wretch like me, by one such example to secure thousands from future ruin. (*Falls on his knees*)

During Corder's last speech, the Spirit of Maria Marten rises at back. Bell tolls. Characters form picture. Blue fire.

The End

The String
of Pearls
(Sweeney Todd)

GEORGE DIBDIN PITT

GEORGE DIBDIN PITT (1799/1855)

The origins of the many Pitts and Dibdins in the late eighteenth and nineteenth centuries remained inextricably confused until Charles Dibdin the Younger's Memoirs were made available to the Society for Theatre Research in the 1950's by a Dibdin family descendant, permitting George Speaight to unravel at last the complicated relationships. His 1956 edition of the Memoirs for the STR allows, with the aid of the Dictionary of National Biography, the following to be extracted:

Charles Dibdin the Elder (1745/1814) deserted his wife in 1767 to live with Harriet Pitt, a dancer at Covent Garden, by whom he had two children, Charles and Thomas. Harriet already had two children of her own by the actor George Mattocks, Harriet and Cecil Pitt: Cecil, a musician, became George's father. George sometimes dropped his first name, and his half-brothers dropped the Pitt, which adds to the confusion, but I hope it will now be clear that George was not in fact related to old Charles, and that the 'Dibdin' was purely a courtesy assumption. His theatrical antecedents were impeccable, however, for both his grandmother (Harriet) and his great-grandmother (Harriet's mother, Ann Pitt) were popular figures at the Patent houses – Ann was a celebrated beauty, and was painted by no less distinguished an artist than George Romney.

Charles junior was almost as celebrated a song-writer as his father, and his brother Tom wrote almost as many plays as young George; they were both extremely proud of their father, and in his Memoirs Charles junior refers to Harriet and Cecil as his brother and sister, so we may presume that their home life was a happy an affectionate one. Old Ann Pitt looked after the welfare and education of the children with the help of her brother, and there does not appear to have been any undue hardship or poverty in the family. With such a background it was inevitable that George would find his livelihood in the theatre; he doubtless started as an actor and graduated into playwriting, although it was not until 1831 that his first piece is recorded – My Own Blue Bell at the Surrey, where he was probably resident dramatist.

By 1835 he was the stage-manager of the Pavilion, Mile End, and later became stock-author at the Britannia, Hoxton, where he remained until his death in 1855. In 1845 he had sixteen pieces presented at the Brit. (as well as nine at other theatres) and two years later had no fewer than twenty-one plays performed at the 'Great Theatre', plus five at other houses. George Dibdin Pitt was a hack writer of the most rough and ready kind, producing pieces to order with conveyor-belt regularity; many of his works were not so much written as 'nailed-up'. H Chance Newton describes in *Crime And The Drama* (1927) the working methods of a later stock-writer at the Britannia, Colin Hazlewood, who was paid £3 per week:

> *'When I saw that Hazlewood 'wrote' these plays, of course it was hardly to be expected that he would be able to sit down and work out such new dramas in any pronounced literary fashion for such a weekly wage.*
>
> *He had a very good method, however. He used to take in the popular periodicals of the time, such as* The London Journal, The London Reader, Reynolds Miscellany, The Welcome Guest, *and other such publications, alas ! long since defunct. To these Hazlewood added all the 'penny bloods' of his young days, such as* The Boys of England, The Young Men of England, *and all the highwaymen stories and similar cheap books.*
>
> *Hazlewood, or one of us working with him, would run through these periodicals, jotting down the main incidents in the stories thereof, and scissoring out here and there sundry aphorisms, axioms, and moral sentiments and so forth. These were docketed alphabetically, and when Colin (a dear old fellow) was engaged in writing, or in sticking down, a new play for the Brit., etc, he or his assistants would take down from the shelf sundry envelopes containing these aphorisms, such as 'Ambition is', etc, or 'Kindness of heart', etc, and so forth, and would pop these moral, patriotic and other reflections into the play-script then under way'.*

We can safely assume, I think, that Pitt must have had some system of this kind. However, despite this battery-farm method of production, he did write one memorable piece – *The String of Pearls; or The Fiend of Fleet St*, even though this play, like so many on the nineteenth-century English stage, was an adaptation from the French. Other pieces which flowed Niagara-like from Pitt's pen (the final total is incalculable, but it must be well in excess of two hundred) were the famous monster-melo-drama, produced at Sadler's Wells in 1834 and entitled *The Eddystone Elf*, and a horse-drama called *Rookwood* (1840) which was one of many versions of Harrison Ainsworth's romantic idealisation of Dick Turpin.

With the best will in the world, I have been forced to the conclusion that dear old Sweeney, like those other two venerable figures of British folk-lore Robin Hood and St George, is a myth. The efforts of some writers to make him an historical figure are unconvincing; the origins of the legend are lost – it is certain that all those allegedly 'original' sitings of Sweeney's barber-shop and adjacent pie-shop are bogus. H Chance

Newton confidently placed the sanguinary saloon a few yards east of St Dunstan's Church in Fleet St, but he was an incorrigible romantic.

It is possible that there may perhaps have been a barber who cut his customers' throats for their loose change – there have been villains in all walks of life – and it is just conceivable that there may have been a lady who kept a pie-shop and who, in hard times, filled her wares with Long Pig, but the co-operation of these two malefactors to their mutual benefit is entirely a figment of George Dibdin Pitt's imagination, for it was he who first dramatised the gory tale in the form familiar to us today. And he refers to his play as a '*legendary* drama'.

In *A Playgoer's Memories* (1920), H G Hibbert remembers:

When I was a young Londoner I was shown in Fleet Street the very shop of the demon barber – and shuddered to think that meat pies were on sale there. And I read that an enterprising tradesman has again, by way of advertisement, labelled the new building erected on the site as the authenticated abode of the wretch. But in truth I believe there was no such person as Sweeney Todd, for fascinating research has brought me so far back as, and to a full stop with, a French ballad of the Middle Ages . . . It is conceivable that [he] had no more definite original than the hero of a French novel, The String of Pearls, *translated for the Penny Miscellany, they say by George Augustus Sala, and promptly seized by a dozen dramatists. For years Sweeney Todd was a stock favourite at the Coburg, the Britannia, the Pavilion and the Effingham Saloon. Bancroft played Sweeney during his Birmingham novitiate. And the character was in the repertory of every stroller.*

In a tiny volume of strange cases I find the record, professing authenticity, of a 'Horrible Affair in the Rue de la Harpe, Paris' where travellers were said to have been murdered by a barber, robbed, then passed through a subterranean passage to a pie shop next door. The bodies were found by a dog – sometimes 'starred' in the plays – who missed his master.

That this ballad refers to these horrible events taking place about 'the year eleven hundred or so' takes us a long way from nineteenth century Fleet St, but then melodramatists took their plots where they could find them.

It could be argued that villainy knows no frontiers, and that an English barber may well have been prompted by hearing of the old tale to augment his profits by 'polishing off' his better class of customer; H Chance Newton refers to a French crime which was remarkably similar to William Corder's murder of Maria Marten and which occurred at approximately the same time. (An English version of this tragedy by W T Moncrieff, translated from an original by Messieurs D'Ennery and Lemoine, entitled *The Red Farm; or, The Well of Sainte-Marie* appeared at Sadler's Wells in 1842). If, therefore, your patriotic feelings refuse to allow you to believe that one of Britain's best-loved villains owes his origins to a medieval French horror-story, you are at liberty to do so. After all, there are still plenty of cut-throats in Fleet Street today...

Although many others tried their hand at stage-versions of Sweeney Todd – Fred Hazleton and Matt Wilkinson among them – Pitt's remains the best by far, and is interesting in that it features an early example of the villain being foiled, not by the hero, but by the principal comedian, Jarvis. This innovation was subsequently worked to death by other theatre-writers; nearly fifty years later Jerome was still warning the villain to 'beware of the comic man' (*Stage-land*, 1889).

The original stage Sweeney was Mark Howard, described by one writer as 'a very appalling Todd indeed'. Later Cecil Pitt (a younger brother of George Dibdin and an early Jonas Fogg) made a speciality of the role, but the most celebrated Demon Barber of the century was George Yates of the Pavilion, Mile End, who with his large-sized wife, Harriet Clifton, as Mrs Lovett, made as fearsome a duo as a horror addict could wish for in a month of Bloody Sundays!

I have seen various dates given for the original performance at the Britannia Theatre, Hoxton (the theatre to which Dickens devoted a chapter in *The Uncommercial Traveller*) but my own research gives the date as March 1st, 1847.

The String of Pearls. Frontispiece from Dick's Edition, 1883.
(*British Museum*)

THE STRING
OF PEARLS
(SWEENEY TODD)

An original playbill of *The String Of Pearls* can be seen in the British Museum collection, and gives the following cast for the first performance at the Britannia Theatre, Hoxton, March 1st, 1847.

Colonel Jeffrey by Mr J Mordaunt
Captain Rathbone by Mr Arthur
Mr Grant by Mr Clements
Mr Oakley by Mr Colwell
Rev Mr Lupin by Mr F Wilton
Sweeney Todd by Mr M Howard
Tobias Ragg by Mrs Hudson Kirby
Thornhill, alias Mark Ingestre, by Mr Sawford
Mr Parmine by Mr Cecil Pitt
Jarvis by Mr J Gardener
Hector by Mrs Roby
Ben Bluffhead by Mr Macarthy
Ruby by Mr H Pitt
Fogg by Mr Roberts
Constable by Mr Davison
Johanna Oakley by Miss C Braham
Mrs Oakley by Mrs Colwell
Mrs Lovett by Miss Hamilton

The playbill announces that *The String Of Pearls; or The Fiend of Fleet Street* is 'taken from the much admired Tale of that name (founded on fact) in *Lloyd's People's Periodical*. For Dramatic effect, and to adapt the story to general taste, some alterations have been judiciously made, enhancing its interest'.

This mysterious publication *Lloyd's People's Periodical* remains undiscovered. – *M.K.*

Dramatis Personae

As performed at the Britannia Theatre 1847

Sir William Brandon, a Judge, by Mr C Williams
Colonel Jeffery, of the Indian Army, by Mr J Reynolds
Jasper Oakley, a Spectacle-maker, by Mr Elliott
Mark Ingestrie, a Mariner, by Mr S Sawford
Sweeney Todd, the Barber of Fleet Street, by Mr Mark Howard
Dr Aminadab Lupin, a Wolf in Sheep's Clothing, by Mr J Dunn
Jarvis Williams, a Lad with no small appetite, by Mr W Rogers
Jonas Fogg, the Keeper of a Mad-house, by Mr C Pitt
Jean Parmine, a Lapidary, by Mr J Pitt
Tobias Ragg, Sweeney Todd's Apprentice-boy, by Miss Burrows
Mrs Oakley, Jasper's wife, by Mrs Newham
Johanna, her daughter, by Miss Colwell
Mrs Lovett, Sweeney Todd's Accomplice in Guilt, by Mrs Atkinson

Time in representation, one hour and thirty-five minutes

Note: The above cast list is given in the published edition of 1883, and differs in several respects from that given on the original playbill. The play was probably altered in subsequent performances, and it is doubtless the improved version which was eventually published. – *M.K.*

SWEENEY TODD, THE BARBER OF FLEET STREET

Act 1

Scene 1

Interior of Sweeney Todd's Shop. A revolving trap, which has a similar chair beneath, so that whichever side is shown to the audience, the position of the chair and its appearance are the same.

Sweeney Todd discovered dressing a wig, and Tobias Ragg attending him

Sweeney You will remember now, Tobias Ragg, that you are my apprentice; that you have had of me board, lodging, and washing, save that you take your meals at home, that you don't sleep here, and that your mother gets up your linen. (*Fiercely*) Now, are you not a fortunate, happy dog?

Tobias (*Timidly*) Yes, sir.

Sweeney You will acquire a first-rate profession, quite as good as the law, which your mother tells me that she would have put you to, only that a little weakness of the head-piece unqualified you. And now, Tobias, listen.

Tobias (*Trembling*) Yes, sir.

Sweeney I'll cut your throat from ear to ear if you repeat one word of what passes in this shop, or are to make any supposition, or draw any conclusion from anything you may see or hear, or fancy you see or hear. Do you understand me?

Tobias I won't say anything, Mr Todd; if I do, may I be made into veal pies at Lovett's in Bell Yard.

Sweeney (*Starts*) How dare you mention veal pies in my presence? Do you suspect?

Tobias Oh, sir; I don't suspect – indeed I don't! I meant no harm in making the remark.

Sweeney (*Eyes Tobias narrowly*) Very good. I'm satisfied – quite satisfied; and, mark me, the shop, and the shop only, is your place.

Tobias Yes, sir.

Enter Mark Ingestrie, dressed as a sea-captain of the period

Mark By the description, this should be the man I seek. He can doubtless give me some tidings of Johanna, and I can look forward to a happy meeting after an estrangement of many long and tedious years. Good morrow, friend; I have need of your craft. Let me get shaved at once, as I have to see a lady.

Sweeney Happy to be of service to you, good gentleman. Will you be pleased to seat yourself? (*Brushes Mark's hair*) You've been to sea, sir?

Mark Yes; and I have only now lately come up the river from an Indian voyage.

Sweeney You carry some treasures, I presume?

Mark Among others, this small casket. (*Mark produces it*).

Sweeney A piece of exquisite workmanship.

Mark It is not the box but its contents that must cause you wonder, for I must, in confidence, tell you it contains a string of veritable pearls of the value of twelve thousand pounds.

Sweeney (*Chuckling aside, and whetting his razor on his hand*) I shall have to polish him off. Ha ha ha! heugh!

Mark What the devil noise was that?

Sweeney It was only me. I laughed. By the way, Tobias, while I am operating upon this gentleman's chin, the figures at St Dunstan's are about to strike; the exhibition will excite your curiosity and allow me time to shave our customer without your interruption

Tobias goes out

Sweeney Now sir, we can proceed to business, if it so please you; it's well you came here, sir, for though I say it, there isn't a shaving shop in the City of London that ever thinks upon polishing off a customer as I do – fact – can assure you – ha, ha! heugh!

Mark Shiver the main-brace! I tell you what it is, Master Barber: if you come that laugh again, I will get up and go.

Sweeney Very good, it won't occur again. (*Commences to mix up a lather*). If I am so bold, who are you? – where did you come from? – and whither are you going?

Mark You seem fond of asking questions, my friend; perhaps before I answer them, you will reply to one I'm about to put?

Sweeney Oh, yes, of course; what is it?

Mark Do you know a Mr Oakley, who lives somewhere hereabouts? He is a spectacle maker.

Sweeney Yes, to be sure I do – Jasper Oakley, in Fore Street. Bless me, where can my strop be? I had it this minute – I must have lain it down somewhere. What an odd thing I can't see it. Oh, I recollect – I took it into the parlour. Sit still, sir, I shan't be a minute; you can amuse yourself with the newspaper. I shall soon polish him off!

(*Sweeney hands paper and goes out. A rushing noise heard, and Mark seated on the chair sinks through stage. After a pause, the chair rises vacant, and Sweeney enters. He examines the string of pearls which he holds in his hand*)

Sweeney When a boy, the thirst of avarice was first awakened by the fair gift of a farthing; that farthing soon became a pound; the pound a hundred – so to a thousand, till I said to myself, I will possess a hundred thousand. This string of pearls will complete the sum. (*Starts*) Who's there?

(*Sweeney pounces upon Tobias, who has cautiously opened the door*)

Speak – and speak the truth, or your last hour has come! How long were you peeping through the door before you came in?

Tobias Please, sir, I wasn't peeping at all.

Sweeney Well, well, if you did peep, what then? It's no matter. I only wanted to know, that's all. It was quite a joke, wasn't it? Come now, there's no harm done, we'll be merry over it – very merry.

Tobias (*Puzzled*) Yes, very merry.

Sweeney Who's that at the door?

Tobias It's only the black servant of the gentleman who came here to be shaved this morning.

Sweeney Tell the fellow his master's not here; go – let him seek elsewhere, do you hear? I know I shall have to polish that boy off!

(*Whets his razor on his hand. – As Sweeney concludes this speech, Tobias discovers the hat worn by Mark; this he secretes and goes out*).

Enter Jean Parmine

Jean Good evening, neighbour; I would have you shave me.

Sweeney Your servant, Mr Parmine – you deal in precious stones.

Jean Yes, I do; but it's rather late for a bargain. Do you want to buy or sell?

Sweeney To sell

(*Produces a casket and gives it to Jean*).

Jean (*Examining pearls*) Real, by heaven, all real.

Sweeney I know they are real. Will you deal with me or not?

Jean I'm not quite sure that they are real; let me look at them again? Oh, I see, counterfeit; but so well done that really for the curiosity of the thing I will give you £50.

Sweeney £50? Who is joking now, I wonder? We cannot deal to-night.

Jean Stay – I will give you a hundred.

Sweeney Hark ye, friend, I know the value of pearls.

Jean Well, since you know more than I gave you credit for I think I can find a customer who will pay £11,000 for them; if so, I have no objection to advance the sum of £8,000.

Sweeney I am content – let me have the money early to-morrow.

Jean Stop a bit; there are some rather important things to consider – you must know that a string of pearls is not to be bought like a few ounces of old silver, and the vendor must give every satisfaction as to how he came by them.

Sweeney (*Aside*) I am afraid I shall have to polish him off. (*Aloud*) In other words, you don't care how I possess the property, provided I sell it to you at a thief's price; but if, on the contrary, I want their real value, you mean to be particular.

Jean I suspect you have no right to dispose of the pearls, and to satisfy myself I shall insist upon your accompanying me to a magistrate.

Sweeney And what road shall you take?

Jean The *right* path

(*As Jean turns, Sweeney springs upon him. A fierce struggle ensues. Sweeney succeeds in forcing Jean into the chair. Sweeney touches a spring, and the chair sinks with a dreadful crash. Sweeney laughs and exclaims, 'I've polished him off!' as scene closes*)

Scene 2
Breakfast Parlour in the house of Jasper Oakley

Enter Johanna

Johanna Oh, Mark, Mark! why do you thus desert me when I have relied so abundantly on your true affection? Oh, why have you not sent me some token of your existence and of your continual love? The merest, slightest word would have been sufficient, and I should have been happy! Hark, what was that? I'm sure I heard footsteps beneath the chamber window

Colonel Jeffery, enveloped in a cloak, enters

Jeffery I have the honour of speaking to Miss Johanna Oakley?

Johanna Oh, sir, your looks are sad and serious! You seem about to announce some misfortune; tell me if it is not so.

Jeffery Let me pray you, lady, to subdue this passion of grief, and listen with patience to what I shall unfold. There is much to hear and much to speculate upon, and if from all that I have learnt, I cannot, dare not tell you Mark Ingestrie lives, I shrink likewise from telling you he is no more!

Johanna Speak again! – say those words again! – there is hope then – there is hope!

Jeffery You are aware that a quarrel with his uncle caused him to embark in an adventure in the Indian Seas?

Johanna Too well. Alas! it was on my account he sacrificed himself.

Jefferson Nay, good fortune attended that enterprise, and Mark Ingestrie showed me on our homeward voyage a string of pearls of immense value, which he said he intended for you. When we reached the River Thames, only three days since, he left the vessel for that purpose.

Johanna Alas! he never came.

Jefferson No; from all inquiries we can make, and from all information we can obtain, it seems that he disappeared somewhere in Fleet Street.

Johanna Disappeared!

Jeffery We can trace him to Temple Stairs, and from thence to a barber's shop kept by a man named Sweeney Todd; but beyond, we have no clue. It is necessary, Miss Oakley, that I now leave you, but you must promise to meet me –

Johanna When and where?

Jeffery At the hour of six this day week, in the Temple Gardens. I ask this of you because I am resolved to make all the exertion in my power to discover what has become of Mark Ingestrie, in whose fate I am sure I have succeeded in interesting you, although you care so little for the 'string of pearls' he intended for you.

Johanna I suppose it is too much for human nature to expect two blessings at once. I had the fond warm heart that loved me, without the fortune that would have enabled us to live in comfort, and now, when that is, perchance, within my grasp, the heart which was by far the most costly possession, lies buried in a grave – its bright influences, its glorious aspirations quenched for ever.

Jeffery You will meet me, then, as I request, to hear if I have any news for you?

Johanna I have the will to do so, but Heaven knows only if I may have the power.

Jeffery What do you mean?

Johanna I cannot tell what a week's anxiety may do. I do not know but a sick bed may be my resting-place till I exchange it for a coffin. I feel now my strength fail me, and am scarcely able to totter to my chamber. Farewell, sir, I owe you my best thanks.

Jeffery Remember, I bid you adieu, with the hope of meeting you again

(*Jeffery by this time has reached the door of the apartment. He hears some one without, and conceals himself behind it as Dr Lupin enters*)

Johanna Lupin here! (*Aside*) How unfortunate!

Lupin Yes, maiden. I am that chosen vessel whom the profane call 'Mealy Mouth'. I come hither at the bidding of thy respected mother to partake of a vain mixture which rejoiceth in the name of 'tea'. (*detains her*)

Johanna You will allow me a free passage from the room, if you please, Dr Lupin.

Lupin Thy mother hath decided that I take thee unto my bosom, even as a wedded wife.

Johanna Absurd! Have you been drinking?

Lupin I never drink, save when the spirit waxeth faint. (*Takes a bottle from his pocket, and drinks*). 'Tis an ungodly practice. (*Drinks again – offering Johanna bottle*) Let me offer you *spiritual* consolation – hum! ha!

Johanna Bless me! you have the hiccups.

Lupin Yes; I – I rather think I have a little. Isn't it a shame that one so pious should have the hiccups? Hum – h! hum – ha! Damn the hiccups – that is, I mean damn all backsliders!

Johanna The miserable hypocrite!

Lupin The fire of love rageth – it consumeth my very vitals. Peradventure I may extinguish the flame by the moisture of those ruby lips – nay, I am resolved. (*Lupin seizes Johanna*).

Johanna Unhand me, ruffian, or repent it!

(*Jeffery rushes forward, and belabours Lupin with scabbard of his sword, Jeffery escapes through door, Johanna secures key*).

Lupin Help! verily I am assailed. Robbers! fire! help!

(*The household run in armed with brooms, mops, and Lupin exhibits a black eye. On perceiving this, Mrs Oakley screams and faints.*)

Scene 3
Interior of Lovett's Pie-shop in Bell Yard, Temple Bar, front scene

Enter Mrs Lovett and Jarvis Williams, dressed in rags

Mrs L. Go away, my good fellow; we never give anything to beggars.

Jarvis Don't you, mum? I ain't no beggar, mum, but a young man who is on the look-out for a situation. I thought as how you might recommend me to some *light* employment where they puts the *heavy* work out.

Mrs L. Recommend you! – recommend a ragged wretch like you! Besides, what employment can we have but pie-making? We have a man already who suits us very well, with the exception that he, as you would do if we were to exchange, has grown contemptuous in his calling.

Jarvis Ay, that is the way of the world. There is always sufficient argument by the rich against the poor and destitute to keep 'em so; but argifying don't mend the matter. I'll look after another job. (*Going*).

Mrs L. (*Aside*) If he be unknown he is the very man for our purpose. (*Aloud*) Stay, you have solicited employment of me, and I don't see why I should not make a trial of you. Follow me.

Jarvis Where to?

Mrs L. To the bakehouse, where I will show you what you have to do. You must promise never to leave it on any pretence.

Jarvis Never to leave it!

Mrs L. Never, unless you leave it for good and for all. If upon those conditions you choose to accept the situation, you may; if not, you can depart and leave it alone.

Jarvis As Shakespere says, 'My proverty, and not my will consents' (*Mrs Lovett raises a trap-door in front of shop, and points to the descent*).

Mrs L. By this passage, young man, we must descend to the furnace and ovens, where I will show you how to manufacture the pies, feed the fires, and make yourself generally useful

Music – They descend trap, which closes as the scene opens

Scene 4
The Bakehouse. A gloomy cellar of vast extent and sepulchral appearance. A fitful glare issues from the various low-arched entrances in which a huge oven is placed.

Enter Mrs Lovett and Jarvis down the steps

Jarvis I suppose I'm to have someone to assist me in this situation. One pair of hands could never do the work in such a place.

Mrs L. Are you not content?

Jarvis Oh, yes, only you spoke of having a man.

Mrs L. He has gone to his *friends* – he has gone to some of his very *oldest friends*, who will be glad to see him. But now I must leave you a time. As long as you are industrious, you will get on very well; but as soon as you begin to get idle and neglect my orders, you will receive a piece of information that may –

Jarvis What is it? I am of an inquiring disposition – you may as well give it me now.

Mrs L. No; I seldom find there is occasion for it at first; but, after a

252

time, when you get well fed you are pretty sure to want it. Everybody who relinquishes this situation goes to his old *friends*, *friends* that he has not seen for many years! I shall return anon

Mrs Lovett goes out

Jarvis What a strange manner of talking that respectable middle-aged female has! There seems to be something very singular in all she utters! It's very strange! And what a singular looking place, too – nothing visible but darkness. I think it would be quite unbearable if it wasn't for the delicious odour of the pies. Talking of pies, I fancy I could eat one (*Takes a pie off tray, and eats voraciously*). Beautiful! delicious! lots of gravy! (*He suddenly discovers a long hair, views it mysteriously, and winds it round his finger*). Somebody's been combing their hair. I don't think that pie's a nice un
(*Puts part of eaten pie back, and takes another*). This is better! Done to a turn! Extremely savoury! (*Puts his hand in his mouth*) What's this? A bone? No; a button! I don't think I like pies now. How did that button come into that pie! Oh, la! I'm very poorly!
(*At this monent a part of the wall gives way, and Jean Parmine, with an iron bar, forces a passage through the aperture he has made*).
Oh, la! her's one of the murdered ghosts come to ax for his body, and it's been made into pies. Oh, la! Please it wasn't me. I was only engaged to-day.
Jean Silence, my friend; you have nothing to fear! I see, like myself, you have been lured into this den!
Jarvis Since you are flesh and blood, and not a ghost, perhaps you can inform me why such wholesale butchery has been indulged in.
Jean The object of the wretches has solely been robbery, and their victims people of supposed wealth. They have in all cases been inveigled into the shop of an infamous monster, named Sweeney Todd, a barber, residing in Fleet Street; here, by an ingenious contrivance, the unfortunate sufferers were lowered to the cellars beneath the house, murdered, and conveyed to this retreat, where a glowing furnace destroyed every trace of the crime.
Jarvis Well, I never!
Jean We must strike out some plan for our mutual deliverance. We are in Bell Yard, and to my certain knowledge the houses right and left have cellars. Now, surely, with a weapon such as this bar, willing hearts and arms that have not quite lost their powers, we may make our way from this horrible abode. (*Noise*) Hark! some one is approaching. Follow me!

Music – Jean and Jarvis retire through aperture – Sweeney enters

Sweeney Gathering clouds warn the mountaineer of the approach-

253

ing storm; let them now warn me to provide against danger. I have too many enemies to be safe. I will dispose of them one by one, till no evidence of my guilt remain. My first step must be to stop the babbling tongue of Tobias Ragg. Mrs Lovett, too, grows scrupulous and dissatisfied; I've had my eye on her for some time, and fear she intends mischief. A little poison, skilfully administered, may remove any unpleasantness in that quarter. Hum! – ha – heugh! Who's there! (*Turns and discovers Mrs Lovett standing at his elbow*).

Mrs L. Sweeney Todd!

Sweeney (*Calmly*) Well!

Mrs L. Since I discover that you intend treachery, I shall on the instant demand my share of the booty – aye, an equal share of the fruits of our mutual bloodshed.

Sweeney (*With the same air of indifference*) Well, so you shall, if you are only patient; I will balance accounts with you in a minute.

(*Sweeney takes a book from his pocket, and runs his finger down the account*).

Sweeney £12,000, to a fraction!

Mrs L. That is just £6,000 for each person, there being two of us.

Sweeney But, Mistress Lovett, I must first have you to know that, before I hand you a coin, you will have to pay me for your support, lodging, and clothes.

Mrs L. Clothes? Why, I haven't had a new dress for these six months!

Sweeney Besides, am I to have nothing for your education? (*Draws his finger significantly across his throat*) Yes, for some years you have been totally provided for by me; and, after deducting that and the expenses of erecting furnaces, purchasing flour for your delicious pies, etc, etc, I find it leaves a balance of 16s 4¾d in my favour, and I don't intend you to budge an inch till it is paid.

Mrs L. You want to rob me; but you shall find, to your sorrow, I will have my due

(*Mrs Lovett secretly draws a knife – Sweeney starts back on beholding the weapon*).

Now, villain! who triumphs? Put your name to a deed consigning the whole of the wealth blood has purchased, or you perish where you stand!

Sweeney Idiot! you should have known Sweeney Todd better, and learnt that he is a man to calculate his chances. Behold! (*Draws a pistol from his breast fires, and kills Mrs Lovett*)

Now let the furnace consume the body as it would wheaten straw, and destroy all evidence of my guilt in this, as it has in my manifold deeds of blood

(*Sweeney opens the furnace door, a fierce glare lights the stage – he drags the body of Mrs Lovett to the ovens as Act drop falls*)

Act 2

Scene 1
Sweeney's shop

Tobias and Jarvis Williamson

Jarvis At last, Tobias, I fancy I have got to the bottom of this mystery. This house communicates with the next door, and in it Sweeney Todd hides his victims until he gets rid of them in the shape of his juicy confectionery – pies, all hot! By touching a spring in the mantelpiece, the opening to Lovett's house is discovered, but it is difficult to remove alone. I needn't ask if you will lend me a hand?

Tobias I will, indeed; but we must use caution in the proceeding, and watch our opportunity. At present it would be dangerous, as I expect his return every minute.

Jarvis Then I'll make myself scarce at once.

Tobias Hush! I hear footsteps.

Jarvis Talk of the devil, and he's at your elbow. I wonder how he'd eat in one of his own pies!

Jarvis goes out – He has scarcely done so when Sweeney Todd enters hurriedly. He looks suspiciously and attentively at Tobias, who regards him

Sweeney What are you staring at, boy?

Tobias I wasn't staring, sir!

(*Sweeney strikes him*).

Sweeney There's a lesson for you to learn.

Tobias I won't endure it! I won't be knocked about in this way, I won't.

Sweeney You won't, eh? Ha, ha, heugh! have you forgotten your mother?

Tobias You say you have power over my mother, but I don't know what it is, and I cannot and will not believe it. I'll leave you, come of it what may. I'll go to sea – anywhere, rather than stay in such a place as this.

Sweeney Oh, you will, will you? Then, Tobias Ragg, you and I must come to some understanding. I'll tell you what power I have over your mother, and then, perhaps, you'll be satisfied.

Tobias I am persuaded you can do her no injury while I am living to protect her.

Sweeney Last winter, when the frost continued eighteen weeks, you were starving, and Mrs Ragg was employed to attend the chambers of a lawyer in the Temple. He was a cold-hearted, severe man, who never forgave anything in his life, and never will.

Tobias The home was indeed desolate. A guinea was owing for rent, but mother got the money, paid it, and obtained the situation where she now is.

Sweeney Ah, you think so. The rent was paid, but, Tobias, my boy, a word in your ear – she took a candle-stick from her employer to pay it. I know it – can prove it! and I will hang her if you force me by any conduct.

Tobias Liar and calumniator! This infamous charge against an innocent woman has given me a nerve of iron. I utterly throw off the yoke imposed by you upon me, and –

Sweeney Where are you going?

Tobias To the nearest magistrate's – there to denounce Sweeney Todd, and deliver into the hands of justice a designing, cruel and cold-blooded muderer!

Sweeney You have pronounced your doom!

(*A desperate struggle takes place between Tobias and Sweeney – Tobias is overpowered, and the knife of Sweeney is raised as the chair sinks, and Mark Ingestrie rises in its place. His face is deadly pale; his hair is dishevelled, and his clothes marked with blood – Picture*).

Ah! the yawning grave yields up its ghastly inmate to fix my guilt! See, he is there – there he comes to accuse me of the murder. Oh, save me! Let me hence, or it will kill me – ha, ha, ha!

(*Laughs hysterically, as scene closes*)

Scene 2
A chamber in the madhouse at Peckham. Discover Jonas Fogg

Enter Sweeney

Jonas Mr Sweeney Todd, I think, if my memory don't deceive me?

Sweeney You are right, Mr Jonas Fogg. I believe I am not easily forgotten by those who have once seen me.

Jonas (*Pointedly*) True, sir; you are not easily forgotten. What can I do for you now?

Sweeney I am rather unfortunate with my boys. I have got another here who has shown such decided symptoms of insanity, that it becomes, I regret to say, absolutely necessary to place him under your care.

Jonas Indeed – does he rave?

Sweeney Oh, yes, he does, and about the most absurd nonsense in the world. To hear him, one would really think that instead of being one of the most humane of men, I was, in point of fact, an absolute murderer.

Jonas A murderer?

Sweeney Yes, a murderer – a murderer to all intents and purposes. Could anything be more absurd than such an accusation?

Jonas For how long, do you think, Mr Todd, this malady will continue?

Sweeney I will pay for twelve months; but I do not think, between you and I, that the case will last anything like so long. I think he will die like Simkins – suddenly.

Jonas I shouldn't wonder if he did. You may as well introduce me to your patient at once.

Sweeney Certainly; I shall have great pleasure in showing him to you. (*Goes to door*) Tobias Ragg, come into the room directly. Tobias Ragg!

Enter Tobias, pale and dejected

Jonas Quite young!

Sweeney Yes, more's the pity; and *of course* we deeply lament his present position.

Jonas Of course. But see – he raises his eyes.

Tobias Sweeney Todd is a murderer, and I denounce him!

Sweeney You hear him?

Jonas Mad, indeed!

Sweeney Could anyone but a maniac make so absurd an assertion?

Jonas No; it's insanity in its most terrible form. I shall be under the necessity of putting him in a strait waistcoat.

Sweeney I'm afraid mild treatment, which I have tried, only irritates the disease; therefore I must leave you, as a professional man, to deal with the case as you deem fit. But, as time presses, and I have an important engagement to fulfil, good evening. I have no doubt the patient will be properly attended to.

(*Sweeney shakes hands with Jonas, and speaks to Tobias as he goes out*). Ha, Ha! Tobias, how do you feel now? Do you think I shall hang, or will you die in the cell of a madhouse?

Exit

Tobias I don't know who you are, sir, or where I am; but let me beg of you to have the house of Sweeney Todd, in Fleet Street, searched, and you will find that he is a murderer. There are at least a hundred watches, rings, and trinkets, all belonging to the unfortunate persons who from time to time have met their death through him.

Jonas How uncommonly mad!

(*Jonas rings a bell – Keepers enter*).

Jonas You will take this lad under your care, as he seems extremely feverish and unsettled – shave his head and put a straight waistcoat on him. Let him be conveyed to one of the dark, damp cells, as too much light encourages his wild delirium.

Tobias I will die ere I submit to you or your vile myrmidons.

Jonas Then die, for no power can aid you.

Tobias Yes, there is one! (*Points upwards*) Heaven – which fails not to succour the helpless and persecuted.

(*Music – As Fogg and his men advance to seize Tobias, the window is shivered, Jarvis Williams dashes through, and protecting Tobias, confronts the others with his fists – Picture*).

Jarvis Stand off, you cowardly rascals, or I'll put the 'kiebosh' on the whole consarn.

Jonas The 'kiebosh?'

Jarvis Yes, it's a word of Greek extraction, signifying the upset of the apple cart – so – bunk! Tobias – assist me, and we'll lock up these rascals in their own madhouse

Music – Jarvis seizes Fogg by the throat, shakes him violently, and throws him to the ground; he fights the others off after sending one through window – Scene closes in

Scene 3
Front – Temple Stairs

Enter Colonel Jeffery

Jeffery Johanna will be true to her appointment, I have no doubt, though I have little to make known to her with respect to her missing lover. 'Tis strange since our last interview, a feeling to which I have been hitherto a stranger, should have assailed me – is it love? – yes, if Mark Ingestrie be dead, there is no dishonour in the acknowledgement, and a beautiful girl is not to be shut out from the pale of all affection, because the first person to whom her heart has warmed is no more

Enter Johanna

Jeffery Ah! she is here! Your servant, Miss Oakley, I rejoice again to meet you.

Johanna Pardon me if I dispense with the common observances of courtesy, as my mind is ill at ease. Tell me, I pray you, at once, if you bring sad or gladsome tidings.

Jeffery I have heard nothing, my good young lady, that can give you satisfaction concerning the fate of Mark Ingestrie, but I have suspicion that something serious must have happened to him.

Johanna I do sincerely hope from my heart that such a suspicion may be dissipated. I hope it, because I tell you freely and frankly, dim and obscure as the hope is that Mark has escaped the murderous hands raised against him.

Jeffery Do not speak despairingly.

Johanna Have I not cause for despair?

Jeffery You have cause for grief, but scarcely for despair; you are yet young, and let me entertain a hope –

Johanna I dare not. I know your words are kindly spoken, and kindly meant.

Jeffery You may well assure yourself that they are so.

Johanna I will ascertain the fate of Mark Ingestrie or perish.

Jeffery You alarm me by those words, Johanna; pardon me for using that name.

Johanna It requires no excuse; I am accustomed to be so addressed by all who feel a kindly interest in me. Call me Johanna, if you will, and I shall feel a greater assurance of your friendship and esteem.

Jeffery I will avail myself, then, of that permission, and again entreat you to leave the task to me of what attempts may be made to discover your lover's destiny – there must be danger in even inquiring for him, if there has been any foul play – and, therefore, I ask you to let that danger be mine alone.

Johanna I will accord with your wishes thus far, and promise that I will attempt nothing that shall not have the possibility of success attending it. Return here to-morrow at the same hour, and I will divulge to you the scheme I have in view with regard to this terrible mystery

Exit

Jeffery I love her, but she seems in no respect willing to enchain her heart. Alas! how sad it is for me, that the woman who above all others I would wish to call my own, instead of being a joy to me, I have only encountered that she might impart a pang to my soul

Enter Sweeney in a mask and cloak

Sweeney Colonel Jeffery, you are in danger, or I am much mistaken.
Jeffery Indeed! from whom, may I ask?
Sweeney Follow me, and you will soon find out your enemy.
Jeffery I must first know who and what you are before I consent to

be guided by a man who disguises his features by wearing a mask.

Sweeney I wear this mask for other purposes than concealment, which it is not judicious to explain at the present moment.

Jeffery Unless you are more explicit, I cannot, I consider, with safety to myself, consent to accompany you. What is your name?

Sweeney I am a man, and friendly disposed towards you.

Jeffery Nevertheless, this assertion fails to move my scruples.

Sweeney Why should it do so? But since you distrust me, I must leave, and you will remain without the information I was about to afford.

Jeffery Can it be? I am in doubt and fear how to act in this strange intercourse. Stay, my friend; since you say you are a friend to me, have you no token by which I may recognise amity?

Sweeney Yes, an undeniable one
(*Sweeney shows pearls – Chord*).

Jeffery Great Heaven! the string of pearls!

Sweeney Hasten with me to the shop of Sweeney Todd, the Barber of Fleet Street, and you will there learn who and what I am, and more of the owner of the gems than I can tell you here.

Jeffery Say you so? Then I have tarried too long; my impatience to fathom the mystery is so great, that I wish our onward speed could leave the wind behind us. Come, let no further time be lost by discourse

Rushes out

Sweeney So he has the pearls in his possession – good! I can now denounce him, and remove the grave suspicion that attaches itself to the name of Sweeney Todd

Exit

Scene 4
A Court of Justice – Colonel Jeffery, a prisoner

Judge That the prisoner at the bar is either an accomplice in the murder of the unfortunate man, or the actual perpetrator of the deed, there is, strong evidence – his absence from his home without any special reason, and the discovery of the pearls on his person, can lead to no other supposition than he must be in some way connected with the mysterious affair upon which we are adjudicating. What your motive was, prisoner, can be clearly conceived – your victim was the only bar between you and the object of your affection, Johanna Oakley.

Jeffery My lord, circumstances are against me. I can make no defence, can call no witness to prove my innocence – the stranger from whom I received those pearls has failed to make his appearance, and my bare word is nothing –

Judge The statement that you received those pearls from an unknown person in a public thoroughfare, is so improbable, that it cannot for a moment be accepted as truth.

Jeffery Then I must sink into the grave with ignominy, and my name, which has been hitherto untarnished by dishonour, become the scorn of all honest men.

Judge The only chance of life left you, prisoner, hangs on this mysterious letter; but its purpose is so vague that I cannot offer you any hope on that score. (*Reads letter*) 'Let the hand of justice for a moment be arrested, ere sentence is pronounced a witness will appear and confound the guilty in their hour of triumph'. That witness has not appeared, and there is but one other to examine. Let him stand forth

Sweeney Todd ascends witness-box

Jeffery My Lord, you will not take the evidence of this man, who –
Judge Silence! Make your deposition.
Sweeney My lord, I cannot but express my deep regret at being called to testify against one who has held the good opinion of the world, but duty and justice compel me to speak. I had taken into my service a fatherless lad named Tobias Ragg –
Judge So it has been stated in the earlier stages of the trial. Is that boy here?
Sweeney No, my lord! Since the murder of Mark Ingestrie, he can be found nowhere, though a diligent search has been made by the officers. It is supposed that, being an accomplice of the prisoner, he has –
(*A green light burns at the gauze window, and the form of Mark Ingestrie appears for an instant. Sweeney stands transfixed*)
Sweeney 'Twas his form – I saw it distinctly! Can the dead rise from the grave?
Judge Why do you pause, witness? – the Court is waiting.
(*Mark Ingestrie vanishes*).
Sweeney Gone! – 'twas the picture of a distraught brain. Your pardon, my lord – a sudden giddiness, nothing more.
Judge Produce the string of pearls stated to have been taken from the murdered man. (*The casket is produced*) Can you swear to them?
Sweeney Yes; the clasp is so curiously and cleverly devised, you might distinguish it among a thousand.
Judge And you have seen it in the possession of Mark Ingestrie?
Sweeney Have I seen it in his possession? Shame, shame – why do you ask such a question? Do you not see him coming to claim it? Ask him, I say – he is coming towards the judgment-seat
(*The figure of Mark Ingestrie appears behind Judge from panel*).
Look, my Lord Judge, Mark Ingestrie is by your side! Do not whisper to

him. Your ermined robe is stained with blood! Ha, ha, ha!

(*The figure again vanishes*).

Judge Witness, your words are incoherent and wild; your frantic gesture would lead us to suppose that reason had resigned her throne to mad despair. If your nerves are unstrung by the painful office you undertake, retire awhile to recover self-possession.

Sweeney Yes, it was a dark, foul deed; but heed not what you hear, Lord Judge – the prisoner has bought his victim! What! do you still remain, and suffer such corruptness? I feared it would come to this, and through accursed gold – for which men sell their souls and barter their eternal salvation! –

(*The figure of Mark Ingestrie stands beside Sweeney in the witness-box*). Ha, Ha! 'tis useless to deny my guilt; the very dead rise from their cerements to prove Sweeney Todd a murderer! (*Sweeney falls*).

All Mark Ingestrie, living?

Mark Yes, Mark Ingestrie, who, preserved from death by a miracle, returns to confound the guilty and protect the innocent. (*Tableau*)

Curtain

A REMINISCENCE

In 1842 respectable critics did not venture as far east as the Britannia, Hoxton, and so I have been unable to discover any press notices of the original production. However, in 'Two Views Of A Cheap Theatre' (Chapter four of *The Uncommercial Traveller*) Dickens gives his well-known impression of the Britannia, written some fifteen years after Sweeney made his first sanguinary appearance. In the front row of W M 's woodcut for *The Uncommercial Traveller* is a lady plainly suckling her babe (children in arms were admitted free), a practice which Thomas W Erle was still castigating twenty years later in the following account of a performance of *The String Of Pearls* from his *Letters From A Theatrical Scene-Painter*, published in 1880. Unfortunately Erle does not give us the date of his visit to the Great Theatre, but we can suppose it to have been in the 1870's.

The String of Pearls; or, The Barber Fiend of Fleet Street *at the Royal Britannia*

An evening at the Britannia during the run of 'The String of Pearls; or, The Barber Fiend of Fleet Street', *was to sup full of horrors. In the vulgar tongue of Hoxton and elsewhere, a full supper is called a 'tightener'. The expression is course, no doubt, yet suggestive. Abominably so. Going to see* The Barber Fiend *was a tightener of horrors, like a visit to the small room at Madame Tussaud's.*

The plot was as follows. The Barber Fiend murders in succession all his customers who come to him to be shaved, and then, by way of utilising them to the utmost possible extent, as well as of conveniently disposing of their bodies, makes them into pies, upon which such of the characters as are left to carry through the business of the piece, are regaled. A series of effects is produced by successive discoveries in the pies of what may be called 'internal evidence' of the true nature of their ingredients. Thus, one of the consumers finds in the first instance a woman's hair. This is not viewed as a circumstance of much gravity, since it is a matter of

263

A cheap theatre –
Saturday night,
Illustration from
Dickens' 'The
Uncommercial
Traveller'
(*Associate Book
Publishers Ltd*)

common experience that long hairs have an intrusive tendency which induces them to present themselves in combination with most alimentary substances. From buns, for example, they are as inseparable as grit. Lodging-house butter is usually fraught with them, and a marked affinity is developed in their constitution for London bread. Their frequent manifestation in mutton pies is natural enough, since it may so easily occur that the stumps of the horses' tails which supply the meat, may, on the occurrence of any press of business in the trade, be incompletely divested of them. This specific class of mutton is also distinguished by a wiry tenacity of fibre and sinew such as an advocate of 'muscular Christianity' might envy. It is attributable to the fact that the particular kind of 'sheep' which supplies it forms the source of motive power in the cab system of the metropolis.

But to return to the Barber's pies. The discovery of the hair is followed by that of a thumb nail, which appears to give rise to some indistinct, but uneasy, misgivings in the breast of the consumer. He pursues his meal with reflective hesitation, and with a zest which has now been obviously impaired by the operation of disquieting mental influences. The startling revelation of a brass button attached to a fragment of material substance of some kind or other which bears the aspect of having once formed a constituent portion of somebody or other's leather breeches, proves what is called 'a staggerer', and brings the repast to an abrupt and uncomfortable conclusion. The terrors of the scene culminate in the discovery of a full and detailed account of the whole matter set forth on the paper in which the pies had been wrapped. The narrative in question is accompanied by strictures on the conduct of the murderer, ably drawn up by his victims, and a free and explicit confession by himself is also appended to the document. At this point a torrent of fiddles is let loose, which rasp away for some moments with an energy worthy of the crisis.

The Barber is then taken into custody. But not by policemen. Not a bit of it! The R B management knows better than that. Police constables, no doubt, constitute a highly respectable and estimable body of men. Still, when they march in with the mechanical precision of automata, as stiff as a procession of animated lamp-posts, and with countenances fraught with utter unmeaningness, they present, it must be confessed, the very essence of the unpicturesque in effect. And their plain, matter-of-fact, truncheons are but silent and ineffective accessories to a situation. No. A party of supers rush in, attired in the uniforms in which they are accustomed to 'do' the Swedish army in Charles the Twelfth, and let off their muskets with signal intrepidity, firing earnestly upwards, as though anxious to hit some bird or other object which they must be supposed to have descried flitting about up among the gas battens. This light fusillade incidentally brings about the desirable result of creating a strong smell of gunpowder, and the noise throws a collection of urchins

265

at the door of the theatre, who cannot muster their sixpence for the gallery, into paroxysms of excitement to know what is going on inside. Of all the various sad forms of human destitution, perhaps the most affecting to contemplate is that of small boys who hang night after night about the doors of theatres but can't afford to go in.

The apprehension of the wicked barber necessarily brings the drama to its conclusion, and at this point, therefore, all the murdered characters reappear. If it be objected that the supposition of his guilt is weakened by, not to say is absolutely inconsistent with, the bodily presence of his victims – the ipsissima corpora delictorum – all as right and tight as can be, the answer is that the claims of the final tableau are paramount. The scene is then illuminated with red fire. An explanation of the propriety of this enrichment of the tableau is probably to be sought in the notion of its being in some degree typical of the subject-matter of the piece, since it is not within ordinary experience that the action of retributive justice is attended by any such meteoric phenomena. The whole of the characters then joined in a patriotic song, in which the invasion panic, and the discomfiture of the enemy by the gallantry of the Hoxton volunteers, together with any other points which may happen to be of general interest to the community at the particular moment, are very neatly and happily touched off.

Now if that isn't a 'strong' piece, pray what is ? If the reader does not agree with me in so characterising it, I should then be glad to be put in possession of his views as to what is a strong piece. Surely the conversion of one half of the characters in the drama into animal sustenance for the other half is an incident of a complexion sufficiently decided to arrest attention. In the ultimate dénouement of the plot more formidable and perplexing difficulties have to be encountered than even in the case of a certain novel which was published in parts in one of the penny awfuls some time ago. In that instance, the author, on getting into a tiff with the editor of the periodical, brought the story which was in course of publication to an abrupt and absurd conclusion by taking all his characters out in a boat to a spot about midway between Dover and Calais, and there upsetting them into the sea, and drowning them like a litter of mongrel puppies. Subsequently, however, being desirous to publish his work in a separate form on his own account, he became obliged to fish them all up again from the bottom of the sea, and set them to work out a proper conclusion as best they might. But in The Barber Fiend half the dramatis personae have to be resuscitated after mastication and digestion by the other half.

It was a disappointment that there was no call for the author, as I should have liked to have seen the party. His cast of mind must be a sort of

266

combination of *Lady Macbeth's* with that of the editor of the *Newgate Calendar*. He must reside in some spectral and gloomy scene, such as Gower Street, or the immediate vicinity of Cold Bath Fields' Prison, where the picture of desolate and dreary waste which is ever presented to his view is unrelieved by any stray gleam of a cheerful tint. Moreover, the conception and composition of The Barber Fiend must have taken place in his moments of acute indigestion. Perverted fancies of the imagination like this are usually the result of functional disorder in the system.

Joking apart, I think that the representation of such a mass of unnatural and repulsive horrors is extremely wrong and pernicious, and the subsequent astonishing resuscitation of the victims does little to rectify it. If the Drama be 'holding the mirror up to nature', it should also be remembered that there is such a thing, and a very real and common thing too, as holding nature up to the mirror. For the contemplation, or vivid description, of an act of wickedness, frequently, as is perfectly well known, inoculates weak minds with an irresistible impulse to do the same kind of thing. It was in this course that Courvoisier, who murdered his master, Lord William Russell, declared himself to have been brought to the gallows, and there have been many similar instances. Besides which, it isn't the pleasantest thing in the world to sit for an hour or two looking at murders, although they are but sham ones, nor is it in good taste to have too many of them on the stage.

Horace, who is a good authority in such matters, doesn't at all approve of the conversion of the stage into an abattoir. He says

> Ne pueros coram populo Medea trucidet,

which means, being translated, '*Medea shouldn't put her children to death before the eyes of the people*'. And he adds, as if with express reference to The Barber Fiend,

> Aut humana palam coquat exta nefarius Atreus,

'*nor should wicked Atreus cook human flesh in public*'. Of course neither Horace, nor anyone else, would be so absurdly over-particular as to forbid the doing of any deeds of blood whatever on the stage, as, for example, that in the last scene in Rosmunda where Ristori corkscrews her hand and wrist into Mademoiselle Picchiotino's back hair, and then dabs a nasty-looking dagger into the small of her back. Of all situations on the stage that one is the finest and most terrific. It makes the heart of any impressionable spectator give such knocks against the inside of his waistcoat as a peremptory ghost might be supposed to do on getting

267

impatient when the bad man whom it had come to terrify wouldn't wake to be lectured.

But at the Britannia, where the victims are worked off in a mere business-like way by a commonplace dab with a knife, and where the butchering process is not relieved or embellished by any grandeur of attitude or tableau, it would be much better that some such expedient should be made use of as that adopted in the old Greek plays, where the chorus came in and described in chronological order what was to be supposed to have already taken place elsewhere. Or else that Horace's suggestion should be adopted that these little matters should be attended to privately behind the scenes, and that somebody on the stage should state to the audience what he is to be conceived as actually witnessing. If the latter plan were resorted to, a murder would be sufficiently re- presented by any character in the piece keeping his eyes rivetted on the wing, and preserving a display of hot excitement sustained during the delivery of some such interjectional exclamations as the following: 'See ! he relieves him of his head.' 'Now he lets a little daylight into his wind- pipe !' 'By Jove if he hasn't been and whipped a long knife into his heart.' 'Now he fetches him a crack on his skull !' 'That last dig in the eye was a nasty one !' and so on.

Before dismissing the subject of stage murders, one perplexing feature in the mode of their actual perpetration may be adverted to, which is this. When the intending assassin seems to be on the point of putting his purpose into execution, it is often the case that he is standing immediately behind, or close by the side of, his unsuspecting victim, in so very comfortable and convenient a position for sliding a knife cosily in between his ribs, or otherwise surreptitiously administering to him his quietus, that one could almost fancy that a man of infirm moral principle, on finding himself so circumstanced, might actually be impelled to commit a murder which he had not previously contemplated by the mere irresistible temptation of so brilliant an opportunity for working off his man with tastefulness and despatch. It is easy to conceive his deploring in all sincerity the lamentable necessity, imposed upon him by the simple force of circumstances, of knocking on the head the object, possibly, of his cordial esteem, and towards whom he maintains the whole time, without suspension, a feeling of the most genial kindness.

Yet your stage assassin is never found to avail himself of any such advantageous opening thus presenting itself. Instead of that, he makes off to the third entrance, where he pokes his head and body forward, as coarse women do when in a violent paroxysm of scolding, and then hisses forth hostile sentiments, for the express purpose, as it would seem, of *putting the subject of his intended operations thoroughly on his guard. The natural consequence of this is that he becomes involved in a course of wrestling with a desperate man before the accomplishment of his purpose, and he is thereby rendered so breathless that the emphasis of the final 'dai !' is much impaired by lack of steam.*

The proceedings on the stage, of a midnight assassin who finds his victim asleep, are no less inscrutable. He looks at him – starts – recoils – then turns to the audience, and in a whisper fraught with tremendous significance puts them in possession of a circumstance which they have already had abundant opportunity of observing for themselves, namely, that 'he sleeps !' He then proceeds to execute a series of brisk, but elaborate, manoeuvres about the stage, comprising a body of tactics sufficient to carry a small army through an ordinary campaign. I have never enjoyed the advantage of witnessing the perpetration of a murder off the stage, but it would seem to be unlikely that when such transactions take place in real life they are attended by the complicated evolutions above described. They correspond in point of eccentricity to the funny things which some people do on receiving a letter whose contents they are dying to know. They contemplate it externally in every possible point of view, and the aspect which it presents when held topsy turvy would appear to be a source to them of the most animated interest. It is subjected to a protracted course of manipulation, and in that process is done everything in the world to but read.

By the way, I used the word 'enjoy' just now, with reference to witnessing a murder, in the conventional sense in which one occasionally represents oneself to have 'much pleasure' in accepting somebody or other's 'kind invitation', although feeling all the time that it would be a far less severe penance to go and have a tooth out, or listen to a sermon a whole blessed hour long, and scrupulously purged from the slightest semblance whatever of any meaning, than fulfil the engagement. Similarly, it is a common expression among Sussex rustics that So and So 'enjoys' very bad health.

The consummation of a tragical situation at the R B is usually intensified by the tune of 'I loves a drop of good beer', played pensively. Objections might of course be made by tiresome rigorists to the adoption of so genial and festive an air as an accompaniment to proceedings partaking in no degree of a convivial spirit. But those who resort to a theatre in a mean and nasty spirit of petty captiousness are in no proper frame of mind for appreciating the pathetic and touching effects which the management has had an eye to. For my own part, I can conscientiously affirm, in the beautiful kind of language used by speakers at public dinners, that on all these occasions 'my emotions are of such a character as to be unlike anything which they do not resemble'.

The Barber was well played by a Mr B Savile. Dramatic impressions are so strong with me that I should not go out of my way to get my hair cut in Fleet Street just at present. The uncomfortable atmosphere of suspicion and distrust which already envelops the rations of opaque slime and gristle conventionally known as mutton pies is amply sufficient of itself, without the addition of any further unpleasant misgivings which might be suggested by The Barber Fiend, *to discourage one from partaking of those ambiguous delicacies. When I was at school, a man who sold mutton pies to the boys went the way of all piemen, and his son succeeded to the business. It was currently reported and believed that* no funeral ever took place. *This, under the circumstances, was a tremendous fact. For it afforded room for surmising that the expression that the deceased had 'gone the way of all flesh' was pregnant with unusual significance. If it had been stated that he had 'gone to his last home', his place of final rest and his son's mutton pies, might, not impossibly, under the particular conditions of his disappearance, have proved to be convertible terms.*

Stephan played a dumb black boy. Her pantomime was very graceful and pretty, but her appearance in such a character seemed rather like the case of a star fallen from its sphere and turned rushlight. She reversed the ordinary course of Nature by converting herself from a butterfly into a grub. It is a sad misfortune to know that Stephan is not only married, but that her husband has a close interest in cabs. The halo of poetry which encircles a graceful danseuse is rudely dispelled by an acquaintance with such abominably prosaic circumstances as these.

Let me see – who else was there worthy of mention? There was a beefeater who played a conspicuous part. This, I apprehend, was because, the scene being laid in Fleet Street, the colour of the costumes and accessories was unavoidably cold and sombre. This drawback was rectified by the artful expedient of introducing a beefeater, and thus supplying in the most compendious form possible a considerable body of warm colour. Under the circumstances of his appearance, the remarks which were assigned to him were of course on purely general topics, and wholly divested of any connexion whatever with the business of the piece. I was pained to observe the embarrassment to which he was subjected, arising from the obvious fact of his having taken more than was good for him to drink before coming upon the stage. He clutched his halbert convulsively, under the impression that it was a fixed object. His gait, for the same reason, was somewhat devious and uncertain. And in walking he planted each foot down, alternately, with a laboured stamp, as though his path were beset by a series of blackbeetles which he was bent on exterminating by scrunching.

The leading lady in the play was doubtless introduced with a corres-

ponding view to exclusively spectacular effects, since how she was supposed to connect herself with anybody or anything else in the drama was wholly unsusceptible of explanation. She was got up as a shepherdess, or what is known as a 'fidèle Bergère'. Now a shepherdess is clearly a Harris. Who ever saw one out of a picture, or off a piece of china ? Since her duty was simply to form an embellishment of the stage, and to be wholly independent of the transactions which took place there, it was judiciously considered that she might as well be put into the most ornamental guise which suggested itself. She looked, therefore, as if she were a coloured illustration to Theocritus galvanised into vitality, or as if she had stepped out of a book of Swiss costumes.

A low comedian, whose name I didn't attain the advantage of discovering, got a reception, and forthwith addressed himself to give divers sly winks, and execute a series of convolutions of his person, which appeared to be considered as powerful strokes of pleasantry, and brought down the gods. The entertainment was of so rare and subtle a quality that it eluded my best efforts to detect the secret of it, or to participate in its relish. The only notion which his gesticulations conveyed to my mind was that, like Miss Pross, in Dickens' Tale of Two Cities, *he was labouring under an acute attack of 'the jerks'.*

It is desirable that the practice adopted by Hoxton mothers of taking their babies to the theatre should be discontinued. The small miserables are brought out at the end of the evening with their feathers all rumpled, and their poor little eyes all glazed and fishy like those of old debauchees. Their general effect, too, conveys the impression of their having been sat upon, and otherwise exposed to gross personal contumely.

In the Biglow papers, some slaveholder or other talks of wishing to purchase 'a low-priced baby' to bring up. Some of these embryo members of the R B public could only, if offered for sale, be got off at a wretchedly low figure, as damaged articles. Besides, too, their own personal sufferings, they are very undesirable neighbours to sit by. For, in the first place, they are apt to be – well – I forbear to press the details with unpleasant explicitness, and will therefore only say, in general terms – damp.

An artless and impulsive girl, all poetry, warmth, and sensibility, a fresh and fervent product of Nature with the first bloom and gloss still on it, is usually spoken of (and the expression is used in a perfectly commendatory spirit) as 'a gushing young thing'. But when the 'young thing' in question is a baby, and the 'gushing' consists in a profuse secretion of moisture arising from an over-industrious action of the salivatory glands, wherewith the producer slobbers and bedabbles itself till it presents a slimy and gelatinous appearance, which is anything but alluring, one is naturally desirous to keep safely out of the range of contact. Babies, too, as has been observed by somebody or other, in one of their worst failings, resemble Cherubim – namely, that they 'continually do cry'.

These little weaknesses, which seem to be inherent in their constitution, naturally prove the source of obloquy and objection to them in the judgment and feeling of the general public. And it is in these considerations, no doubt, that one may descry the grounds of the hard-hearted complacency, not to say satisfaction, with which the various indignities and vicissitudes to which sham babies in pantomimes are subjected, are viewed by the spectators. For it is some slight gratification to the vindictive feelings with which people are apt to regard infants, to see their little tormentors of real life thoroughly well battered and bullied in effigy. It is for similar reasons that a clown, when he accomplishes the discomfiture of policemen, is always secure of the genuine and hearty sympathies of the turbulent and disorderly spirits in the gallery, who regard the officers of the law as their natural enemies and oppressors. The exclusion, therefore, of babies from theatres should be rigid and imperative.

Very different from the condition of the poor babies is that of the youths in the gallery, who are gifted with a flow of exuberant animal spirits which find a safety-valve in shrill whistlings, reminding one of Virgil's account of the storm, where Œlous lets loose the wind, and

'Una Eurusque Notusque ruunt', *etc, etc.*

Since the temperature up in their sixpenny heaven is so high (there was a fat little boy up there who I thought would have been melted and had to be taken home in a gallipot), they find it 'cool and convanient' to sit without their coats. They evince, too, a noble independence of bearing and sentiment towards the swells in the body of the house (who are in this case the counter-skippers of Kingsland and Dalston) by turning their backs to the chandelier, and sitting along the gallery rail like a row of sparrows on a telegraph wire. In this position they confront their friends in the back settlements, and exchange with them a light fussillade of badinage, *principally couched in idiomatic expressions of remarkable vigour and terseness, which is sustained with much animation during the time that the curtain is down between the pieces.*

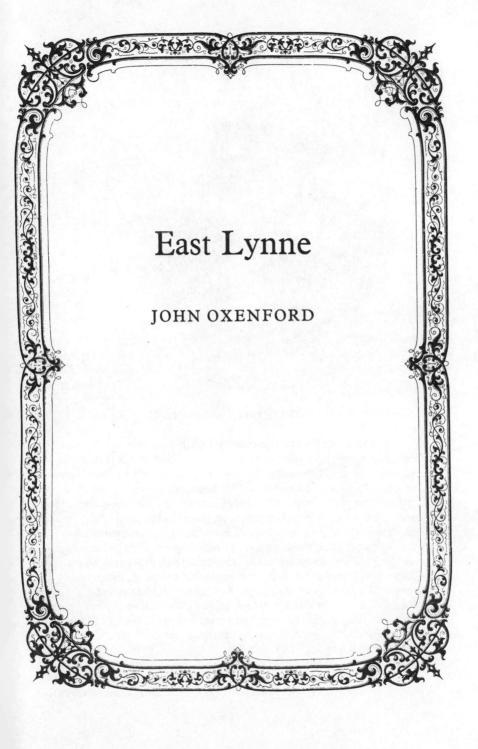

East Lynne

JOHN OXENFORD

John Oxenford
(*Enthoven Collec-
tion*)

JOHN OXENFORD (1812/77)

Oxenford's early life is curiously like that of so many nineteenth-
century playwrights: humble beginnings, articled to a solicitor, almost
entirely self-educated, and a flair for languages – in this case German,
Italian, French and Spanish as well as Latin and Greek. Despite his legal
studies, Oxenford wrote the money market columns for the *Times*,
assisted by his uncle in whose office he worked after qualifying, besides
somehow finding the time to become a noted amateur mathematician.

Again the parallel with other dramatists can be seen in his volumin-
ous contributions to many of the periodicals and magazines of the day.
Unlike his peers, however, he had some claims to be an intellectual – he
translated a number of foreign authors of stature (including Calderon,
Goethe and Molière), edited a German-English dictionary, and was the
first in Britain to appreciate and write upon the philosophy of Schopen-
hauer. Nor did he ignore his native language, for he produced prose and
poetry of 'much facility', and was described as one of the 'ripest and most
variously endowed scholars of our time'.

It is strange that such a widely-read and culturally aware man should
have been attracted to the lowest forms of the drama, but such was the

case. He wrote some ninety stage pieces which included (especially in his early days) all the usual farces, burlesques and melodramas on well-trodden themes. Guy Fawkes, Jack Sheppard, and the example of his work included here, *East Lynne*, were three of his subjects; he also wrote a large number of libretti for long-forgotten operas. Most of this output was not of course original – even his Jack Sheppard play, first seen at the Queen's Theatre in 1873 under the title of *Old London* was 'prepared' from the French. Even Oxenford must have been a little ashamed of this one, for the author was given out as one Frederick Boyle.

His first stage-piece was *My Fellow Clerk*, which appeared at the English Opera House in 1835 and attracted little interest, but his second, given at the same theatre in the same year, was *A Day Well Spent*. This was much more successful, being published and frequently performed on both sides of the Channel.

Sometime about the year 1850 John Oxenford became the dramatic critic of *The Times*, a position he held for over a quarter of a century. A very kindly and amiable man, his value as a critic was lessened by his excessive soft-heartedness – he couldn't bear the thought of hurting anyone's feelings. As he wrote himself, 'none of those whom I censured ever went home disconsolate and despairing'.

Perhaps Oxenford's main claim to fame is that it was in his *Ivy Hall* (yet another adaptation from the French) that Irving made his London début in 1859. Irving, however, was so disappointed at the minuteness of his role (six lines) that he asked to be released from his contract.* Not that Oxenford took the slightest offence, for with his characteristic good nature he was subsequently to extol in the most extravagant terms Irving's performance in *The Bells* (1871), and referred to his *Richelieu* two years later as 'nothing but genius'.

In 1875 Oxenford was received into the Roman Catholic Church, and at about the same time retired through ill-health. He died at 28 Trinity Square, Southwark, on February 21st, 1877, a life-long bachelor.

East Lynne and *Uncle Tom's Cabin* are unquestionably the most renowned melodramas on both sides of the Atlantic, with the former offering the prime example of the erring heroine. Lady Audley,† it will be remembered, went raving mad, Nelly Armroyd in *Lost in London* died miserably, and poor Lady Isabel loses her life and her child as well – when a heroine sinned, it was essential that she pay for her transgressions. Later adventuresses, as they were called, were Wilde's Mrs Cheveley and

---

*Irving had appeared in Oxenford's drama *The Porter's Knot* in the previous year at the Olympic, Edinburgh

†From Angela Braddon's three-volume novel, *Lady Audley's Secret*, 1862

Pinero's one and only Paula Tanqueray, but by this time such 'ladies-with-a-past' were allowed to arouse a modicum of compassion, and even occasionally to live more or less happily ever after.

Mrs Henry Wood's* most famous novel, *East Lynne*, appeared in 1861, and was immediately pounced upon by scores of recorded and unrecorded dramatists and burlesquers. The first stage adaptation in this country of what can perhaps be called the first High Society melodrama was by W Archer (not William Archer, the critic – heaven forfend!) and produced at the Effingham Saloon, Whitechapel, in 1864 under the title of *The Marriage Bells; or The Cottage on The Cliff*. Other mutilators of this lachrymose work were Gus West, Charles Embley, Ned Albert, J Pitt Hardacre, Lilla Wilde, Herbert Shelley, and T A Palmer. It was this last adaptor who introduced into the dialogue the most famous line in melodrama, 'Dead! Dead! And never called me mother!' This version is the best known, probably because it was published by French's, but it is pretty poor stuff, even by the standards of the time. I have chosen Oxenford's, not because it is a particularly superior piece, but because it was an earlier version (1866, at the Surrey) and because of the intrinsic interest in his work.

Lady Isabel was of course a gift for leading ladies, among them Caroline Heath (Mrs Wilson Barrett) in Frank Harvey's version at the Olympic in 1879, and Avonia Jones (Mrs Gustavus Brooke), the American wife of the eminent tragedian, who made the success of her career in the role.

*née Ellen Price, 1814–188?

276

EAST LYNNE

Dramatis Personae

As first performed at the Surrey Theatre
February 5th, 1866

Earl Mount Severn by Mr C Butler
Captain Levison by Mr E F Edgar
Archibald Carlyle by Mr J Fernandez
Justice Hare by Mr Maclean
Richard Hare by Mr Henry Haynes
Mr Dill by Mr Henry Thompson
William by Miss Charlton
Isabel/Lucy by Miss N Newham
1st Policeman by Mr Callbrook
2nd Policeman by Mr Harris
Lady Isabel Carlyle and
Madame Vine both by Miss Avonia Jones
Miss Cornelia Carlyle by Mrs Moreton Brooks
Mrs Hare by Mrs G Howe
Wilson by Miss C Newham
Suzanne by Miss A Newham
Barbara Hare by Miss Rose Ogilvy
Joyce by Miss Stafford

Act 1
Scene 1: *the garden of Justice Hare's house*
Scene 2: *a country view*
Scene 3: *an apartment in East Lynne*

Act 2
Scene 1: *the Blue Parlour in East Lynne*
Scene 2: *a room at an inn in Grenoble*

Act 3
Scene 1: *the apartment in East Lynne*
Scene 2: *a street in West Lynne*
Scene 3: *the nursery at East Lynne*

Act 4
Scene 1: *the street in West Lynne*
Scene 2: *Lady Isabel's apartment in East Lynne*

EAST LYNNE

Act I

Scene I
The garden of Justice Hare's house. Barbara is discovered

Barbara No, he never cared for me, and was I in the grave tomorrow I should soon be forgotten. I almost wish I was there now . . . why can I not forget the dream of my youth ? Years have passed since he brought his wife to the house of her fathers; her children gather round him and still my old infatuation is as strong as ever. Oh, this weary misery!

Enter Mrs Hare

Mrs Hare Barbara!
Barbara Mother.
Mrs Hare You are sad, my child. Ah, no wonder! This suspense about my poor Richard is unbearable. Not one word for so long to say whether he is alive or dead to his father, as you know too well, I dare not breathe his name.
Barbara My father seems more incensed against him than ever.
Mrs Hare As long as the suspicion of murder clings to him his father will be his bitterest foe. Hush – he comes this way

Enter Justice Hare

Barbara Are you going out, father ?
Hare Is that any business of yours, young lady ?
Mrs Hare I suppose you are going to see your old friend, Mr Carlyle ?
Hare Then you suppose wrong. My old friend, as you call him, does not stand so high in my good books as he did before he married the stuck-up penniless daughter of that bankrupt Earl. I suppose he thought that having bought East Lynne he was bound to take the livestock with it.
Mrs Hare Mr Carlyle saw how unhappy the bereaved Lady Isabel was at the house of her haughty relation, Lady Mount Severn –

Hare Yes, and to rescue her he sacrificed himself.

Barbara Sacrificed!

Hare He ought to have married you, Barbara. I'm sure you always had a sneaking fondness for him.

Mrs Hare Husband, you quite embarrass the girl.

Hare Well, perhaps I was wrong. Woman is one of the puzzles I could never rightly make out . . . but what do you think of his keeping that good-looking scamp Captain Levison always sauntering about his house? I tell you what, Mrs Hare, you are not quite so good-looking as you were a few years ago, and in your best days you were not a patch upon Lady Isabel, but hang me if I should like to see a fellow like that Levison dangling about you even now!

Mrs Hare Husband, you are in a strange mood today. I hardly know whether to call it good or bad.

Hare Well, whatever it is, my constitutional walk will take it off. Will you go with me? (*Going*).

Mrs Hare Yes, perhaps you'll call at the Carlyle's. Little William is said to be ill . . .

Exeunt Justice and Mrs Hare

Barbara Captain Levison! That rumour that he was attached to Lady Isabel . . . it is possible that her love for him is not altogether extinguished in spite of her marriage with Archibald Carlyle. No, no – I will dismiss the fancy, it is unworthy of her and of me

Richard appears

Who is that strange man? Who and what are you?

Richard Do you not know me, Barbara?

Barbara My brother! O, Richard, how you terrify me! I am rejoiced to see you alive, but still, the risk you run in venturing here –

Richard I know, Barbara: I risk my neck, neither more nor less. Still, I can't live for ever as I have been living; I could better myself if I had a little money. That's what brings me here. I watched till I saw my father go out of the front door. I suppose he is as deeply incensed against me as ever?

Barbara Quite. You know his stern sense of justice.

Richard I tell you that I had no more to do with Hallijohn's murder than you had.

Barbara Mother always says it was Bethel.

Richard Bethel is a poacher, but of that black job he is as innocent as the babe unborn. It was Thorne who murdered Hallijohn.

Barbara I never heard the name – who is Thorne?

Richard I don't know. Nobody knows Thorne but Affy Hallijohn, the murdered man's daughter.

Barbara For shame – do not mention the name of that creature before me.

Richard I wish I had never heard it myself: that girl has been the curse of my life. Oh, Barbara, I feel exhausted. I think a glass of father's old port might do me good.

Barbara You shall have it. (*Going into the house*) Poor Richard! Poor outcast! (*Exit*).

Richard In the place of my birth, almost beneath my father's roof, and forced to conceal myself like an escaped felon. (*Walks up-stage*)

Enter Captain Levison

Levison I should like to have a peep at this cottage beauty . . . nobody here ? (*Sees Richard*) My good young man, this I believe is Justice Hare's house ?

Richard Yes, sir – (*Recognises Levison. In terror*) Oh! (*Cowers*).

Levison What the deuce – ? No, on second thoughts it may be best not to enquire further. (*Exit*).

Richard (*Dazed*) I could not be deceived . . .

Enter Barbara with glass and port decanter

Richard Thanks (*Swallowing hastily*) – another! Barbara . . . sister . . . I have seen him!

Barbara Whom ?

Richard That man – that murderer, Thorne!

Barbara Why did you not follow him instantly ?

Richard Because my joints were stiffened, my feet had no power of motion; because I felt as one who looks upon a ghost!

Barbara Richard, is this an illusion ? Do not deceive me.

Richard I see you still doubt my innocence.

Hare (*Calling from within the house*) Barbara!

Barbara Father's voice – he has returned! Fly – fly!

Richard But how shall we meet again ?

Barbara The grove – at ten tonight.

Hare (*Within*) Barbara! Barbara!

Richard (*Going*) You wil not fail ? (*Exit*).

Barbara Poor Richard. I will believe him

(*As she goes into the house, the scene changes*)

Scene 2

A country view

Enter Levison

Levison I wonder who that was? He stared at me as if I was a hobgoblin, but I didn't recollect his face . . . humph! That fool Carlyle is very kind in letting me hide myself from my creditors, and flirt with my old flame Lady Isabel, but I wish to heaven his house was situated somewhere else. Anyone who would recollect the particulars of my last visit to this neighbourhood would be awfully inconvenient . . . (*Exit*)

Enter Dill and Cornelia Carlyle

Cornelia Mr Dill, you may talk till the sun rises tomorrow, you won't alter my opinion. I don't like her, I tell you, and there's the long and short of it.

Dill Miss Cornelia, you are a sensible woman, and I mean to pay you a high compliment when I say that I almost look upon you as a lawyer in petticoats.

Cornelia Much obliged, Dill.

Dill Don't mention it. Now what astonishes me is that you can indulge in such absurd prejudices against Lady Isabel.

Cornelia If my brother chose to indulge in such a superfluity as a wife, why couldn't he take one after my pattern? He was a fool to marry her, there's no doubt about that.

Dill Recall, Lady Isabel is the daughter of an Earl.

Cornelia A pretty Earl, who died so immensely in debt that his very body was arrested!

Dill More shame on them who committed the outrage. Well, poor Lady Isabel was forced to hire as a dependant with her father's kinsman and successor, the present Lord Mount Severn. Your brother rescued her from the oppressor, purchased the mansion of her father's ancestors and made her the mistress of it. Where is the folly, Miss Cornelia?

Cornelia To tell you the truth, I am afraid that the folly is in me and that my brother is a fine noble creature whom I don't appreciate half so much as I ought. It was only natural if I looked upon Lady Isabel as a sort of usurper when she gained affections that had belonged to me alone.

Dill Yes, and I'll bear in mind that every one of the fair sex loves to wear the etceteras* and that consequently when there are two women to one pair of continuations we may look out for squalls. Bye the bye, having accompanied you so far I must hurry to the Office to complete a marriage settlement. Ta–ta! (*Exit*).

---

*In the original MS this was 'breeches'

282

Cornelia It is a very humiliating thing to say, but I am afraid that to my brother's wife I'm a nasty, cantankerous, ill-conditioned old creature. I'll mend! I'll reform and be pleasant – ah, but to begin to be pleasant at my age when one has gloried in being despotic for so many years – it's hard work after all! (*Exit*)

Scene 3
An apartment in East Lynne

Joyce and Wilson are discovered on

Wilson Well, Lady Isabel is such a dear creature. I can't make out why her last maid left her.

Joyce She said that Miss Cornelia's manners were too rough for her delicate feelings. For my part I could never have left such a darling as our Lady Isabel. I suppose as you quitted the Hare's you find her a great deal better than Miss Barbara?

Wilson Well, Miss Barbara was very good at first, but her temper has sadly changed.

Joyce Indeed!

Wilson They do say that Miss Barbara had secretly picked out Mr Carlyle for herself and that consequently she looked upon our dear Lady Isabel as –

Enter Lady Isabel

Isabel Wilson, you can leave the room.

Wilson Thank ye, my lady. (*Aside*) Oh, gemini! (*Exit*).

Isabel What was Wilson talking about?

Joyce Oh, I scarcely know, my lady. You see, she lived with the Hares, and was rather finding fault with Miss Barbara's temper, and servants will gossip –

Isabel That's enough! You need not tell me any more. The Hares are nothing to me. Leave me, Joyce.

Joyce Yes, my lady. (*Aside*) She heard more than she ought or I'm not a Christian woman! (*Exit*).

Isabel Barbara, yes, that was the name I heard. The name of the woman whose image is ever present to my mind – as that of my evil genius. And why? She once loved Archibald, that is all! Is there the faintest whisper that he ever returned her love? No – I am the only cause of my own wretchedness. Oh, husband, I will believe in you. My trust in you as my Rock of Safety

Enter Carlyle

Carlyle Isabel, my love!

Isabel Archibald!

Carlyle You seemed lost in thought.

Isabel I was, for I was thinking how I am indebted to you to an extent I can never repay.

Carlyle Say not you are indebted. If you are happy I am more than repaid. When first you consented to become my wife, you told me that if you did not exactly love me then, you might learn to in time. The time has arrived, hasn't it, Isabel?

Isabel Long ago – if the love you require is a love founded on the deepest esteem, a love that has not sprung from mere caprice but is the result of earnest admiration, such is mine.

Carlyle Well, you do not describe a very Romantic passion, but –

Isabel Perhaps if I tell you that my love is strongly tinged with jealousy...

Carlyle Oh, jealousy I grant is romantic enough! Pray, do you even find an object for this interesting passion?

Isabel Oh, dear, yes. I am getting tired of – Captain Levison's stay here. He seems to interrupt our domestic tranquillity.

Carlyle Nay, I thought he was rather a favourite of yours. Even if it were otherwise, we could hardly refuse shelter to a friend who wishes to conceal himself from his creditors.

Isabel True, true.

Carlyle At all events, if your jealousy is limited to Captain Levison, it will not –

Isabel Archibald, you have long been acquainted with the Hare family?

Carlyle Certainly. Our fathers have been friends for I don't know how many generations.

Isabel I dare say you used to meet oftener than of late?

Carlyle Oh, yes, a great deal oftener. They have not gone out much since that terrible affair of Richard's.

Isabel I suppose you knew Richard from childhood, and – Barbara, too?

Carlyle Yes! They used to call me their old brother.

Isabel Was Barbara pretty as a child?

Carlyle The sweetest little thing you can imagine.

Isabel Of course, she is extremely handsome. Everybody can see that...

Carlyle Isabel, why this unusual tone?

Isabel I don't know – is it unusual? (*Pause*) Archibald, did you – did you – ?

Carlyle Well! I am all attention!

Isabel Did you ever love Barbara Hare?

Carlyle So that's the drift of this long cross-examination, is it? My beloved Isabel, I never loved but one woman in the world and that woman

I made my wife.

Isabel Archibald, of late my love has grown until I feel you are so precious to me that if you ventured to deceive me even in thought, everything – my soul's welfare – would be lost.

Carlyle My dear child, don't distress yourself in this way. I never thought of loving her, I assure you. Stay – I think I hear my sister coming.

Isabel She must not see that I have been weeping. I'll retire. (*Exit*).

Carlyle Dear, doating creature!

Enter Cornelia

Cornelia Pretty goings-on, very pretty indeed!

Carlyle Why, sister, you seem quite agitated, quite in a fluster.

Cornelia Prepare for something astounding. The dress-maker has actually sent a new dress. There, I see you don't believe me.

Carlyle I should be very unreasonable if I doubted you, when I ordered the dress myself.

Cornelia You ordered it? Oh, very well, go to Ruin your own way! I'll give you another piece of my mind. I hate Captain Levison, and for a man I think him rather good-looking. Couldn't you contrive to give him fewer opportunities of talking with Lady Isabel?

Carlyle Silence, Corny!

Cornelia I will not say another word, except that I look upon Captain Levison as a mocking, smooth-faced undermining scoundrel! There! (*Exit*).

Carlyle Poor Corny. What a taste the ladies seem to have for jealousy, to be sure

Enter Barbara Hare

Barbara Oh, Mr Carlyle!

Carlyle Barbara Hare!

Barbara I am so glad to find you at home. None can aid us like you, with your legal knowledge and experience. My poor brother Richard has re-appeared!

Carlyle Indeed!

Barbara I have advised him to state his whole case plainly to you. I will bring him to the grove at ten this evening, near this house. Can you be there?

Carlyle Well, in such an emergency I can't refuse. But I suppose I may explain the cause of my absence to Lady Isabel?

Barbara No, no – when my brother's life is at stake I cannot trust anyone with our secret, till all is cleared

Levison enters unseen

Carlyle Be it so, then.

Barbara Mind – 10 o'clock – the grove. (*Exit*).

Carlyle Rather an unlucky coincidence this appointment, and Lady Isabel's avowal of her jealousy ... hum ... how shall I contrive it ?

Enter Dill, with lawyer's bag

Dill Oh, if you please, sir, as Farmer Coulter is obliged to go to London in a hurry, I brought him from the office that he may execute the deed here.

Carlyle Where is he ?

Dill In the Blue Parlour, sir.

Carlyle Very good. (*Aside*) How shall I contrive it ? (*Exit*).

Dill (*Sees Levison, who has advanced*) Holloa, Captain Levison ! Fine evening.

Levison Very, Mr Dill.

(*Dill goes out, with his bag*)

Well, I think I can turn this secret assignation between Barbara and virtuous Mr Carlyle to good account ... that they mean no harm by their meeting I'll be sworn, but that I can make harm of it I am positive

Enter Lady Isabel

Levison Ah, Lady Isabel, you have not – ? No, of course, you have not – you came another way.

Isabel Have not what, Captain Levison ?

Levison Have not met Miss Barbara Hare ?

Isabel Has she been here ?

Levison Oh, yes, but her business seemed to be with Carlyle rather than you. They conversed together very privately.

Isabel They were aware of your presence ?

Levison Well, to confess the truth –

Isabel To confess the truth you have condescended to play the part of a dishonourable eavesdropper – of a paltry spy !

Levison Lady Isabel, the manner in which facts are obtained, unworthy though it be, does not invalidate the facts themselves.

Isabel Too true – too true – oh !

Levison And though I appear laden with the hideous sin of ingratitude, you will find some extenuation in the circumstance that your husband transformed Lady Isabel Vane, the virgin idol of my boyhood into Lady Isabel Carlyle, the wife of the rich country lawyer; that he has secured a heart which was once not wholly indifferent to me, and which when I remember those few happy days at Boulogne I sometimes flatter myself is not altogether indifferent to me now.

286

Isabel Cease, Francis, cease! Leave me – leave me, I implore.

Levison I obey. (*Aside*) I do leave you to watch the assignation in the grove. (*Exit*).

Isabel What a frightful state of doubt is this! Is there no truth in the world – is even Archibald deceitful?

Enter Carlyle

Carlyle Isabel, I have an appointment tonight – how pale you look!

Isabel Do I? I am sure I know not why. Go, as you have an appointment. It is rather late, is it not?

Carlyle (*Aside*) It would be best to tell her all, but I dare not betray Richard's secret. (*Aloud*) In our profession there are secrets which we cannot divulge even to those to whom we confide our whole happiness. Goodbye for an hour or so, Isabel, perhaps tomorrow you will know all. (*Exit*).

Isabel His manner is confused. There is something more than ordinary business in this – Gracious Heaven! Everything tends to confirm my worst suspicions!

Enter Cornelia

Cornelia Oh, Lady Isabel, I hope you will excuse the liberty – while the dressmaker was here with your new dress, I availed myself of the opportunity to countermand the new frock you ordered for Miss Isabel.

Isabel I will bear this intereference no longer! Recollect that though I am the wife of a country attorney I am still the daughter of an Earl!

Cornelia Gracious me! Have your own way, Lady Isabel. When the country attorney is brought to ruin, I hope you'll be able to live on the family coronet! (*Exit*).

Isabel These petty annoyances and this great misery will drive me mad!

Enter Levison

Levison Lady Isabel, I need not ask if Mr Carlyle's here. I have just seen him in the grove.

Isabel Very likely. He has gone out on business.

Levison Oh, indeed? He told you that he had to meet Barbara Hare?

Isabel No, no, he did not tell me that. This is a falsehood!

Levison Nay, I do not ask you to believe me. Simply trust your own eyes. (*He takes her up to the window*) There, look towards the grove: you see two figures, a man and a woman, engaged in earnest conversation –

Isabel These are strangers. I care not who they are.

Levison (*Gives her a telescope*) Perhaps with the assistance of this glass –

Isabel (*Takes it*) How my hand trembles . . . (*she looks. With a shriek*) True, true! I am deceived – wronged – outraged!

Levison You cannot remain under the same roof with this sordid hypocrite –

Isabel Oh!

Levison Perhaps soon, even hypocrisy will cease. He is not very careful now . . . perhaps Barbara Hare will be his avowed mistress in the face of Lord Mount Severn's daughter!

Isabel Horror! Horror!

Levison Fly with me, I say! Fly, my own love! Let not another moment be lost!

Isabel I will! A charnel house is preferable to this accursed mansion. Take me where you will, only take me hence!

Levison In a few minutes a chaise will be at the gate. (*Aside*) Victory! Mine! Mine! (*Exit*).

Isabel I will not think. I will not reflect – thought might drive me from my purpose and I might stay here to endure new wrongs. No . . . I'll just write a line. (*Sits at desk and writes*).

Enter Joyce

Joyce My lady – are you ill?

Isabel Who's that? Ah, my good faithful Joyce . . . if anything should happen to me, Joyce – promise that when I am gone you will stay at East Lynne and take care of – my children.

Joyce I certainly will, my lady. But why talk in this way?

Isabel No matter; you have promised – you won't forget, Joyce?

(*Levison returns and makes a sign. A piano is heard off-stage*).

Isabel What is that music?

Joyce It's only Miss Isabel.

Isabel The dear child . . . just go to her, Joyce, tell her to play some other tune. That air strangely affects me now.

Joyce I will, my lady. (*Aside*) What can be the matter? (*Exit*).

Isabel Another moment and I should have forgot my wrongs. Levison, take me where thou wilt! Guardian angel or tempting devil, I am yours for ever!

(*As she half faints, Levison picks her up and carries her through to the garden*)

Re-enter Joyce

Joyce Why, where in the world is she? Here's her scarf . . . who has gone through the conservatory . . . those strange words of hers! Why did I not understand them? She will destroy herself! Help! Help! Help!

Enter Cornelia, Carlyle and Miss Isabel

Cornelia Good gracious! What's the matter? Is the house on fire?
Joyce My lady! My lady! She is killing herself I am sure.
Cornelia Joyce, are you in your senses?
Carlyle (*Picking up the note*) But what's this?
Joyce Please, sir, I saw her writing that. I hope she did not write it to say she is dead!
Carlyle (*Having read*) No, no . . . she is not dead . . . that is not the misfortune

Enter Justice Hare

Hare I say, Mr Carlyle, I don't trouble you often, but just as I was leaving the club a chaise with Captain Levison and Lady Isabel dashed past me as if it was going to the – ahem!
Cornelia and Joyce Levison!
Carlyle Enough, enough! Don't tell me more at present, dear old friend.
Miss Isabel But papa, don't cry! What is the matter?
Joyce Hush, hush, Miss Isabel.
Carlyle No, not Miss Isabel: for the future – Lucy. While I am living the name of Isabel shall never again be uttered within the walls of East Lynne

Act 2

Scene 1
The Blue Parlour. Carlyle is discovered, the note in his hand

Carlyle A strange fascination! This scrap of paper has more interest for me than any book in my library. (*Reads*) 'When years go on, and my children ask where their mother is, and why she left them, tell them that you, their father, goaded her to take this desperate step'. What was this imaginary wrong that she avenged by the commission of a deadly crime? Strange fatality! The great misery of my life is involved in impenetrable mystery

Enter Cornelia, sneezing

Cornelia Oh, dear! Do you want anything, Archibald? I think of going to bed. Indeed, with a cold like mine, I ought to have been in bed long ago.

Carlyle By all means take care of yourself, Corny. Good people are scarce, you know.

Cornelia I've heard of an excellent remedy. It's to double a flannel petticoat cross-wise, and put it over the night-cap.

Carlyle Try that by all means, Corny. You'll secure a charming head-dress, at any rate.

Cornelia Ah, it's all very well, but I can only sa- sa- say (*Sneezes*) Good-night! (*Exit*).

Carlyle How are the mighty fallen . . . (*Moves to window*) I wonder whether it's still snowing?

(*Richard appears at the window. He opens it*).

What's this? An intruder – ? Richard Hare!

Richard (*Entering*) Yes, miserable Richard Hare. Richard the outcast. I've cut away from London at a moment's notice. Would you believe it, that scoundrel Thorne, that murderer, has had the brazen impudence to set the police upon me!

Carlyle Strange indeed!

Richard Some days ago, I was talking to a cab-driver at one of the stands. I do a job now and then to get a crust of bread. Well, who should come to the very stand but that Thorne! His glance met mine, but in another second, he jumped into a Hansom and wheeled out of sight like a flash of lightning.

Carlyle And you are sure this was Thorne?

Richard Certain positive. But there's more to come, sir. A day or two afterwards I saw him at the entrance to Tattersall's; so I walked up to him and said I, 'I want your name!' He changed colour. 'Young man' said he, 'you have watched me more than once and as there happens to be a policeman in sight' – and he points to a policeman on the other side! Without more ado off I go, down one alley, up another through all the back slums of London. At last I reached my lodgings, and chancing to look out of the window saw the very policeman standing right over the way! I felt that London, big as it is, was too small for me, so I sneaked out of the house, and escaped him.

Carlyle Really, Richard, there is something so strange about your story that even your best friends can't help being suspicious. It seems that all your misfortunes have arisen from your senseless passion for that worthless girl Affy Hallijohn.

Richard Yes, sir! That's quite right, and in spite of my father's opposition, I believe I should have married her when I came of age, aye, and in spite of her love for *him*.

Carlyle Her love for whom?

Richard For Thorne, who used to come and visit her stealthily at dusk, when he thought Affy's father was from home. On the evening of the sad affair, I went to Hallijohn's carrying my gun which he wanted to borrow. I reached the house by a wood path, and Affy came out of the house in a confused sort of way, telling me that just then she could not admit me. Well, I gave her the gun for her father, but I had a suspicion Thorne was there, so I kept lurking about the premises. In about 20 minutes I heard a shot, and almost directly afterwards a man came tearing along the path from the cottage, and if that man was not Thorne, I'll –

Carlyle You followed him?

Richard On the contrary, I ran towards the cottage, hurried up the steps and stumbled over the body of poor old Hallijohn who lay dead with my gun by his side, discharged. I ran away, and never showed my face near the spot again.

Carlyle I must own, my poor Richard, that for an innocent man you took the most wonderful pains to look like an assassin.

(*Knock at the door*).

Richard What's that? Hide me!

Enter Cornelia with a flannel upon her head and a candle in her hand

Hallijohn's ghost by all that's horrible! (*Runs off*).

Cornelia A strange man by all that's shocking! (*Runs off. Carlyle follows laughing*)

Scene 2

A room at an Inn in Grenoble

Isabel and Suzanne are discovered on

Suzanne Now, don't go vexing yourself in that way, Miladi. No doubt Monsieur will soon return.
(*Sound of whip*).
There's the diligence. Yes, and here is Monsieur. You will be happy now, Miladi.
Isabel Happy!
Suzanne (*Opening door*) This way, Monsieur. Miladi has been anxious about you.

Enter Levison. Exit Suzanne

Levison Anxious, eh? I'm flattered. (*Offers to salute her but she repulses him*) Hey day! Is this the welcome a fellow receives after travelling hundreds of miles through such horrible weather?
Isabel Nay, for one reason you are welcome. I intended to have written but often it is easier to come to a point in conversation than by letter. I wish to deal with you quite unreservedly without concealment or disguise. I must request you to deal so with me.
Levison What do you mean by deal?
Isabel When you left in July you solemnly promised to return back in time for our marriage. You know what I mean when I say in time.
Levison Yes, yes, I promised, but when in London I found myself so overwhelmed with business that I could not get away –
Isabel You did not intend to return in time for the marriage – nay, you could easily have married me before your departure.
Levison What fancies you take up!
Isabel A few days after you had left this place, one of the maids who had been arranging your clothes showed me a letter which she had found. That letter contained the information that Archibald Carlyle had obtained the divorce without opposition!
Levison Well, Isabel, as you drive me into a corner I will tell you the plain truth. I am no longer plain Captain Levison. The death of my uncle has made me the representative of an ancient and respected Baronetcy, and were I to compromise the dignity of my family, to marry a divorced woman –
Isabel I assure you that were you to propose to marry me tomorrow I would refuse you, for I cannot fancy any calamity so dreadful as that of being compelled to pass my life with you. Oh, may Heaven help all who may be tempted as I was!
Levison Come, come – half the temptation at least lay in your outrageous jealousy of your husband and that Barbara Hare.

Isabel Outrageous jealousy!

Levison Most outrageous, and most unreasonable. I am convinced Carlyle never thought of the girl in the way of love – there was a business secret between them.

Isabel You shameless reprobate, you!

Levison I plead guilty, but don't forget, my dear Isabel, that in love as in war all stratagems are fair. By the bye, is my room ready?

Isabel You have no room here. These apartments have been transferred into my own name and cannot offer you accommodation.

Levison Well, if you intend a regular break-off, so be it. And I don't know that you are altogether wrong, Isabel, for a cat and dog life would be simply miserable. However I cannot see you starve; let us fix on some amount to be remitted half-yearly.

Isabel Sir Francis Levison, what do you take me for? I am still Lord Mount Severn's daughter.

Levison For a person who must live, and who, having no fortune, must receive assistance from someone.

Isabel At all events I will not receive it from you.

Levison Very well, very well. If you happen to change your mind, a line addressed to me at my bankers will find me.

Isabel I shall not change my mind, and as we, I believe, have no more to say we will part at once. (*Rings bell*).

Levison So, henceforth, we are mortal enemies.

Isabel Rather say utter strangers

Suzanne enters

Suzanne, open the door for Sir Francis Levison.

Levison Some might think this scene rather humiliating, but when I reflect what an easy escape I have had I cannot help considering myself a devilish lucky fellow. (*Exit, followed by Suzanne*).

Isabel And for this man, this cold-blooded, heartless, shameless wretch, I have sacrificed a husband, children who doated on me, honor which is a woman's priceless jewel. Merciful Heaven, give me strength to bear the punishment I have righteously deserved!

Enter Suzanne

Suzanne Please, Miladi, there is an English gentleman who wishes particularly to see you.

Isabel Admit him

(*Exit Suzanne*)

Lord M-S (*Off*) I know I am right

(*He enters*)

Isabel My cousin, Lord Mount Severn!

Lord M-S Yes, even so, Isabel. Where is that scoundrel who has brought disgrace upon us all?

Isabel We have parted for ever.

Lord M-S I am glad there's an end to that connection at any rate; but now, Isabel, I am the head of a noble family of which you are a not very honourable member and I am bound to see that you do not sink even lower than you are at present. How do you mean to live?

Isabel I am selling my jewels. Before they are exhausted I shall endeavour to gain a livelihood by, perhaps, teaching.

Lord M-S But Mr Carlyle tells me that you did not take away any jewels or anything else when you eloped.

Isabel You have seen Archibald – Mr Carlyle?

Lord M-S Of course I have. A man who might almost be regarded as a benefactor to our family, and who had received such a deadly blow. Isabel, what demon prompted you to sell yourself to that bad man, Levison?

Isabel He knew, my husband knew.

Lord M-S He does not know to the present moment. You left a note which neither he nor I could understand.

Isabel I believed that his love was no longer mine, that he had deserted me for another.

Lord M-S What do you mean by 'deserted'? He was with you, he is at home still with his children, which is more than can be said of their mother.

Isabel There is a desertion of the heart.

Lord M-S Desertion of a fiddle-stick! I tell you that in word, deed and thought no man was ever more thoroughly devoted to woman than he was to you.

Isabel I saw my husband and Barbara walking together secretly by moonlight.

Lord M-S On the evening of your flight – exactly. They were conversing about Barbara's brother who lay under a suspicion of murder, and whose presence in the neighbourhood they were forced to keep secret. Oh, Isabel, how utterly you have lost yourself!

Isabel Oh, spare me! I can bear no more.

Lord M-S Well, then, we'll proceed to business. On my return to England I shall settle upon you £400 a year, and you may draw it quarterly.

Isabel I do not deserve this kindness. One question – is my husband ... is Mr Carlyle well?

Lord M-S In bodily health, yes.

Isabel And my children?

Lord M-S Your name is never mentioned, but the children

remember you with affection. A faithful servant of yours, named Joyce, will not allow you to be forgotten.

Isabel Thank Heaven! And the children are well?

Lord M-S Lucy, as they now call her, is well, but little William is drooping. (*Pause*) I can't bear this any longer. (*Puts down pocket book on table*) Heaven protect you. (*Exit*).

Isabel It is consumption, the hereditary curse of our family . . . my boy is dying . . . I shall never see him more. Suzanne! Suzanne!

Enter Suzanne

Pack up my trunks. We must leave this hateful place.

Suzanne Leave Grenoble? O, for where, Miladi? For where?

Isabel I know not. I care not – anywhere. Oh! My heart is broken! Why do I not die! (*As she weeps passionately, the curtain falls*)

Avonia Jones (*Enthoven Collection*)

Act 3

Scene 1
An apartment in East Lynne, as for Act 1 Scene 3

Cornelia is discovered seated

Cornelia Oh, dear, oh dear, it's astonishing how women fall off when they marry my brother. There was not a nicer girl in all the country than Miss Barbara Hare, but now she has turned into Mrs Barbara Carlyle, I feel my affection for her getting less and less

Enter Joyce, red-eyed

Ah, Joyce, you've been crying. A tiff with your new mistress, I suppose?
Joyce No, it's the sight of that poor little William.
Cornelia Ah, poor little thing. His mother left him the family consumption if she left him nothing else. I tell you if ever I become a mother – good gracious, what am I saying! My mind revolts at the horrible supposition! I dare say even you, Joyce, were not altogether pleased by my brother's taking a second wife?
Joyce Well, Miss Cornelia, I cried a little and sighed a little, I'm free to confess. But how conscientiously master behaved. Though he had a divorce and might have married immediately, he would not make Miss Barbara his wife till he was a real widower – till he read in the newspapers how poor Lady Isabel was killed by that horrible railway accident in foreign parts.
Cornelia Ah! I, for one, was grieved to the heart at poor Lady Isabel's death.
Joyce Partly, because it caused Mr Carlyle to take another wife, eh, Miss Cornelia?
Cornelia Partly on that account. I don't like the present Mrs Carlyle half so well as Lady Isabel with all her faults

Enter Justice Hare, Barbara and Carlyle

Hare I'm glad you talked him over, my dear. I'm glad you showed a little of your father's obstinacy and would not give up your point. We want such a man as you to represent us, Mr Carlyle.

Barbara Yes, dear husband, it is your duty to present yourself as a Candidate.

Carlyle Well, thanks to your kind persuasion, I am a Candidate. Still, I fear I can scarcely command the time.

Hare Stuff o' nonsense! You have stuck to business the best part of your life, and a pretty penny you have made by it, and it's hard if you can't now spare a few weeks for the good of your country!

Cornelia A pretty figure he'll cut in Parliament! Why, he's not a good hand even at a common after-dinner speech! Oh, Archibald!

Hare It's too late, I'm afraid, Miss Cornelia, for unless the printer and bill-sticker have been very remiss in obeying my orders 'Carlyle Forever' is already posted on every wall.

Cornelia Is it? Then I'll soon have it down again! Joyce, bring me my large gingham umbrella – the one with the hook at one end and the sharp point at the other. I'll let them see!

Enter Dill

Dill Oh, Mr Carlyle! Oh, Miss Cornelia! Oh, Justice Hare! Here's a pretty business!

Hare What's the matter, now, man?

Dill: There's another of them. There is another Candidate for West Lynne!

All Another Candidate!

Dill He is no other than – you'll scarcely believe it – than Sir Francis Levison!

Carlyle Surely that man cannot venture to show his face here?

Cornelia I shall explode!

Hare I shall burst!

Dill Bless your innocent hearts, there are some people who can face everybody, just as a brass-knocker can bear all weathers.

Hare Oh, he won't come!

Dill He is here already. He arrived by train last night, and what is more he is supported by the ministerial interest. We are insulted, all of us.

Hare Confoundedly insulted!

Cornelia Outraged! Outraged!

Carlyle Well, sister, shall I withdraw from the contest?

Cornelia Withdraw, indeed? I'll disown you for a brother if you do!

Hare Carlyle for ever! I'll go at once and beat up recruits for another meeting at the Boar's Head!

Dill I'll go with you.

Cornelia And I too!

All Carlyle for ever!

Exeunt Cornelia, Joyce, Hare and Dill.

297

Carlyle Poor Corny! She fancies she's a strong-headed woman, and does not know her own mind for two minutes together. But Barbara, how silent you are – and how sad you look.

Barbara Yours is a noble nature . . . will you forgive me if I tell you the cause of my passing melancholy? When I saw the cloud pass over your brow at the mention of that wicked man's name, I fancied – pray, pardon me – that it arose from something like a feeling of jealousy. And then I thought that jealousy is a sign of love . . . and then a suspicion arose within that the old love for Lady Isabel, your first wife, might not be quite extinct. Pray pardon me, Archibald.

Carlyle Folly, folly, Barbara! You must not dwell on that subject or you will displease me much. The unhappy woman expiated her crime by a horrible death, and I desire that she may never be named directly or indirectly again.

Barbara I have offended you.

Carlyle No, no, there . . . (*Kisses her*) . . . it's all over now. Let us change the theme. I think you said the new governess has arrived?

Barbara (*Rings bell*) Yes, she has. She is under the care of Joyce in the room we have assigned to her

Enter Joyce

Oh, tell Madame – Madame –

Joyce Madame Vine –

Barbara Yes, tell Madame Vine we shall be happy to see her.

Joyce Yes, ma'am. (*Exit*).

Barbara I hope she will turn out well. You have a high opinion of Mrs Crosby's judgement –

Carlyle The very highest, and Mrs Crosby, as you know, writes from Germany that she had Madame Vine with her for two years as a governess, and that she regarded her as quite a treasure

Enter Isabel disguised as Madame Vine

Carlyle Madame Vine, I presume. (*Offers his hand*) Perhaps you had better defer the performance of your duties until you have recovered from the fatigue of your journey.

Isabel No, no, I would rather begin at once. Let me see the children as soon as possible.

Carlyle This anxiety promises well. Goodbye for the present, Madame Vine. I will leave you and Mrs Carlyle to manage matters between you. (*Exit*).

Isabel (*Aside*) Gracious Heaven, give me nerves of steel!

Barbara Well, Madame Vine, welcome to East Lynne, I hope you will find your residence here agreeable. Have you lived much in England?

Isabel In the early part of my life, yes.

Barbara You lost your husband some years since ?

Isabel Not many years.

Barbara And you have no children living ?

Isabel I have no children now.

Barbara Ah, your losses have been very terrible. You are not aware perhaps that the children of whom you will have the charge are not exactly mine, but the children of Mr Carlyle's first wife. Joyce tells me the children often talk of her in secret.

Isabel The darlings – no doubt lest your feelings should be wounded.

Barbara No, it is their father's order that their mother's name should never be mentioned.

Isabel Strange...

Barbara As you cannot live in this part of the world without hearing the story from someone, I may as well tell you that Lady Isabel quitted her husband and children under disgraceful conditions, with a paramour.

Isabel I fancy I have heard the story. She is dead now.

Barbara Yes – a railway accident.

Isabel A just retribution.

Barbara Let us hope she was spared time to repent of her sin. But what is the matter ? How pale you look !

Isabel I am naturally pale – think nothing of it. The children: are they amiable, affectionate ?

Barbara You will find Lucy, the elder of the two, a very interesting and intelligent girl; as for the younger one, William, he's a charming little fellow, but I fear he is not long for this world.

Isabel How does Archi – how does Mr Carlyle endure the prospect of losing him ?

Barbara Calmly though sadly, as he endured his first wife's desertion.

Isabel Perhaps he did not love her ?

Barbara Madame Vine, she was his idol. He himself told me that although he had obtained a divorce he would never have married if Lady Isabel had lived.

William (*Off*) Mamma! Mamma!

Barbara That is poor little invalid William

Enter William with Joyce

William Oh, Mamma! (*Tries to run to her; stumbles and is caught by Isabel, who shrieks*).

Isabel You doubtless think my conduct strange, but this little boy so strongly reminded me of one of the children I have lost.

Barbara I perfectly comprehend the feeling.

William Mamma, may I ride to town with you today ?

Barbara I am not going out today, and if I were, the air is too keen for you. Take him back to the nursery, Joyce.

Joyce Certainly, ma'am. (*Aside*) What violent emotion ... (*Exit with William.*)

Carlyle enters.

Carlyle Excuse me, Madame. Barbara, come with me into the parlour. Richard is below – the strangest story! I think the man Thorne is found at last.

Barbara Heaven be praised if the poor lad is exculpated! Madame Vine, I trust you will make yourself at home. East Lynne is not very large and you may soon grow familiar with every corner of it. (*Exit with Carlyle*).

Isabel Familiar with East Lynne, with the home of my girlhood, of my wedded life . . . here I reigned the proud and happy mistress of the mansion, and the honoured wife of a noble husband, and hither I return a humiliated outcast. Here I find my husband wedded to another – oh, no more, no more! Gracious Heaven, let me die! My punishment is greater than I can bear!

(*As she kneels, the scene ends*)

Scene 2
A street in West Lynne placarded 'Carlyle Forever!'

Enter Richard and Dill with two policemen

Dill (*To policemen*) Just stand on one side. He's almost sure to come through this street. (*Policemen retire*) Now, Richard, you are sure you are not mistaken?

Richard No, Dill, I never was mistaken about the identity, but while I had no evidence I was afraid to come forward; now we have Bethel's testimony we are all right.

Dill Very well – oh, here comes our honourable friend ... (*Richard retires*)

Enter Levison

Welcome to West Lynne.

Levison Ah, my respected old friend – how d'ye do, Mr Dill? I suppose you are still with Mr Carlyle?

Dill Yes, Sir Francis, thank ye. When I have a good master I know how to stick to him, though some wives don't know how to stick to good husbands.

Levison Smart as ever, Mr Dill. You are working against me, of course?

Dill Well, sir, I'm doing my little best – everyone to his own party.

302

Levison Sound morals, friend Dill, exceedingly sound. I say, do you think they will like me down here?

Dill Well, Sir Francis, one says 'What! Has that scoundrel Levison the impudence to shew his ugly face here again? The rascal ought to be kicked down the High Street!' 'And flogged at the cart's tail!' adds a second. 'Don't you think we ought to duck him?' suggests a third, whereupon a fourth gravely replies 'Most assuredly!' Pray don't misunderstand me, Sir Francis – it's not I who say all this, oh dear me; I'm only repeating the talk of low people.

Levison Of course, and I can perceive by that pleasant giggle that the report gives you infinite pain. Then altogether you don't think the voters will have me?

Dill Well, I should say they will not. But there's one consolation, Sir Francis: if the voters won't have you, somebody else will.

(*Gives a signal to policemen, who advance*).

1st Policeman Sir Francis Levison, I arrest you.

Levison Arrest me? Stuff!

1st Policeman You are charged with the wilful murder of George Hallijohn.

Richard (*Advancing*) Yes, villain! Assassin! It is proved that you and Thorne, the lover of Affy Hallijohn, are one!

Levison (*Struggling in the grip of the policemen*) Scoundrels, do you dare – ?

1st Policeman Now, Sir Francis, you had better take it easy. (*They secure him*).

Levison I say, Mr Dill – if you are passing the Goose and Gridiron, just drop in and tell my committee that I hope to be with them in half an hour. (*He is led away*).

Dill Ha! I'm afraid that worthy Baronet's time will be too much occupied to allow him to pay due attention to the interests of the nation

Exeunt Dill and Richard and the scene closes

Scene 3
The Nursery at East Lynne

William is discovered lying on a couch, with Lady Isabel near him

William No, no, I try to hold the figure, but it fades, fades away. I have nearly forgotten what mamma – I mean my own mamma – was like. They say a wicked man took her to some foreign country . . . have you seen her?

Isabel Yes.

William What did she say?

301

Isabel She said that though she was parted from her children, she trusted that she would meet them in Heaven.

William Perhaps I should not know her . . . will it be long before I die?

Isabel Oh, my child, Heaven grant it may be very long.

William No, I think not, for they are always crying round me . . . I do not want to live long. I want to be with Mamma

Enter Joyce and Lucy

Oh, how my head wanders . . . oh, Lucy – Joyce: Madame Vine has met mamma, and she talked about us . . .

Joyce (*Aside*) Is this true, Madame?

Isabel (*Aside*) No, no, I only spoke to quiet the child.

William Take away the light, Joyce – I like dark. Thank you, thank you . . . Good-night, Joyce . . . Good-night, Madame Vine . . .

Joyce We are not going to leave you. (*Aside*) The child is dying, Madame. (*Aloud*) This way, Miss Lucy, this way. (*Leads her to the door*).

Isabel Dying . . . was I spared on that horrible night? Have I risen from the maimed and the dead only witness a scene like this . . . ?

William Mother! Mother!

Joyce I will fetch her.

Isabel No, not Barbara Hare. William, William! Look at me; do you know me? (*She throws off her disguise*).

Joyce My mistress! Great Heaven!

William Mamma! Mamma! My own Mamma! (*He dies*).

Isabel My boy! My boy! Say that word again! He is dead – dead!

Joyce Oh, my lady!

Isabel Come back to me, my own boy . . . call me Mamma . . . once more . . . kiss me a farewell . . . !

Picture as the act-drop falls

Act 4

Scene 1
A street in West Lynne

Enter Cornelia and Barbara as shouts are heard off

Cornelia They have come to some conclusion.
Barbara This is indeed an anxious moment

Enter Dill

Dill Well, ladies, it's all over. Have you heard the news yet?
Barbara No, pray speak!
Dill Your brother, Richard, is acquitted.
Barbara Thank Heaven! Then the murderer will meet his doom on the scaffold.
Dill Come, it won't be quite so bad as that. Levison thought that by his attentions to Affy Hallijohn he was conferring an honour on the family – the old man took a different view of the case; there was a dispute, but Hallijohn was not slaughtered in cold blood. Under the circumstances our honourable Candidate is lightly visited with transportation to a penal settlement for life. (*Exit*)

Enter Richard, Justice and Mrs Hare

Richard Dear Barbara – it's all right!
Mrs Hare My poor persecuted boy! (*She embraces him*).
Richard Mother, dear Mother!
Hare Richard, my lad ...
Richard Ah!, father dear –
Hare No, don't call me anything of the kind. I'm an infernal old fool, and what's more a confounded old brute. I'm sure you can't forgive me, Dick.
Richard I do with all my heart and soul

Enter Levison handcuffed and guarded

303

Levison Good morning, Miss Carlyle. Present my compliments to that worthy attorney your brother, with my congratulations on his Election. You may add that I am in possession of a lock of Lady Isabel's hair which I shall be happy to return to him, if he'll visit me in my next place of abode. Officers, let us move on. Ta-ta, Miss Carlyle – ta-ta!

(*Exit Levison with guard*).

Cornelia Oh, the brazen monster! I really believe that wretch was bad enough to try his tricks upon me . . . if he had not encountered Lady Isabel . . . ! (*Exit*)

The scene closes

Scene 2
Isabel's apartment at East Lynne

Isabel is discovered in an armchair; Joyce in attendance

Joyce (*Aside*) She is dying, poor lady . . . the secret will not be kept much longer.

Isabel I must see them. I must see my dear, good husband and my poor child once more. I cannot die till then.

Cornelia (*Outside the door*) Joyce, how is Madame Vine? Is she any better?

Joyce (*To door. Calling softly*) No, I grieve to say, no.

Cornelia Then I ought to see her.

Joyce (*Aside*) And my lady is without her disguise! (*Aloud*) No, you must not –

Cornelia (*Entering*) Must not? I like that – you could let in a doctor and I'm as good as a dozen. (*She goes to the armchair*) I'm sorry to hear that – Lady Isabel!

Isabel Oh! Miss Carlyle, is it you? Do not reproach me . . .

Cornelia No, Lady, I don't reproach you. I pity you.

Isabel You can see that my sin is crushing me beneath its deadly weight.

Cornelia Nay, Lady Isabel, I have a sin on my conscience that often gives me a deal of trouble. I was harsh and exacting – was I in any way the cause of your leaving East Lynne?

Isabel No, on my soul you were not. My crime is to be attributed to my own bad suspicious temper, and to the temptations of a villain.

(*Shouts are heard off*).

What is that?

Cornelia Some of the people returning from the trial. Richard Hare has been acquitted of a crime of which he has long been suspected.

Isabel Ah, I remember. That was the fatal mystery which occasioned so much wretchedness.

Cornelia The real murderer was – Sir Francis Levison!

Isabel I knew to my cost he was a bad man, but a murderer . . . ! (*She faints*).

Cornelia Oh, dear Lady Isabel! I have killed her! Oh, forgive me!

Isabel (*Recovering*) I forgive you. It is right that I should know ere I die how utterly vile was this man for whom I sacrificed my noble husband . . . could you not let me see him once more? I cannot die without his forgiveness.

Cornelia Joyce, desire your master to come here at once. (*Exit Joyce*).

Sustain yourself, my poor penitent child. The most trying moment of all is at hand. Heaven give you courage to support it.

Isabel Merciful power, endow me with strength!

Enter Carlyle

Carlyle I understand from Joyce that you desire to see me here.

Cornelia Yes, Madame Vine is very ill. She has something of importance to communicate. Speak to her. (*Exit*).

Carlyle Madame Vine, I am much grieved – Lady Isabel!

Isabel Archibald . . . I – I could not die without your forgiveness. You turn from me – you refuse it! Nay, forgive me! I was long confined to my bed in consequence of that accident, but when I had regained a little strength, I felt that I could not stay away from you and my children – the longing for you was killing me. I never knew a moment's peace after I quitted you.

Carlyle Oh, why did you go?

Isabel Do you not really know?

Carlyle It has always been a mystery to me.

Isabel I thought you were false to me, that your love was given to another; and in my sad jealousy I listened to the temptings of that bad man who whispered to me of wrongs.

Carlyle Isabel, I never was false to you in deed or in thought.

Isabel No, I was mad – and my crime was madness, nothing more. Surely you will forget and forgive? I could almost sink into the earth with remorse and shame.

Carlyle Would I could forget the shame you have bestowed on me and on my children.

Isabel Oh, I know! I have not a claim to forgiveness save that of my intense suffering. But think what I have endured! How I have lived in this house with your other wife – think what it was to watch the dying moments of my little William; when the darling boy lay dead it was Barbara's petty grief you soothed, not my great agony – the agony of a mother. Heaven knows how I have lived through it all – oh, my husband! Say once more that you forgive me!

Carlyle I pity, I pardon you; I will strive to forget all but our happy days.

Isabel My strength fails me . . . your fondness for your new wife will not lessen your love for our surviving child?

Carlyle She is as dear to me as ever.

Isabel Only one word of love . . . my heart is breaking . . .

Carlyle May Heaven bless you, and give you rest, my own dear Isabel!

Isabel We shall meet again in another world, and live together for ever and ever. Our little William awaits us now. Keep a little corner of your heart for your poor, lost Isabel.

Carlyle Yes, yes . . .

Isabel Are you going to leave me?

Carlyle No, no – you are faint. Let me call assistance. (*Rings bell*).

Isabel Too late – this is the faintness of death. Oh, it is hard to part . . . farewell, my own beloved husband

Enter Lucy and Joyce

Carlyle Farewell, my own Isabel!
Isabel Till Time has given place to Eternity . . . (*She dies*)

Tableau. Curtain

THE PRESS

Illustrated London News, February 10th, 1866:

The Surrey has given the note not only of preparation but of progress by the production of a new piece on Monday, and by the appearance of Miss Avonia Jones as the heroine. It appears that Mr John Oxenford had reduced Mrs Wood's novel of East Lynne *to the conditions and limits of a drama, and that Miss Jones had taken it with her to Australia and elsewhere, winning on colonial stages a high reputation in the character of* Lady Isabel. *The quality of Miss Jones's acting is well known to the English public, in consequence of her appearance, a few seasons ago, at the Adelphi, when she sustained the part of Medea in the American version of that tragedy. Her style is somewhat monotonous, but set off with attitudes which are certainly picturesque, and with a pathos which at the climax is frequently effective. The story of* East Lynne *is so well known to our readers that it would be impertinent to repeat it. Suffice it to say, therefore, that it is divided into four parts. The first consists of the lady's jealousy of her husband, her temptation, and final elopement; the second shows her parting from her betrayer; the third, her visit to her child; the fourth, her repentance and death. In all these situations Miss Jones acted with power and emphasis, at least in the culminating portions of the scenes and situations; but, from the want of a middle tone in her voice, the conversational parts are so clouded that it is difficult to catch the sense of the dialogue. Miss Jones, however, is an actress of force, and her appearance on the Surrey stage is an indication of a proper kind of ambition in the management which merits encouragement.*

The Illustrated Sporting and Theatrical News, February 10th, 1866:

Mr Shepherd is proving that he intends to turn to good account the splendid new theatre which has been raised for him out of the ruins of the one over the fortunes of which he so long held successful control. On Monday evening he played a trump card as an indication of the sort of hand he holds, and we have no doubt that he will find he has played it with the best effect. The engagement of Miss Avonia Jones, after that lady's protracted absence from the London stage, is in every way calculated to give emphasis to the opening arrangements of his new campaign. With politic liberality he has gone to one of the leading dramatists of the day to furnish a drama worthy the circumstances of the occasion, and in East Lynne *he may be proud of having given to his transpontine patrons a play that would have met the most exacting demands of a West-end audience. The adapter of the present version of Mrs Wood's famous novel is Mr John Oxenford, who has done his work with the effectiveness of a thoroughly skilled artist. We do not know how far he may have been indebted to the highly popular version of the story produced in America, the chief character of which has been, we believe, frequently sustained there by Miss Avonia Jones, but whether wholly or only in part his own as to construction, the piece which bears his name is well worthy of his reputation. It is in four acts of medium length and sets forth the more touching incidents of Mrs Wood's story with perfect distinctness and with very strong dramatic effect.*

[Here follows a summary of the plot]

In this bald outline of the plot we have said nothing of minor characters and incidents, of which there are a considerable number, all necessary to the complete development of the story. The principal interest of the piece centres in Lady Isabel, *whose terrible position the audience are led to sympathise with in an extraordinary degree by the extremely pathetic acting of Miss Avonia Jones. It is a very long time since we have seen so many tearful eyes follow the mimic sorrows of a heroine. These tears are the most striking acknowledgment of the actress's power, a far higher tribute than the vehement applause which greeted her throughout the piece, but more particularly at the end of the third act. In this act is represented the death of* Archibald Carlyle's *son (very nicely played by* Miss Charlton) *in the arms of his mother, whom he knows only as his governess. The wild burst of agony with which the unfortunate mother throws herself upon the lifeless body of her child is indescribably pathetic and makes a profound impression on the audience. As a whole, the piece is extremely well played. Two or three of the minor characters are sustained in a remarkably praise-worthy manner, special praise being being justly due to Mr Henry Thompson for his rendering of* Mr Dill, *an old confidential clerk of* Archibald Carlyle. *The mounting of the piece is in the very best taste; indeed everything that care and money could do for it has evidently been done. That* East Lynne *will prove a great success we have no doubt; we are quite sure that it is worthy to enjoy a long run. The pantomime of* King Chess; or, Tom the Piper's Son and See-saw Margery Daw *concludes the evening's entertainment. Throughout the week the house – which for its own sake is worth a visit – has been crowded.*

Lost at Sea

H J BYRON
and
DION BOUCICAULT

H J Byron 'Illus-
strated London
News', 1884. (*Vic-
toria & Albert
Museum*)

HENRY JAMES BYRON (1834/84)

H J Byron was a remarkable man by any standards: in a quarter of a century he produced over two hundred dramas, pantomimes, ballets, comedies, spectaculars, operas, burlettas, and above all the numerous farces and burlesques by which he is remembered today. Despite this vast output, he plagiarised less than most contemporary theatre-writers – his dramas especially were noted for their originality. In the year of his death he was voted the most popular dramatist of the day in a poll run by Henry Labouchère's magazine *Truth*;* he collaborated with all the prominent dramatists of the day – F C Burnand, W S Gilbert, Dion Boucicault – and indeed his name and influence are inescapable in all writings of the time.

A second cousin to Lord Byron, Henry was born in Manchester in January 1834 of middle-class parents, his father being then British consul

---

*At this time Labouchère was also Radical MP for Northampton

at Port-au-Prince. He was originally intended for the practice of medicine and for a time studied at this profession. Thespis beckoned, however: he joined a provincial touring company, and later began his astonishing output with *Richard, Coeur de Lion*, a burlesque unsuccessfully mounted at the Strand Theatre in 1857. Family pressures must have been brought to bear, for the following year he entered Middle Temple to read for the Bar. Now began the stream of pieces (not to mention a three-volume novel), principally for the Strand,* which were to make him a legend in his own comparatively short lifetime. His first great hit was a burlesque of Pocock's *The Magpie, or The Maid?* for Marie Wilton at the Prince of Wales (Tottenham St) in 1865, the same year in which he became the first editor of *Fun*.

Two years later he went to Liverpool where he ran – disastrously – three theatres, returning to London in 1874 to take over the Criterion. In January of the following year his *Our Boys* opened at the Vaudeville, and achieved the astounding run of four years and three months, a record run which was not to be broken for over forty years; this piece was regularly revived, and was still occasionally performed by amateurs as late as the 1920's, yielding a small income for Byron's daughter.

H J Byron was renowned in his day for his wit, although one might be forgiven for doubting this from the welter of cumbrous puns with which his comedies and burlesques and pantomimes are saturated. Their very titles give the flavour: *The 'Grin' Bushes, The Lady of Lyons, or Twopenny Pride and Pennytence, The Corsican 'Bothers'*, and *Ali Baba, or the Thirty-Nine Thieves, in accordance with the Author's Habit of Taking One Off!* As one writer observed, 'There is not a classical story, nursery tale, opera or drama to which he has not applied a sacrilegious pen'. Another wrote 'as an actor Byron attempted little. A quiet unconsciousness in the delivery of jokes was his chief recommendation to the public'. Faint praise indeed, although Gilbert thought sufficiently highly of his acting ability to include him in the cast of his comedy *Engaged* (1881), the only known instance of Byron's appearing in any play other than by himself since his very early days in the theatre. H G Hibbert said of him that 'he rejected make-up, and would step from a cab on to the stage, a tall, handsome, heavily moustached man, who was hardly ever known to lose his temper, who was universally beloved for his charm and wit'.

And a final word from Augustin Filon: 'he wrote a million nonsensical things but not a single indecent thing' – which must be another record of some sort.

---

*This was not the present-day Strand Theatre, but a much smaller house pulled down in a road-widening scheme for the approaches to Kingsway

DION BOUCICAULT (1820?/90)

In Dion Boucicault we reach the apotheosis of melodrama; he was the one man who raised the genre almost to the level of an art form, and is the only melodramatist whose plays are remembered today on both sides of the Atlantic – even if they are nearly all adaptations, translations and plain borrowings; indeed, he is virtually the only playwright between Sheridan and Robertson whose works remain in the repertory. *London Assurance* which he wrote at about the age of twenty-one was a sensation when first seen at Covent Garden in 1841, just as it was when revived in 1970 and again in 1972 by the Royal Shakespeare Company; *The Shaughraun* gave him a part wonderfully suited to his Irishness as it did for Cyril Cusack in Dublin in the 1960's (also seen at the Aldwych during one of Peter Daubeney's World Theatre Seasons), and *The Colleen Bawn** – the first 'sensation' drama – based on Gerald Griffin's novel *The Collegians* is still regularly performed by fit-up and small touring companies in Ireland to this day. Its first production in England at the Adelphi Theatre in 1860 netted no less than £45,000 for the author, and was burlesqued by countless lesser hands, including, inevitably, H J Byron.

Dionysius Lardner Boucicault (or Bourcicault, or Boursiquot) was born in Dublin on an indeterminate date under dubious circumstances. It seems fairly certain that he was the illegitimate son of the family's lodger who later assumed a degree of responsibility for the boy's welfare and education, for it was at London University that Boucicault studied under a 'Dr Lardner'. But despite his English schooling, he never lost his thick Dublin brogue, which always limited his range as an actor.

Boucicault began his career in the theatre at Brighton under the name Lee Morton. Here he had his first piece staged at the Theatre Royal in 1838; this was *A Legend Of The Devil's Dyke* – he was ever adept at suiting the play to the locale. His version of *Les Pauvres de Paris* was first produced as *The Poor of New York*, then as *The Poor of Liverpool*, finally reaching the Metropolis as *The Streets of London* (1864).

In 1839 Boucicault was acting at the Haymarket, and the following year was engaged by the Queen's Theatre, Tottenham St (later the Prince

---

*The full text is included in George Rowell's 'Nineteenth-Century Plays', 1953

314

Dion Boucicault, Vanity Fair, 1882. Spy cartoon.
(*Victoria & Albert Museum*)

of Wales). In 1841 *London Assurance* took the town by storm, and Boucicault used his own name (if it was his own name) thenceforward. But it was at the Princess's under Charles Kean's management from 1852 onwards that he laid the foundations of his fame as an actor and dramatist, although the Irish plays were not to emerge until his first visit to the United States.

For the Princess's in Oxford St he wrote, amongst others, *The Vampire* (with himself as the bloodsucking monster, without make-up but with Irish accent!) which was full of those startling effects and mechanical innovations for which he was to become so celebrated, *Louis XI* and *The Corsican Brothers*, both adapted from Casimir Delavigne, and both splendidly mounted and played by Kean. *The Corsican Brothers* was an especial favourite of Queen Victoria's (she was later to see *The Colleen Bawn* three times) and was still in Irving's repertoire the week he died fifty-three years after its first production.

Boucicault's social conscience occasionally led him on to very thin ice: *The Octoroon* (New York, 1859) was one of the first plays to deal, however obliquely, with what is now called the 'colour problem', *Arrah-na-Pogue* (1864, 'Arrah of the Kiss' – a rebel secret sign) and *The Shaughraun* (1875) featured the dangerous theme of Fenianism, *The Long Strike* (1866) denounced capitalism, and *The Rapparee* (1870) attacked the Protestant William of Orange – for Boucicault was passionately devoted to Home Rule. On one occasion he fell right through the ice by singing 'The Wearing o' The Green' at the Gaiety at a time when Anglo-Irish relations were particularly strained. The actor-author was hissed off the stage for his temerity.

In 1863 Boucicault lost a great deal of money in management at Astley's (he was neither the first nor the last to come to grief at this notoriously unlucky house) and lost £10,000 of someone else's money with a fairy extravaganza at Covent Garden called *Babil & Bijou* (1872). It is said that he fled to America before the curtain rose in order to escape his backer's wrath. But whatever his peccadilloes, he was a charming and hospitable man, witty and brilliant in conversation, and was 'popular in all circles, Bohemian or otherwise'.

Dion Boucicault was the first dramatist to demand a share of the box-office receipts instead of accepting a lump sum per performance or for the copyright; he made sundry technical and scenic innovations – notably the Corsican trap – and claimed, with some justification, to have 'discovered' Irving whom he engaged in Manchester in 1866. Irving stipulated that if he should prove his worth, he should have the offer of a London engagement. In Boucicault's *Two Lives Of Mary Leigh* Irving did indeed make his mark, and it was in his original role of Rawdon Scudamore in this play (retitled *Hunted Down*) that the future leader of his profession first impressed London audiences at the St James Theatre later that year.

Boucicault was an absolute master-craftsman; his dialogue is taut and the construction of his myriad pieces shows a consummate flair. He was highly individual, stylish and inventive, despite the undeniable fact that hardly anything he wrote was entirely original. 'Sensations' featured in nearly all his plays: in *The Colleen Bawn* there is the famous dive into the sea, in *The Shaughraun* a similar water rescue, in *The Octoroon* a ship blows up and the villain is convicted by the evidence of a photographic plate, in *The Long Strike* the hero is saved by a telegraph message; *Flying Scud* (1866) featured the Derby, no less, and *Formosa* (1869) the Boat Race! *Foul Play* (1868) offered another wrecked ship, *Pauvrette* (1858) an avalanche; in *Rescued* (1879) the villain controls a swing-bridge over which an approaching train is to pass, while the heroine struggles to alter the points...

Boucicault was also a noted stage-manager, prompted by the improvement in scenery, dressings, costuming and general production standards of Charles Kean and J R Planché with whom he was associated at various times. Like them he was much concerned with the unifying of a presentation; his productions had a discipline, a style and an overall polish which we might describe as 'professional'. He paid great attention to trick effects and to lighting, thus helping to inaugurate the end of the actor's ages-long domination of the stage and the beginning of 'director's theatre'. The latest gadgets and inventions were dragged into his pieces (as noted above) either to forward the plot or simply for display – he has been described as being like a child with a Pollock's Toy Theatre, always looking for ways to change and alter even when he could not (or did not wish to) improve the drama as such.

He was an instinctive writer whose comedy retains its effervescent sparkle and gaiety and whose plots are laid out with an unerring sureness of touch. Literature and fine writing did not attract him; he was fundamentally a man of the theatre and a man of his time. In short, Dion Boucicault was a hack – but the very best hack that the melodrama ever produced.

His first visit to New York was in 1853, caused by his despair at ever being able to amass a fortune from playwriting in England (he only received £300 for *London Assurance*); in 1876 he settled permanently in New York, repudiating his wife (Agnes Robertson, Charles Kean's adopted daughter) in order to make a second 'marriage'. There he remained, apart from occasional visits to London and a short trip to Australia, where he married his third wife. He ended his days in New York sadly, as a poorly paid teacher of drama, although his influence on the American Theatre was incalculable.

All his four children – two sons and two daughters – were connected with the stage at one time or another; Dion junior became a much respected actor-manager in London, and Nina is chiefly remembered today as the original Peter Pan.

I have deliberately chosen not to include one of Byron's or Boucicault's better known pieces; but as I wanted to include an example of the work of these two celebrated authors, and as space is limited, I thought I would kill two birds with one stone by abridging a piece which they wrote in collaboration.

'Lost' plays were always popular – *Lost A Sovereign*, *The Lost Child*, *The Lost Letter*, *The Lost Shilling*, *The Lost Son*, *Lost in London*, *Lost And Found*, *The Lost Bride of Garryowen*, *Lost By A Head*, *The Lost Fortune*, *The Lost Husband*, *The Lost Inheritance*, *Lost In The Snow*, *The Lost Letter*, *The Lost Overture*, *The Lost Son Found*, *The Lost Ship*, *Lost £30,000*, *The Lost Will*, etc, etc. *Lost At Sea; A London Story* contains all the ingredients for success: the 'loss' theme, a mention of the sea, and a location which could be changed as required.

LOST AT SEA

Dramatis Personae

As first performed at the Adelphi Theatre*
October 2nd, 1869

Walter Coram by Arthur Stirling
Lord Alfred Colebrooke by J D Beveridge†
Jos. Jessop by George Belmore
Rawlings by Mr Atkins
Franklin by C H Stephenson
Smyly by Eliza Johnstone
Griffiths by Mr Skinner
Dr Thorpe by C Locksley
Jones by Mr Tomlin
Gabriel by C J Smith
McKay by Mr Hawthorne
Bidder by Mr Cooper
Grey by Mr Romer
Katey by Miss Rose Leclerq
Laura Franklin by Miss Lennox Grey
Mrs Jessop by Mrs Leigh Murray
Mrs Pybus by Mrs Stoker
Lady by Miss E Turtle
Newsboy by Miss Stoker
Boy with 'Echo' by Master Sidney

Also a crowd of supernumeraries

---

*Some of these characters have disappeared in this abridgement

†This was J D Beveridge's first appearance in London; he was in general favourably received, although his slight Irish accent which he was unable completely to disguise, caused some comment.

LOST AT SEA

Act 1

Scene 1
An elegant room in Franklin's villa at Acton. Griffiths, a servant, is arranging table

Enter Franklin in his dressing-gown, leaning on the arm of Laura

Laura There, papa! That little walk in the garden will give you an appetite for breakfast. It is nearly nine o'clock.
Franklin (*To servant*) Has Mr Rawlings arrived from town with my letters?
Laura Why do you worry yourself about your business! The doctor ascribed your illness to over-work and anxiety. (*A bell rings*) Ah, there comes your cashier, Mr Rawlings. See, already you turn pale! – your hands tremble! – sit down! Why are you so troubled?

Enter Rawlings with a leather letter-bag

Franklin Good morning, Rawlings!
Rawlings Good morning, sir; good morning, Miss Franklin.
(*Laura bows coldly to him, and while he opens the bag at table, she and her father speak aside*).
Laura I don't like that man.
Franklin You are mistaken in him; I have daily proofs of his devotion.
Laura So have I; but you mistake their object.
Franklin Leave us, Laura.

(*Rawlings goes to open door for her. He bows; she goes out*).

Franklin (*Eagerly*) Well?
Rawlings The 'Bombay Castle' is lost!
Franklin Lost!
Rawlings Gone to the bottom, with every soul on board!
Franklin Thank heaven! (*Rises*) I am saved!

319

Rawlings It is a respite, at least, for some months.

Franklin There is no doubt that Mr Coram was a passenger in the vessel?

Rawlings Not the remotest

(*Franklin buries his face in his hand and sits*).

What is the matter, sir?

Franklin The joy that I feel at this terrible disaster is that of a murderer! This man, Coram, whom I have never seen, confided to my firm great sums of money for investment; and because I have misappropriated his funds to mend my broken fortunes – because I have robbed him – I feel rejoiced at his untimely death!

Rawlings Let us not reproach Providence with a capital offence! Had he presented himself –

Franklin I must have acknowledged myself a fraudulent bankrupt.

Rawlings But Mr Coram has executors – someone will represent him.

Franklin No – he has no relatives in England. He was a waif whom fortune floated out to India, where he accumulated his vast wealth. Here are his letters: you will see that he has led a solitary, retired life, buried in a distant district of Nepal.

Rawlings He may have neglected to leave a memorandum of the money deposited in your bank – or such may have been lost with him. There exist no traces of the large sums we have received.

Franklin And in a year or two our firm will have re-established its affairs on a firm basis. Then – then Rawlings –

Rawlings Then, sir, we can afford to be honest.

Franklin And I can afford to repay your fidelity.

Rawlings (*Aside*) I mean you shall, and handsomely. Nothing less than a share in your bank, and the hand of your daughter, will satisfy me.

Franklin (*Opening a letter*) What is this? A letter from Walter Coram! My hand shakes! – my sight is troubled. Read it.

Rawlings It is dated from India, a month before his departure. Be calm, sir; it is only a letter advising us of his intention to send part of his baggage by way of the Cape, addressed to our care, at the bank.

Franklin Has it arrived?

Rawlings No, sir

Enter a servant

Servant Lord Alfred Colebrooke!

Enter Lord Alfred. Exit Servant

Lord A. Ah! my dear Franklin! how is our Pall Mall Croesus this morning? How do, Rawlings?

Franklin You enter like a ray of sunshine. Laura will be so pleased to see you.

Lord A. My dear sir, before I indulge in Laura again – I have to submit to you a very grave piece of news.

Franklin Indeed!

Lord A. Fact is, my brother Bob, the Duke – the best of fellows – who for twenty-two years has lived quite contented with me for an heir, has altered his mind.

Franklin What do you mean ? He cannot disinherit you – the estate goes with the title.

Lord A. Unfortunately it does; because the young vagabond whom my sister, the Duchess, has just introduced into the family might have had the dukedom, if he had only left me the estates.

Franklin The Duke has a son and heir!

Lord A. Yes. Bob has written me such a kind letter about it – he is so glad, and so sorry – so full of pride and sympathy. By Jove, sir, such a brother is worth the fortune I have lost. Hello, Croesus! – what's the matter ?

Rawlings Excuse me, my lord, but the large sums advanced to you by our firm remain uncovered!

Lord A. Pardon me, my shares in the Polgelly Mines and the Mexico Gas –

Rawlings Are not worth the stamps upon them!

Lord A. Why, then I owe Mr Franklin –

Rawlings Upwards of forty thousand pounds!

Lord A. By Jove! – you don't mean that! Why did you not tell me of this ?

Franklin Your relation to Laura forbade it, and your expectations were good security. (*Rises*) But do not reproach yourself. This news did somewhat affect me at first, but I beg you to accept the amount we have lent you as an instalment on Laura's fortune. I will send her to you.

Lord A. How can I repay your generosity ?

Franklin Make my child happy. (*Exit*).

Lord A. I don't feel quite comfortable under this arrangement. It is splendid on the old boy's part, of course. But, 'pon my life, I think I should prefer Laura without a shilling – she would appear to belong to me; now, I seem somehow to belong to her – and not in a nice way.

Rawlings You are quite right, my lord. Mr Franklin is on the verge of bankruptcy, to which extremity you have assisted him.

Lord A. I – I –

Rawlings He deceives you and his daughter! This illness was caused by the state of his affairs! Ruin and disgrace beset him! There is but one issue from his difficulties! His fortune may be retrieved if you oppose no obstacle to the plan.

Lord A. I oppose! I would go to the devil to save the dear old boy. What can I do ?

Rawlings Withdraw your pretensions to his daughter's hand. If you marry her you will squander the last valuable asset of which her father can dispose – her person.

Lord A. Yes, I see. She might marry a man whose wealth would prop the falling house while her father's fortunes were under repair. I'm in the way.

Rawlings Pardon the blunt address of a man of business.

Lord A. I appreciate it gratefully – you are right in your commercial way – not very delicate, but quite right.

Rawlings (*Going*) Good morning!

Lord A. (*Takes his hand*) Thanks, dear Mr Rawlings, many thanks!

(*Exit Rawlings*).

£40,000 in debt! To pay which I have my lieutenant's commission in the Life Guards, and an allowance of £400 a year from my brother Bob

Enter Laura

Laura What's the matter, Alfred ?

Lord A. There's a good deal, Laura! To begin with – I am ruined – and I have given your father a commercial crisis.

Laura And yet he speaks of you so kindly!

Lord A. I suppose you have heard, Laura, you can never be a duchess ?

Laura Papa has just told me all about it. Do you think I regret it ?

Lord A. We must not think of marrying, Laura; I can't afford luxuries in the place I am going to.

Laura Alfred, are you serious ?

Lord A. Rarely, my dear; but I – I am rather so now. I must sell my commission, and pay the proceeds to your father. I must borrow from my brother £10,000, and pay that off my debt to the bank, and then I go out to Brazil.

Laura Are you mad, dear ?

Lord A. I don't think so. You see, the Count d'Eu, the Commander-in-Chief out there, is a great friend of ours. I hope he will give me a regiment, or put me on his staff.

Laura And me, Alfred – what's to become of me ?

Lord A. I would ask you to wait for me, if I thought I was worth waiting for; but I'm not worthy of a girl like you!

Laura And you propose – deliberately and coldly – to – to – sacrifice me to your pride ?

Lord A. No, Laura; if I could share your wealth, my love is mean enough to be tempted with you as a bribe. But our marriage means your sharing my poverty. It means your father's ruin. We have a painful duty to perform, my dear, but if we are worthy of each other, we must do it – we must say Farewell.

Laura Yes, yes! I know! Oh! how good you are! You think of him when I am forgetful and ungrateful. Yes, we must part – (*Embracing him*)

– mustn't we?

    Lord A. Yes! – Ah! but this is not the way to begin.

The scene closes in

Scene 2

Jessop's dispensary, a low-class quack's shop. Over the window and door, 'Jessop, Herbalist, and Dealer in Cures'

Smyly, a boy, enters. He is dressed as a pill-box and has handbills for distribution

    Smyly (*Calling off*) You jest wait, then, till I gets out o' my drum'
I'll let you know who's Jessop, and who's Jim Smyly! 'Tain't no wonder
the boys chivies me! This here rig is wuss than wot I was born in in the
workhouse. Blessed if the werry cab-horses don't shy at me. (*Sings*)
    Oh, valkin' in the Zoo, Is the rowdy thing to do.
    Ri too ral looral loo, That's hall I hever noo

Enter Mrs Jessop

    Mrs Jessop Is that the way you earn your bread, you wagabone, not
to speak of eighteenpence a week reg'lar? Oh! the expense and eddication
lavished on that boy by my husband, the doctor, nobody knows!
    Smyly No, they don't! Look'ee here, Mrs Jessop, I can't gaff like
this here no longer!
    Mrs Jessop Jim Smyly, when I looks at you, I'm surprised to hear
you talk so! To think of the gruel we took you from, and the cold meat and
potatoes you gets every day! For you ain't a boy; you're a happetite! If
there's a thing I can't a-bear, it's hingratitood! My husband, the doctor, is
away on business in the country for a month, but –
    Smyly In the country! oh, my eye! in the Home Hoffice Hotel, at
Clerkenwell, you mean – got a month for practisin' physic without a
license!
    Mrs Jessop (*Crying*) Oh, you unfeeling boy! –
    Smyly Here! – I didn't mean to turn the water on! (*Opens a trap-
door in the top of his pill-box, and takes out a rag of a handkerchief*) There –
blow your nose, and don't bear no malice – the old man's time will be up
in another month, and then he'll come home! (*Exit*).
    Mrs Jessop While Jessop has been in trouble, that boy has been
making up the remedies – wot he have given to the public I'm sure I don't

323

know – but I never takes up a noospaper without a cold prespiration – and my heye nat'rally goes to the hinquests. (*Exit*)

Enter Jessop, his hair cut short

Jessop How astonished the family will be to see me arrive home a month before my time is out! Not more astonished than I was this morning to get my discharge

Enter Rawlings

They said at the prison as someone had interested themselves about me. Who could it have been?
Rawlings Can't you guess, Joe?
Jessop Rawlings!
Rawlings Yes. It is not because my fortunes have gone up in the world since I was in your service yonder as book-keeper that I forget you.
Jessop You! you get my release!
Rawlings One of the customers of our bank is obliged to me, and I made him use his influence. What's the matter with you?
Jessop I'm trying to guess why you took all this trouble to get me out of prison. Come, what is at the bottom of this?
Rawlings What a brute you are, Joe!
Jessop Cut it short, and lay it open.
Rawlings Franklin and Sons are insolvent. We have been in daily expectation of the arrival of a gentleman from India who is our largest depositor. We must account to him for eighty thousand pounds.
Jessop That will put your shutters up, I suppose?
Rawlings It would have that inevitable effect; but a week ago, late at night, I was alone in my private office at the bank, balancing my cash, when four cases arrived, bearing the well-known initials of our customer. They were directed to our safe keeping until his arrival. Those cases contain his papers, his correspondence, and values to a considerable amount.
Jessop How do you know that?
Rawlings This morning I broke them open.
Jessop What will the owner say when he arrives?
Rawlings He will never arrive. He went down in the 'Bombay Castle' mail-steamer.
Jessop Lost at sea! But he has got relatives to look after his leavings?
Rawlings Not a soul!
Jessop Then this money the bank holds in charge – it will lie there till somebody turns up to claim it?
Rawlings To-morrow he will present himself at our bank, to our consternation, and he will in person assure us of his wonderful escape.
Jessop Oh!

324

Rawlings He will be furnished with all his vouchers, and with our own letters written to him during the past five years. I found them in the cases now lying in my private room in the bank. He will deposit with us £5,000 of India Stock, and £12,000 miscellaneous securities, which now are locked up in my safe.

Jessop Lord, Jack! – stop and let's take breath! twelve and five, £17,000. What sort of a fellow is this Walter Coram going to be?

Rawlings A man much about your size – not unlike you, but bronzed with the Indian sun – grey-haired, and remarkably taciturn – he employs his time chiefly in reading this diary, which I found amongst his papers. (*Produces a black book*) A curious book, in which he has entered his daily doings and thoughts for years past.

Jessop (*Reads*) 'My diary, from 1844, Walter Coram; born in the Foundling Hospital, London. August 15, 1823'. This is a big thing! How much?

Rawlings One hundred and forty thousand pounds!

Jessop And – and – my share!

Rawlings Halves!

Jessop Seventy thousand pounds!

Rawlings A new life in America unfolds itself before you!

Jessop Far from my creditors and from Mrs J J!

Rawlings To work then! You must start for Southampton by the five o'clock express; in three hours hence you can telegraph Mr Franklin the news of your arrival in England. The cases must be removed from the bank at once. We were closing as I left. I can put them in a cab and store them here.

Jessop It is a bold stroke for fortune, Jack.

Rawlings Nothing venture, Joe, nothing win. (*Exeunt*)

Scene 3
Jessop's back shop and sitting room. Smyley behind a small counter, is pounding drugs in a mortar. Mrs Jessop is preparing tea, cutting bread-and-butter

Mrs Jessop Can't you hold your noise and pound easy? Don't you know we have got a hinvalid lodger up stairs?

Smyly The neighbours will think the business is a-falling hoff if they don't hear summat a-goin' on!

Enter Katey

Mrs Jessop Well, Katey, how is your patient to-day?

Katey So well that he can be removed now. He seems quite loathe to leave us, mother.

Smyly I should think he wos. Four meals a-day, and the back hattick all to hisself, and to be nussed and coddled by you! only try me at it.

Mrs Jessop Hold your tongue! this is no concern of yours.

Smyly Ain't it? didn't I see the 'Ansom cab go to smash at the corner of our lane? Didn't I have the gentleman brought here on a shutter instead of to the hospital?

(*Shop bell rings*)

There's the shop. (*Jumps over the counter*) Oh, it's old Mrs 'Obbs – her baby's bad agin, I suppose. (*Exit*)

Mrs Jessop Katey – your patient is cured of one pain, but he hev catched another, my dear.

Katey What d'ye mean?

Mrs Jessop Ain't you woman enough to see what's the matter with him? He loves you, Katey!

Katey Nonsense, mother!

Mrs Jessop It's no nonsense, my dear, and it is only fair to our lodger to let him know as other parties has a priorer claim on you.

Katey Do you really think that this stranger cares for me?

Mrs Jessop I do – and what's more, I wouldn't say no to him in a 'urry. Mr Rawlings ain't been nigh this house for three weeks. As he gets hon in the world, he's been a-cooling off towards you. Why haven't he married you, now he can afford it?

Katey I don't know. I am content to love him and to wait, and I won't hear him abused, mother.

Mrs Jessop Don't be so wiolent – don't be a firework!

Katey Then don't speak against my John.

Mrs Jessop Why don't he come to see you – 'specially now your father is in trouble?

Katey Mr Franklin is ill; and all the work of the Bank falls on John

Enter Walter Coram

Mrs Jessop Good day, Mr Walter; proud to see you well.

Walter I almost regret my recovery, for I have spent the happiest hours of my life under your roof.

Mrs Jessop (*Aside*) There! ain't that plain enough for any girl? I'll leave 'em alone.

(*Shop bell. Exit Mrs Jessop*)

Walter I shall never forget your kindness!

Katey And I shall be sorry to say good-bye, Mr Walter!

Walter I am going out into the world, where I have not a single relation! I have no home! I never felt the want of a companion until you shed a light into my obscure life, and made me feel that I am alone.

Katey Surely you have some friend.

Walter Not one!

Katey No friends – no relatives – that is strange!

Walter Thirty-five years ago I left the Foundling Hospital a nameless orphan to earn my bread as light porter. One night when passing through St James's Park in a heavy rainstorm I overtook a gentleman to whom I offered my umbrella. He accepted a share of it only, and as we jogged along he inquired who and what I was. The next day he sent for me, gave me a sovereign and a letter to the manager of the Agra Bank. Here they employed me as messenger, then I rose to be clerk; in that capacity I was sent to India, where eventually I started in business on my own account.

Katey And during all these years you have not found a man whom you could make your friend?

Walter I lived in a distant district of Nepal, far from society.

Katey But not from women whom you could love?

Walter I never met one until now – do not be angry with me if I am abrupt. I am old enough to be your father, but if you could –

Katey Oh no – don't say what you are going to say. Oh! I am so sorry, dear Mr Walter. I would give you the love you so well deserve, but indeed I can't!

Walter You love another person, then?

Katey Yes – devotedly. I love him so, that the feelings I have excited in you seem to reproach me with having been false to him.

Walter No, my dear Katey, you have not given me encouragement, and it was your modest reserve first gained my affection

Enter Rawlings

Katey Dear John, I knew you would come at last.

Walter This is the gentleman of whom you spoke?

Katey Yes.

Walter Then, sir, I have to offer you an explanation. I have just made this lady an offer of marriage, which she declined in such a manner as to increase, if possible, the esteem and admiration I entertain for her. I congratulate you, sir. (*Aside*) I don't like his looks, but 'tis natural I should not.

Rawlings Your admiration needs no apology, sir, and I am sorry you found me in possession of the heart you prized.

Smyly (*Looking in*) The cabman wants to know if he is to take down the luggage?

327

Rawlings Yes. (*Smyly disappears*) Have you any place where you could stow away some cases for me for a few days?

Katey If Mr Walter would not mind them lying in his room.

Walter I am about to vacate it.

Rawlings Excuse me then, Katey. (*Exit*).

Walter What is your lover's name?

Katey John Rawlings. He is cashier in the house of Franklin and Company.

Walter Franklin! – the banker?

Katey Do you know the firm?

Walter Yes – that is – slightly. I have heard of it

Enter Smyly and a Cabman, carrying a black case

Smyly Leave it there. (*Exeunt Smyly and Cabman*).

Katey I am sure you will like him – he will stop to tea. I should wish you to like him as much as you like me. (*Exit*).

Walter Possible – not probable. I wonder what he is. (*Sees the case*) Ha! – why that case is exactly like one of those I sent from Ceylon by long sea to London!

Re-enter Smyly and the Cabman, with a second case

Smyly Number two! (*Exeunt*).

Walter (*Examining the case*) The address has been removed. 'Tis singularly like! Stay – (*Taking out a bunch of keys*) – I have the keys of these chests. (*He fits the key in the lock*) It fits the lock! (*He raises the lid*) My own papers – my books – mine! – here – am I dreaming? – there are my letters too – what can this mean? Have they discovered my arrival here? Is this a jest? (*He locks the box*) We shall see

Re-enter Cabman with a third case, followed by Mrs Jessop, Rawlings and Katey

Rawlings That will do – there – (*Pays the cabman*).

Cabman Thankye, sir (*Exit*).

Walter You lost your keys, I presume?

Rawlings No; the cases are not mine – they belong to a gentleman who has just arrived from India, after escaping most wonderfully from shipwreck on his voyage home. Very fortunately he had sent this part of his effects by another route – so he wrote to me this morning to open his cases and send him a large sum of money and bills which were in his portfolio.

Walter Oh! And where is he now?

Rawlings At Southampton.

Mrs Jessop Now, gentlemen, the tea is ready

Enter Smyly, with a tea-kettle

Katey Come, John, dear, how delightful it is to sit beside you again.

Walter (*Aside*) This man is in earnest! There is some impostor at work, who believing me to be dead, is about to represent me, and obtain possession of my fortune. Is this man his dupe or his accomplice?

Rawlings You forgot, Katey, to introduce this gentleman to me.

Katey So I did. Mr Walter – Mr Rawlings.

Rawlings I hope we shall be better acquainted.

Walter I feel sure we shall. Now, my dear sir, perhaps during tea you will favour us with the romances of the shipwreck?

Rawlings With pleasure.

Walter What is your hero's name?

Rawlings Coram.

Walter Coram! I am all curiosity.

Smyly Order! – hush! – order there in the gallery – order!

(*As Rawlings prepares to begin the story, the act-drop falls*)

Act 2

Scene 1

The villa at Acton. House and garden. Griffiths, the butler, is arranging a small table on one side. Laura advances

Laura Place the table there, and then tell the gentlemen that coffee is served here – in the garden

(*Exit Griffiths*)

Why does not Alfred leave the men to their wine? I'm sure he could steal away if he liked

Alfred enters

Lord A. Ah! what a relief!

Laura What do you think of our visitor, Mr Coram?

Lord A. Candidly? Well, candidly, Coram is a cad.

Laura I won't have him abused, Alfred! His money has already re-established the Bank, and since his arrival my father's health has been restored as if by a miracle. I am sure the particulars he related of his escape from shipwreck were quite thrilling.

Lord A. Very. That man don't inspire me at all.

Laura You are very ungrateful then; for now Papa assures me that all anxiety about his affairs is past, and there can be no excuse for your departure.

Lord A. Your father deceives you. The panic in the city to-day has paralyzed credit.

Laura I wish you would think less of money and more of me.

Lord A. Your father relies on the support of this man, Coram. I have no faith in him, Laura. He is a vulgar, low-bred fellow!

Laura I see how 'tis; you wish to release yourself from me, Alfred; you desire to find some excuse to be rid of our engagement. I have seen that for some time. (*The gatebell rings*) If you love someone else, tell me so

Enter Griffiths, who crosses to the gate, and opens it

Lord A. You don't believe in what you are saying.

330

Laura Yes, I do. Why, then, are you so reluctant to hope? Why, if you loved me as I love you, you would beat out one single grain of hope until you gilded our future lives with it. You don't wish to hope. Very well! Good bye! Go!

Lord A. I think I had better. (*Exit into house*).

Griffiths (*Speaking to one outside the gate*) Yes, sir, Mr Franklin is at home; but he is at dinner, with some friends.

Laura Who is it, Griffiths?

Griffiths A gentleman, miss.

Laura How provoking! Ask him to walk in

Enter Walter Coram

Walter I would not intrude –

Griffiths This is Miss Franklin. (*Exit Griffiths*).

Walter I wished to remind Mr Franklin of a service he rendered me over thirty years ago. My name is Walter; but he will not remember me, though I cannot forget all I owe my benefactor.

Laura I will tell him – pray take a seat. (*Exit*).

Walter I like that girl – she has the honest blue eye of her father! So! my double is in possession already. I heard of his arrival – traced him to this house, and could not restrain my curiosity to see what he is like

Enter Laura and Lord Alfred

Laura (*Clinging to his arm*) Don't be angry with me, Alfred, there's a dear – I won't do it again.

Walter (*Aside*) I see how it is with those two young ones

Enter Franklin and Rawlings

Franklin Mr Walter, I really forget the occasion on which we met.

Walter Do you remember a poor youth to whom you gave a sovereign and a letter to the Agra Bank some thirty years ago?

Franklin Surely – surely – but you are not that orphan boy?

Walter Here, attached to my watch-chain is that coin – it has been my talisman. As you pressed it into my hand, you said, 'Go into the world, boy, be as honest as you look, and you will prosper'. I have prospered, sir, and I have come to tell you that your good-nature has not been thrown away, nor your faith in me misplaced. That is all I have to say; and I thought the pleasure it would give you to hear it would excuse my intrusion. (*Bows and offers to go*).

Franklin (*Taking his hand*) Stay, Mr Walter, I cannot allow you to deprive me of this pleasure so soon. You must join our little party here. This is my daughter, Laura. Lord Alfred Colebrook, Mr Walter. (*Introduces them*). Mr Rawlings.

Walter We have met before.

Rawlings Why did you not tell me that you were obliged to our Mr Franklin?

Walter Because I desired the matter should reach him from my own lips

Enter Jessop, dressed as Coram – bronzed face, small white whiskers, white hair

Franklin This is my good friend, Mr Walter Coram – Mr Walter. (*Introducing them*).

Walter (*Affecting surprise*) Walter Coram! That name is quite familiar to me!

Jessop (*Aside*) The deuce it is!

Walter Have you ever been in India?

Jessop India! Of course. (*Hesitating*) India – to be sure – I never was anywhere else. (*Confused*) Ha! ha! quite so!

Walter I thought I could not be mistaken.

Rawlings (*Aside*) Jessop is turning pale!

Walter I should have recognized you at once.

Jessop (*Relieved*) Would you, really? – I shouldn't – that is – time changes a person.

Walter You recollect Futtehpoor, in 1858?

Jessop (*Aside*) Who is he?

Walter In the month of February?

Jessop Was it February – I thought it was in March.

Walter No, we were relieved in March.

Jessop So we were. (*Aside*) I wish I was relieved now.

Walter We could not have held out for another day. (*To the others*) Forty families, nearly all civilians, shut up in Colonel Fraser's compound, and completely surrounded.

Jessop On every side! (*Aside*) Oh, dear! there's nothing about all this in the diary! Your face begins to come back to my recollection – yes – it dawns upon me.

Franklin How strangely people meet in this world!

Jessop Very strangely. (*Aside*) I wish they didn't

The servants enter with liqueurs, and hand coffee

Rawlings (*Aside to Jessop*) Recover yourself – your emotion is visible.

Jessop (*Aside to Rawlings*) I should think it was! There's nothing about Futtypooh in the diary. This fellow is an impostor. I feel very uneasy.

Rawlings He said he recognized you!

Jessop Yes – but we know he didn't!

Griffiths hands a telegram to Franklin on a salver

Franklin (*Opening the telegram*) Excuse me. (*Reads apart and then to Rawlings*) Rawlings the business is important!

(*The servants go out. Jessop goes into the house and is seen drinking*)

Laura Then we shall leave you. (*Exit, with Lord Alfred and Coram*)

Franklin (*Reads*) The Bank of England refuses to advance specie on the deposit of Consols.

Rawlings We shall be able to meet any run that our customers can make upon us thanks to the deposits of Mr Coram.

Franklin He seems to have taken an extraordinary liking to you.

Rawlings He is full of strange whims which we must take care not to thwart

Jessop returns

Franklin How much I owe you, Rawlings! (*Exit*).

Jessop What was he talking about? Does he smell a rat about me?

Rawlings Not he! I have a plan to secure us from all exposure in case of any accident.

Jessop The deuce you have?

Rawlings I must marry this man's daughter! Franklin will not prosecute his own son-in-law. You must propose the alliance.

Jessop Are you going to throw over our Katey?

Rawlings Our safety demands the sacrifice. We are in for it now!

Jessop *I'm* in for it, you mean! I see your game, Jack. If I was caught, you would swear that you were deceived about me like any body else. You'd leave me in the hole!

Rawlings Recollect the stake Jos! – £70,000! You must make your support of the Bank conditional on his acceding to your humour, for you are a whimsical fellow, mind, and you are not to be crossed; you have taken an absurd fancy to me.

Jessop He'll never believe that.

Rawlings He will! he does!

Griffiths enters to remove the coffee service

Come this way and be sure you follow the instructions I give you

(*Exeunt*)

Smyly's head appears over the wall

Smyly My eye! what a swell place! I say Miss Katey, if you could only see it from here! No, I don't see Mr Rawlings nowhere, but here's a

Johnny. Psit! whew! here! (*Griffiths looks round*) Up here, stoopid!

Griffiths What are you doing there? Get down, directly.

Smyly I am saving you the trouble of hanswerin' the bell. Is Mr Rawlings here?

Griffiths Yes he is.

Smyly (*To Katey outside*) Johnny says it's all right.

Griffiths (*Opening the gate*) Whom do you want? Come in.

Enter Katey, Smyly disappears

Katey (*At the door*) I will wait outside, if you please. Would you give Mr Rawlings this letter, and tell him Miss Jessop wishes to see him for one moment.

Griffiths Remain here. I will let him know. (*Exit*)

Enter Smyly

Katey There can be no doubt, Jem, that my father was really liberated?

Smyly Didn't old Mrs Danel's see him last Monday, walking down our lane past her house, as plain as I see you?

Katey What has become of him?

Smyly See! here come two gents! step aside, Miss Katey, and let 'em go by! (*They retire into the shrubbery*).

Enter Franklin and Jessop

Franklin You cannot be serious in your proposition concerning my daughter.

Jessop I wish to secure the fortune as well as the happiness of my friend. He loves your girl! You never suspected that, did you?

Franklin No – but – I fear – she perceived it; in fact, she said as much.

Jessop Well?

Franklin She entertains an aversion for him she cannot overcome.

Jessop Would she not take your affairs into consideration?

Franklin (*After a pause*) Yes, she would; and that is why I ask you to spare her. I will not pretend that your assistance at this moment is of small importance to me. No: it is vital, Mr Coram. I make this confession to place my child under the protection of your generosity. Had I to choose between my ruin and her sacrifice – you know, sir, I could not hesitate.

Jessop I'm an obstinate fellow.

Franklin But a generous one. Come, let us finish the claret.

Jessop I will join you. (*Exit Franklin*).

Smyly (*Looking out of the shrubbery*) Tho guv'nor hisself here, dressed up and play-hacting!

334

Katey (*Looking out*) It cannot be my father – that gentleman's hair is white.

Smyly That's the heffect of prison diet. But what's his game? Hist! here comes Mr Rawlings. (*They retire*)

Re-enter Rawlings

Rawlings Well?

Jessop It's no go, Jack – the girl won't have you at any price.

Rawlings Then you must force it upon her; and, if necessary, she must know that it is not ruin only, but disgrace – fraud – felony that hangs over his head.

Jessop Why do you want to marry the girl that hates you?

Rawlings Because I love her – yes – I love her the more passionately because she does hate me. The little love I once felt for Katey is dead and gone a year ago. I never felt for her one tithe of the passion with which the contempt of this haughty girl inspires me.

Jessop Well – if I had no other motive but to save my infatuated girl from such a man as you are, John Rawlings, I'd do it.

Rawlings There's only one fault in your character, Jos, and that is, you will mix up sentiment with business. (*Exeunt into house*)

Smyly appears

Smyly Oh, please don't, Miss Katey! What shall I do? She's been and gone and fainted dead off! There's some water on the table in there – that 'ud fetch her to. (*Runs towards house*)

Enter Lord Alfred

Lord A. What are you doing? How came you here?

Smyly There's a young woman in here 'as fainted.

Lord A. Where is she? (*Enters the shrubbery*).

Smyly He picks her up like a baby. (*Enters the shrubbery*). She has come round! there! It is all right now. (*Looks round*) The road is clear. (*He opens the gate*)

Katey appears, Lord Alfred's arm around her

Lord A. You are better now?

Katey (*Crying*) Yes; I – I wish I wasn't – oh! I wish I was dead – dead. (*Falls sobbing convulsively on his shoulder*).

Lord A. Come – don't give way like this. It won't do at all, you know.

Smyly She can't hold up. I'll never get her to the end of the lane where the busses pass.

Lord A. I'll go with her

Re-enter Laura. As Lord Alfred helps Katey out at gate, Laura sees them and stands amazed. Smyly, looking after them, is going out

Laura Stay! what girl is that, and what brings her here?

Smyly Well, miss, she come after her old sweetheart, and little hexpected to find as how he was a-going to be married to the young lady here – that's you, I suppose, miss. The poor thing keeled right over, she did, 'cause they've been a-courting these two years – that's all! Good evenin'! (*Exit*).

Laura Alfred for two years past has maintained this affair! Oh, I cannot believe it! (*Goes to the gate and looks out*)

Enter Rawlings, with a letter in his hand

Rawlings Katey, here!

Laura (*Looking off*) How tenderly he bends over her! His arms are round her! He presses her hands! Ah!

Rawlings (*Aside*) She is gone! Has Laura seen her?

Laura I see why he relinquishes me so easily, and I – I have loved that man!

Rawlings Miss Franklin – Laura – you are ill!

Re-enter Lord Alfred by the gate

Lord A. What is the matter, Laura? (*Advances to her*).

Laura Nothing. I am very well. Come, Mr Rawlings.

She turns away, clinging to Rawlings, leavingqLord Alfred surprised; the scene closes in

Scene 2
A room in Jessop's house

Enter Mrs Jessop

Mrs Jessop There's nine o'clock gone, and Katey ain't got back. Mr Walter, too, is out. I am that lonely – for there's nothing at home except that shop-bell. (*Shop-bell*) There it is! (*Looks off*) Oh, it's Jem Smyly and my girl. Oh, whatever is been and 'appened?

Enter Smyly and Katey

Bless my 'eart, how white she do look!

Smyly Bring a chair – quick – and stop quakın'.

Mrs Jessop Of all the wulgar boys – what can you hexpect to get out

336

of a workhouse! Did you find out anything about your master?

Smyly Yes – no – we thought we did – but it turned out – (*The bell rings*).

Katey Oh, to hear what I have heard! – see what I have seen! My life is shattered – my heart is broken!

Enter Rawlings

Rawlings I received your letter, Katey, but you had gone before I – what is the matter?

Katey Nothing. I am very weak and ill.

Mrs Jessop No wonder. We are kep on the boil night and day about Jessop.

Rawlings (*To Katey*) You have learned nothing?

Katey Have you?

Rawlings No. I was unaware of his release.

Katey Yes – true – I forgot that. (*To Smyly*) Leave us, Jem. (*Exit Smyly*). John, there is something you have wished to tell me for some time past, is there not?

Rawlings Yes, Katey, there is. My affairs are in a hopeless state. I could see no issue out of the ruin around me; when this morning, Mr Franklin proposed to give me a share in the business if I would become his son-in-law.

Katey His daughter loves you, then?

Rawlings I wish I could return her passion.

Katey Oh! (*Covering her face with her hands*).

Rawlings I accepted his offer. If I cannot share my life with you, I can share my fortune. A part of the wealth she brings me shall be yours.

Mrs Jessop Well – he can't say no fairer than that, I'm sure.

Rawlings (*To Mrs Jessop*) Jessop has deserted you. I feel sure you will never see him again; but while I live she shall never want a penny. Come, Katey, we must make a sacrifice – say you won't forget me.

Katey Go your way! and good bye, John. We shall not meet again. I shall not trouble your schemes, nor cross your crooked path. Mine lies another way. Good bye. (*Exit*).

Mrs Jessop There! I was just as bad about a dozen young fellows afore I took Jessop. She'll marry and get over it.

Rawlings (*Giving her money*) Here's a fifty-pound note! Could you not shut up the shop at once, and go down to some quiet seaside place – take a house – let lodgings? I think change of scene would do her good. (*Going*).

Mrs Jessop I'm sure, sir, we can't do better nor take your advice – for which I'm not ungrateful. Good night, and thank you, which is more than Katey had the grace to say.

Rawlings Good night! (*Exit, followed by Mrs Jessop*)

337

Re-enter Katey

Katey He is gone, and there's an end! There's an end! It can't be love I feel for that man – it can't be – and yet I would die for him. I am mad! (*The bell rings*) Hush! someone enters the shop. It's Mr Walter! he loves me, heaven bless him! ha! ha! that's it. I cannot love those who love me, and I cannot hate those that hate me. I must steal out by the yard and through the side alley. (*Exit*)

Scene 3
A street – night

Enter Smyly and Walter Coram

Smyly She is after no good, I tell yer! Why did she creep out by the back yard, and slip away like a thief? I saw her.
Walter Yonder she sits, poor thing! She recognized her father, you say?
Smyly It worn't that as broke her 'eart; she's know'd *him* for what he is this long time! But when she heer'd Rawlings turn hisself hinside out, it bleached her werry 'eart, it did!
Walter How she must love that scoundrel!
Smyly Never trust me, sir, if she's not bent on some mischief to herself.
Walter If so, why did she not execute her design as she crossed Lambeth Bridge?
Smyly She 'adn't made up her mind 'ow to do it; but sudden it come across her, and she started up and hurried down here.
Walter Why, then, does she sit there so still and irresolute?
Smyly May be she's a-thinking of the past, and saying good-bye to some things – me, perhaps! Look! – she's on foot again! (*Exeunt*)

Scene draws, and discovers –

Scene 4
The Steamboat Pier at the foot of Hungerford Bridge. The pay-offices

During the following scene the traffic of cabs, omni-buses, waggons, etc, is maintained across Westminster Bridge. The dark form of a barge, with sail set, floats slowly up the river, it lowers the mast to pass under the bridge. A locomotive and train passes across the Railway Bridge above. These incidents occur at intervals

Katey (*To the Money-Taker*) The next boat down the river ?

Money T. In half an hour! (*Shuts the slide of his pay-place sharply*).

Katey (*Repeating mechanically*) In half an hour! (*Goes up*).

Boy Buy a Hecho, miss – only a ha'penny – third edition. Do, miss, I 'aint sold a paper to-day, and me and my little brother there 'aint tasted a toothful o' food since yesterday mornin'.

Katey Here! (*Empties her pocket*) Take it – take it all! All but the price of my ticket! (*Gives him money*).

Boy I say, missis, you don't mean to gi' me all this here silver ?

Katey Yes – I shan't want it – go!

Boy Don't you want a paper ?

Katey No – nothing! (*The Boy goes off slightly*).

Boy (*Aside*) She didn't empty her pockets for nuffin'. Here's a matter of six shillings; she don't know what she's a-doin' of! I'll stick to her – she shan't hurt herself if I knows it. I ain't been a Jack-in-the-water since afore I could walk for nuffin'!

Enter Smyly and Walter Coram. They stand behind Katey and on each side

Smyly This is no place for you, miss. (*Katey starts*).

Katey You – Jem! you here!

Walter You must come home, Katey.

Katey No, no! No more!

Smyly You're ill, miss, and you're a-goin' to take the wrong physic, that's all.

Boy (*Aside*) There's somebody after her.

Walter If you do not value your life, give it to some one who does; don't throw it away.

Katey Oh, I cannot return to a life where every hour has its separate torture, and every moment is a dread!

Walter I know the fraud in which your father and lover are confederates, and they little suspect that detection has been walking arm-in-arm with them! I am Walter Coram! I am the man who was lost at sea! I am the individual your father impersonates – whose place in life he has taken!

Katey You! You!

Smyly My eye!

Walter Unfortunately, I have no means of identifying myself. I am unknown in London. They have gained possession of all my documents and effects!

Katey If you cannot prove your own identity, you can prove my father's imposture – he is too well-known in London.

Walter I cannot prove the complicity of Rawlings. He is not yet in my power; but he will be.

Smyly Lord! – if I had such a fish as what he is on my hook, wouldn't I play with him!

Walter I am led to suspect that they are resolved to hold destruction over Franklin's head, and compel his daughter to sacrifice herself to save her father. A cheque, bearing my name, will be presented to-morrow at the bank – drawn for an amount which they know to be larger than the firm can pay. This will oblige Mr Franklin to close his doors. It is bankruptcy!

Katey And for my sake – yes! for love of my worthless ungrateful self – you would spare my father?

Walter Oh! Katey, if you bid me, I will spare your lover too.

Katey Do not think badly of me if my sore and bruised heart pleads for him! Do not punish him for my sake! But I know you will not – you are too good – too generous. But have I the right to ask? Oh! why can't I love you? (*They are going out*).

Boy (*Looking after them*) Ah! she's a hescaped lunatic, and them's her two keepers!

End of Act 2

Act 3

Scene 1
A room in Franklin's house. Lord Alfred waiting

Enter Griffiths

Griffiths Miss Franklin begs you will excuse her, my lord; she is not well enough to receive you.
Lord A. Pray convey to her my regret for having disturbed her.
Griffiths Will your lordship call again?
Lord A. I fear not, Griffiths; I am going away – rather – and – oh, Griffiths, as I mayn't see you for some little time, here's the Christmas-box I shall owe you when that time comes round. (*Gives him a five-pound note*).
Griffiths Thank you sincerely. Oh, here's master! (*Exit Griffiths*)

Enter Franklin

Franklin What's the matter with Laura?
Lord A. She thinks – that is, we both think, sir, that we had better part.
Franklin Nonsense! The storm that breaks over London to-day finds me well-prepared to meet it. Let our relations remain unchanged, I beg.
Lord A. May I ask you if any important event occurred last night – anything likely to have affected your daughter deeply?
Franklin Yes; Mr Coram made me a proposition, which I rejected promptly.
Lord A. It concerned Laura?
Franklin He proposed that she should marry Rawlings! In fact he offered to lend me a hundred thousand pounds if I would consent to their union

Enter Laura

Laura I – I beg pardon – I thought papa – that is, I did not know your lordship was here.

341

Franklin What is all this – have you quarrelled?

Laura I am quite satisfied now that a marriage with a person in Lord Alfred's position would be imprudent.

Franklin Laura, I profess to you I am astonished – but it is your affair.

Laura Exclusively, papa. I release Lord Alfred. He argued very fervently that it was our duty to part.

Lord A. Yes, I did endeavour to bring her to this resolution.

Laura You said so, my lord; but at the time I did not believe you.

Lord A. It is quite right. I leave for South America to-morrow. Here Mr Franklin, is an order on Cox to pay you the price of my commission, when sold. I have sent in my papers to the Horse Guards. I have a reversion, which I have directed my lawyer to sell. I cede to you those shares of mine, which are not so valuable as Mr Rawlings stated. That done, I believe I shall still remain your debtor for £12,000, including interest. Here is my brother's bond for the amount. (*Hands him the papers as he mentions them*) Good-bye sir! (*Turning to Laura*) Miss Franklin, I thank you from my heart for the happiest hours of my life. Farewell! (*Exit*).

(*Laura buries her face in her hands*)

Franklin Are you mad, Laura; or do you think men of that stamp of nature and breed of soul are to be called off the stand of society like cabs, when wanted; or have you ceased to love him?

Laura No. (*Sobbing*) You see I have not! I can't help it! Oh! he has deceived me – and I hate him! Oh – he – he does not spend all his happy hours with me, papa; there's – another one.

Franklin Oh, oh! another affair?

Laura Two years old – I've seen her – in his arms – she fainted when she heard of our engagement; for he had deceived her, of course!

Franklin Hem! hem! My dear – in that case, I really think when a young man in his position is a – endeavouring to relinquish a – or settle – a – a – a previous claim – of a – a – delicate nature –

Laura Indelicate – sir!

Franklin She had fainted! Humanity, my dear – decent feeling –

Laura Decent, sir! Can you find such language to excuse –

Franklin No, my dear – no. I don't excuse him. Let him go. I'll say no more; let us forget him.

Laura I dare say he will spend his last hours very happily with this girl.

Franklin Don't torture yourself with any such reflections.

Laura No; better wipe him out altogether.

Franklin Much the best plan. Wipe him out.

Laura I hate persons who pretend to a feeling while another occupies their heart – who pretend to love when they are indifferent –

Franklin Don't be so hard upon 'em, dear: human nature is weaker than you are aware of.

342

Laura Oh, papa, I do love him so; bring him back to me – do, on any terms.

Franklin Such was my intention, dear.

Laura Oh, you dear – dear – dear. (*Embracing him*) I cannot tell what possesses me – is it love ? – am I mad ?

Franklin Nature has provided a remedy for your pains.

Laura What is it – let me have it ?

Franklin Marriage, my dear. (*Exeunt*)

Scene 2

Lombard Street. A crowd of persons encumber street. A Policeman stands at Franklin's door. A file of persons are waiting their turn to enter Franklin's; another file are going into Sterling's. Clerks, Messengers, and Telegraph-Boys pass in and out of the Banks

Gent Control yourself, my dear – do – I beg – in half an hour our turn will come round. Surely we shall get our money.

Lady Oh, Charles, how can I help trembling when our children's lives – their bread – depends upon that half-hour !

Enter the Newsboy

Boy Last edition of the 'Telegraph' – the last list of failures – one penny ! (*Sells paper*).

1st Tradesman (*Buying paper*) This is a fine harvest for you, lad, eh ?

Boy I should think it wos – I ain't made such a day's work – no never. I wish it wos panic all the time

Enter a Man, drawing a cart, on which are two iron-bound boxes, guarded by two Policemen

All Gold ! – bullion !

Policeman Make way there ! By your leave !

Widow What is it ? – what is it ?

Clerk Gold ! Specie from the Bank of England !

All Where is it going ? To the Guarantee Bank ? To Sterling's ? To Franklin's ?

Policeman Stand back, there !

A lane is made. Two Porters enter from Franklin's and, under Rawlings' directions, the boxes are carried in

Rawlings (*To the Crowd*) I am desired to acquaint you that, instead of closing at the usual hour of four, this firm will keep its doors open until

343

six o'clock, to accommodate those depositors wishing for cash. (*Disappears*).

2nd Tradesman Franklin is all safe! I shall go home!

Tradeswoman Do you think so? I have left my four little ones all alone!

Enter Franklin

2nd Tradesman Here he is!

Franklin Allow me to pass! You need not fear for your money, my good friends, we are amply provided to meet you. (*Goes inside*)

All Three cheers for Franklin and Sons! Hurra!

A Clerk from Sterling's enters and posts a paper on the door. He re-enters, the doors close, and the shutters being to move up

Lady What is it, Charles?

Gentleman (*In clerical dress, reads the notice*) 'Sterling and Bond are obliged to suspend payment; and while their books undergo audit, they reckon on the indulgence of their customers'.

A low wail comes from the crowd. The Lady faints. Scene changes

Scene 3

The interior of Franklin's Bank. Rawlings and the Clerks are actively employed in paying out to the crowd of applicants who pour in at door

Rawlings (*Reading a cheque*) Two seventy-six and fourpence. How will you have it?

1st Tradesman Two in hundreds – rest in gold.

(*Rawlings counts out money*).

2nd Cashier (*Simultaneously with the above, reading a cheque*) Sixteen pound four and ten. (*Pays the boy who waits*)

Jessop enters the parlour during the above. He then peers through the partition into the Bank. He signals Rawlings, who enters by door in the partition, which he closes behind him

Jessop Well!

Rawlings Are you prepared? Have you the cheque?

Jessop Yes, there it is. (*Hands him a cheque*).

Rawlings £20,000! That will serve to break us. We shall not have half this amount in the till. What are you afraid of?

Jessop The consequences, Jack! This is forgery! It is transportation for life, John! Norfolk Island!

Rawlings No; 'tis £140,000! 'Tis the Island of Monte Cristo, Jos! You will present this cheque. I shall beg you to wait while I carry it to Franklin. When he sees himself face to face with ruin, he will subscribe to any terms.

Jessop Still, there stands the forgery, like the executioner.

Rawlings Fool! You know we can't pay this cheque – it must be returned to you. Then you will destroy it.

Jessop True! I forgot that! I think we are safe!

Clerk (*Opening door in partition*) You are wanted, Mr Rawlings

Rawlings passes quickly into Bank. Enter Franklin

Jessop I feel as if I was going to walk over Niagara on a tight-rope! If I fall, he shall stand half in. I'll take him down with me. Oh, lud! my heart is in my throat, and I can't swallow it! (*Exit*).

(*Franklin passes into Bank-parlour through the door in partition, preceded by Rawlings, who looks round first to see that Jessop has gone*).

Franklin Good! You say we have £14,000 still left?

Rawlings But we have withdrawn the last of our specie from the Bank of England.

Franklin Terrible times, these, Rawlings! How much I owe to Mr Coram – or perhaps, I should say, to you! but your interests are henceforth mine. I receive you into partnership; that is settled. There was another proposition made by Mr Coram.

Rawlings I am not aware of it.

Franklin I am glad of that, for it was absurd – unreasonable.

Rawlings No doubt, sir. He is a strange, wilful man. There is no reliance on him – (*Aside*) as you will soon discover.

(*A Clerk hands Rawlings a cheque, exit clerk*)

Franklin Already two-thirds of my customers have withdrawn their funds – fortunately, the larger depositors remain firm.

Rawlings The Ernest Assurance Company draws for its entire account, £8,300.

Franklin Pay it!

Rawlings 'Twill run us close.

Franklin We have no choice. (*Rawlings returns to the Bank*). I reckoned on the public companies standing by us. Oh, heaven, if after all I should not escape – if –

Enter Walter Coram into bank parlour by back door, he carries a small black bag

Franklin Mr Walter!

Walter Yes, Mr Franklin, I come to return you the good service you once did me. While in India I contracted, amongst other habits of the people there, one of carrying about my person a round sum in precious stones and valuables. It was fortunate I did so, for I have been able to make up a sum of £25,000, which I have brought here in this bag. I hope it comes in good time to meet any unexpected pressure upon your firm

Enter Jessop into the bank, he confers with Rawlings across the counter

Franklin My dear sir, I cannot express my gratitude. The trivial assistance I rendered you –

Enter Rawlings

Rawlings Ruin, sir! Mr Coram has presented this draft for £20,000. (*Hands Franklin the cheque*).

Franklin Did you beg him to see me?

Rawlings He said you knew the alternative.

Walter Yes, Mr Franklin knows it; but here's an alternative, my dear Mr Rawlings, the gentleman outside there does not perhaps expect. Pay him, there's the money!

Rawlings Pay – pay him?

Walter Ask him how he'll take it. (*Rawlings is about to take the cheque*). No! I'll take that, if you please. It's a sort of security – an acknowledgment.

Rawlings Of course – then I am to – to –

Walter Pay him his money – nothing is more simple.

Rawlings Exactly – as you say – nothing – is – more – simple

(*Takes the money up and goes out with it, into Bank*).

Walter This cheque is a forgery – that man is an impostor. He is no more Mr Coram than I – no – I mean than you are.

Franklin An impostor! – impossible. But he is receiving your money!

Walter Leave him to me, sir – I'll not lose sight of him. (*Exit hastily*).

Jessop (*In the bank, aside*) What's the matter with Jack, he is as pale as magnesia! Why don't he give me back the cheque

(*Rawlings place rolls of bank-notes on the counter*).

Jessop (*Aside*) He's never going to – to – to pay me!

Rawlings 10, 11, 12, 13,000, 14, 15, 16, 17, 18,000. I must give you the rest in gold.

Walter (*Beside Jessop*) You will want a policeman to see you home with this. Here, officer, attend to this gentleman

Tableau

Scene 4
A room in the Charing Cross Hotel

Enter Jessop

Jessop There is something wrong! What did Rawlings mean by paying me this money? There's a screw loose. The policeman waited upon me until I reached the door – I felt as if I was in custody – I dared not send him away – I have ordered my bill – I'll leave London – I'll go to the end of the world!

Enter a Porter, with bag and portmanteau

Thank you – leave them there! (*Exit Porter*) I must secure this money. (*Opens the portmanteau*) What's this? (*Takes out morocco case*) I never examined this trunk before. (*Reads the label on the case*) 'Bolton and Cleaver, Photographers, Calcutta!' the portrait of the defunct, no doubt! My likeness!

Enter Rawlings

What's the matter?
    Rawlings That fellow Walter entertains some suspicions. What is he? Who is he? this inscrutable lodger of yours who lives in a back attic, yet can command £20,000? Did you notice how he watched us as I paid you the cash?
    Jessop No. I was too astonished – and looked to you for explanation.
    Rawlings I dared not show a sign! Walter has some suspicion.
    Jessop He may know the dead man! and if so –
    Rawlings Why did he pretend to recognize you? He would have exposed our game then and there!
    Jessop Stay; Here is a photograph. I found it in this trunk amongst his cravats. See, his initials are on the case. How does it open? So. (*He opens the case and looks at the photograph*) Ah!
    Rawlings What's the matter?
    Jessop Look there! (*Hands him the picture*).
    Rawlings Why this is – the portrait of – the devil! – 'tis Walter, your lodger! Have we been his dupes – his playthings? Has he been deliberately waiting upon us?

347

Jessop Watching our little game, Jack, until we went in for forgery, and now he is down upon us.

Rawlings I can scarcely believe my senses! This Walter Coram escaped then?

Jessop My lie turned up true. It is horrible!

Rawlings Why has he concealed his existence? I see! Because we possessed the only means by which he could identify himself, and he found you in possession. Yes, yes! He has not discovered himself to Mr Franklin – therefore to all the world. (*Pauses*) Jos!

Jessop Jack?

Rawlings We have only one way to defeat him now.

Jessop I don't see it.

Rawlings He is dead – lost at sea.

Jessop That is, he ought to be.

Rawlings He must be – what he pretends to be – dead. Don't drop your jaw like an idiot! This man is angling for our lives. We are in his power. And he means to crush us both.

Jessop (*Aside*) There's a red glare in his eyes like a danger-signal.

Rawlings He sleeps in your house tonight!

Jessop I suppose he does. What then?

Rawlings Amongst your herbs and drugs at home you must have some good strong narcotic.

Jessop Laudanum is the basis of my 'Baby-Settler'. It is certain detection. Don't attempt it, Jack.

Rawlings I'll attempt nothing that will leave a trace detection can follow up. An accident will happen to-night, and in it the unknown and unclaimed man will disappear. Direct me where I can lay my hand on this drug.

Jessop The bottle on the shelf on the shop-door is labelled 'Opium Water'. You don't mean –

Rawlings To poison him! I'm not such a fool! I told you he shall disappear.

Jessop I don't want to know how. I leave it entirely to you. Oh dear! As a doctor I ought to be accustomed to this sort of thing. But what am I to do? Remain here?

Rawlings No. You must aid me to remove your wife and Katey from the house, so that your lodger may sleep there alone to-night. Alone – d'ye hear?

Jessop Yes.

Rawlings How shall we manage to get your wife out of the way?

Jessop I wish you could tell me. I've been trying these many years, but she won't go.

Rawlings You must resume your own shape.

Jessop Oh! I am to reappear! Where am I to turn up?

Rawlings You must write to me from Dover – where you await their arrival by the mail-train this evening. I'll see them off.

Jessop Ah! you are a city man, and you are accustomed to desperate games.

Rawlings We are playing for our lives now, Jos. It is touch and go.

Jessop Let it be go, Jack; let it be go, as far as I am concerned! I'm out of my depth.

Rawlings Cling to me. I'll fetch you through! I'll land you. (*Exeunt*).

Jessop But *where ? where ?*

Scene 5
Walter Coram's room in Jessop's house

Coram and Katey discovered

Katey How could I have loved that man!

Walter My dear Katey. Pardon me, if I have purposely exposed the object of your infatuation to your contempt.

Katey I forgive the pain you inflicted on me for the motive. You loved me, and love is a Jesuit – it always thinks the end sanctifies the means.

Walter Oh, Katey, why can you not return some of the tenderness I feel for you ?

Katey Perhaps I could – if you were less worthy of being loved. I must get more used to goodness before I dare to take such a liberty with one so much above me

Enter Smyly

Smyly Hist! They've been and made another move.

Walter Who ?

Smyly The guv'nor has come to life!

Walter Is he here ? (*Rising*).

Smyly No; but Rawlings is. He have brought a letter from him, as he is a readin' to the old woman downstairs.

Walter If your father has thrown off his disguise, there is some bad scheme on foot

Enter Mrs Jessop, with a tray containing coffee-things

Mrs Jessop You'll excuse me being so long Mr Walter, but I've had such a turn. My Jessop have turned up, sir.

Walter I congratulate you.

Mrs Jessop At Dover he is, my dear; where he wants me and you to jine him – There's Mr Rawlings a-waiting below, who is a-goin' to see us off by the mail-train.

Katey To-night, mother?

Mrs Jessop Yes, my dear; but I must go for the coffee-pot, which I left on the fire. You'll excuse me, but I am so flustered with this here news and so upset. Bless my heart! (*Exit*).

Walter Your father is not at Dover, nor has he left London.

Katey Perhaps he intends to leave the country with the money they have already shared.

Smyly That's it!

Walter Then why has he sent for me? They do not dream of the possibility of detection – their audacious plot has been too successful.

Katey What shall I do?

Walter Follow your father's directions implicitly, silently!

Re-enter Mrs Jessop, with the coffee-pot, she has her bonnet on

Mrs Jessop Go, Jim – put up the shutters, lock the shop-door, and bring me the key. (*Exit Smyly*) I 'ope, sir, you won't take it ill of us leaving so sudden – but here is Jessop's letter to Mr Rawlings, and you'll see how persumptive he is about our going.

Walter (*Reading it*) Well, I shall make myself as comfortable as possible until I hear from you. My compliments to your husband. You can leave me Smyly?

Mrs Jessop Certainly! Mr Rawlings wants the use of him for this evening!

Re-enter Smyly

Smyly The shop is shuttered and locked up – there's the key.

Mrs Jessop Which I leaves with you, sir! (*Hands it to Walter*) We can get out by the side-door, which shuts with a spring-lock – so you will be obliged to let Jim in when he returns, if you please, sir!

Walter I do not mind being left alone. Farewell! (*Aside to Katey*) Do not fear!

(*Exeunt Smyly, Katey, and Mrs Jessop*).

What can be the new direction of their scheme? They cannot have the least suspicion of my existence – if they had, I should apprehend some mischief in this solitude – this lonely house. Are they gone? (*Goes to the window and looks out*) There is Katey, her mother, and the boy, but I do not see Rawlings. Oh, there he is in the yard! – what did he lag behind for? – he closes the door – that's right – they are gone. (*He takes from his trunk a brace of pistols*) I think I can take care of myself. I have a singular instinct for the approach of danger – (*pours out his coffee*) – rather a pleasant sensation than otherwise. (*Drinks*) I recollect when I was travelling in Oude – What a curious taste this coffee has! – ha! – quite odd. (*Tastes it*) Very strange – surely I recognize – it can't be. (*Smells the coffee-pot*) It is! – 'tis opium; I can't be mistaken. What does this mean? This coffee drugged! By whom? Ha! Rawlings was left alone – down-

350

stairs – he – he! They reckoned without the lodger, who is an old opium-eater. I have not tasted anything so delicious since I left India. (*Tastes it*) But why drug me? They can't suspect – they must – yes; they have found some clue. But how – what?

(*A red light is visible under the door in flat*).

They surely dare not attempt my life! No; they are cowards both. They have the pluck of impostors, not of assassins.

(*Smoke and fire begins to appear through the cracks of the floor*).

What's that? It is fire – the place is on fire! (*Runs to the door*) Good heavens! the door is bolted on the outside! Ah, Rawlings – this is his work! The window! (*Runs to it*) 'Tis barred, barred! See, the whole house is in flames below! I could not escape now by the staircase, it is full of fire. By this room? (*Unlocks the door of room*) No; that window is secured; I am caged!

(*Cries are heard in the street. The scene is closed in*)

Scene 6
The exterior of Jessop's shop, as in Act I

Enter Smyly and Katey, hurriedly

Smyly I tell you there is sommet wrong, miss. I found the bottle o' laudanum standing on the counter. And Rawlings came out of the house looking as pale as a sheet

Enter Tradesman

Tradesman Where is the fire? My house next door is filled with smoke, and we hear the voice of a man crying for help

(*The upper windows of Jessop's show red*).

Look! – there! – you are on fire.

Smyly The doors are locked!

Katey Break in the doors!

Smyly No, don't; that will let the draught in. He can escape by the windows.

Katey He can't – he can't – they are barred!

Smyly Let us through your house! From your roof we may reach ours, and get at him.

Katey Oh! he saved my life. I'll save his, or perish with him. (*Exeunt*).

(*The scene draws and shows the roofs of houses. The two back-windows of Jessop's, at one of which Coram is vainly trying to wrench away the*

351

bars. *Fire and smoke surround him, and burst from below. The trap-door on adjoining house is opened. Smyly climbs on to the roof, and then helps up Katey. Smyly crawls along the sloping roof, on to Jessop's house. He helps Katey. They begin to tear away the tiles from above Coram's room, until a large hole is made. Katey leaps down into the room as the brass helmets of two firemen appear over the roof, carrying hose and a ladder. As they come in answer to the frantic cries of Smyly, the Act-drop descends)*

End of Act 3

Rose Leclerq
(*PhotographicCol-
lection, Victoria
& Albert Museum*

Act 4

Scene 1

Franklin's villa at Acton, Franklin seated

Enter Griffiths

Griffiths Lord Alfred Colebrooke, sir.

Franklin Alfred! I thought he was on his way to Paraguay.

Enter Lord Alfred. Exit Griffiths

Lord A. So I was. I had reached Southampton when this telegram overtook me.

Franklin (*Reads it*) 'Return. Papa needs a true and reliable friend. For his sake I forgive your falsehood and treachery. Come back at once. – Laura'.

Lord A. I forfeited my passage and returned at once. What has happened?

Franklin Rawlings has thrown aside the mask. He has informed Coram that I have made a fraudulent use of the certificates and scrip lodged with me in trust. And this morning I have received an intimation from the Mansion House that a warrant had been applied for to arrest me

Enter Laura

Laura O Alfred, how could you desert us at such a moment?

Lord A. My presence here seemed rather to be an obstacle to the only course open to you to release your father from difficulty.

Laura It released you also from a difficulty. I know all about the girl whom you have deceived for two years past.

Lord A. I cannot conceive whom you allude to

Enter Griffiths

Griffiths (*Announcing*) Mr Walter Coram, sir, and Mr Rawlings: and if you please, sir, they are accompanied by –

Laura Whom?

353

Griffiths Two officers, miss

Enter Rawlings and Jessop

Rawlings Not yet, Griffiths. They will remain outside until they are wanted – Mr Franklin will call them in.
Lord A. You speak, sir, as if you were master in this house!
Rawlings Perhaps I am!

(*Exit Griffiths*)

Your lordship may not be aware of the peculiar position in which Mr Franklin finds himself?
Lord A. I have been informed of every circumstance, I believe.
Laura It still depends on me, sir, whether my father is conducted from his home to prison. Is that the meaning of your presence here, and of the law's hesitation?
Rawlings (*To Jessop*) I think, Mr Coram, the lady has expressed your views?
Jessop That's about it.
Franklin Mr Coram, I am willing to give up into your hands my business – my property, everything to satisfy the debt I owe you; but I will not sell my own flesh and blood.
Rawlings This is your resolve? You have well weighed the consequences?
Laura No! no! he has not – not yet

Enter Griffiths

Griffiths Mr Walter Coram, sir.
Rawlings Eh! who?
Jessop What! who d'ye say?
Griffiths Mister – Walter – Coram, – sir

Enter Walter Coram. Exit Griffiths.

Rawlings (*Aside*) He has escaped!
Jessop Fire won't burn him – water won't drown him –
Franklin What am I to understand, sir?
Walter That my name is Walter Coram – that I did not take passage in the 'Bombay Castle', nor was I lost at sea – that on my arrival in London I found my place in the world occupied, my name appropriated, and my property in the possession of that man! (*Points to Jessop*)
Jessop I must go and consult my legal adviser. Come –
Walter I confess, gentlemen, I have just come from your hotel, where I have laid violent hands on your luggage, and abstracted from it

354

these £20,000, the proceeds of your friend's cheque.

Rawlings This is robbery!

Walter It *is* robbery, and you are the thieves!

Rawlings I presume, sir, you have come provided with evidence to substantiate your claim? Satisfactory proof?

Walter I hope you will find it so

Enter Griffiths

Griffiths Mrs Jessop, Miss Jessop, Mr James Smyly

Enter Mrs Jessop, Katey, and Smyly. Exit Griffiths.

Rawlings Your wife! – Katey! – Jem – here!

Jessop (*Subsiding*) Oh, Lord – we're swamped!

Laura That is the girl I saw in your arms. Will you deny your knowledge of her now?

Lord A Hush, my dear, and listen.

Mrs Jessop Oh! Joseph! I know all about it, now.

Franklin Who is this person then?

Katey My father, sir – Dr Jessop, of Love Lane, Lambeth.

Smyly Herbalist and dealer in cures.

Jessop Appearances are unfavourable. Yes – I go so far as to – say – eh, Rawlings?

Rawlings You hold the game in your hands, Mr Coram; throw down your cards.

Walter Let me see – fraud, forgery, arson, and conspiracy to murder. When a bill wherein such things are charged is presented against a man, do you know the coin in which it is paid?

Rawlings Yes; life for life. But you don't mean to exact that payment – I see you have some reason for sparing us.

Walter Here it is. (*Takes Katey's hand*).

Katey O father! for my sake, because I am your daughter he spares you. (*To Rawlings*) Because you have occupied this heart – unworthy tenant though you were – he spares you – the memory of my love is your sanctuary.

Walter Gentlemen, the 'Mercury', 1,500 tons, A.1, for Swan River direct, sails from Gravesend to-morrow. You will proceed by that commodious liner to Australia – and never set foot beyond the limits of that colony, if you value the lives I spare.

Jessop But – this – sounds like –

Rawlings Transportation for life. That's a settler, Jos.

Jessop Two settlers, Jack. We've got to behave as such. But a new life unfolds itself already – a vista where new associates, new family ties –

Walter Your wife consents to be your companion.

Jessop (*Aside*) Oh – lord! the vista dissolves –

Laura Alfred, can you forgive me the foolish suspicion ?

Lord A. My dear Laura, I don't see how all this improves my position in the least.

Walter I think it may, my lord, if my old friend will receive favourably a proposition I have to make; that is, to receive me into partnership, and accept you in the like capacity as the husband of his daughter.

Franklin No. Let me retire and leave the field to you, Mr Coram, and to you, my lord – you will redeem and uphold an old city name which you have rescued from disgrace.

Smyly I wonder what is a-goin' to become of me.

Katey While I have a home, it shall be yours, Jem.

Walter There, boy. (*Hands the sovereign which is at his watch-chain. to Smyly*) Take that sovereign, and these words, with which I went abroad into the world. 'Be as honest as you look, and you will prosper'. Wherever in the wide world you may be, whether afloat or ashore, keep your eye on the guiding star, Truth, and you'll never come to grief on land –

Katey Nor be Lost at Sea

Curtain

THE PRESS

The Times, October 5th, 1869:

Lost at Sea, *the new drama of Messrs Boucicault and H J Byron, was brought out at the Adelphi on Saturday night, and was received, with much, though not unmingled applause.*

The absence of the word 'original' from the play-bills might suggest a belief that Lost at Sea *is borrowed from the French, while, on the other hand, the structure of the piece, involving perpetual changes of decoration, looks English to the last degree. The position of the gentleman whose maritime calamity is recorded in the title will probably recall to some minds Mr Charles Dickens' latest novel,* Our Mutual Friend; *but the details of the book are altogether different from those of the play, and a theory that the latter is a compound result, derived from many sources, will, in all likelihood, be an approximation to the truth.*

The story has the advantage of being perfectly intelligible to every capacity. The evanescent boundary between good and evil, where battles for and against rehabilitations are so readily fought, is never approached. There are no virtuously vicious or viciously virtuous persons, whose doubtful merits drag 'Paterfamilias' into print, and make him ask whether the morally pure air of London is to be infected by the moral fogs of Paris. The good are good, the bad are bad; the spade is a spade, and, in accordance with the nature of spades, is not remarkably brilliant. The crimes committed are of that thoroughly wholesome kind that never calls a blush to the cheek of real or imagined innocence, being simply fraud, forgery, and attempted murder. The jade must be sadly galled indeed who could wince at these. Perhaps at the present moment the only person in all Europe who could find the subject offensive is M Traubmann of Parisian notoriety.

[Then follows the usual long outline of the plot]

. . . The interest of this piece is mainly derived from the adventures of Rawlings *and* Jessop *who are admirably sustained by Messrs Atkins and Belmore, the latter representing with great humour, but with some exaggeration, the humiliating position of a miserable wretch who is a*

357

*villain against his will, the former portraying the cool, daring, un-
scrupulous scoundrel, to whom conscience is a thing unknown. Though
the strong points in* Katey's *character are well carried out by Miss Rose
Leclerq, we can hardly sympathise with her passion for such a heartless
rogue as* Rawlings, *especially when she herself is ready to give him up,
after a certain amount of persuasion; and still less do we care for* Laura
*when she becomes jealous without inquiring into the ostensible cause of
her jealousy.*

As a 'sensational work' Lost at Sea *is sadly weak. Pieces in which a
powerful dramatic situation is accompanied by striking scenic accessories
are those by which 'sensation' as it is called, is most effectively produced.
Here, however, the action that occurs before a distant view of West-
minster-bridge (which is not so good as it was meant to be) might as
well have occurred before an ordinary pair of flats. Here, too, while
the fire, which brings the third act to a close, is a first-rate fire, the
circumstances of the rescue appeal but faintly to the eye.*

Certain omissions will, we think, be found indispensable. The levity of
Mrs Jessop, *who thinks that* Rawlings *acts very handsomely when he
offers to maintain her daughter, while he is the husband of another,
suggests an offensive position, which is by no means in harmony with the
general tenour of the plot, and which caused a strong expression of
disapprobation on Saturday night. Equally unfortunate was a scene
which caricatured the stoppage of a bank in the immediate neighbourhood of Mr Franklin's establishment, and is, moreover, utterly
superfluous.*

*The rise of the drop scene was loudly commended at the end of every act,
and the two authors were called and cheered at the end of the piece, but
many hisses were mingled with the applause, and it may reasonably be
doubted whether a permanent success has been attained.*

*The Prince and Princess of Wales, arriving immediately after the
commencement of the play, were universally welcomed by the audience,
who rose from their seats to greet them.*

The Theatrical Journal, October 6th, 1869:

*Adelphi
On Saturday night this house was again opened, when the per-
formances commenced with a new drama, by Messrs Byron and
Boucicault, entitled* Lost at Sea, *being most successfully rendered by
Mr Belmore, Mr Stirling, Mr Stephenson, Mr Atkins, Miss Rose
Leclercq, Mrs Leigh Murray and Miss Eliza Johnston, especially
distinguishing themselves. A Mr Beveridge, new to London, made*

Lost At Sea. Playbill of first production, 1869 (*Guildhall Library*)

a very favourable impression as a young nobleman. A fine scene, in which an attempt was made to burn alive the man whose unexpected appearance threatened to baffle the scheme of the conspirators produced much effect and is likely to remain a memorable scene in the recollections of playgoers. Other scenes in various parts of London were not less favourably received. Of the piece we may say it is interesting throughout. At the commencement of the performance the Princess of Wales advanced, followed by the Prince to the Royal Box. This – one of her first appearances, if not her first appearance at the production of a new piece – was warmly welcomed by the crowded audience which was loud in its demonstrations of gratification. Further criticism upon the piece and the actors we must defer.

An extremely lengthy notice for *Lost at Sea* in *The Era* of October 10th, 1869 is interesting for the following brief quotation which shows a long-vanished custom:

'*A crossing scene, representing Villiers-street, Strand, with a perspective glimpse of Gatti's Concert Hall,* is not particularly suggestive of the places named; but the night view of Hungerford-bridge and the Thames, from the steamboat-pier and landing-stage, is very well painted, and the artist, Mr Hawes Craven, was quickly summoned to personally respond to the applause evoked*'.

---

*Now the home of the Players' Theatre

Eugene Aram

W G WILLS

W. G. Wills
'The Critic',
1898. (*British
Museum*)

W G WILLS (1828/91)

William Gorman Wills was born at Blackwell Lodge, Kilburry, Co Clare, on January 28th, 1828, the son of a country gentleman who dabbled in literature and poetry. At the age of seventeen he entered Trinity College, Dublin, and (although he did not take a degree) showed an early leaning towards the literary arts by winning the vice-chancellor's medal in 1845 for his poem *Poland*, and by contributing to an ephemeral magazine called *The Irish Metropolitan*.

However, his talents lay more in the use of the brush than the pen, and he later received a modicum of training at the Royal Hibernian Academy. In 1862 he came to London where his efforts to earn a living as a writer at first met with little success. But later that year his story *The Wife's Evidence* attracted the attention of the magazines; this mild triumph was insufficient to support himself and his newly-widowed mother, so in 1868 he decided to revert to portrait painting. He took a studio at 15, The Avenue, Fulham, and was soon the darling of the *haut ton* – after an exhibition he was even summoned to Osborne to draw the Royal grandchildren.

His first attempt at writing for the stage was an adaptation from a German piece, but his second, *Man o' Airlie*, provided a fine part for Hermann Vezin at the Princess's in July, 1867, who encouraged his dramatic endeavours and produced two more of his plays; Vezin also introduced him to Colonel Bateman who was later to engage Wills as resident dramatist at the Lyceum (for £300 per annum) at about the time Irving was establishing himself as the leading actor of the day. For Irving, Wills wrote *Charles I*, *Eugene Aram*,* and (with Percy Fitzgerald) *Vanderdickan*, which was based on another favourite melodrama theme – the Flying Dutchman. Wills and Irving were both arch-Romantics, and exactly complemented each other.

The next ten years saw Wills writing a quantity of very inferior work, mostly quasi-archaic verse plays in which he took little interest after submitting the manuscript. He rarely attended rehearsals and never attended any of his own first nights. His real interest lay in oils – he once referred to himself as 'a poor painter who writes plays for pence', which underlines his scale of priorities. After his mother's death in 1887 he moved his studio to Walham Green where he lived in a state of picturesque squalor, often writing in bed. He died in Guy's Hospital on December 13th, 1891 : he was unmarried.

W G Wills' generosity and absent-mindedness were legendary – he is said to have once boiled his watch in mistake for an egg, and was totally unreliable with regard to social invitations or obligations of any kind. One obituarist wrote of him 'his Bohemian life, his impassioned character, his hasty methods of production, gave him in the distance the look of genius. But it was a misleading look . . . his pieces are founded upon conceptions which crumble away upon analysis, and the versification is too poor to veil or redeem the weakness of the dramatic idea'.

Wills wrote about 40 plays, mostly dramas and tragedies, and of these the majority were adaptations, including versions of *Jane Eyre*, Goethe's *Faust*, *Black-Eye'd Susan* (as *William and Susan*), and *The Vicar Of Wakefield* – in which Olivia became one of Ellen Terry's most popular roles. His *Jane Shore* provided Caroline Heath (Mrs Wilson Barrett) with such a heavily emotional role that after playing it continuously for ten years her mind gave way and she died deranged at the age of 52. Wills also showed a facility as a balladist: his are the words of *I'll Sing Thee Songs Of Araby*.

Thomas Hood's celebrated dramatic poem *The Dream Of Eugene Aram, Murderer*, was first published in 1829; two years later Bulwer-

---

*Irving had previously performed Hood's original poem as a solo recitation

Lytton expanded it into a novel, and it was this rather than the original verse-narrative which attracted the attention of so many dramatists. However, Dutton Cook wrote: 'With Lord Lytton, Mr Wills has ignored the circumstance that Aram, who was fifty-five at the date of his death, left behind him a wife and a family of three sons and three daughters; and the dramatist, with even less adherence to truth than the novelist, has dispensed with the trial and execution of his criminal-hero, and permitted him to escape at last almost unpunished and undisgraced'.† Thus spake the Victorian moralist – in Wills' version Aram dies of remorse in appalling agony of mind the morning of his wedding-day, but nothing would satisfy Dutton Cook, it seems, other than the full obscenity of legal slaughter.

Ten years after Wills' version was first seen at the Lyceum in 1873, he abridged it into one act as *The Fate Of Eugene Aram* for Irving's farewell programme before his first American tour. I have been unable to trace this MS and so offer here my own abridgement.

Eugene Aram was born in Yorkshire in 1704; a self-educated man, he had a remarkable facility for languages, and worked variously as bailiff, clerk, usher and schoolmaster. He returned to Knaresborough where in 1745, at St Robert's Cave just outside the town, the infamous deed was perpetrated. It was not until thirteen years later that he was apprehended for the crime; the following extract is taken from the Folio Society's 1951 edition (by the then Sir Norman Birkett) of the *Newgate Calendar*, originally published *circa* 1774:

> *When the morning appointed for his execution arrived, the keeper went to take him out of his cell, when he was surprized to find him almost expiring through loss of blood, having cut his left arm above the elbow and near the wrist, with a razor; but he missed the artery. A surgeon being sent for, soon stopped the bleeding, and when he was taken to the place of execution he was perfectly sensible, though so very weak as to be unable to join in devotion with the clergyman who attended him.*

> *He was executed near York on the 6th of August, 1759, and afterwards hung in chains on Knaresborough forest.*

> *Such was the end of Eugene Aram: a man of consummate abilities, and wonderful erudition: the power of whose mind might have rendered him acceptable to the highest company, had not the foul crime of murder made him only an object of pity to the lowest!*

---

*Bulwer-Lytton himself attempted a stage version but abandoned it after two acts

†Nights at the Play, vol i (1883)

How such a man, with abilities so superior, could think of embruing his hands in the blood of a fellow-creature, for the paltry consideration of gain, is altogether astonishing! It does not appear that he had any irregular appetites to gratify, or that he lived in any degree above his income. His crime, then, must be resolved into that of covetousness, which preys like a viper on the heart of him that indulgeth it.

From this vice, so repugnant to all the feelings of humanity, may the God of Benevolence protect us!

Henry Irving. A rare early photograph from the author's collection, taken *circa* 1875

EUGENE ARAM

Dramatis Personae

As first performed at the Lyceum Theatre
April 19th, 1873

Eugene Aram by Mr Henry Irving
Parson Meadows by Mr W H Stephens
Houseman by Mr E F Edgar
Jowell by Mr F W Irish
Joey, his son, by Miss Willa Brown
Ruth by Miss Isabel Bateman

*Original overture, incidental music and anthem (sung by
a choir of boys off-stage) by* Robert Stoepel

The action takes place during one summer night, 1759

Note: On the front of the Lyceum programme for the original
production is the following:

*The Author has invested this well-known personage neither upon the
popular novel of the late Lord Lytton nor upon the famous poem of
Tom Hood, but mainly upon tradition*

EUGENE ARAM

Act 1

Scene: The garden of the Parsonage. A village in Yorkshire

Jowell and Joey are discovered making garlands and nosegays

Jowell When you are going to be married, Joe, and the gardener as follows me is dressing out your wedding posies, bring a good conscience to your wife, then you'll have all the neighbours putting on their best, and the Parson cutting down the whole summer fall of flowers for you. Marry, as you and I knows on, Joe, have a bad wife, and a bad conscience, and that's a pair of vixens, with this differ, Joe, that the conscience grows easier, and the wife grows crabbeder, the longer they live. So you look out, Joe, and let me know your views in time. How old are you, Joey?

Joey Eight years old, father.

Jowell Dost know the difference between a good conscience and a bad 'un, Joe? Eh? A good conscience is first rate company, always awake – all eye and ear, and a mere trifle of a tongue. A bad conscience, Joey, is like baby at home; it sleeps all day, and then wakes up with a squall!

(*Sings*)
'She was sweet when I met her first,
'Tis apples be red and plums be blue;
Some wives are kind, but most of 'em curst,
'Tis oh! the brown ale is bonny to brew!'

Enter Houseman during the latter part of the song through the gate

Houseman Good morning, friend.

Jowell Morrow to you, master.

Houseman Flowers to sell?

Jowell They're for the church yonder, master: we're going to have a wedding. Our good schoolmaster is going to marry the parson's daughter. Aye! and a bonny bride she'll be – a sort of poor man's angel! A creature so sweet as 'ud give a man a weak brain to be always a-considerin' upon her.

Houseman I dare say, friend, you won't object to earn a trifle now and then, outside your work?

Jowell Well – no, master; not when the day be done.

Houseman I don't want your time, friend; I want that spade there, just for an hour or so.

Jowell My spade, master?

Houseman Aye, your spade. Just as you have a taste in flowers, I've got a taste in spars and specimens.

Jowell Why – you've the very same fancy as his reverence the parson yonder. He has lumps size o' that! of crystal and spar on his parlor chimney-piece.

Houseman Aye, aye, that's the sort of thing! That's what I came for. (*Takes out money*) There's a shilling, friend, and lend me your spade. And a pick if you have one handy.

Jowell That I will.

Houseman Perhaps that lad would leave them for me, eh? (*Gives Joey penny*) Leave the tools your father will give you at . . . you know Saint Robert's cave?

Jowell Saint Robert's cave! Oh, you've heard of it?

Houseman Oh, yes. Who hasn't? Is it far?

Jowell Two meadow fields from t'quarry.

Houseman Well, let your lad start at once and leave the things in the cave. He can return for them about – what's the hour? Four, is it? Let him come about eight. You'll find the tools in the cave.

Jowell Don't answer, lad: you run. Know where to find tools? Off wi' you! (*Exit Joey*).

Houseman How far is the nearest inn from here?

Jowell The H'Owlet at Bradford – but Bradford is a long way from here.

Houseman That's awkward! Could I hire a horse?

Enter Parson Meadows

Jowell A horse? Not very like; since two men were hanged for horse-stealing here, the neighbours are shy of lending their beasts to strangers.

Parson Can I be of any service, sir? You were enquiring?

Jowell Here's a gentleman, your reverence, come a-picking up the stakalites here about; and is on his way to the dropping cave.

Parson Sir, I should be happy to further your researches –

Houseman I am sure you are very good: my researches just now were confined to the very ordinary matter of a good Inn for the night.

Parson Then I'm afraid you have rather a long and dangerous ride before you.

Houseman As they say in the country, if I ride I must ride two nags at once.

Parson What! Go afoot? Have you no horse?

Houseman Well, I had one. He jogged along with me steadily enough till we were well out of reach of bed or victual, and then the brute fell dead lame.

Parson Dear, dear! What is to be done? Eh, Jowell? Have we a horse fit to ride?

Jowell Why, your reverence, we sold the brown roadster at t'fair this morning. And the mare is at grass without a shoe to her feet.

Parson It would give me very great pleasure, sir, to offer you – I beg to say I am the clergyman of this parish; my name is Meadows, sir. I may not be able at such short notice to offer you a very comfortable bed –

Houseman My dear sir, any corner –

Parson We'll do better for you than that, sir. Your name, if I may venture – ?

Houseman Er – er – Coleman.

Parson (*Offering his hand*) Who knows, Mr Coleman, but in entertaining a stranger, I may find a future friend unawares?

Houseman I hope so, sir, I'm sure; and I accept your offer very gratefully.

Parson Sir, you do me great honor – great pleasure. Now, Jowell, take those flowers to the church, Ruth is waiting for them.

Jowell Aye, parson, aye. (*Aside*) If I knows a daw from a pigeon, he be not an angel anyhow.

Parson The fact is, my dear Mr Coleman, my house is rather upset just now. You notice our little festive preparations? A wedding, sir! The parsonage, tomorrow, may not be a very quiet place for a gentleman of your pursuits, but I think I may say you will find in my future son-in-law a man of the rarest parts, and yet secluded and unknown.

Houseman You quite alarm me, parson.

Parson Of my daughter, it does not befit me to speak –

Jowell Since her blessed mother died, six years a-gone, not such a angel of a lady-bird ever lit of a rose leaf!

Parson Tut-tut! You forget yourself, Jowell. (*To Houseman*) I am going up to the church, sir; will you accompany me?

Houseman Thank you, parson, I have this little expedition in hand; I have but a few hours to spare for this idleness; but for that –

Parson Do not apologise. We may expect you to tea at six?

Houseman Not till quite eight, I fear, my dear sir.

Parson Well, then, we shall have something ready for you. I am quite impatient to show you my specimens. You go to the Dropping Cave?

Houseman No, to Saint Robert's.

Parson Oh, you won't find stalactites there; but the caves are quite close to one another. Now which is the shortest way ... let me see ...

Jowell (*To Houseman*) What name, sir?

Houseman Houseman – I mean to say Coleman. Coleman –

Coleman !

Parson Ah, yes! By the grave – yes, yes. Come, sir, I will put you on your road. This way, Mr Coleman. Those wonderful chemical secretions which it takes perhaps a century to form (*etc, etc. Exit, with Houseman*).

Jowell Oh, indeed! Coleman – Coleman – *Coleman !* But his name is Houseman . . . Houseman ? Where did I hear that name ? Houseman . . . and a-goin' to St Robert's cave, wi' a pick! The very spot I found this gowden coin. (*Produces coin*) Eh, Jowell, there be summat there worth raising – there be buried money there! I'll fetch that pick and spade myself. (*Looks off*) But here comes Mr Aram, in a brown study, as usual. He's going to meet his lady-bird! (*Exit*)

Enter Aram

Aram How long ago it seems! Again I'm here
To part with her once more – and only once –
First I shall see her at the church's porch;
And each first glimpse of her is precious.
'Tis just the hour when I should hear the choir;
At any moment now their hymn may rise.
Their anthem angel-plumed, take flight to me
From yonder gray church tower. (*Goes to sundial*).
Oh! in the endless, trackless drift of days
Which fall like dust-flakes on the pyramids,
May one day of my life pass unrecorded,
Leave no more trace than Time upon this dial!

Enter Ruth

Ah! Ruth, at last!
Ruth At last ? You have not waited long ?
Aram It seemed long, or it was long – I scarcely know.
Are your duties over in the choir ?
Ruth My duties ? Eugene, *they* begin tomorrow.
The choir is waiting till the sun gets lower, it seems more solemn.
Oh, Eugene, I am so vexed. My father has invited a strange man.
Aram Indeed ?
(*Long pause*).
Ruth Eugene – I've often wished to ask one question.
Aram A question! Do you mistrust, or fear ?
Ruth Fear and mistrust! My only fear could be
That you should cease to love me; for, my love,
I have no gifts but only love and truth.
I might mistrust myself, but never you.
In you I have such boundless confidence –
Such blind belief, that, in my daily prayers
I ask forgiveness for such trust in man.

Aram You said there was a stranger ? Who is he ? What sort of man ?

Ruth I have forgot the name. He has some interest in the Knaresborough crystals.

Aram Ah yes! Ah yes! Well, what's this question ?
Sit there and ask me all that's in your heart. Well ?

Ruth There is some grief – some haunting melancholy,
Which enters with you and goes out with you.
Another might not see it, but I watch you
Almost unconsciously, and know you closer
Than you might think.

Aram So – you take fancies, Ruth ?

Ruth It is not fancy. I am sure some trouble
In your past life weighs upon you – some regret.
Confess to me. Come, tell me – some old care ?

Aram Nay, Ruth, I am not sad today –

Ruth No, no – you shan't escape.
You must confess; what is this melancholy ?
I don't mean now, but since I knew you first,
From the first evening father brought you home.
Since then I've noted you, and I have seen
That – struggle as you might – there was a weight,
A shadow, or a pain, I know not what.

Aram Oh, love, say this for me; I did not come
To steal your heart, or link it to the lot
Of my most loveless life! It grew on me –
Before I heeded, love had grown on me.
I had not courted it – the comfort came,
And filled my spirit with unbidden smiles;
And round my life, before I knew it, Ruth,
Stole the green shelter of your love for me.

Ruth And as for me – I saw in you
A life as gentle, blameless, and as pure
As blows the wind o'er beds of lavender

(*Pause. The light is fading*).

Aram You see this ring ?
Look at it well.

Ruth Why – it has lost its stone! It's quite valueless.

Aram And yet I prize it
Beyond all rubies: 'twas my father's ring!
I love it now for what it has been –
For some tender memories –
For an unreasonable fondness. I will wear it
Even unto the end – whatever the end may be.
Oh! Could you love me still
If I had lost my honor, and good report ?

Ruth Yes, dearest. Ever wear this empty ring,

For it is gold, although the gem is gone!
  Aram Yet answer me: if I –
  Ruth Hark to the music!
  (*A hymn sounds off*).
  Choir 'As the gracious evening falleth
  In a bland and dewy calm,
  So upon the heart that calleth
  For thy pardon, come with balm.

  Now the heart that once did harden
  Softness to sweet penitence;
  As we leave the sound of pardon,
  Life's long sorrow fleeth hence'.
  Aram Does it sound like penitence . . . like pardon?

The curtain falls

Act 2

Scene: the drawing-room in the Parsonage. Aram and Parson are discovered playing chess: Ruth is working at a table

Parson It is not that – it is not only that;
Not the mere tribute of respect for you.
This testimonial these poor people send
Comes from the heart of my parishioners.
  Aram It is my move ... well ... there.
  Parson Are you not pleased?
  Aram Well, sir, it is a pleasure two parts sad. A eulogy unmerited.
  Parson Nonsense! What modesty is this? I move my knight.
  Ruth Where is this lovely testimonial, father? Remember! *I'm* to
read it out to him!
  Parson Nay, nay – 'tis hidden. I'm to read it out.
  Ruth Oh, hidden is it? (*Looking about the room*) I've a knack of
finding ...
  Aram (*Concentrating on the board*) You cannot move it – you uncover
check.
  Parson Ah! now I see my danger. (*Moves a piece*).
  Ruth (*Triumphantly*) I have found it!
Now, Eugene, listen, I will sound your praises.
  Aram Dearest, not tonight. (*To Parson*) Check!
  Parson Ah! You have lost your queen!
  Aram Ah! Ruth, you're not, by many, the first woman
Has lost a battle for a general. (*Moves a piece*).
  Parson I see it! There – check-mate!
  Ruth Now then, you are at liberty to listen: (*Reads*).
'To our kind and loving schoolmaster,
The friend of our children!
In the play-hour, a teacher – in the school-hour, a companion!
Whose consolation has softened many a trouble;
Whose wisdom has averted many a loss;
Whose spotless life has been at once a reproach
To us, and an example!'

(*Exit Aram, abruptly*).

Eugene! Come back!
  Parson This is his modesty. I'll send him back to you, and make

some preparations for the stranger. (*Exit*).

    Ruth Though he has left the room I seem to see him, and am content.
In his dear presence all is well with me;
Yet, with great happiness comes oft time fear.
If he should weary of me when he finds
I know so little. But he shall not know;
I'll read the books he loves, and so wise thoughts
Shall come – strange tenants! – to my girlish brain

    (*Houseman appears behind at window and taps*).

I'll never question him; for once he said
That happiness died of a question – what's that?

    Enter Houseman by window

Your pardon, sir, I did not hear your step.
You are our stranger guest.
    Houseman I'm sorry you were startled.
Happy the man whose lot tomorrow 'tis
To claim such charming ministry for life.
    Ruth Were Mr Aram here –
    Houseman Aram?
    Ruth His thanks were given in better words than mine,
But not more heartily.
    Houseman Did Mr Aram once live in Lynn?
    Ruth I know but little of his former years,
But in a moment, Eugene will be here.
    Houseman What! Eugene Aram? 'Tis my old acquaintance …
Eugene Aram! A name I have not uttered for these fourteen years!
    Ruth I should so like to hear tales of his youth!
Was he reserved – abstracted – as a boy?
    Houseman Reserved? No, quite the opposite –
    Ruth Oh, tell me all you recollect of him!
    Houseman All! No, Miss Meadows, it would never do
If women could know all before they married.
Why, we might have no weddings … he had
His little weakenesses, like all of us.
    Ruth His weaknesses!
    Houseman In fact, I may congratulate Miss Meadows
On making convert of a youthful sinner,
And pulling the wild feathers from his wing.
    Ruth You said just now he was a friend of yours!
You may hope first to dim an everlasting star
As injure Eugene Aram's stainless name!
    Houseman What if a lady once did try with him,

And he was as infatuate as you?

    Ruth It is not true! I'll ask him if it's true! (*Cries*).

    Houseman Young lady, pray accept apology;
I did not mean to make a lover's quarrel

Enter Parson Meadows

    Parson Why, Ruth, a tear? My darling, what is this?

    Ruth Father, this stranger has hinted such things!

    Houseman Forgive me, sir. Your daughter misconceived my friendly
words.
I spoke of Eugene Aram as a youth,
Whom I knew well in other happier days.

    Parson Of his youth, Mr Houseman, we know little –

    Houseman Coleman.

    Parson Pardon, sir. My servant said you gave the name of House-
man.
No doubt 'twas some mistake.
Will you accompany me to the parlour,
There's some refreshment served?

    Houseman Thank you, parson, it is welcome.
'Tis time, I think, to make a good retreat.
I am a blunderer. (*Exeunt Parson and Houseman*).

    Ruth 'He . . . he was as infatuate as I?'
Then she was false – she dallied with him!
If he had charged him with the blackest crime
I'd meet the slander with a patient smile,
But he has hinted at another woman!
I wish – I wish I'd never met that man.
    (*She moves up sobbing to chair at back*)

    *Enter Aram. He slowly moves to the piano without seeing Ruth; he
sits and sings the following, accompanying himself.*

    Aram 'Oh, cling to the heart you have chosen,
Let your love be a life 'during vow;
If its current should ever be frozen,
'Tis worthless and frivolous now.
You love him – be sure to be near him,
If to pain or to sickness he bend;
To watch and to soothe and to cheer him,
Oh! love, and love on to the end'
    (*Sees Ruth, who comes running to his side*).
Ruth! What, tears, love – tears?

    Ruth Oh, Eugene, search your memory –
Those precious words which you have said to me:
Are they not twice-told music?

That other woman!

    Aram What woman?

    Ruth The stranger! He knows you and you know him.

    Aram The stranger?

    Ruth Who was she?

    Aram (*Sighs. After a pause*) Ruth, I was one who worshipped long ago,

Some blood-stained idol, and looks shuddering back,

From the bright confines of a blessed creed.

Sit here.

I was a silent child, and motherless,

And I grew to a distempered youth,

Experienced in unhappiness.

You were a child, and I a youth of scarcely twenty years –

And she, that other woman, is long dead!

    Enter Houseman

    Houseman Aram!

    Ruth: The man!   (*Together*)

    Aram (*Aside*) Houseman!   (*Aloud*) Do I know you?

    Houseman You should, sir. Look again.

    Aram You are a stranger to me.

    Houseman But you are not to me. Aram, I'd speak with you.

    Aram Some other time.

    Houseman This evening. It may be something which concerns you nearly.

    Aram (*To Ruth*) Leave us alone awhile.

    Ruth No, no, Eugene. Let me stay.

    Houseman Our talk, young lady, is not for your ears. Take my advice.

    Aram This lady, sir, needs no advice from you.

    Ruth I must forget I am a wayward girl,

And be a woman fit to share your cares.

(*To Houseman*) Pray pardon me. (*Exit*).

    Aram (*Aside*) Now nerve of iron, and brain of ice,

Or in this closing of the door, I close

The door of Heaven. (*Aloud*) Now, sir, your business?

    Houseman You don't remember an old friend?

    Aram Sir! I remember you,

As one whom I should shun, and know no more.

Let's end it. What have you to do with me?

    Houseman I know what we have had to do together.

    Aram I'd have you, sir, speak low, and to the point,

Remembering what you are and what I am. (*Shuts window*).

    Houseman Aram, I tell you –

    Aram Do you threaten, sir?

Houseman Yes, if you put me to it, Eugene Aram.
Your life is on my lips. Ah! You wake up . . .
    Aram Fool! Do you take me for the trembling dupe
That lets the horse-leech fasten on his throat
In hopes that, when it bloats, 'twill drop away ?
    Houseman Come, let me reason with you.
You have respectability and credit;
Why should not I, the lesser criminal –
    Aram Criminal! There is a world between our acts.
The Lion boldly strikes his prey,
But the Hyena comes back to plunder!
What brought you hither ?
    Houseman My motive, Aram, in returning here
Was not with hope of meeting you:
You might, for all I know, be dead and sainted.
I came in hope to find some buried guineas!
You understand me – in Saint Robert's cave.
This paltry chatelain was all I found –
'Tis nothing. See – her name is on the gold.
    Aram You play your cards, sir, very carelessly
To show the ghoulish booty you have rooted
This very evening from your victim's grave.
I take my stand forthwith, here, face to face.
No, not a coin – no, not a word to stay you.
    Houseman 'Tis a stale game, no doubt, this buying silence.
But it will last as long as guilt exists.
So long as one man holds another's life
At hazard of a word. My evidence –
    Aram Off to the market place, and shout it forth!
The beadle, fool, will clap you in the stocks.
I meet your malice, Houseman, with a smile.
    Houseman A deuced uneasy smile as e'er I saw.
    Aram Do you think to frighten me ? Your evidence!
Why, shape it as you please – it brands you thief!
Your evidence! An unknown vagabond,
With a false name, and a suspicious past,
How could it touch me ? I defy you!
What have you to tell ? The only witness
A body in Saint Robert's Cave,
Of which you know too much, which you have rifled.
    Houseman A word from me might mar your bliss with Mistress
Ruth . . .
    Aram Houseman, your villainy is blind – is mad!
Threaten my life and I may hold my hand
From harming you; but slander me to her
And I'll find sudden means to silence you;

379

Too long your presence desecrates the place.
Go, take it hence. Already, aye, already
I found your poisoned trail upon her heart.
Rob me of this one blessing I possess,
And I may rob the gallows of its due

Enter Parson Meadows

(*With a sudden change of voice*).
I have lived here, sir, a secluded student
These many years; my goings in and out
Are known to all. Sir, in charity,
As having known you, I would warn you here
That slander and imposture do not thrive
In honest Knaresborough.
    Houseman No, murder seems to thrive.
You, Eugene Aram, have you ever heard
That dead men break their graves and rise again ?
    Parson (*Interrupting*) Dead men ?
    Aram You stand, sir, in the presence of a magistrate.
I charge you, Richard Houseman, with complicity
In a robbery, with one Daniel Clarke!
    Parson Oh, Eugene, here! Beneath my roof!
    Aram Ask him – did he not fly in company with Clarke,
And was he not his close associate ?
    Parson But we need witnesses and circumstance.
    Aram I could supply those at the proper time,
But I forbear to prosecute.
My simple motive was to draw his fangs,
And to convince you of his utter falsehood.
(*To Houseman*) Go, sir! You see he's silent! For the future
Avoid my name and neighbourhood

Enter Jowell and several servants with lanterns

    Jowell Your reverence! Your reverence!
    Parson Why, Jowell, what's the matter ?
    Jowell Your reverence, here is foul murder
Just come to light!
    Parsons Murder ?
    Jowell Your reverence, I followed this here stranger
Into Saint Robert's cave. When he came out
He walked off briskly to the Parsonage.
He'd been picking there some hours –
The tools were left behind, and a fresh mound of clay.
Some six feet long I cleared away

380

Until my spade grated upon a skull!

  Parson A skull?

  Jowell Aye! The skull of Daniel Clarke!

  Parson Daniel Clarke. Aram, you know that story –

  Aram I do, sir, well.

  Parson Why, that was –

  Jowell Fourteen years ago.

  Parson Aye, just six years before I settled here.

And this is the skull you say of that same Clarke.

What is your evidence?

  Jowell Why, this old knife:

His name is cut on it. I found it at the place

Where he'd been digging. (*Indicating Houseman*) I know him now!

I didn't know him first, but he is Richard Houseman, his old companion,

And his murderer!

  Houseman 'Tis false! The murderer of Daniel Clarke stands there!

(*Pointing at Aram*).

  Aram Be not misled by Jowell's foolish tale.

This is no murder! An old robbery –

  Parson Aye, but the skull Jowell says he found?

  Aram There is no cave without its mouldering tenant;

This special cave we know Saint Robert owned,

It was his home in life, his vault in death.

  Jowell But Mr Aram, here was violence!

The skull was drove in by some heavy weapon.

  Aram Nay, nay, 'twas the over-eager spade –

  Jowell No, no. I could dig clean round a tulip's root,

And never graze it.

  Parson But what of the knife with Daniel Clarke's initials?

  Aram The knife dropt from the breast of that man Houseman –

His old comrade's knife. Had it lain in the cave

These fourteen years, it would be cased in rust.

  Jowell 'Twas yellow as a slice of cheese

Until I flaked it off to read the name.

Come, judge of it yourself.

You'll see below, not twenty steps from this,

The mortal relics of Daniel Clarke.

I've brought them here myself to show you, parson.

  Aram What! Dragged to light a holy hermit's bones?

Pardon my heat – 'tis thoughtless sacrilege!

  Parson I share your reverence for an honoured grave.

Yet, in the cause of justice we must waive

Our gentler sympathies, and seek for truth.

Come, Aram, we will go and look.

You, Mr Houseman, in your obvious interest will not object to –

  Houseman I, sir? Surely not. And Mr Aram – ?

Aram I will follow, sir. I will follow. Pray go before

(*Exeunt Parson, Jowell, Houseman and servants*).

At last! At last!
Oh, clay and granite, could ye not have kept
The secret now so long entrusted you ?
They wait! It waits!
In dreams I have been with it, sped forth to it.
Under gray clouds stabbed with the ruddy light,
And met it in the cave, struck it once more
And then awakened with a smothered cry!
Dare I see the reality ? I see it.
I think I see it now, there, through the wall :
White, long, so thin, so grimly terrible!
'Tis painful, this fear! Fool! Man yourself.
There, shake it off! What, trembling at dead bones ?
I will walk forth with indifferent mien,
And I will speak – oh, Heaven! – *must* speak aloud.
If I delay, I'm lost! This swaggering wretch,
He has more nerve than I. I'd tear it out,
This guilty panic, but it poisons all –
My blood, my heart, my brain! Oh, I must go . . .
Oh, Ruth! Oh, Ruth! (*Looks in mirror*)
There, there – be calm! I look more like myself.
There, there! I'll go – be calm! I'll go! I'll go!
    (*Exit Aram as the curtain descends*)

Act 3
Scene: A church-yard at night. Aram is discovered on stage

Enter Houseman

Houseman Well, I have weathered many a stormy day,
But never was I in such mortal pinch.
Aram, you wrestled well with me today;
Now, a wisp trips you. Fool! Frightened by a skull!
One look upon those relics, which I handled,
And there he stood, the culprit, struck midway
With the paralysis of guilty fear!
Lord! How he fled away!
I'll hasten on to Lynn,
If only to anticipate discovery – (*Going*).

(*Aram rises*).

Great God! Out of what grave have you risen?
Aram What did I say? Did my face look like guilt?
The torpid cold is still upon my fingers
That touched the chill and bleachéd thing.
I muttered something as I staggered out.
Was it confession? Houseman, has she heard?
Houseman I've done with you – you rave! I think you're mad!
Aram I heard you laugh a light and careless laugh.
And I – I have not laughed these many years.
How have you got contentment all these years?
How kindly time and guilt have dealt with you.
Houseman The law deals not so kindly – have a care!
Aram How did you drug your mind? With drunken revel?
Was it debauchery and riot? I have lived
A life of purity and winnowed thought,
And the foul spot showed fouler for the white.
Houseman (*Aside*) His brain is turned!
Aram I'll give you all I own! All, all!
But teach me how to quell this endless ache . . .
Houseman You're mad! Why – sleep it out . . . cut out your heart!
Farewell! Farewell! (*Exit.*)
Aram If I had but his peace . . . an hour ago
I had within my heart a joy as radiant

383

As that which burst upon the pardoned thief
On his first day in Paradise!
Since I looked on that sight, a numbness creeps
Around my heart. Does my brain wander?
How bitter cold it is. As one who feels a pain in sleep,
Scarce knowing it is pain, takes fantasies
Of what would give him ease, so I believe ...
I will confess. To whom? I look above!
I, Eugene Aram, a despairing man,
In the presence of the Great Confessor here,
I confess!
There is a dumbness in the vaulted sky;
There is a blindness in the starry waste! Mercy! Oh, grant me mercy!
There is no aid, no balm, no ear to heed
In all the throneless sky! Death, blind and black,
God's face is turned away from me tonight

    Enter Ruth

    Ruth It cannot be; it cannot be that he is fled!
I've that within which tells me he is near.
I heard his spirit call me in my room:
'Ruth! Ruth!' Twice in my heart an anguished voice
Not formed on mortal tongue. Oh! Heaven guide me!
    (*Sees Aram*).
Who's this? My Eugene! Speak! I, Ruth, am here!
He's ill! He's dying! Help!!!
    (*Aram lifts his head*).
    Aram Ruth? Ruth?
    Ruth Yes, Ruth.
    Aram Thrust me away from you – thrust me away from you.
    Ruth Oh, this is cruel!
    Aram Oh! My lost love, on me be all the stain;
On me the judgement and the penalty ...
Let not God's hand, which presses upon me,
Crush, with the guilty, the poor innocent.
Go in, go in, and leave me. (*She holds him in her arms*).
    Ruth Oh! Trust me – tell me all! Give me your burden.
I am a simple girl, but mine is love
That is not worn alone for happy days,
But, like the eider down, for icy blasts.
    Aram Ruth! Do you know what you would ask of me?
I loved another woman long ago –
Wrap me about, I am very cold –
And staked my soul for her.

Houseman – the stranger – and Clarke, his friend, were partners;
Both nearly bankrupt! Houseman, a reckless gambler,
The other, Clarke, a man of gallantry:
He took her from me . . . that was easy said . . .
Oh! What a speechless wrong was in the word!
She knew him shallowly, she knew me well;
He brought her straws – smiles, jests, and fulsomness –
I, wealth more than the Eastern kings could bring:
All the deep, tender passion of my youth!
There was an outcry of a robbery,
Of gold and silver plate borrowed by Clarke
Upon pretence of his approaching marriage
With her – my love! – that he might make brave show before her friends.
His house was closed, he and the plunder gone.
I went to visit her – no, not in triumph,
For I had sworn to see her never more!
I found her, a lost woman!
Her honor, like a diamond, burnt to charcoal,
The priceless changed to dust, no more to shine.
Oh, God! What demon's work! What bankruptcy!
Of soul and body in that weeping wreck
So late life of my life!

(*Throws himself on the ground*).

    Ruth There is no word of terror you can speak
But I will answer with a word of love.
    Aram I left her. Straight into my soul there passed
The soul of Cain; my will was not my own.
I neither slept, nor ate, nor sat me down
Till all was plain, and I was on his trail!
I tracked the robber down.
Saint Robert's cave – I tracked him to its mouth.
I heard him speak within, and heard a clink
Of hammer beating out his spoil!
There, at my very foot, there lay a spade!
I grasped it –
    Ruth Look in my face – I do not shrink from you.
    Aram I looked within, and by the lantern's glare
I saw two men: Houseman was one;
The other, Clarke, half-turned, foiled, tremulous.
Oh! There are moments when God holds the scales . . .
I faltered for a moment – the cold wind
Whispered 'Pity' and a bird that chirped
Touched a heart's nerve, and softened me.
I had refrained, but that the wretch held up
A woman's ornament – her name upon it,

And read it with a mock. I sprang within,
Confronted him, and shouted 'Coward! Thief!'
And – clave him down! I struck and struck again.
I only saw beneath my furious blows
Some writhing vermin – not a human life!
Great God! This moment I can hear his cry
And see the wild quenched gaze he fixed on me.
    Ruth Eugene! Eugene!
    Aram We buried him – his partner Houseman saw the deed,
And was content to take the booty, and to part.
Last night that secret grave gave up its dead . . .
My sin has found me! My tale is done,
And the cold strikes my heart . . . You shrink from me.
    Ruth I shrink? Aye, as the magnet from the steel.
There, rest on me.
I kiss your forehead – there's no stigma there,
No stain of blood – 'tis as spotless as my own.
    Aram Put my hair from my eyes – I cannot see you.
    Ruth There's nothing there . . . can you not see me, love?
You are worn and wearied, but you are not ill?
    Aram No, no; I am at peace.
Come in – together we will see your father;
Come in! the early cold strikes at my heart.

    (*Aram tries to rise, but falls back*).

    Ruth Your face seems altered . . . why do you smile?
    Aram Oh, Ruth! I shall not die a death of shame.
    Ruth No: you shall live –
    Aram My hair . . . push it aside . . . I see you faintly.
    Ruth What change is this? Oh, love, there steals a pallor across your
cheek . . .
    Aram 'Tis but the morning light.
    Ruth Why is your voice so hollow?
And still that phantom smile. What is it, love?
Your fingers loosen! Oh! . . . you are not dying . . . ?
    Aram No – dying? No . . . ! My youth is back again . . .
    Ruth What is this? I see within your eyes
My dying mother's look – the last farewell!
    Aram Oh! Love, we will not breathe that word 'Farewell' . . . !

    (*Soft music begins*).

Hush!
    Ruth It is the morning choir . . . Oh, try to rise. I'll help you . . .
    Aram Oh, Ruth! The gate is open . . . I am gone.
    Ruth Oh, God! His smile is fading!
    Aram I would find
My burial in your arms – upon your lips,

Irving as Eugene Aram. (*Enthoven Collection*)

My only epitaph; and, in your eyes,
My first, faint glimpse of Heaven!

(*The anthem peals out. Morning is now apparent. Aram dies*)

Tableau. Slow curtain

THE PRESS

From *The Bells to King Arthur* by Clement Scott, published in 1896, a critical record of productions at the Lyceum Theatre, 1871–1895 (pp. 25–33)

Eugene Aram.
We honestly own, and as candidly confess, we feel to the full the responsibility of sitting down at a late hour, with a mind naturally excited, after witnessing a performance which we guarantee many hundreds who are now fathers of families cannot trump in excellence – though they summon up their recollection since childhood – to attempt the most difficult task of explaining the play of Eugene Aram, *by Mr Wills, and the acting of* Eugene Aram, *by Mr Henry Irving. We will discard, if you please, all stereotyped phrases and formulas. It is nothing to say* Eugene Aram *is a success.*

. . . What we wish emphatically to point out, and at once, is this: Eugene Aram *is no ordinary play. The acting of Mr Irving is no ordinary acting. . . Let those who will have every play made good in the end, and who would banish tragedy from the boards, avoid the Lyceum and* Eugene Aram. *Let those who believe the theory of Mr Boucicault, that an English audience must have a goody-goody termination to their amusement, steer clear of the new play.*

. . . But in all charity, let those who have some kindly feeling towards English dramatic art, in spite of innumerable difficulties, remain behind and see Eugene Aram. *Let them linger awhile, and note carefully the performance of Mr Irving . . . We have here photographed the mind of* Eugene Aram, *the mind of a man who has murdered another fourteen years ago, the mind of a wretch who has hoped to live down conscience, the mind of a poor devil who is flung once more amongst roses and love, as just as he is smelling the flower it falls to pieces in his hand.*

The play concerns three scenes in the after-life of an undetected murderer. In the first, haunted with dismal recollection, he still clings to life and hope. . . . We are in the Vicar's garden at Knaresborough, on the eve of the marriage of the Vicar's daughter with Eugene Aram, *the schoolmaster. . . . This act is purely idyllic and contemplative. It shows us*

Aram's *present life, and allows us a glance at his past career. The story has commenced well, is replete with charm, and, even by the unenthusiastic, is pronounced pretty.*

The second act is dramatic, for here Aram *meets his old accomplice,* Houseman, *who has come down to dig in the cave, and therefrom to extract some treasure which will frighten* Aram *into giving hush-money. . . . It is a splendid battle between these desperate men, and the acting here is almost as good as any in the play.* Houseman *is a bully, and destitute of sentiment. But* Aram *has his way. His arguments to* Houseman *are unanswerable, his threats are terrible.*

From this instant, the whole tone of Aram's *demeanour changes, and from being a white-hot, passionate man, he is a hang-dog, beaten, defeated fellow. This is a splendid change on the part of the actor, and, if we mistake not, will be accepted as a triumph of Mr Irving's acting in this most difficult scene. It was so sudden and complete, it electrified the audience, and the play was deservedly stopped for the applause.* Eugene Aram *has little more to say. He makes a wild appeal on behalf of the very* Houseman *he has previously accused. He accounts for the presence of the bones in an ingenious, but improbable, manner. He refuses to accompany the discovering party, and begs to be allowed to remain behind awhile, and when behind, left alone with his conscience, once more he gives himself up to a noble soliloquy, with which Mr Irving brings down the curtain, after such acting, as surprised as much as it delighted. It is a soliloquy of the craven man, looking at his haggard face in the glass, and fearing to gaze upon the bones of his victim. It made, deservedly – with all its delicacy, its thought, its study of attitude, and picture – a deep impression on the audience.*

The third act will provoke much controversy. It is, in reality, one tremendous soliloquy, and the excellence of Mr Irving's acting is at once pronounced with the statement that it held the audience almost from the commencement.

The play may be horrible, but such acting will not be dismissed by future intelligent audiences, in spite of the elaboration of the end of so terrible a life. That the actor could get variety out of such an unrelieved scene is marvellous. It is all on his shoulders, but again and again the interest revives. The confession was listened to with the deepest attention, and the oncoming death, now at the tomb, now writhing against the tree, and now prostrate upon the turf, brings into play an amount of study which is little less than astonishing, and an amount of power for which credit would have been given to Mr Irving by few who have seen his finest performances. We feel we have but incompletely given an idea of the high thought and judgement given in the play, or of the varied excellence of

Mr Irving's acting.

The other characters – with the exception of Houseman, *played with excellent discretion and praiseworthy contrast by Mr Edgar, and* Ruth, *prettily rendered by Miss Isabel Bateman – were of minor importance, though both intelligently rendered. Mr W H Stephens was the genial old* Vicar, *and Mr Irish the talkative gardener. The scenery and decorations even surpassed the artistic care of the Lyceum. No one will forget that summer garden of roses; the quaint old furnished interior or the sombre church yard with its overhanging yew-trees, and the distant view of Knaresborough expressed by a most poetical artist. The scenery comes from Mr Hawes Craven and Mr Cuthbert.*

Mr Wills has executed a difficult task in our humble opinion remarkably well, and Mr Irving's successful career has never shown such a stride as this in the right direction. The task of the play is herculean for any actor; and once more Mr Irving has triumphed.

The Times, April 21st, 1873:

Eugene Aram *at the Lyceum.*
Rarely is a theatrical audience, save on some festive occasion indicated by the Almanack, so anxious as the crowd which on Saturday evening filled the Lyceum Theatre to overflowing. Yet nobody acquainted with the present state of the theatrical atmosphere expected that it could be otherwise. Not only was Charles I *one of the most thoroughly successful and generally impressive pieces of the winter season, but it was a work of a new kind. The patrons of the drama are much more earnest and numerous than they were 20 years ago, and any amount of interest could be fully accounted for by the fact that* Charles I, *withdrawn after Friday's performance, was to be replaced on Saturday by another play, written by the same author, and sustained by the same principal actor. The importance attached to the actor must not be overlooked. The success of* Charles I *is closely associated with that of Mr Henry Irving, who was comparatively in the background three years ago, but whose progress is now anxiously watched as an upward career to which none can assign a possible limit.*

Having disposed of Saturday's audience, itself a spectacle, we came to the play, Eugene Aram. *In some respects it is the very reverse of its predecessor.* Charles I, *like the 'histories' of Shakespeare, comprised the changes of many years, and consisted of four striking acts, the result of somewhat fanciful groupings, connected together rather by the imagination of the spectator than by the art of the dramatist. On the other hand,*

Eugene Aram is marked by truly antique severity of construction. Changes of character, indeed, occur, but they never take us out of the one Yorkshire parish; the unity of time is observed with a strictness which even a French critic of the old school would not have required, the events presented throughout the piece being supposed to occur within little more than 12 hours, while as for that law of unity of action, the validity of which all parties agree to recognize, it is not more rigidly observed in Œdipus Tyrannus *than in* Eugene Aram. *The fact that the foundation of the story, as testified by the title of the play, was the record of a murder which in the course of the last century was committed in the neighbourhood of Bradford, perhaps led some among the audience to expect a melodrama highly spiced with visible assassination, with the semblance of a real criminal court, and, perhaps, a procession to the gallows; but as well might any one who hoped or feared that anything of the sort was coming have looked out for one of Madame Tussaud's waxen murderers in the sculpture-room of the British Museum. There is no murder whatever during the course of the action either before or behind the scenes, and, far from anybody being hanged, nobody is brought to trial. The author of* Eugene Aram *has worked in his own way as he did when he wrote* Charles I, *though the ways of work in the two cases are widely diverse, neither regarding the* Newgate Calendar, *the powerful ballad of Hood, nor the elaborate novel of Lord Lytton. None of these supplied the* Eugene Aram *that he required, so he made one of his own.*

In one particular, however, the author of Eugene Aram *shows his identity with the author of* Charles I. *If in the latter many appeals are made to the eye by elaborate groupings, while in the former there are none, there is this quality common to both, that the interest they excite is of a psychological kind. It is not so much the exhibition of incident as the development of character under exceptional circumstances which is contemplated by the author. Whether the principal figure be King* Charles *or Schoolmaster* Eugene, *it is the inner rather than the outer man that Mr Wills presents to his spectators. Herein, whether his form recedes from or approaches the antique, he remains truly English, or, to speak more largely, Teutonic.*

When the curtain rose on Saturday we found ourselves looking at one of the most real gardens ever planted on any stage, even by Mr Hawes Craven.

[Here the customary précis of the plot]

Mr Irving's delineation of the fall from a haughty defiance of daring to a state of hopeless humiliation is not to be surpassed in force and elaboration.

The action of the play is now virtually over. Houseman *has been released, and in the third act we find him in the churchyard, when his attention is arrested by the sight of a dark body under a spreading tree, which presently developes itself into the form of* Eugene, *so weird and ghastly that the vulgar reprobate shrinks from the spectacle with horror. Left alone, the fallen man who has seen the corpse is in a still more harrowing condition. He has made up his mind that all chance of forgiveness is denied him, but presently receives a sad consolation from the visit of his beloved* Ruth, *to whom, as a guardian angel, he makes a full confession of his guilt. The murder was committed under extenuating circumstances, comprising atrocious wrongs inflicted by his victim on the woman he fondly loved, but the weight of conscience has at last crushed him, and he dies in the arms of* Ruth, *who, as she had promised in a merry mood, remains devoted to the end. What we have described in a few lines forms the substance of a long soliloquy, occasionally interrupted by the remarks of* Ruth. *We could not without quotation convey a notion of the vigour with which this is written, nor even with a quotation could we convey a notion of Mr Irving's marvellous representation of the various phases of mental agony undergone by the wretched criminal. As the curtain falls the sun is rising, and the anthem is again heard in the church. The change from happiness to woe has occurred in the time intervening between the afternoon of one day and the dawn of the next, and yet the downward course has been clearly indicated step by step, without so much as a gap.*

A burst of admiration followed the termination of Eugene Aram, *and this had a remarkable effect, following, as it did, upon the breathless attention with which the scene had been watched. If the conclusion of* Charles I *gained a portion of its celebrity from the abnormal quantity of tears shed in the sometimes apathetic stalls, the death of* Eugene *was equally remarkable for the blank terror which it seemed to diffuse – a terror, be it observed, produced by purely dramatic means apparently of the simplest kind. Throughout the play not so much as the composition of one elaborate living picture is attempted. When the stage is occupied by the fewest persons, the drama is at its strongest.*

Our opinion of the admirable acting of Mr Irving has been briefly expressed in the course of our narrative. His is the figure that chiefly absorbs attention, but the high merits of Miss Isabel Bateman in a part that depends on the exhibition of a gentle nature placed amid untoward circumstances must not be overlooked. Her gaiety in the beginning is spontaneous and unaffected; her devotion is always manifest, and the terrible death of Eugene *would lose half its effect were not the despairing sufferer contrasted with the meek, resigned being, who watches over him in his last moments. The other parts are less important; but we may commend Mr Edgar for his appropriate roughness as* Houseman*; Mr*

W H Stephens for his bland respectability as the Vicar; *and Mr Irish for his characteristic performance of the gardener,* Jowell.

The drama is one which could be played with scarcely any accessories at all; but of this peculiarity no advantage is taken at the Lyceum. The garden in the first act, to which we have already referred, could not have been more completely elaborated if the manager had intended to succeed by dint of decoration only, and nearly the same may be said of the church-yard in the third act, with the tall spreading tree in the centre of the stage. The whole performance indicated unexceptionable management, and no more than justice was done when, after the artists had appeared before the curtain, a call arose for Mr Bateman.

The following rather sour little notice appeared in the *Stage,* ten years later:

On Thursday, July 19th, 1883, was played here for the first time, in one act, the play by W G Wills, entitled: Eugene Aram
Eugene Aram by *Mr Henry Irving*
Parson Meadows by *Mr H Howe*
Richard Houseman by *Mr W Terriss*
Jowell by *Mr S Johnson*
Ruth Meadows by *Miss Ellen Terry*

If Mr W G Wills's drama, Eugene Aram, *as originally produced at the Lyceum Theatre on April 19th, 1873, erred in being too long, just the opposite fault is to be found in the play as acted here on July 19th last. It is at all times a difficult task to attempt to compress a three-act play into a one-act sketch, and in this particular case the compression has not been successful. The play was found to have lost its dramatic force and significance, the story became vague and uncertain, and the acting was entirely spoiled in consequence. Mr Henry Irving's* Eugene Aram, *always a powerful and vivid psychological study, was reduced into a dramatic sketch, and nothing more; yet it was as artistically treated as ever by the actor. Miss Ellen Terry, as graceful and pathetic a* Ruth Meadows *as ever took the stage, had no chance whatever.*

Dan'l Druce

W S GILBERT

WILLIAM SCHWENCK GILBERT (1836/1911)

William Schwenck Gilbert (the 'Schwenck' was his godmother's surname) was born at 17, Southampton St, between the Strand and Covent Garden, on November 18th, 1836, the only boy in a family of five. The first event of note in his life was his kidnapping by brigands in Naples at the age of two. He was ransomed by distraught parents for £25, a circumstance which has been seen to account for the more bizarre aspects of some of his plots.

In 1857 he graduated from London University with the degree of BA, and entered the education department of the Privy Council office. During four uncongenial years in this post he began contributing to various magazines (notably H J Byron's *Fun* in which *Bab Ballads* first appeared and *Punch*) as a humorist, theatre critic and story-writer. Although he appears not to have received any formal training, he illustrated many of his own articles, also two of his father's books.

An unexpected legacy of £300 in 1861 enabled him to leave his 'ill-organised and ill-governed office' and to read for the bar. He joined the northern circuit in 1866, but was conspicuously unsuccessful as a barrister. Only his pen earned him a 'decent income'.

His career in the theatre began in 1866 when Tom Robertson recommended him to the lessee of the St James's Theatre. At short notice he produced *Dulcamara, or The Little Duck and the Great Quack* (a burlesque version of *L'Elixir d'Amore*) which was produced on Boxing Day, ran for several months was was twice revived. Further burlesques – *La Vivandière, or True To The Corps* based on *La Figlia del Reggimento* and *The Merry Zingara, or the Tipsy Gipsy and the Popsy Wopsy* based on *The Bohemian Girl* – enhanced his reputation, and the next few years saw a steady stream of burlesques, farcical plays, sketches and musical extravaganzas. In 1867 he married Lucy Agnes Turner, the daughter of an Indian Army Officer: there were no children – the character of Dorothy Druce is said to represent how deeply he felt this lack.

The year 1871 was a milestone in his career; he wrote *Pygmalion and Galatea*, a romance in stiffly artificial verse which was a colossal success – in his obituary in the *Daily Telegraph* he is said to have made £40,000 from this one piece alone. This same year also saw his first collaboration with (Sir) Arthur Sullivan on a burlesque called *Thespis, or The Gods Grown Old*. In 1875 they produced *Trial By Jury* at the Royalty Theatre, in 1877 *The Sorcerer* at the Opèra Comique, but their first sensational success came the following year with *HMS Pinafore* at the same theatre.

Gilbert designed the sets and costumes for his productions, and also directed the performance, in which capacity he was the strictest of martinets. With Tom Robertson (whom he considered as his master in this respect) he brought a fresh approach to the notion of 'stage-management' as it was called. Before rehearsals started he would work out every move with the aid of a model stage; all exits and entrances, gestures, dances and even make-up were minutely regulated, and he brooked no diversions from his instructions. Later ideas of stage discipline, exhaustive preparation and rehearsal owe much to his pioneering work.

He wrote some 50 farces, burlesques, and a handful of dramas as well as the fourteen Comic Operas with Sullivan, plus ten or so other musical pieces with other composers, among them Frederick Clay and Edward German. His burlesques were perhaps slightly less silly than those of his contemporaries (although full of facetiousness and puns) since he endeavoured to direct his heavy irony at Victorian life, customs, fashions and institutions as well as other plays, currently popular novels and operas. In fact his knighthood is said to have been delayed until after Victoria's death by his disrespectful treatment of the House of Lords in *Pirates of Penzance* and *Iolanthe*.

Gilbert built the Garrick Theatre, contributed munificently to theatrical charities, and purchased the house and estate of Grims Dyke at Harrow Weald, Middlesex. It was in his own lake in the grounds that he rescued a young woman from drowning on May 29th, 1911. The exertion brought on a heart attack, which proved fatal.

Of his dramatic plays I have selected *Dan'l Druce* for its power and genuinely emotional strength. The sombre mood of the piece and the rhetorical dialogue do not smother the excellence of the construction; even the predictability of the outcome does not result in any loss of interest. The characterisation is unremarkable, but the climax is only reached after several heart-turning twists which leave one breathless. There is the usual outrageous coincidence, well-spoken ingénue, noble-hearted hero, and honourable representative of the gentry. The lustful, blackhearted villain is unusual in that he is a plebian, being but Sir Jasper's bailiff. Dan'l himself is an example of the Good Old Man of Jerome's *Stage-land* who spends his life being subjected to the hammer-blows of Fate, but his passionate outbursts are so authentically drawn by Gilbert that he demands and, I submit, receives - our respect and profoundest sympathies. When he realises that he is once again to lose his daughter, his agony of mind would melt a heart of stone.

However, the play was not especially successful, and ran for barely three months, although it was popular with provincial leading men and had a brief revival at the Prince of Wales Theatre in 1894.

Hermann Vezin was forty-seven when *Dan'l* was produced, having been born in Philadelphia in 1829. His first engagement in this country was at the Theatre Royal, York, and in 1859 he took the Surrey for a Shakespearean season for six weeks, in which he scored a particular success as Macbeth. He later stood in for Irving in this role at the Lyceum, when Irving was ill for a week. Such was his success again that Irving presented him with a diamond ring and a cheque for £120. He died in 1910.

Marian Terry made her first appearance at the Haymarket Theatre as Dorothy, and it made her reputation. A younger sister of Ellen Terry, she had made her début as a professional actress at the Theatre Royal, Manchester, as Ophelia in Tom Taylor's version of *Hamlet* in 1873. Marion Terry was born in 1856 and died in 1930 – although there seems to be some doubt about her birth-year, which might have been 1853.

The Mr Forbes-Robertson who played Geoffrey was of course (Sir) Johnston Forbes-Robertson, who was born in 1853 and was therefore twenty-three years of age when *Dan'l Druce* was produced. This was only two years after his first professional appearance (as Chastelard in *Mary Stuart* at the Princess's Theatre) and it laid the foundations of his tremendously successful career. Although he had started out in life as an artist – he trained for a time at the Royal Academy School of Art – his good looks, voice and deportment soon established him as the foremost romantic juvenile lead of the day. He joined Irving at the Lyceum for the first time in 1892, and went on to become, under his own management, the Hamlet of his generation. He also presented Shaw's *Caesar and Cleopatra* in the United States and Britain, Caesar being one of his most

Herman Vezin (*Photographic Collection, Victoria &*
Albert Museum)

popular roles. His name will always be linked with Jerome's *Passing of the Third Floor Back*, a role he detested. He died in 1937.

Gilbert disliked intensely the Mr Odell who played Reuben, and claimed that his poor performance was to a large extent responsible for the comparative failure of the piece.

DAN'L DRUCE

Dramatis Personae

First performed at the Theatre Royal, Haymarket
Monday, September 11th, 1876

An incident in the First Act was suggested by George Eliot's novel
Silas Marner

Sir Jasper Combe, a Royalist Colonel, by Mr Howe
Dan'l Druce by Mr Hermann Vezin
Reuben Haines, a Royalist Sergeant, by Mr Odell
Geoffrey Wynyard, a Merchant sailor, by Mr Forbes-Robertson
Marple by Mr Braid
Joe Ripley, a Fisherman, by Mr Weathersby
Sergeant, of the Parliamentary Army, by Mr C Allbrook
Soldier, of the Parliamentary Army, by Mr Fielder
Dorothy by Miss Marion Terry

The first act takes place shortly after the Battle of Worcester.

There is an interval of fourteen years between the first and second acts

Act 1 : *a ruined hut on the Norfolk coast*

Act 2 : *Dan'l Druce's forge*

Act 3 : *interior of Druce's cottage*

DAN'L DRUCE, BLACKSMITH

Act 1

Scene. Interior of Dan'l Druce's hut, a tumble-down old shanty, of the rudest description; with very small wood fire. The whole place is as squalid and miserable as possible. Wind and snow without. Rain and wind heard each time the door is opened. Night

Ripley (Without) Hullo! Dan'l, art within? *(Knocks)* Dan'l, I say, open, will you? *(He kicks the door open)* Why, the hut's empty. Where's the old devil gone, I wonder? Come in master, out of the storm

Enter Marple

Don't be afeard. *(Marple shuts door)* He'll be a bit rusty, to be sure, at our coming in without leave, but that'll blow off sooner than the gale outside.

Marple Is the man away?

Ripley Nay, he's hauling up his boat on the beach, maybe, or taking in his nets, and making all snug and taut for the night; and well he may, for the devil's let loose, and there'll be mischief afore morning. The devil likes these Norfolk coasts, burn him!

Marple And so Jonas lives here.

Ripley Jonas? No, Dan'l – Dan'l Druce.

Marple Well, Dan'l Druce, if that's what he calls himself. It's a strange hole for such a man as he!

Ripley It's a fit hole for such a dog as he! A surly, scowling, drunken, miserly, half-starved cur! Oh, take my word for it, it's a fit hole for such as he. There's only one fitter, and I wish he was in it.

Marple Stop that cursed red rag of yours, will you? I am this man's brother.

Ripley (Aside) Well, you've got the family tongue in your head, anyhow. If you're his brother, maybe you know how he came to live here all alone?

Marple Maybe I do.

Ripley They say that before he came here – a matter o' three or four years since – he was a decent sort o' body enough, a blacksmith, I *do* hear, but he got struck half silly like through some bad luck, and he's been a changed man ever since.

Marple Oh, they say that, do they?

Ripley Well, I don't know what he *was*, but I know what he *is*; that's enough for me. The scowlingest, black-browdest, three-corneredest chap *I* ever see, 'cept as regards children, and the littler they are the more he likes 'em, and they likes him. That's odd, ain't it?

Enter Dan'l Druce. He has a bundle of nets over his shoulder, and he is half tipsy. His appearance is that of a man of fifty, but haggard with want. His hair is long and matted, and he has a beard of some days' growth on his chin

Dan'l Hullo! Who's that? Joe Ripley, eh? Nothing to lay hands on *here*, Joe Ripley. And thou'st brought a friend, eh? Didst thee think there was too much plunder for a man to carry that thou'st brought an ass to help thee?

Ripley Hold thy peace, man. I want nowt of thine. I've brought thee money for thy two nets.

Dan'l Where is it?

Ripley And here's a man as says he's thy brother. I found him in the village, so I brought him to thee.

Dan'l Gi' me the money.

Marple Dost thou not know me, Jonas Marple?

Dan'l Dead. Dead three years ago.

Marple Ay, thou gavest thyself out as dead, that *he* might make an honest woman of her.

Dan'l Thou liest, she *was* an honest woman, for all she left me. 'Twas him that stole her, God bless her! Jonas Marple died the day she left him. I'm Dan'l Druce.

Marple And if Jonas *be* dead, hast thou no word of welcome for Jonas's brother?

Dan'l None! (*To Ripley*) Gi' me the money. (*To Marple*) How didst thou find me?

Marple I was in the town on law business, and I heard men talk of such a one as thou, and I asked and asked, and found out that thou wast the brother who used to work wi' me. I've come to ask thee to come back to us, and be the man thou wast wont to be. Come, throw off thy present self, thou canst not be worse!

Dan'l Not worse! Why, man, I'm a king, alone here! What, back to the world, the hollow, lying world? Not I! Back to the rock on which my ship was wrecked? Not I! See here – I've lived here nigh upon four years, and 'cepting some such gaping fool as him (*Indicating Ripley*) I've seen no soul, and no soul's seen me. I've lived on the fish I've caught, the garden I've dug, and I've saved money by the nets I've made. I've no hopes, no cares, no fears. And thou askest me to go back to the bitter black world that blighted this poor, harmless life. No!

Marple Well, as thou wilt, Jonas.

Dan'l Dan'l – that's my name. Dan'l Druce. Jonas Marple died the day his wife left him.

Marple Thou art sadly changed: it's fearsome to see a good, honest, hearty soul changed into the white-faced ghost of what he was.

Dan'l Does it seem so strange to thee ? Hast thou e'er known what it is to set thy heart night and day on one object, to dream of it, sleepin' and wakin', to find the hope of it weavin' itself into thy life so that every deed of thy hand has some bearin' on it ? So did I hope and pray to be blessed with a little child. When *she* left me (curse him!) I gave over the love of my heart to the next best thing – gold and silver, gold and silver. Ay, brother, I love my gold as other men love their bairns. I've prayed a thousand times that my gold might take a living form, that the one harmless old hope of my wrecked life might come true.

Marple The age of miracles is past, Jonas. Stay where thou art, and Heaven forgive thee, Jonas Marple.

Dan'l (*Sternly*) He's dead! Now go

(*Marple, after a pause, shrugs his shoulders, and exit with Ripley*).

Dan'l Ay, he's dead, dead, dead! He died then, that the blackest devil that ever cursed this earth might put her right with the world. Heaven send he has done so! And the bairn! It was promised to me –
(*Opens a hole in the floor in front of stool, and takes out a bag of money*). This is my bairn now. Here's a child that'll never grow up to bring sorrow on its dad's head, that costs nowt to keep, and never grows so big but you wish it bigger – my bairn! Lie here, my beauty, lie there in peace; I'll never wake thee but to add to thy life, my bairn, my beautiful golden bairn

The door is suddenly burst open, and Sir Jasper Combe enters hurriedly followed by Reuben as if pursued. They are both dressed in torn and faded Royalist uniforms; Sir Jasper an officer, Reuben, a sergeant. Reuben carries a child of three or four years of age, wrapped in a cloak, so as not to be seen by Dan'l. They close the door and listen for their pursuers. Reuben places child on locker

Who and what are ye, jail-birds ?

Jasper Listen to me, my friend! We are Royalists, and you, miserable man, have harboured us, Heaven help you! If we are taken here, I, he, and thou will surely hang – I and he for our sins against the Parliament, thou – for thy virtue in aiding, abetting and comforting us. Dost thou clearly understand me ?

Dan'l (*Taking up an iron bar from the fireplace*) Go your ways, both

405

of you; or as I am a man I'll brain ye with this bar!

Jasper The very thing! (*Wrenches it easily out of his hand and barricades the door with it, while Reuben shows Dan'l a pistol*) Now master, listen to me. We are desperate men in a desperate strait, and little disposed to stand on ceremony, as you may perhaps have remarked. We are flying for our lives, and we desire to cross to France, where my lady is, and where we shall be safe. You have a stout boat on the beach; when this accursed gale shall have blown itself out you shall have the distinction of working us across to the opposite coast.

Dan'l Who, in the devil's name, are ye?

Jasper I'm a cavalier colonel, a trifle out of repair, and a thought begrimed, maybe, but that'll wash off. This is my regiment, the King's Dragoons (*Indicating Reuben*). Come, doff thy hat, Reuben, for thou'rt all that's left of it! Now, what food have you got?

Dan'l I've no food – I'm a beggar.

Jasper Here's a coin – our last – go and get bread, meat and drink. Now be off, or Reuben here shall whip you with his sword-flat till he drops. And, mark me, if by word, deed or sign you do aught to give a clue to our hiding-place, I'll burn the hut to the ground, and everything in it.

Dan'l But –

Jasper Not a word. Be off, and do your errand – and mind, no treachery, or – (*takes a burning log from the fire and holds it over the hole where Dan'l's money is concealed*).

Dan'l Put that down, for the love of Heaven! I'll see what I can do, I'll see what I can do. (*Exit*).

Jasper Whew! I've brought the old devil to his senses. What a life is this! Was ever a poor dog so hounded about from pillar to post as Jasper Combe? And for no better reason than that he is a gentleman, and loves his king! Is the child safe?

Reuben (*Uncovering the child, and bringing it down*) Ay, sir, thanks to my cloak.

Jasper A dozen times we might have got away but for being hampered with this squalling abomination. Well, there's no help for it. My lady would have gone mad had I returned to her without it. She is devotedly attached to the child.

Reuben My mother always disliked me and kept me at a convenient distance. But *she* was a Scotchwoman and not liable to be imposed on.

Jasper Whew! How cold it is. I'm chilled to the marrow of my bones. Bring an armful of logs and make a merry blaze, for I ache as though I were trussed in a suit of thumbscrews

(*Exit Reuben*)

Here's a plight for the Lord of Combe-Raven! Stripped of an ancestral mansion and two thousand acres; hunted to his death by broad-brimmed bloodhounds – separated from his pretty wife by some two hundred miles of barren land and stormy water, and saddled with a confounded brat that hampers his flight, let him turn whithersoever he will! By the Lord Harry!

(*Stamps impatiently; his foot starts a board over Dan'l's hoard*).

Ha! Why what's this? Not gold? (*Takes out some*) Gold – and in profusion! Here's a way out of our difficulties, if Combe-Raven were but the man to take it. (*Closing hole*) Lie there – I'll not meddle with thee

Enter Reuben in breathless haste

Reuben Sir! We must fly – the old man has played us false! I hear the horses' hoofs in the distance –

Jasper A thousand devils wring his damnable neck! Run to the boat – get her ready for the sea. I'll join thee at once and we'll launch her together.

(*Exit Reuben. Jasper watches him out, then quickly turns to the hole*).

So – this changes the aspect of affairs. Old fool, thou hast betrayed us, and this is fair plunder. (*Takes it out of the hole*) With fair luck we may beat across to France tonight, but the child – again a clog on our movements! She would surely perish in an open boat on such a night as this. There is no help for it – I must leave her here – this locket will serve to identify her (*Putting a locket and chain on her neck*) – and I'll reclaim her when I get across. They'll never harm a child!

Enter Reuben hurriedly

Reuben Sir, sir, the troops are upon us – they're not two hundred yards off –

Jasper I'm coming. (*Exit Reuben. Jasper writes on a piece of paper, and pins it on the child's dress*) So – lie thou there, and God help thee, little one. I'm loth to leave thee, but it's for life and death – for life and death!

(*Jasper leaps through the window as Dan'l and a Sergeant with four soldiers, in Parliamentary uniform, enter at the door*).

Sergeant Where are thy prisoners, the sons of Belial?

Jasper They were here, but the noise of thy horses' hoofs has alarmed them. I warned thee to tether thy beasts afar, and proceed silently.

1st Soldier See they are putting off from the beach.

Dan'l My boat, oh, my boat!

Sergeant Bring down the Philistines, Nahum; a steady shot under the fifth rib, and may the Lord have mercy on them!

1st Soldier I will even smite them hip and thigh! (*He fires through the window*) Missed! Nay, they're beyond range. May Heaven mercifully overwhelm them in the great waters!

Dan'l (*Sees hole in floor*) My gold – my gold! They've stolen it; they've robbed me! Sixty golden pounds! all I had – all I had! and it's gone! My child! My child! They've stolen my child!

Sergeant Nay, man, see, they child's safe enough, and a bonny lass she be.

407

Dan'l Eh? Why, what's that?

Sergeant Thy Child! Come, man, be thyself; the child's safe enough. (*Places child on ground*).

Dan'l That's not mine. My gold is my child!

Sergeant Here's a paper, and some words writ on it.

Dan'l Read – read – I cannot read.

Sergeant 'Be kind to the child, and it shall profit thee. Grieve not for thy gold – it hath taken this form'.

(*Music*).

Dan'l (*On his knees taking the child*) A miracle, a miracle! Down on your knees, down, I say, for Heaven has worked a miracle to save me. I prayed that this might be, but scoffers mocked me when I prayed, and said that the days of miracles were passed. My Heaven-sent bairn, thou hast brought me back to reason, to manhood, to life!

(*Soldiers crowd round him. 1st Soldier offers to touch the child*).

Hands off, hands off! Touch not the Lord's gift! Touch not the Lord's gift!

(*Tableau*)

Act 2

Scene. The interior of a picturesque old forge. Dan'l Druce, a hearty-looking old man of sixty-four, is discovered hammering lustily at a piece of red-hot iron

Dan'l (*Laying down his hammer*) Whew! That job's done. Eh, but I'm that breathed, surelie. Mebbe I'm growing old. Well, a body can't hope to live sixty-four year, and leave off a young un arter all. 'Twouldn't be fair on the boys – no, nor the gals neither – eh, Dorothy?

Enter Dorothy running

Dorothy Oh, father, thou shouldst see the Green, by Raby's End. The village is brave with banners and garlands. And Master Maynard, the constable, is mounted on an ale cask to receive Sir Jasper Combe, who should pass on his way to Combe-Raven in half an hour. I have heard that he is a grave gentleman of goodly presence and beyond measure kindly. He is a righteous landlord, too, so folk say, and giveth largely to the poor.

Dan'l I shall be right glad to welcome him, but I'll not go to Raby's End to do it.

Dorothy Art thou wearied, father?

Dan'l Growin' old, lass, growin' old. It's one o' those blessings that allers come to him that waits long enough. But if old age will leave me strength enough to pull at a pipe and empty a tankard, why, that's all I ask. My lass can do the rest.

Dorothy As I have been to thee so will I be to the end.

Dan'l There's no saying, Dorothy. Thou'rt comely, lass, and there's mor'n one within a mile o' this who'd give his right arm to carry thee away to t'other side o' the sunrise.

Dorothy Nay, thou art unkind. Did I not tend thee when thou wast hale and strong, and shall I desert thee now that thou hast most need of me?

Dan'l (*With emotion*) My lass, Heaven knows I never needed thee more than when thou wast left at my hut fourteen year since. But I've news to gladden thee – thine old playmate Geoffrey Wynyard is returned from sea, and is now on his road from Norwich to see thee.

Dorothy Geoffrey returned? Oh, I am right glad! Oh, indeed,

409

father, I am right glad!

Dan'l See to him when he cometh, for he'll bide here wi' us. (*After a pause*) My darlin' – thou'lt never leave me?

Dorothy Never, while I live!

Dan'l God bless thee, my child! (*Kisses her and exit*).

Dorothy Geoffrey returned! and Geoffrey a stalwart mariner and grown to man's estate! I can scarce believe it! Of a truth I could weep for very joy! Pity that I have not my new shoes, for they are comely; but they do compress my feet, and so pain me sorely. Nevertheless, I will put them on, for it behoveth a maiden to be neatly apparelled at all seasons.

Enter Geoffrey

Geoffrey Mistress Dorothy!

Dorothy Geoffrey! Oh, Geoffrey!

Geoffrey How thou art grown! A woman! By my right hand, a very woman!

Dorothy Yes, Master Geoffrey, I am a woman now!

Geoffrey And a fair one, Mistress Dorothy. Nay, 'tis but truth; and truth is made to be told. May I not say that thou art fair?

Dorothy Yes, Master Geoffrey, if thou thinkest so in good sooth.

Geoffrey In good sooth I do! It seems but yesterday that we tossed hay together in the five acre field, yet three years have gone.

Dorothy It seemeth more.

Geoffrey Dorothy, I love the sea dearly. There is but love that is stronger in my heart – one love for which I would yield it up for ever and ever. Dear Dorothy, I have loved thee, boy and man, for ten years past; and I shall love thee, come what may, through my life.

Dorothy Oh, Geoffrey – Geoffrey! I know not what to say!

Geoffrey Fear not for thy father, for I will quit the sea. Sir Jasper has offered to make me his secretary, and that is why I have come. But say nay, and I must needs go to sea again.

Dorothy Oh, Geoffrey – let me think – let me think! Do I love thee? I cannot say. Truly thou art dear to me, for I am rejoiced when thou comest, and I am sorely grieved when thou goest. Is that love?

Geoffrey Dorothy, let us inquire into this. We will suppose that I have given up the sea – that I have bought a little farm near at hand, and that I have come to live here, close to thee and thy father, for the rest of my life. Canst thou see the picture I am painting?

Dorothy Ay. It is a pleasant picture.

Geoffrey Living here, close to thee, I naturally see thee very often.

Dorothy Every day?

Geoffrey Twice – maybe thrice – a day – for my horses need much shoeing, and I always bring them to the forge myself. Is that pleasant?

Dorothy Very pleasant. And on Sabbath thou takest me to church?

Geoffrey Ay, save only when some other village gallant is before-

410

hand with me and offers to escort thee thither, and in such case I am fain to take Farmer Such-a-one's daughter Susan instead.

Dorothy Is she fair?

Geoffrey Very fair.

Dorothy Then thou wouldst not.

Geoffrey And wherefore not?

Dorothy Wherefore not? Oh, go to Susan if thou wilt, Geoffrey. It is not for me to hinder thee!

Geoffrey Well, then, I wouldst not. And so we live on – very, very happy, for, say a year. But a change is at hand. My crops fail, my cattle die, and one evil night my homestead is burnt to the ground, and I am penniless!

Dorothy Oh!

Geoffrey So there is nothing for it but to go to sea again, for three long years!

Dorothy No, no, Geoffrey – oh no!

Geoffrey Months pass by and no news of me. The village seems blank at first without me, the walks to church seem long and lonely, and the evenings sad and cheerless. At last come tidings of a wrecked ship – thine heart beats quickly, for the name of the ship is the name of mine. Of all the crew but one man is saved, and that man's name – is not Geoffrey Wynyard – for Geoffrey has gone down to his death in the dark waters.

Dorothy (*Throwing her arms round him*) No, no, Geoffrey, be silent. I cannot bear it – have mercy, for I cannot bear it!

Geoffrey And dost thou love me?

Dorothy (*Bashfully*) Oh, Geoffrey! (*Hiding her head in his bosom*).

Geoffrey Art thou happy there, Dorothy?

Dorothy Passing happy! And thou?

Geoffrey Passing happy. (*He places a ring on her finger*).

Dorothy Oh, Geoffrey, what is this?

Geoffrey A ring that I have brought thee from Venice, where there are cunning workers in such matters. Let it stay there in earnest of another ring of plainer workmanship that is not beyond the craft of our English goldsmiths to fashion.

Dorothy But I know not if I may wear it. It is a vanity – but it is very beautiful. See how it shineth! Oh, pity that I may not wear it, for in truth it is very beautiful.

Geoffrey Thou hast a silver chain with thy mother's locket on thy neck. Wear it on thy chain. Will it be a vanity if it is concealed beneath thy kerchief?

Dorothy Nay; for none will know of it. See, the locket shall be thine, and thy ring shall take its place. (*Detaches locket and gives it to him. He kisses her*)

Enter Dan'l Druce. They all stand confused

411

Dan'l (*After a pause, sighs deeply*) Tell me all about it, my pretty.

Dorothy Dear father, Geoffrey hath told me that he loveth me, and would fain take me to be his wife –

Dan'l Ay, ay, lass – go on –

Dorothy He loveth me very dearly, father, and will quit the sea to bide with us here.

Dan'l Go on –

Dorothy He loveth me so dearly that it would sadden his life if I were to wed with another.

Dan'l Well?

Dorothy So, dear father, as I would not cause him sorrow I will not wed with another.

Dan'l So soon! so soon! Dorothy, oh Dorothy, the hope and stay of my poor old life! my saving angel! my saving angel! It's hard to part with thee, Dorothy. I'm but a thankless man. It was to be, and 'twould better fit me to rejoice that thou hast found a brave and honest man to tend thee when I am gone. Get thee within, and dry thy eyes. I'll do thy weeping for thee, Dorothy!

(*Exit Dorothy into the cottage*).

It's come sudden, my lad, it's come sudden, and I doan't rightly know how to shift wi'out her. I was a hard and bitter man when she was left with me fourteen years since – for I'd been cruelly warped – I was cruel and hard, but I couldna sit glowerin' at mankind wi' her little arms round my neck, and her soft cheek agin' my wicked old face. Then it come about that Dolly must be taught her Bible; so, wi' a shamfaced lie on my tongue, I borrowed a good book, and we spelt it out together. And many's the time as the old half-forgotten words come back to me, bit by bit, and I called to mind when I'd first learnt 'em as a child, I laid my head down on the book, and wept like a woman. And as it was for me to teach her right from wrong, I learnt as I taught, and the Light come to us together, and such as I am – hale, hearty and happy – livin' by the sweat o' my brow – owin' no man, fearin' none, and lovin' all, why she has made me, God bless her!

Geoffrey And thou has never seen her father since?

Dan'l No; though for years I never passed a strange face but I peered into it – for I knowed every line o' his, though I never heerd his name. Knowed it! Why, it burnt it my eyeballs, so that I see it in the dark. After a while (but it was a weary while!) the thought come that mayhap he had perished in the gale, yet the old fear comes back, odd times, and, oh, Geoffrey, it's like enough she'll be taken from me yet

Enter Dorothy from cottage

Dorothy Oh, father, a gentleman whose horse hath cast a shoe hath need of thy services.

Dan'l A gentleman, eh?

Dorothy It is Master Reuben Haines, Sir Jasper's bailiff. He passed this way twice before when thou wast away at Norwich.

Dan'l Come Geoffrey, and lend me a hand. I'll see to his horse.

Geoffrey kisses Dorothy and exit with Dan'l into yard. Enter Reuben from cottage

Reuben Good morrow, pretty Mistress Dorothy! We have not forgotten one another, I see! And how has time sped with thee since I saw thee last? Has it crept, crawled, drawled, dragged and dawdled for lack of a certain merry old man who whiled away a certain half-hour with thee two months since with curious quip, quaint retort, and surprising conundrum? Dost thou remember that half-hour, Dorothy?

Dorothy Sir, I do indeed remember your coming; but as for your sayings, I understood them not. Is – is Sir Jasper at hand?

Enter Dan'l Druce, unobserved, at back

Reuben He will be here anon. Some village clowns are plaguing him with an address – a scurvy long one, and writ in very false jingle.

Dan'l Nay, sir, but if Sir Jasper deserve all that men say of him, he will scarcely hold in scorn that which poor humble folks have writ in his praise.

Reuben Who is this old gentleman?

Dan'l I am Dan'l Druce – no gentleman, but a hard-working blacksmith, very much at your honour's service. I'm a punctual tenant, sir, and I fear no man. Dorothy, draw this gentleman some ale while I look to his horse. (*Exit*).

Reuben (*Dorothy going*) Nay, do not go. Never heed the ale. I'd rather take a long look at thy pretty face than a long pull at thy village brew. Come hither, Dorothy.

Dorothy Nay, sir, I –

Reuben I have news to tell thee, Dorothy – thou art a kind of wife of mine, for I have, in a manner, married thee – intellectually and reflectively; or, as one may say, in a mental or moral sense have I married thee. (*Aside*) A quip!

Dorothy Sir, I do not rightly understand thy talk, but it seemeth to me that thou makest a jest of solemn things.

Reuben Nay, if thou wilt be my wife, I will so coll thee, coax thee, cosset thee, court thee, cajole thee, with deftly turned compliment, pleasant whimsy and delicate jest – I will so edify thee with joyous anecdote, tales of court and camp, tales of love, hate and intrigue, tales of murder, rapine and theft, merry tales, sad tales – (*Takes her round waist*).

Dorothy Nay, sir, I pray you, remove your hand! Sir, I pray you, desist!

413

Enter Sir Jasper

Oh, sir, defend me from this wicked man.

Jasper Why, Reuben Haines, thou art at thine old tricks again! If thou sayest or doest aught to anger this gentle maiden, I'll lay my whip across thy shoulders, as I have done oft times ere this.

Reuben (*Aside*) We are virtuous now, but time was when we would have angered her in company.

Dorothy Nay, sir, I pray you, bear with him. Whenever he cometh to the forge he sayeth such strange things that I fear he is sorely afflicted, and not to be held accountable for his deeds.

Jasper (*Laughing*) Why, in truth, I sometimes think so too. (*To Reuben*) Get thee to the inn, sir; we shall be there tonight: as for the whipping, why the maiden's intercession hath saved thee this once.

Reuben She pleadeth for me! Bless their hearts, they're all alike! They all plead for me! (*Exit*).

Jasper And now, pretty maiden, tell me, who art thou?

Dorothy So please your worship, I am Dorothy Druce, only daughter of Dan'l Druce, the blacksmith, and your worship's tenant.

Jasper He's a kind father to thee, I'll be sworn.

Dorothy He is kind to me and to all.

Jasper And thou tendest him very carefully?

Dorothy Yes, indeed. We love each other with a love that passeth all telling.

Jasper Dorothy, I once had a little child who promised to grow up to be just such a pretty lass as thou. But we – we were separated many years ago, and I have never seen her since.

Dorothy Poor gentleman!

Jasper Poor indeed – for I declare to thee, Dorothy, that I would give all my substance, were it ten times what it is, to have her with me in my old age.

Dorothy Indeed, my heart bleeds for your worship.

Jasper Her mother died of grief – and – and I would fain make amends, I would fain make amends! Yes, Dorothy, it would have gone hard with me but I would have made her love me!

Enter Dan'l

Who is this good fellow?

Dorothy It is my father, of whom I spoke to your worship. Father, this is Sir Jasper Combe.

Dan'l At your worship's service, Sir Jasper. I've naught to say, sir, but what's been said by better men – 'welcome to Combe-Raven'. I'll go bail my daughter Dorothy's said it already.

Jasper Indeed, she has given me a very kindly greeting, Master Druce. I was telling thy daughter how I came to be wifeless and childless;

and how, desolate as I am, I envy thee thy good fortune in having so fair a little nurse to cosset thee in thine old age.

(*During this speech Dan'l has gradually recognized Sir Jasper. He is stupified with terror*).

Take care that she be not taken from thee one of these days.

Dan'l (*Still stupified*) By whom ? Taken from me by whom ?

Jasper Oh, never fear me, Dan'l – by some far younger man than I ?

Dan'l Ay, ay – to be married. Ah, mebbe, mebbe!

Jasper There, be of good cheer, man; I did but jest, to be sure. (*Aside*) To think that those few light words should have so shaken him. Master Druce, I'm an old man now, and a very grave and sober old man too. I had a fair young wife once; she had eyes like thy daughter's eyes. There's a strange whim in my head, but I'm an old man, and – and – and – may I kiss thy little daughter ?

Dan'l (*Much moved*) Ay, ay, thou – thou mayst kiss her if thou wilt! (*Dorothy goes up to Sir Jasper, who kisses her on the forehead*).

Jasper God bless thee, maiden. Dan'l Druce, I thank thee! (*Exit*).

Dorothy Oh, father, I grieve to think how solitary the poor gentleman must be, all alone in so vast a house, with neither wife nor child to solace him in his old age!

Dan'l Did he tell thee of his child ?

Dorothy Ay, when he told me how he lost the maiden many years ago, and how he has vainly sought her ever since, my heart yearned to him, for the tears glistened in his eyes.

Dan'l Nay, thou knowest him not. He did not deal rightly by the girl. He left her to perish – to perish, Dolly – that he might save his own life. He is rightly served. The sins of his youth are visited upon him in his old age. It is just, it is just. *I* would not have quitted *thee*, my child, my child!

Dorothy In truth, I am very sure of that. I cannot think that there is in this world peril or necessity so dire as to part us twain!

Dan'l Thou'lt never leave me, Dolly ?

Dorothy Never!

Dan'l Come what may ?

Dorothy Come what may! (*He kisses her. Exit Dorothy*).

Dan'l Oh, it's hard, arter so long; for the heart o' my body is not so dear to me as yon poor little girl! Oh, Dolly, it canna be right – arter so long – it canna be right

Enter Geoffrey

Geoffrey Why, Master Druce, thou hast tears in thine eyes!

Dan'l Ay, lad, and cause for 'em in my heart! Geoffrey, there's a heavy blow come on me. I – I told thee of the cruel thankless father who left my girl wi' me – my Dorothy – *thy* Dorothy –

Geoffrey Yes!

Dan'l I – I have seen him, Geoffrey! Here – here I have seen him! Him as thou art to meet – that's Dolly's father!

Geoffrey Sir Jasper! Impossible!

Dan'l Yes, I tell thee, 'twas him. He didn't know me – *but I knowed him !* Geoffrey – my only hope lies wi' thee. Thou must wed Dorothy – ay, at once too. He cannot take her from *thee* – and we will all go hence to a place of safety – tomorrow – tomorrow!

Geoffrey Master Druce, if this man, Sir Jasper Combe, is indeed her father, bethink thee – the poor lone gentleman hath paid a bitter price for his wickedness. Grief and penitence have wrought a great change in him, and the laws of Heaven and of man give him a right over her that none may gainsay.

Dan'l And have I earned no right in these fourteen years ? Why, think what she is to me! what we are to each other! We are life and death, body and soul, all in all to each other. And now thou wouldst have me say to this unworthy man, 'Here is the daughter that thou didst abandon in thy peril. For fourteen years I have reared her as mine own; but as thou did beget her, so take her'. It may be that this is my duty, Geoffrey Wynyard, but I canna do it – I canna do it.

Geoffrey Thy case is a hard one – it is not for me to judge.

Dan'l Moreover, bethink thee, thou lovest her. If this man, her father, reclaims her, he will take her from thee, and raise her to a station as far above thine as thine is above hers.

Geoffrey Art thou so sure that Sir Jasper is indeed her father ?

Dan'l That's true! that's very true! I know not that he *is* her father! I cannot tell that. We judge men by their deeds, Geoffrey, and not their words. He may have lied. Come, that's well thought of, Geoffrey! But we'll go hence, Dolly and I – no one shall know – thou shalt join us later; and when thou and she are married, and he cannot take her from thee, why then, maybe, we'll – oh, Geoffrey – thou wilt not betray me – thou wilt not betray *her !* Promise me that!

Geoffrey I promise!

Dan'l Remember, Geoffrey, thou'st promised! (*Exit*).

Geoffrey In truth I am in a sore strait, for Sir Jasper is a man of proud blood, who would laugh to scorn such humble love as mine. And oh, Dorothy, if thou art taken from me, why, my life may go too!

Enter Reuben

Reuben Why, whom have we here in Dorothy's house ? A whelp, a very whelp, cur, or puppy to be whistled to, scowled at, whipped, beaten with sticks and slapped with the flat of the hand!

Geoffrey Your servant, sir. Who are you ?

Reuben Why, sir, I am an old horse-soldier, and yet not so very old neither but that I can wield quarter-staff or give the Cornish fling as well as another. One who has so snicked, chipped, chopped, slashed, cut and carbonaded with sword, pistol, arquebus, petronel and what-not, that he'd make no more of passing a rapier through that boy's body of thine than of spitting a penny herring. And now, sir, who are *you*?

Geoffrey Why, sir, I am a sailor, and I hate brag.

Reuben Come, come, civil words, young master, lest we quarrel; and when *I* quarrel grave-diggers strip to their work. Dost thou know this Dan'l Druce?

Geoffrey I do.

Reuben A comfortable old man, they tell me, and one who can portion his pretty Dorothy. And talking of pretty Dorothy, we have here a bauble or locket, or, as one may say, a trinket that belongeth to her, I'll go bail. (*Picking up locket which Geoffrey has dropped*).

Geoffrey Sir, that locket is mine.

Reuben It is very like – it is very like, yet for that I have but thy word. If the trinket be thine, describe it with circumstance, and I will give it up to thee

Enter Dan'l unperceived. He listens in great agitation

Geoffrey It is fashioned like a heart, and bears an inscription 'To the best loved of all' and it is dated seventeen years since. It is a love-token, sir, and I desire you to yield it up without further parley.

Reuben Why, surely, I should know this locket well. From whom did you receive it?

Geoffrey (*Taking it from him*) That is a question I have no will to answer. It is a token of bethrothal – let that suffice.

Reuben But it don't suffice. Do you know who I am? I am bailiff to Sir Jasper Combe –

Geoffrey Sir Jasper Combe!

Reuben Ay, and I recognize that locket as one that he placed about the neck of his missing daughter the very day he abandoned her. Come, sir, from whom did you receive it? To whom are you betrothed?

Enter Dorothy at back. Dan'l stops her, and motions her to be silent

Geoffrey I decline to say.

Reuben Shall I hazard a conjecture? Thou art here, making free in the blacksmith's forge. The blacksmith has a daughter – her name is Dorothy. Shall we say that it is to Dorothy that thou art betrothed?

Geoffrey What, Dorothy Druce? No, no, Master Bailiff, not Dorothy Druce!

(*Dorothy expresses surprise and pain*).

It is true that I have laughed and jested with Dorothy, but you know how we sailors have a special licence for such frolics. We mean nothing by them. It is said of us that we have a wife in every port –

(*Dorothy weeps on Dan'l's bosom*).

Reuben Ha! Thou art a shameless young reprobate by thine own showing. It will go hard but Sir Jasper will elicit the truth. We shall meet again. (*Exit*).

Dan'l So, Geoffrey Wynyard! The blow that is to bring me to my grave has been dealt by thine own hand! Oh, slayer of human life, are there no laws to fit such crime as thine!

Geoffrey Master Druce – indeed, I knew not –

Dan'l Thou knewest not! Will the last years of my poor old lonely life be less desolate because thou knewest not! (*Taking up hammer*) Geoffrey Wynyard, there are injuries that no laws can measure, and wi' them we deal ourselves, and wreak our vengeance wi' our own right hands.

Dorothy (*Kneeling*) No, no, father, yield not to thy wrath. He hath denied me – he hath dealt lightly with my love – and there's an end. Oh, harm him not, oh, harm him not! Pardon him, even as I pardon him; and let him depart in peace.

Dan'l Ay, ay, thou recallest me to myself. Geoffrey Wynyard, thou hast spoken lightly of my child, thou hast denied her who gave thee her heart. It was ill done. Quit my roof and let me see thee no more. I – I pardon thee. Go.

Geoffrey Master Druce, have pity –

Dan'l Go!

Geoffrey Dorothy, one word. Hear what I have to say.

Dorothy Geoffrey, thou hast denied me. I love thee – but – thou must go!

(*Geoffrey goes out sadly. When he has gone, Dorothy falls sobbing at Dan'l's feet*).

Dan'l My child! My child!
(*Music*)

Act 3

Scene. Interior of Druce's cottage. Time evening. Dorothy is discovered pale and weak, sitting by the fire, reading an old and tattered letter. Dan'l is discovered at back – he has a bundle and stick in his hand as if prepared for a journey. He is pale and anxious

Dan'l Eventide, and he's not yet come to claim her. It's hard to have to creep away like a thief in the night, but that it should ha' come through him whom I loved like a son, it's doubly hard. (*Looking at Dorothy*) Poor maiden! She thinks him false to her. Well, it's better so. I'll keep that thought alive; 'twill account for much that I cannot explain. One word would lift that sorrow from her gentle heart; but it must not be spoke – not yet – not yet! What art thou reading lass?

Dorothy It is the letter he wrote to me from Morocco, two years since. Oh father, it's hard to bear. And to vaunt his unfaithfulness in the ears of a very stranger! It was a cruel boast – for I loved him with all my heart! It is hard to bear, for he had truth in his face, and I doubted nothing!

Dan'l Trust no faces, Dolly – they lie – they lie.

Dorothy Nay, but it is not like thee to say these bitter things.

Dan'l More like me than thou wottest of, Dolly. I have told thee what I was afore thou camest to me – the past fourteen year are gone like a dream, and I'm waking from it, Dolly, I'm waking from it. (*Takes up his bundle*).

Dorothy Why, father, art thou going away?

Dan'l Ay, lass – we're both going away.

Dorothy Tonight?

Dan'l Tonight. Make thy bundle, for time presses.

Dorothy But whither are we going?

Dan'l Whither? What odds whither, so that we leave this place! Get thy bundle quickly. I'll tell thee more anon.

Dorothy As thou wilt, father. (*Aside*) Tonight! Oh, Geoffrey, Geoffrey, this is indeed the end! (*Exit*).

Dan'l Poor child, poor child! My heart smites me for deceivin' her – for harmful as he's been to me, he never had thought for aught but her. I'm a'most sorry I was so rough wi' him – he did not know – but the harm's done, and there's no undoin' it! So, old forge, the time has come when thou and I must part for ever!

Reuben has entered and heard the last line

Reuben What, Dan'l Druce, on the eve of a journey? Nay, thoul't take no journey tonight I promise thee.

Dan'l Reuben Haines, art thou here to take her from me?

Reuben No, Master Dan'l, I am *not* here to take her from thee – and yet, in a sense, *yes*, Master Dan'l, I *am* here to take her away from thee. Weigh these words well, and store them away in the museum of thy mind, for he hath no wisdom who tells the plain truth, and he hath no need to tell the plain truth who hath wisdom enough to do without it. It is a paradox.

Dan'l To the devil wi' thy chop-logic. Speak out, and let me know the best and the worst. Does – does thy master know?

Reuben He does *not* know, as yet. And why does he not know? Because the mighty should be merciful – and I have refrained.

Dan'l If thou art not mocking at my sorrow, speak plainly.

Reuben Then observe. I am a Potent Magician, or, if thou preferrest it, a Benevolent Fairy, who hath certain gifts to dispose of. On the one hand, I have Family Union, Domestic Happiness, and Snug Old Age – on the other, Blank Misery, Abject Despair, and Desolation. Which shall I give to Sir Jasper, and which to thee? Now, I am a pleasant old gentleman – well to do – not so very old neither, yet old enough to marry. Dorothy and I are good friends; she listens to me when I talk, which many won't. How say you? Come, give me *thy* daughter, and I will give thee Sir Jasper's daughter. (*Aside*) Ha! ha! It is neatly put. It is a quip.

Dan'l Give thee my Dorothy! No, no, it canna be – she is promised. No, no, I canna do that – I canna do that!

Reuben Reflect. Sir Jasper will take her from thee for ever; he will drive thee from thy forge, and thou wilt be a desolate old vagabond, while she is learning day by day to forget thee, and to give her love to another.

Dan'l Nay – stay – one moment – give me time to think. How am I to do this thing? God forgive me!

Enter Dorothy

Dorothy, my child, come hither. I have somewhat to say to thee. I – I am not long for this world, and when I am gone – oh, Dorothy, bear with what I have to say! This man – this Reuben Haines – he loveth thee, and would make thee his wife.

Dorothy Oh, father –

Dan'l Ay, I know what thou wouldst say – thou lovest Geoffrey, but bear in mind, he loves thee not – he did deny thee – he loveth other women. This man, he – he is not a young man – he is of sober age and a man of good substance. Oh, Dorothy, my child, have pity on me!

Dorothy I cannot answer – I am lost in wonder.

Dan'l It is for thine happiness as well as for mine. If thou didst but know! If thou didst but know!

Dorothy Father, I know naught of this man but what is ill – nevertheless, as thou hast been to me as my father, and I to thee as thy child, bound in all lawful things to obey thee, so will I obey thee even in this.

Reuben It is dutifully spoken. It is a bargain. Set thine heart at rest – it is settled.

Dan'l (*Furiously*) Ay, it is settled. Get thee hence, now, and for ever, and do thy worst. Dorothy, forgive me – 'twas but for a moment I wavered – I am strong again now. (*To Reuben*) Thou hast a master – thou owest him a duty. Go, do it – I'll do mine. We will wait here, she and I, and when the blow comes, we'll bear it together.

Reuben Dan'l Druce, I warn thee –

Dan'l And I warn thee, Reuben Haines! Get thee hence – take thy damned face out, I tell 'ee, lest I do that which none can undo. Go! Do thy worst!

Reuben Brave old man! There is sore tribulation in store for thee, likewise much bitter wailing and anguish without end. Yet thou shrinkest not. It is well done, and damme, I honour thee for it. Brave old man! (*Exit*).

Dorothy Father, thou wast wont to tell me thy sorrow – hide not from me the source of this bitter grief. Who should comfort thee if I may not?

Dan'l My child, I've naught to hide from thee now. The reed on which I leant is broken – and –

(*Knock*).

Who's there?

Geoffrey (*Without*) Master Druce!

Dorothy It is Geoffrey.

Dan'l He had best not see thee. Get thee hence, I'll open to him.

Dorothy Father, deal gently with him, for the love I bear him. (*Exit*)

Dan'l opens the door. Enter Geoffrey

Geoffrey Master, Dan'l, I'm going to sea. I have written to refuse the post that Sir Jasper would have given me, and I am going tonight. I come to pray your pardon for the sorrow I have brought upon your home. Give me that before I go.

Dan'l Ay, I pardon thee, my lad. Thou didst not know. Heaven prosper thee. Is that all?

Geoffrey I have something to ask about – about Mistress Dorothy.

Dan'l Too late! She is not mine to give. Her father – he's coming fur to take her from me, and I'm waiting here for the blow to fall. I'm waiting here for my death!

Geoffrey Master Dan'l, when I'm gone and there's many a mile of stormy water betwixt us, I should have a lighter heart if I knew that someone would tell her that I'm not so bad and cruel and heartless as she

421

thinks me – if someone would tell her that it was for *her* sake, and thine, that I denied her. That's all I've got to say.

Dan'l My lad, if it lay wi' me, I'd give my girl to thee wi' a light heart; but, my poor lad, it doan't lay wi' me now. He's coming fur to take her from me!

(*Knock*).

At last! at last! Sir Jasper is here. Get thee within there

(*Exit Geoffrey into inner room as Dan'l opens door and admits Sir Jasper and Reuben*)

Jasper So, Dan'l Druce, thou art the man who for fourteen long years has hidden my daughter away from me!

Dan'l I crave your mercy, for I knew not her father's name till today.

Jasper Yet it would seem that, having learnt it, thou wouldst nevertheless have fled with her, had this good fellow not arrested thy flight.

Dan'l Truly in the bitterness of my grief I had thought to flee with her, but my better self prevailed, and I stayed.

Reuben Credit him not, sir, for he lieth. He was in the very nick of departure when I interposed and did bid him await your honour's commands.

Dan'l Nay, sir, this man – this traitorous man – offered to keep the matter from you for ever if I would consent to give him the child to wife.

Jasper (*To Reuben*) Art thou indeed guilty of this treachery?

Reuben Why, sir, there is a measure of truth even in this fellow's speech, inasmuch as I did say it, but I did it but to try him. It was, as it were, a subtle essay in pursuit of the grandest of all studies – the conduct of a man under the influence of extraordinary temptation. I am a philosopher.

Jasper Thy philosophy shall be severely tried. Deliver thy books and papers to Master Geoffrey Wynyard, whom I appoint steward in thy place. Begone!

Reuben But, sir – consider –

Jasper Begone, I say, and let me see thee no more!

Reuben (*At door*) I am a philosopher!

Jasper Begone! (*Exit Reuben*). Now Dan'l Druce, if thou hast aught to say in defence of thy conduct, I am prepared to hear it.

Dan'l Aught to say? No, sir, I've naught to say worth saying. Thou'st seen the maiden – thou'st seen how fair she is – how good she is – how pure and gentle, tender and true she is. We've bin all in all to each other; and at the thought o' losin' of her my poor old heart's almost broken in twain. I dunno as I've any more to say. No, sir, that's all.

Jasper I am sorry for you – but you have brought this grief upon yourself; you have been guilty of gross injustice both to myself and to the girl.

Dan'l (*Furious*) What!

Jasper Knowing as you did that enquiries would certainly be made for the child, you nevertheless stole away, and left no clue as to your destination.

Dan'l Knowin' as I did! How did I know – what was there for to tell me? Was it the love that her father showed for her when he left her to perish on that stormy Norfolk coast? Why, he set *his* life afore hers! That he might live he left her to die! Why, she was well quit of such a father!

Jasper Dan'l, I spake harshly – I am sorry for it. You are right. That she was not my child, but a step-child, matters nothing. I loved her mother dearly. It was my duty to protect the child, and I basely forsook my trust. It killed her poor mother, who loved her beyond measure, and on her deathbed I swore to search out the child that I might make amends – and now that after many years of weary searching I have found her, shall I yield her up, even to you?

Dan'l (*Calls*) Dorothy, my child, come hither

Enter Dorothy

I ask your pardon, sir, if I call her my child still, for she's bin more than that to me! Dolly, my lass, there's a change in store for thee, a grand change; thou'rt a lady, ay, a great lady, too. I allers knowed thou wast a lady. (*To Sir Jasper*) She doesn't talk like us common folk, sir! This gentleman, Sir Jasper Combe – he's come to claim thee – he's thy father, Dolly, think o' that! And Dolly, he's – he's goin' to take thee from me – only to Combe-Raven, where I'll come and see thee often. (*To Sir Jasper*) Thou'lt let me come and see her odd times? (*To Dorothy*) And thou'lt come and see me, and there'll be grand doins then, eh, Dolly? There, there, go to thy father – he'll be a kind father to thee, and he'll love thee well, never doubt it – and – and I shall love thee too, and thou'lt have two fathers 'stead o' one, Dolly, that's all! (*She is about to speak*) Doan't speak! doan't speak; for God's sake, doan't speak! (*He rushes out. Dorothy stands dumb with surprise*).

Jasper Dorothy, I am indeed he who should stand to thee in the place of a father. Dorothy, I am childless and alone, wealthy, honoured, and of good repute, yet alone in my old age. Dorothy, come to me – come to me!

Dorothy (*Who has been sobbing through this speech*) Oh, sir, he has been so good to me, and I love him with all the love of my heart. It cannot be that after all these long years of tender love I am to be taken from him now. Oh, it will kill him! I cannot leave him now! Oh, sir, if thou hast no care for him, yet for the love of my mother have pity on me!

Jasper (*After a pause*) I had thought my atonement was at an end, but my bitterest punishment is yet to come, and I am to suffer it at thy hands. So be it – it is just! Thou art free to go to him who has been more

423

to thee than many fathers.

Dorothy Heaven bless thee for those good words! Sir, thou hast spared his life. When his wife left him it drove him to the very verge of madness, and this last blow would have ended his life!

Jasper Did his wife leave him?

Dorothy Alas! yes, many years since – before I was sent to him.

Jasper And he loved her very dearly too?

Dorothy So dearly that he called me Dorothy because he read her name in my eyes.

Jasper Dorothy! Was that her name?

Dorothy Ay, Dorothy Marple, for that is rightly my father's name. But to save her good fame he gave out that he was dead, and he took the name he now bears.

Jasper (*Aside*) My sin has borne bitter fruit! Oh, Dan'l Druce, give me thy pardon! Dorothy, for the sake of the Dorothy who is dead, give me thy pardon!

Enter Dan'l Druce

Master Druce, Heaven has interposed to save me from unwittingly working on thee a deep and bitter injury. Take the child that is thine own in the eye of God and of man.

Dan'l Why, sir – Dorothy, my child – is he not goin' to take thee from me?

Jasper Think of the deepest injury that man's wickedness has ever wrought on thee, and place it to my account.

(*Dan'l thunderstruck*).

As I have sinned, so before Heaven I am atoned! (*Exit Sir Jasper*).

Dan'l (*As Sir Jasper's meaning breaks upon him*) Stay! Come back. Oh, source of all the sorrow I have known. Oh, black and bitter curse of two poor lives! Thy life for hers – thy cursed life for hers!

Dorothy Father, be merciful, spare him – be merciful – be just. He has wronged thee, but he has suffered and will yet suffer. As I have prevailed to turn thee to mankind, so let me, thy daughter – thy daughter indeed – thine own flesh – *her* own flesh – prevail against this one surviving sorrow. Spare him and pardon him – for her sake and for mine. (*Kneels*)

Enter Geoffrey

Dan'l Oh, Dorothy, dead and in Heaven, when God took thee He left an angel behind to plead for thee and for this man! It is Heaven's voice – my anger has gone out of me!

Geoffrey Dorothy, wilt thou believe now that it was for thy sake that I did deceive thee? Wilt thou believe, now, that I love thee truly and beyond all earth?

Dorothy Geoffrey, forgive me – forgive me! I acted in haste! I knew not what I did!

(*They embrace*).

Geoffrey My darling! (*Kisses her*).

Dorothy Art thou happy, Geoffrey?

Geoffrey Passing happy! And thou?

Dorothy Passing happy!

Dan'l Druce, Blacksmith scene from the end of Act 1.
(*Enthoven Collection*)

THE PRESS

The Sunday Times, September 17th, 1876:

The sphere over which Mr Gilbert's labours extend is much enlarged by his latest play. Hitherto he has confined himself to comedy, or to depicting such emotions as 'Fancy can beget on youthful thoughts'. In Dan'l Druce, Blacksmith, *he deals with the world of fact, and depicts the influence upon average natures of those sorrows which in varying shapes are the lots of all. His venture is a success, not only as regards the intrinsic merits of the piece he has written, but also in the hold it exercises upon the public. No drama with so little that appeals to vulgar tastes or sympathies has during recent years obtained a triumph so complete. Melodrama is, of course, the head under which Mr Gilbert's piece must be classed. It is, in fact, a domestic drama, with an historical, or rather a romantic background. As it stands, it may be classed with such works as* The Wife's Secret, All for Her, *and similar pieces; a very little alteration would, however, bring it into the same class as* The Man o' Airlie *or* The Porter's Knot. *Why Mr Gilbert has chosen to bring on the stage the Cavaliers, with their slouch-hats and love-locks, and the Ironsides, with their cropped heads and steel helmets, may exercise those who have a taste for needless investigations. It is enough to state he has done so, and has turned to profitable account in more respects than one the opportunities thus afforded him.*

The period at which the play commences is immediately subsequent to 'Worcester's crowning mercy', and the catastrophe is brought about by the Restoration. No attempt is made to obtain capital out of the struggle then waging. The scales of justice are held with even hand, and it is difficult to surmise on which side are the sympathies of the writer. It appears, indeed, that Mr Gilbert has been influenced in the choice of an epoch mainly by the consideration that the defeat of the Cavaliers and their return with the restored King supplied him with an easy way of accounting for a child being lost for some years and then reclaimed.

[Here follows a lengthy recapitulation of the plot, including quotations]

A love-quarrel which, not very rationally, has sprung up between Dorothy *and* Wynyard *is then patched up, and the play ends with a*

426

tableau of reconciliation.

The interest in this story is strong and healthy. There is some clumsiness of workmanship which might easily be remedied. A very little care would at once obviate the stagey device of the lost locket, and the quarrel between Dorothy and her lover might, with no great difficulty, be strengthened so as to furnish more serious ground for anxiety. These blemishes are, however, comparatively unimportant, and the play, on the whole, in invention, construction, character, and dialogue, is good work. The principal character, Dan'l Druce, is drawn with much care, and is a fine and patient study. This part was rendered with the amplest power and capacity by Mr Vezin, who, of late years, has seldom been seen to equal advantage. The varying phases of grief and emotion were depicted with singular skill, and an absolutely electrical effect was produced in the closing scenes. For once this excellent artist is provided with a part suited to his talents. The love-scenes, which are delicious, are done ample justice to by Miss Marion Terry and Mr Forbes Robertson. The former played with much tenderness and refinement. Her air of unconsciousness was admirably worn, and was so good in all respects, it is difficult to imagine a rendering more effective. Mr Robertson looked picturesque, and acted with great tact and taste. He is overcoming a tendency to sway about too much, and is rapidly becoming an excellent actor. One hint more must be taken by him. He must not show his teeth too much. Mr Howe gave, with perfect quietude and repose, the part of Sir Jasper. In a character intended apparently to parody some of the comic personages of Shakespeare, Mr Odell displayed a burlesque drollery which only requires restraining to do good service. In the opening piece, of Love in Humble Life, *Miss Maria Harris gave a sprightly and attractive rendering of Christine.*

The Daily Telegraph, September 13th, 1876:

If there be any meaning in the honest ring of genuine applause, then is Dan'l Druce, Blacksmith, *destined to be a drama which will make its mark. Courtesy and good-nature combined prescribe a formula of congratulation of which recently we have all become somewhat weary. Chance points are cheered, the curtain falls amidst fitful excitement, and the author is treated to an inquisitive summons; but to the accustomed ear such cheers sound hollow, and such welcomes may be regarded as a mockery of success. It was different with* Dan'l Druce, Blacksmith. *When the sentiment was ennobling and true, when the diction seemed nervous and energetic, when the acting reached a special point of excellence, the applause came out with a spontaneity and force which are impossible unless an audience is thoroughly touched. Mr W S Gilbert is well accustomed to the honour of a call before the curtain, but he has seldom looked so thoroughly pleased with his reception, and seldom heard, both on his own behalf and on that of those who have so well carried out his ideas, sounds of a more emphatic approval. It is not likely, notwithstanding the pleasure which was so strongly marked on Monday night that the new drama will pass without comment. Fastidious taste may complain that the play is too consistently in the minor key; keen critics will discover a cloudy gloom at odd times, which undoubtedly does make itself felt; habitual fault-finders may resent the choice of period, and maintain that the human motive would have been as strong now as after the battle of Worcester; and careless cavillers may possibly tilt at some of the dialogue, and the one comic character on which Mr Gilbert has evidently bestowed infinite pains. But when the mist of criticism has passed away, we believe that the strong sunshine of approval will be found, with its warm and encouraging rays. We are not so rich in original dramatists as to be able to withhold consideration from conscientious work, and the mark made in this play by nearly everyone concerned in the interpretation of it is not a matter of everyday occurrence. For let us hasten to declare that* Dan'l Druce *is not what is technically known as a one-part play. The lion's share of the praise will no doubt be devoted to Mr Hermann Vezin, whose intelligent idea of the leading character is only equalled by his brilliancy of execution. It will be a pleasure to describe the picturesque appearance of the lean miser idolising his money-bags, and a delight to recall the scene where the fond father, in a speech of suppressed emotion which was a masterpiece of art, yields up his adopted child. But, excellent as it was, there are treasures in the play beyond the acting of Mr Vezin. We shall have to tell of the manly performance of Mr Howe, giving precisely the correct weight to the story, and no more; of the genuine and sympathetic art of Mr Forbes Robertson, who touched everyone in the farewell scene of a broken-hearted lover; and with sincere pleasure it will be requisite to linger on the acting of Miss Marion Terry, whose grace, refinement, simple earnestness, and maiden modesty at once made sweet* Dorothy Druce *one of the most charming characters in modern dramatic fiction. Since Mr Robertson wrote* Play *and gave us a boy and girl lover in the ruins of the Alte Schloss, no such pretty love-scene has been written as that now interpreted by Mr Forbes Robertson and Miss Marion Terry in the true appreciation of its idyllic character.*

[Here follows a précis of Acts 1 & 2]

So far the play has not advanced so quickly in interest as might have been expected. The quips and cracks of the comic Royalist sergeant, Reuben Haines, who is now Pistol, now Malvolio, now Touchstone, now Nym, do not assimilate with the story. He jars upon the sentiment and breaks upon the interest at unfortunate moments. The character might, no doubt, have been played with more quiet humour than by Mr Odell, but we do not think that the most accomplished comedian could have

428

reconciled the character to the play. This was one great drawback to the act, and the other was the termination of it, which was scarcely so clear as could have been hoped for. It was natural, no doubt, that Dan'l Druce should be vexed that the secret came out through the accidental loss of the locket; but he would scarcely push his irritation so far as to banish the lad and make the girl think her lover a traitor. And besides, it is not reasonable to suppose that Geoffrey would not have explained his innocence. At that time, when the secret was out, there was no reason why Dorothy should not have been told that Sir Jasper was coming to claim her, and that Geoffrey was an honest man. The act as written closes with a theatrical situation, as distinct from a situation which legitimately follows from motive and reason. But, gloom and humour and this last difficulty apart, the acting all along has made a marked impression on the audience. Mr Hermann Vezin is accused of an excess of vigour in old age and a too constant repetition of the same keynote as that which is touched in the first act; but then at this point no-one knows what is to follow, or presumes that further on there is a better period for the requisite change. The character is one of extreme difficulty, and it is in this second act that the actor evidently feels the weight of his task. But there are no two opinions about the delightful freshness of Miss Marion Terry's acting – the first strong and undoubted sign of a valuable career. The love-scene was played with an unconscious innocence delightful to behold, and the pathetic pleading, whenever employed, was true and natural.

The third act revives the interest in a marked manner, and a surprise is in store for the audience which the most far-seeing could scarcely have expected. The impertinent pretensions of Reuben Haines to the hand of Dorothy as the price of his secret are rejected with indignation, and now Dan'l Druce sits waiting his doom. He is to lose his idol. Sir Jasper comes to claim the child he has sought out for so many years, and, to the astonishment of all, owns that Dorothy is not his daughter, but his step-child. The missing link is at once supplied. Sir Jasper is the man who ruined the life of Jonas Marple [Dan'l Druce] and when he left the infant in the Norfolk cottage, he unconsciously gave the old man his true daughter – his own flesh and blood. So now every section of the story is conveniently fitted in, and the curtain appropriately falls with Dorothy clasped in the arms of her lover.

From every quarter good acting comes in the last act. The prize of all, and indeed the great dramatic coup of the play, was made by Mr Vezin when he tells Dorothy another father has come to claim her, and keeps down his great grief with a superhuman effort. The tears are in his eyes, but they hang there; the tears are in his voice, but it never breaks. The lips tremble with emotions, but the strong man still asserts himself. 'This gentleman, Sir Jasper Combe, has come to claim thee - he's thy *father, Dolly, think o' that. And he's going to take thee from me, Dolly, where I'll come and see thee often. Thou'lt let me come and see her odd times? There, then, go to thy father; he'll be a kind father to thee, and he'll love thee well, never doubt it; and – I shall love thee too, and thou'lt have two fathers 'stead o' one, Dolly – that's all. Doan't speak! doan't speak! for God's sake, doan't speak!' At this point came down such a burst of applause as has not been heard in a theatre for years. An audible silence was broken by one triumphant shout. The actor had touched the whole house, and had brought home the situation to every heart. He was called again and again. In fact, the whole act was a succession of acting triumphs, and though this great point turned the whole scale in favour of the play, it would be possible to write very much in praise of Mr Forbes Robertson's farewell, Miss Terry's true pathos, and the manly confession delivered to perfection by Mr Howe. The confession of Sir Jasper, spoken as it was, presented the play with this righteous moral, and rendered eloquent the rapacity of the contented Dan'l Druce, 'Oh, Dorothy, dead and in heaven, when God took thee he left an angel behind to plead for thee and for this man. It is Heaven's voice. My anger has gone out of me'. In so excellent a work, and in the discussion of acting of such conspicuous merit there must be much which we have inevitably passed over. But we leave a good play and meritorious art to the attention and the applause of innumerable playgoers.*

Trilby

PAUL M POTTER

Paul M Potter,
'The Critic'
1895. (*British Museum*)

PAUL M POTTER (1853/1921)

Paul Potter was American by nationality, although born in Brighton, Sussex, on June 3rd, 1853, when his father was headmaster of King Edward's School, Bath. I have been able to discover little about him other than the facts given in the various editions of *Who's Who in the Theatre* published before his death in London on March 3rd, 1921, at the age of 67.

He would seem to have been primarily a journalist; from 1876–1883 he was foreign editor of the *New York Herald* and then London correspondent for the same journal for a year. He then became the dramatic critic until 1887, and in 1889 joined the editorial staff of the *Chicago Tribune*.

He wrote some two dozen plays, of which all the later ones were translations from the French and which, according to the *Stage Year Books*, seem to have remained largely unperformed. Of those that did reach the stage, few achieved any measure of success. His *Parasites* (based on Emile Fabre's *La Rabouilleuse*, itself based on a Balzac story) only ran for twenty nights in May, 1910, despite a first-class production at the Globe and a cast which included Arthur Bourchier and Constance Collier.

In 1895 Potter's stage adaptation of George Du Maurier's *Trilby** was presented in Philadelphia on its pre-New York tour. At the time Beerbohm Tree was touring the States with his own company and happened to be in Philadelphia; with him as manager and secretary (in both of which offices he was by his own admission conspicuously inept) was his half-brother, Max Beerbohm, who went to see *Trilby* to report upon its possibilities. His verdict was that the piece was 'utter nonsense', and there the matter rested until some weeks later when Tree, having one evening free the night before returning home to England, himself decided to see *Trilby* which had by then reached New York. When the curtain fell on the second act he immediately sought out Potter and secured the British rights.

In September of the same year, Tree first appeared as Svengali at the Theatre Royal, Manchester, and on October 30th the play opened at the Haymarket Theatre in London. It was to be Tree's most celebrated role, and the one which is as readily associated with his name as is Irving's with Mathias.

Herbert Beerbohm Tree was born in London on December 17th, 1853, of German parents. He dabbled in amateur dramatics, and forsook his father's business as a merchant when offered a professional engagement in 1878. As a character actor he quickly attracted attention, and by 1887 was well enough established to go into management at the Comedy Theatre, moving later that year to the Haymarket where he was in residence for ten years. He then crossed over the road to Her Majesty's, and it is his tenure of this theatre until 1917 on which his lasting fame is founded. Here he created lavish productions of spectacular proportions and scenic splendour unsurpassed even at the Lyceum.

Although as an actor Tree could not approach Irving's stature, he had a dynamic presence and a gift for comedy which particularly suited the more strongly-marked 'character' roles in which he was so popular. His Malvolio and Falstaff were especially admired, as were his Fagin and of course his Svengali, but the more retrospective roles such as Hamlet or Richard II did not suit his essentially robust personality.

In 1882 he married the actress Helen Maud Holt by whom he had three daughters – Viola, Felicity and Iris – and to whom he was notoriously unfaithful. In 1904 he founded the Royal Academy of Dramatic Art, and received his knighthood in 1909. He died in London on July 2nd, 1917, at the age of 63.

---

*Published in 1894, this was the second of three novels reflecting Du Maurier's years as an art student in Paris. He lived from 1834–1896

Tree as Svengali (*Enthoven Collection*)

Dorothea Baird as Trilby (*Enthoven Collection*)

435

Dorothea Baird, the original Trilby in this country, was born at Teddington on May 20th, 1875. An extremely intelligent girl, she took an honours degree at Oxford, where she also began her stage career with the University Dramatic Society. At her first interview with Tree her only professional engagement had been a year with Ben Greet's Shakespearean company, but her beauty, charm, youth and obvious talent outweighed her lack of experience. Her performance – and her bare feet – caused an overnight sensation almost as great as Tree's 'great hairy spider', and established her reputation. She later joined Irving's company, and in 1896 married his elder son, H B Irving. She retired from the stage in 1913, and died in 1933.

TRILBY

Dramatis Personae

As first performed at Haymarket Theatre, London
October 30th, 1895

Svengali by Mr Herbert Beerbohm Tree
Talbot Wynne, '*Taffy*', *by* Mr Edmund Maurice
Sandy McAlister, '*The Laird*', *by* Mr Lionel Brough
William Bagot, '*Little Billee*', *by* Mr Patrick Evans
Gecko by Mr C M Hallard
Zouzou by Mr Herbert Ross
Dodor by Mr Gerald Du Maurier
Anthony Oliver by Mr Berte Thomas
Lorimer by Mr Gayner Mackay
Reverend Thomas Bagot by Mr Charles Allan
Colonel Kaw by Mr Holman Clark
Trilby O'Ferrall by Miss Dorothea Baird
Mrs Bagot by Miss Frances Ivor
Madame Vinard by Miss Rosina Fillippi
Angèle by Miss Cicely Turner
Honorine by Miss Agnes Russell
Mimi by Miss Olive Owen
Musette by Miss Sadie Wigley

Supernumeraries, dancers, etc

Act 1: A studio in Paris

Act 2: The same

Act 3: Foyer of the Cirque des Bashibazouks, Paris

Act 4: As Acts 1 & 2

The Time: The 1850's

I am greatly indebted to Noël Woolf of Samuel French Ltd for kindly allowing me to use the original prompt copy for my abridgement.

TRILBY

Act 1

An Artist's Studio in Paris, the Latin Quarter, decorated picturesquely. There are three entrances. It is late on a November afternoon

The stage is discovered empty. The voice of the concierge, Madame Vinard, is heard calling off

Mme Vinard Monsieur Billie! Monsieur Billie! (*Entering*) Here's a telegram. But where is he, then, this Litrebili?
(*As she moves to go, she bumps into Taffy who enters carrying a large log*).
Ah, pardon. Mille pardons, Monsieur Taffy.
Taffy Not at all, Mme Vinard. My fault. What's the matter?
Mme Vinard Here is a telegram for Monsieur Billee.
Taffy Hand over. I'll deliver it. (*He puts the log on the fire*) More trouble, I suppose.
Mme Vinard Trouble, M Taffy? Why, never have I seen three happier people than you, M Sandy and M Litrebili.
Taffy (*Stirring up the fire*) You're a good sort, Mme Vinard, but you don't know everything.
Mme Vinard No, but I know that you go every day to the Morgue. Oh, it's horrible.
Taffy A fellow must find inspiration somewhere.
Mme Vinard And you paint the most dreadful subjects: drowning, murder, the guillotine – ugh! But I know why – why you go to the Morgue. It is because you are in love!
Taffy Eh?
Mme Vinard In love with Trilby!
Taffy Shut up!
Mme Vinard And you're afraid to let M Sandy and M Litrebili know it. And you're afraid to ask Trilby to marry you. Bah!
Taffy Fermez vous!

439

Mme Vinard And my husband – who is fond of you all as I – well, he says you're nothing but a great big baby!

Taffy There's not a minute to lose. (*Aside*) I'll tackle Trilby, and know my fate

(*The Laird is heard singing outside*).

You see, Mme Vinard, I'm not very good at proposals – hullo, there's the Laird! I'll get him to coach me. Meantime, Madame Vinard, just you shut up about it, will you? And – and – I'll get some dry logs. (*Going*) You understand – fermez vous! (*Exit*)

Enter the Laird, still singing

Mme Vinard Bonjour, M Sandy.

Laird (*In very bad French*) Bon jour, Mme Vinard.

Mme Vinard But how gaily you are dressed, M Sandy!

Laird (*Scotch accent*) Benighted Gaul though you are, dinna you ken that when my eponym, the Laird of Cockpen, went wooing, he took especial pains with his attire?

Mme Vinard You are going wooing, M Sandy?

Laird I come from the Flower Market, Mme Vinard, and am about to lay these white violets at her still whiter feet. (*Puts them on mantelpiece*).

Mme Vinard At whose feet? Ah, mon Dieu! Not – not – at Trilby's?

Laird And pray why not?

Mme Vinard Take care, M Sandy. You know, Trilby might refuse you; she might love another.

Laird What! In that case I should call my trusty claymore to my aid and lay that 'other' low!

Mme Vinard Ah, vous êtes feroce, M Sandy! Well, I must go. I have to see Mâitre Guerin, the lawyer, about that wretch Svengali's rent. Bon jour, M Sandy. (*Exit*).

Laird Bong jour, Mme Vinard. (*Sings*)

Enter Taffy, carrying another log

Taffy Hello, Sandy! (*Puts log on fire*).

Laird Ha, my bold militaire! (*Carries on singing*).

Taffy Sandy, I say, do you notice anything odd about me?

Laird Nothing. (*Continues singing*).

Taffy Shut up!

Laird Eh?

Taffy I want your advice. I know you'll laugh, but I don't care. Sandy, I'm in love.

Laird In love!

Taffy Come: how do you propose to a girl?

Laird I'll be frank with you, Taffy. I've been propounding that momentous question myself –

Taffy You! No! By Jove, that's rich!

Enter Mme Vinard

Mme Vinard Oh, messieurs, messieurs, what shall I do? What shall I do?
Taffy What's the matter?
Laird Qu'elle est la matière?
Mme Vinard Oh, Svengali – M Svengali – he will drive me mad! Every week for three months he has promised to pay his rent. I give him credit – he gives me nothing but ze bad language – I have myself to pay ze landlord. What shall I do?
Taffy Give him the sack.
Mme Vinard What?
Laird Donnez lui le sac.
Mme Vinard I have told him I will no longer cook his omelette au sauerkraut.
Taffy What does he say?
Mme Vinard He says my house is not respectable. That you paint from the altogether – you understand?
Taffy Yes, I understand perfectly. Tell him that in the eyes of art, nothing is so chaste as the nude.
Laird And tell him that in the eyes of the artist all beauty is sexless.
Mme Vinard Bon. And M Svengali, he say again would Messieurs the Englishmen be so good as to advance him the money to pay the rent?
Taffy Tell Svengali we'll see him blowed first!
Mme Vinard Eh?
Laird Dites lui nous le verrons soufflè d'abord.
Mme Vinard See him blowed first? Soufflè d'abord? C'est une Anglais ...

Enter Billee, much excited

Taffy Why, Billee, what's the matter?
Billee She's sitting at Durien's upstairs – that's all! Trilby!
Laird and Taffy What!
Billee Before all those ruffians!
Taffy For – for the figure?
Billee Yes.
Taffy It's monstrous!
Laird It's a scandal!
Mme Vinard But in the eyes of art nothing is so chaste as the nude ...
Taffy Oh, shut up!
Mme Vinard And all beauty is sexless to the artist ...
Laird Oh, get out!
(*Bell rings off*)

Mme Vinard Ah, that is M Svengali's ring – I tell him now. See him blowed first! (*Going*) Soufflè d'abord. Ha ha! On y va! On y va! (*Exit*).

Taffy (*To Billee*) Here's a telegram Mother Vinard left for you.

Laird This won't do about Trilby. We must stop it.

Taffy Quite right. We will. What is it, Billee?

Billee Nothing much. My mother and uncle have gone to Florence. They want me to join them there.

Taffy Why, young 'un, you wouldn't desert two old pals.

Billee I may have to – I've done with this beastly Paris for ever. To think of her sitting for the figure! It's awful! (*Paints furiously*) By Jove!

Taffy (*Exercising with dumb-bells*) By Jove!

Laird (*Punching a punch-ball*) By Jove!

Taffy She's a good sort all the same.

Laird I shall never forget how she nursed me through that typhoid.

Taffy She might have lived in guilty splendour if she liked.

Laird But she prefers to earn her own living.

Billee And cook our dinners for us.

Taffy And darn out socks for love.

Laird And pawn our watches for us.

Trilby (*Outside*) Milk below!

Taffy Here is Trilby. Billee, not a word about her posing, mind.

Trilby (*Closer, calling*) Milk below!

Laird Ontray!

Enter Trilby

Trilby (*With mock salute*) Salut, mes enfants. The top of the morning to you, boys.

Laird Trilby, recevez l'assurance de ma considération très distinguée.

Trilby (*Pulling his whiskers*) At puis, zutalots-tarra-pat-a pouffe – Houp la! (*Strikes pose*).

Laird Ventre bleu! Sacré nom de Dieu!

Trilby How terribly you do swear, Sandy dear. (*Kicks off her slippers*).

Laird How you go on, Trilby.

Trilby Would you like me to go off?

Laird and Taffy No – no!

Trilby Billee don't want me . . . do you, Billee? What's the matter, Billee? You look as sad as though Taffy had tried to tell you a funny story. Well, life ain't all beer and skittles, and more's the pity. But what's the odds as long as you're happy! (*Pirouettes and sits*).

Taffy We – we'd give a good deal to have your light heart, Trilby.

Trilby You wouldn't give as much for my head – for I've – oh! – such a pain in it. Neuralgia in the eyes or something. There's only one thing that can do me any good – it's awful – but do you know, Svengali can stare at me and point his finger at me, and smile and show his teeth, and – brrr! – all my pain is gone.

Taffy Svengali! He fears neither God nor man.

Trilby He's a rum un', ain't he?

Billee What a ruffian!

Laird But what a genius! He can make divinest music out of a common street song.

Taffy Yes, but for all that, I wouldn't have anything to do with him. Svengali walks up and down the earth, seeking whom he may cheat, betray – man, woman, child or dog, he's as bad as they make them

Enter Svengali

Svengali Ho, ho!
(*Trilby screams slightly*).
Bon jour, ma belle.

Laird We were just talking of you, Svengali.

Svengali You flatter me.

Billee Come, Svengali, play us some music.

Svengali No, I will not. They have insulted me. They have dared to ask me for my rent. The canaille! I will not bear it. A dirty two hundred francs. What is two hundred francs? Have you two hundred francs, my friend?

Taffy No, but you have two hundred francs of mine. If you can repay me, it will be devilish convenient.

Svengali Do not insult me, or I shall be very angry.

Taffy Would you be insulted by five francs?

Svengali Five francs? To me? You dare – ! Well, well (*Takes money*) I will repay you – that will make two hundred and five francs ... the pig dog! To insult me with five francs! Bah!

Taffy Trilby has a touch of neuralgia.

Trilby Ah ha! La grande Trilby ... well, well, I will make music for you, and take away your pain. Gecko shall make music for you, too. My friend Gecko, he waits outside. (*Calls*) Come in, Gecko; we will play for the pig dogs

Enter Gecko with violin

Gecko plays the violin like an angel – I teach him myself – we are two angels. (*Kicks Gecko*).

Trilby You carry your wings inside for convenience.

Svengali En v'la une originale! (*Moves to piano with Gecko*).

Trilby (*To Billee*) Are you angry with me?

Billee You have hurt me – awfully – awfully ...

Trilby How? What have I said? What have I done?

443

Svengali What shall I play ? I know what you English like – 'Annie Laurie'. (*He plays 'Annie Laurie' in a grotesque manner*).

Laird Do you sing, Svengali ?

Svengali No, I cannot sing. (*Playing 'Rosamunde'*) but I can teach singing – the bel canto.

Taffy Is the music doing you good, Trilby ?

Trilby What's that you're playing ?

Svengali It is called the Rosamunde of Schubert, mademoiselle. Rosamunde was a Princess of Cyprus, and Cyprus was an island.

(*Gecko joins Svengali in Schubert's 'L'Adieu'. Long pause*).

Are you fond of music, mademoiselle ?

Trilby Oh, maie aie, I should rather think I was. My father used to sing like a bird. He was a gentleman and a scholar, my father was. His name was Patrick Michael O'Ferrall. He was a member of Trinity College, Dublin. He used to sing 'Ben Bolt', he did. Do you know 'Ben Bolt', M Gecko ?

Gecko I have that facility, mademoiselle.

Trilby I can sing it. Shall I ?

Laird Taffy, you must put a stop to this. You know she can't sing a note in tune.

Taffy Don't sing, Trilby. They are only making fun of you.

Svengali The head – does it still ache ?

Trilby A little.

Svengali Sit down – I will show you something that will cure your pain better than music.

(*Trilby sits. Svengali brings a chair and sits facing her*).

Look me in the white of the eyes.

(*He fixes his eyes on hers, then makes passes on her forehead and temples*).

See – she sleeps not. But she shall not open her eyes. Ask her.

Billee Can you open your eyes, Trilby ?

(*Trilby strains to open her eyes*).

Svengali She shall not open her mouth. Ask her.

Billee Speak to me, Trilby.

(*Trilby tries to speak*).

Taffy This is that devil's trick – hypnotism. Release her, man – release her! (*Grabs Svengali from behind*).

Svengali Ah! If you are so imbecile – pig dog! Well, I will set her free. Awake!

Trilby (*Jumping up*) Oh, maie aie! The pain is gone!

Svengali Did I cure her ?

Taffy All the same, if I catch you at those games again, I'll accommodate you with a much needed bath in the river.

Svengali Ha, ha! That's funny!

Trilby Why ?

Svengali Mme Vinard was telling me the story. While you were sitting for the 'altogether' upstairs at Durien's – our Englanders were furious, and poor Litrebili ran downstairs white with rage to tell the story: he was furious!

Trilby Furious – at what? Furious because I – is this true, Billee? Is that the reason you would not speak to me?

Billee Yes, that was why.

Trilby I never dreamed that there were any objections to my sitting – it was as natural for me to sit as for a man. And all the time that I was running your errands, cooking your food, mending your clothes, I shocked and disgusted you – you despised me!

Laird No, Trilby, no! Listen to me –

Trilby I will never sit again as long as I live – not even for the face and hands, let alone the 'altogether' – and I hope never, never to see any of you again! (*Exit*).

(*Svengali laughs*).

Billee Boys, that settles it – I've made up my mind: I will go to Florence. (*Exit*).

Laird Svengali, you are destined to be hanged. (*Exit, shaking his fist*).

Svengali That's more than can be said for your pictures, my friend.

Taffy And when you're on the gallows, I'll come and make a sketch of you! (*Exit*).

Svengali (*Laughing*) You add a new terror to death, my friend. You are my good friend, eh, Gecko?

Gecko Such as I am – second violin at the Gymnase – I owe it to you.

Svengali Have I money, my Gecko?

Gecko Pas ça!

Svengali Have I debts, my Gecko?

Gecko Mme Vinard does not permit us to forget it.

Svengali I – I, Svengali, who have to borrow five francs from the pig dog for my dinner, am going to make millions!

Gecko How? How?

Svengali I am telling you a secret, my Gecko. The great composer Litolff told Meyerbeer that the most beautiful voice in all Europe belongs to an English grisette who sat for the 'altogether' in the Latin quarter. That beautiful voice is Trilby's.

Gecko She is quite tone deaf!

Svengali Bah! I have tested her voice.

Gecko But she has not learned to sing.

Svengali We will teach her, together, morning, noon and night – six, eight hours a day – you shall see a miracle! I can make Trilby do my bidding – you saw me cure her pain just now.

Gecko She can no more sing than my violin can play itself.

Svengali Her's will be the voice; mine the knowledge – mine the genius. Trilby shall be the greatest soprano the world has ever known, and

I – Svengali – will see that world prostrate itself in admiration at my feet

Trilby enters timidly

Is it not so, Trilby?
  Trilby Haven't heard a word. I – I was looking for my friends.
  Svengali There is not an Angliche here.
  Trilby I knew they had no one to get their dinner for them, the dear
boys. (*Calls*) Milk below!
  Svengali Wunderschon! It comes straight from the heart; it has
its roots in the stomach – pardon, mademoiselle, will you permit that I
look into your mouth? (*Takes candle*) Ach, Himmel! Wunderbar! Mon
Dieu! The roof of your mouth is like the dome of the Pantheon. The
entrance to your throat is like the middle porch of St Sulpice when all the
doors are open on All Saints' Day. And not one tooth is missing – thirty-
two British teeth as white as milk and as big as schknuckle spoons. And
inside your beautiful big chest, the lungs are made of leather. Pardon – say
ninety-nine. (*Lays his ear to her bosom*).
  Trilby (*Shouts*) Ninety-nine!
  Svengali Ach. Himmel! Ungeheim! Stomach voice – wonderful!
And you have a quick, soft, susceptible heart – all that sees itself in your
face. Yes . . . but when I play to you the 'Adieu' of Schubert, you turn
another way – you roll your cigarette – you look at Litre Billee – you do not
look at Svengali – Svengali, who looks at you with all his eyes and all his
soul.
  Trilby I wish you wouldn't stare at me like that, Svengali . . .
  Svengali Ah, ha! The day will come when you will stare at me –
when I shall be the famous Svengali, and hundreds of beautiful women –
Prinzesses, und Contesses, und serene English Altessen – shall fall in love
with me, and shall invite me to their palaces, and pay me a thousand
francs a day to play to them . . .
  (*He is behind Trilby, who is looking straight at the audience*).
. . . but Svengali will not look at them, he will look inward at his own
dream, and that dream shall be all about Trilby – to lay his heart, his
genius, at her beautiful white feet. And you shall see nothing, hear
nothing, think nothing but Svengali, Svengali, Svengali . . . remember all
these things, my Trilby – I will have millions, millions! Come, my
Gecko, we will go and borrow five francs from Durien upstairs – that will
make ten francs for my dinner
  (*He takes Trilby's hand, gloats over it and kisses it. The arm falls
heavily to her side. Svengali awakens her with two quick passes of his
hand; he and Gecko exeunt on tiptoe*).
  Trilby (*Mechanically*) Svengali . . . Svengali . . . Svengali . . . he
seems to have thrown some spell on me . . . (*Rouses herself*) How silly I am
– I was forgetting. I came to get them their dinner, the dear boys . . .

Enter Taffy

Taffy Trilby! You have forgiven us?

Trilby (*Bashfully*) I – I – it was nearly dinner time, and I knew how hungry you would be getting, and –

Taffy Trilby, I feel – er – the moment has come to – er –

Trilby I know you want to scold me, Taffy. You've been like a brother to me, dear Taffy.

Taffy Yes, brother's all right – but brother isn't what I want. I thought – you might think – in short – oh, it's no use, Trilby: I love you! I adore you! I want you to marry me – make me the happiest fellow on earth!

Trilby Taffy . . . I'm more grateful to your goodness than I can say, and – and – I love somebody else. (*Her head is on his bosom*).

Taffy (*Aghast*) Who is it!

Trilby Billee . . .

Taffy Billee! Little Billee! By Jove . . . oh, by Jove! Have you accepted him?

Trilby He proposed to me nineteen times, and I said 'no' for his sake. I don't think I should have the heart to say 'no' to him the twentieth time. And you'll help us to get married, won't you, Taffy? We'd never marry without your consent, for you've taken a father's place to us both.

Taffy Now, I'm her father . . .

Trilby And you'll say 'yes', Taffy? Ah, do say 'yes' – say 'yes' . . .

Taffy Billee's a smart little chap, and isn't half bad . . . I suppose I'll have a devil of a fight with his mother about it. It's all right, Trilby – I'll say 'yes'.

Trilby (*Nestling close*) You dear, dear Taff!

Enter Laird

Laird Hello!

Taffy Hello! We – er – were just making overtures of peace.

Laird Wouldn't mind playing a part in that overture myself.

Trilby We've agreed to forget and forgive, havn't we, Taffy? And as dinner's nearly ready, I'm going to get another log for the fire. (*Exit*).

Laird Taffy – he's gone. Billee.

Taffy Where to?

Laird Florence. He packed his things, slipped out at the back, and took a cab for the station –

Taffy When is he coming back?

Laird Never – the wee fool's in love with her.

Taffy And she with him.

Laird (*Aghast*) Eh? Are you daft?

Taffy No, she just told me. Sandy, this is going to break her heart. We've got to bring him back.

Laird He caught the first train for Florence. No mortal power can overtake him –

Enter Trilby with log which she places on the fire

Taffy (*Aside to Laird*) We'll tell her all about this in the morning – mum's the word tonight. (*Aloud*) That's a regular Yule log, Trilby.

Trilby Yes, I feel so cold and odd – as though I wanted to cry.

Taffy This stupid model business upset you.

Trilby Do you really believe that Billee has forgiven me? Where is he now?

Laird Oh, Billee ... Didn't he go to buy some wine?

Trilby Oh, how the wind whistles! And Billee's out in the snow in his light shoes. I must build up the fire before he gets back.

Laird (*Aside to Taffy*) How she loves that shrimp!

Trilby Whose violets are these?

Laird They – they were left for you – by Billee.

Trilby (*Kisses flowers*) Dear white flowers. Then he *has* forgiven me!

Enter Mme Vinard with wine

See, Mme Vinard, the violets that Billee bought me?

Mme Vinard M Billee did not buy them – M Sandy bought them.

Trilby Sandy! Why did you – where's Billee? Ah, you have been deceiving me all along. Billee isn't coming back to dinner – he hasn't forgiven me. Taffy, tell me the truth: has Billee gone away?

Mme Vinard Why, M Litrebili has gone to his mother in Florence. (*Exit*).

Trilby (*To Taffy*) Why did you let him go? You envied our happiness! No, Taffy, no – I beg your pardon, dear – I don't know what I am saying – but Billee won't leave me like this. I can't live without him. Sandy, you have always told me the truth – will Billee come back?

Laird He has asked us to send his pictures to Florence.

Trilby Then I shall never see him again – never, never! To think of it makes me sick with shame and misery. Ah, Sandy, Sandy, I shall go mad and die. (*Sobs*).

(*Door flies open: enter Billee, followed by Mme Vinard*).

Billee! They – they told me you were gone!

Enter Svengali and Gecko

Billee I tried to go, but I left my heart behind, and I had to come back to find it. Trilby, will you marry me? Answer me, Trilby?

Trilby God forgive me – yes! And you have come back for good?

Billee For life. (*He embraces her*).
Svengali (*Aside to Gecko*) We will see, My Gecko – we will see
(*Billee and Trilby sit on couch. Svengali goes to the piano; he and Gecko play 'Plaisir d'amour' then 'Messieurs les étudiants'*).
Trilby Svengali... Svengali...

Curtain

Act 2

The same, one month later. Christmas Eve. As the curtain rises 'Auld Lang Syne' is heard off stage where a dinner party is in progress

Enter Angèle, dressed as a grisette, from the party

Angèle (*Crossing stage*) Mme Vinard! More wine!

Enter Honorine

Honorine Am I late, Angèle?
Angèle Ah, it is you, Honorine. They are calling for more wine.
Honorine Who is in the party?
Angèle Zouzou and Dodor, Anthony and Lorimer, and the Angliches.
Honorine And all to celebrate the wedding of Trilby and Little Billee?
Angèle Oui, ma chére. They are to marry tomorrow in yonder church of St Nicholas. Where's Svengali?
Honorine He's angry at being invited after dinner.
Angèle Svengali's only asked to play music for people to dance to. Trilby declares he's a big, black spider, and he is

Enter Mme Vinard

Mme Vinard Girls, to the dining-room, quick – there are visitors!

(*Angèle and Honorine each take a bottle from Mme Vinard and exeunt*).

Entrez, madame. Entrez, monsieur. I have sent for M Litrebili

Enter Mrs Bagot and her brother-in-law, Rev Thomas Bagot

Mrs Bagot So this is the studio where my boy works. Picturesque, is it not, Thomas?
Rev Bagot Remarkably picturesque! (*Examining nude*) Fine copies

450

of the antique!

Mrs Bagot And this foot – this foot, scratched in outline in the wall. What is that?

Mme Vinard That, madame? Oh, that is a little sketch by M Litrebili.

Mrs Bagot My poor boy. To think that he is working so late at night –

(*Noises off*).

What is that?

Mme Vinard A little party in the next apartment.

Mrs Bagot We thought he was so busy – he did not answer our telegram of a month ago. He has not even written. We finally became so anxious about the dear boy that we determined to plan a little surprise and come to Paris unheralded. Madame Vinard, you take so much interest in my son that you will be glad to hear of his forthcoming engagement.

Mme Vinard Engagement, madame?

Mrs Bagot To a young English lady.

Svengali (*Entering*) Come, my Gecko, come. We will play for the pig-dogs.

Mme Vinard (*Confused*) This way, Svengali – the party is in here.

Svengali (*To Mrs Bagot*) They have insulted me. They have dared to ask me for my rent. But we could not refuse, hein, Gecko? We could not refuse to make music while they drowned the latchkey of Litrebili in the punch-bowl... (*Exit with Gecko*).

Mrs Bagot Drowning his latchkey!

Mme Vinard Ma foi, madame! This Svengali is crazy!

Mrs Bagot Drowning my son's latchkey in a punch bowl – Thomas, do you understand?

Rev Bagot (*Who has been copying in a sketch book*) A classical phrase. I remember it in Apuleius – or was it Petronius Arbiter? It is symbolical of drinking the bridegroom's health

Svengali re-enters unperceived

Mrs Bagot (*To Mme Vinard*) Has my son never told you of a young lady, highly connected, and of his intention to conform to our wishes and marry her?

Svengali (*Coming down*) Mme Vinard, the big bullock of an Englander demands the punch.

Mme Vinard Punch! Excuse me, madame. I will soon be back. (*Exit*).

Mrs Bagot Pardon, sir, are you the husband of madame?

Svengali I? No, I have not that honour. I am the musician of the wedding-party, given in honour of my friend, M Litrebili.

Mrs Bagot In honour of my son!

Svengali Your son? Pardon, madame. Ah – you are the mother of –

451

my felicitations! Your son has taste. He has chosen well.

Mrs Bagot Chosen whom?

Svengali Miss Trilby O'Ferrall. The most beautiful grisette in the Latin quarter.

Mrs Bagot I – oh! – I – Thomas! My salts! Water! (*Sitting*).

(*Rev Bagot bustles round her*).

Svengali Ah, how I am maladroit! What have I said?

Rev Bagot Strange as it may seem, sir, Mrs Bagot's son, my nephew, has preferred to conceal the matter from his relatives.

Svengali Ah! Undutiful!

Rev Bagot So that, in short, we are compelled to ask a stranger – who *is* Miss O'Ferrall?

Svengali Her father was son of famous Dublin doctor, who was friend of George Fourth. He had all virtues but one. He drank like fish. He came to Paris – tumbled down, down, down – and when he was right down in gutter, Trilby's mother pick him up.

Rev Bagot This is very dreadful.

Svengali Trilby's mother was Scotch, like the pig-dog Sandy. She wore – you know – the tam-o'shanter, and Trilby's father married her, and died of Scotch. And the mother died also – of grief, or Scotch, I do not know. Trilby was brought up anyhow – à la grâce de Dieu – and made money by washing clothes.

Mrs Bagot Washing clothes!

Svengali And boarded with Père Martin, the rag-picker – a very respectable rag-picker – and finally settled down in the Latin quarter as model.

Rev Bagot Model of what? Head, hands, feet?

Svengali (*With gesture*) Altogether.

Rev Bagot This is very, very terrible ...

Svengali Do not grieve, my reverend, do not grieve. That is her foot scratched on the wall – there. It is the masterwork of Litrebili. There is only one foot in all Paris like it – and that is her other foot.

Rev Bagot (*Crossing to examine it eagerly*) Abominable!

Mrs Bagot (*Faintly*) And – her life – has that been irreproachable?

Svengali (*Shrugging*) Madame, she is a model – perhaps not of virtue – mais, que voulez-vous le quartier Latin, n'est-ce-pas?

Mrs Bagot Thomas, advise me – what can we do? How can we stop this hideous marriage?

Rev Bagot I suggest that if we could learn how the French law stands ...

Svengali There is a lawyer at the corner – he is a friend of mine – here is his card. Tell him I recommend you – I, Svengali, the famous musician.

Mrs Bagot I don't know, sir, how we can thank you. My grief has evidently touched you.

Svengali It has, madame.

Rev Bagot (*Producing pocket-book*) I trust, sir, you may be rewarded. (*Looks inside, then puts it away again*) If not now, hereafter

(*Exeunt Mrs Bagot and Rev Bagot*).

Svengali Hereafter? Bah! A bird in hand is worth a pig in a poke

Enter Gecko

Gecko They are coming; they wish us to play a wedding march.
Svengali There will be no wedding, my Gecko. Mamma has gone to Mâitre Guérin!

Gecko looks surprised. Svengali sits at piano; he and Gecko play a wedding march. Wedding party enters in burlesque dignity. Mme Vinard enters with bowl of punch

Omnes A la mariee! Madame Vinard! The punch, the punch!

(*They all crowd round the punchbowl. Billee and Trilby slip off stage*).

Taffy Come, boys, the quadrille!

(*They all dance gaily; when dance and merriment reach a climax, enter Mrs Bagot and Rev Bagot*).

Billee's mother!

(*The music and the dance stop; all but Taffy and Laird scuttle off comically. Svengali goes last, chuckling*).

Mrs Bagot I'm so sorry, Mr Wynne, if we interrupted your dance.
Taffy Not at all, Mrs Bagot. Christmas, you know. Bound to observe the season.
Laird You'll excuse me, Mrs Bagot, but I have an important appointment with the Austrian Ambassador – I hope to see you in the morning. In the meantime, I beg to wish you a merry Christmas. (*Exit*).
Mrs Bagot Mr Wynne, we are in great distress.
Taffy No? Sorry – won't you sit down?
Mrs Bagot Mr Wynne, we know the whole truth. We know that this marriage would ruin my son –
Taffy I can't say I agree with you, Mrs Bagot. You don't know Trilby. You may think it strange, but on my word of honour, she's about the best girl I ever met – the most unselfish, the most –

Rev Bagot Very pretty, I suppose?

Taffy Very – but that's nothing. She has a good heart, a beautiful nature, and I wish to heaven she had chosen me instead of Billee

Enter Trilby

Trilby Mrs Bagot, they – they told me you were here. (*Extends her hand*).

Mrs Bagot (*Rising and ignoring hand*) You are Miss Trilby O'Ferrall?

Trilby Yes.

Mrs Bagot You are beautiful – beautiful indeed. You wish to marry my son?

Trilby I refused him for his own sake – he will tell you so himself – I am not the right person for him to marry, I know that. But he vowed he would leave Paris if I persisted in refusing him – so – so I was weak, and yielded. Perhaps I was wrong.

Mrs Bagot If you are so fond of him, will you ruin him by marrying him? Will you drag him down, possibly ruin his career, separate him from his sister, his family, his friends?

Trilby Mrs Bagot, I love him so.

Rev Bagot You love him! Love him! Let me tell you, Miss O'Ferrall, that if he marries you, his home will be closed to him. And in after years, when you come to witness his poverty, his despair, and know that you – and you only – are to blame, you will feel some of the pangs his mother feels today.

Trilby You are right. This time I will be strong. Mrs Bagot, I give you my promise – I will not marry your son.

Taffy (*Taking her hand*) And I give them my promise – that you *shall*.

Trilby Taffy! ⎫
Mrs Bagot Mr Wynne! ⎬ (*Together*)
Rev Bagot Mr Wynne! ⎭

Taffy Mrs Bagot, I love the boy as much as anybody, and if you, his mother, want to break his heart, I, his friend, won't let you. Billee has promised to marry Trilby – he has taken his oath before the world, and if he breaks his word, I – I'd break his head!

Rev Bagot Your attitude in this matter, Mr Wynne, compels us to resort to extremities. We have just come from the office of a notary. From him we have learned the French law of marriage. In the case of a youth under twenty-five, no union is valid without the consent of the parents, or, if one of the parents is dead, without the consent of the surviving parent. Mrs Bagot refuses her consent to this marriage.

Taffy Why you infer – I beg your pardon, Mrs Bagot, I nearly called him a worm.

Rev Bagot Jane, give me your arm.

Mrs Bagot Good night. Some day you will understand. (*Exit with Rev Bagot*).
Trilby Oh, Taffy, what have you done ?

Re-enter the wedding party except Billee

Laird It's all right – the Austrian Embassy's gone.
Omnes Hooray!
Taffy Don't cheer. They threaten us with the law. Billee's under twenty-five – his mother's consent is necessary.
Anthony What's to be done ?
Zouzou I suggest, what you call it ? – evasion – elopement.
Laird It might be wise – English law is different from the French.
Taffy Then to England we'll go.
Laird We'll have carriages here at midnight – drive post-haste to the Northern railroad – be across the Channel before noon tomorrow and get the marriage legally celebrated by nightfall.
Omnes Hooray!
Taffy Billee is waiting at the church. Trilby will wait for us here. Boys, let thoughts of Lochinvar inspire you, and strike for England, home and beauty!
Dodor Attention! Form battalion! March!

(*They all march off noisily except Trilby and Svengali. Trilby remains seated; Svengali bolts the door and makes hypnotic gestures. Trilby feels his presence and attempts to rise but is unable to do so*).

Svengali So, at midnight we say goodbye, my Trilby.
Trilby I shall be thankful to leave Paris behind.
Svengali You do not listen to me, my Trilby – you turn away when Svengali speaks to you; you still think of Litrebili, eh ? Sleep, ma mignonne – sleep . . .).
(*He staggers, overcome by the effort of hypnotising her*).
Do you hear me, Trilby ? Trilby, do you hear me ?
Trilby Yes . . .
Svengali Then you will do as I bid you. You will rise. You will go into the dining-room; you will wait there till I call for you. I will it! I will it! (*Trilby exits*) Ach! My strength, my genius – my life is passing into hers. If I take not care, it will kill me

Enter Gecko

Gecko Trilby! Where is she ?
Svengali She leaves Paris at midnight; she and I – and you, my Gecko.
Gecko I ?

Svengali You see, I know your secret – you love her.

Gecko Yes, I love her – I would rather die than let a moment of unhappiness come to her.

Svengali Pah! What happiness would she find with Litrebili? She has the artist-nature – the beauty of a queen; and shall she pine away among the swine of an English village?

Gecko No ... if I thought she would ever forgive me ... Svengali, I have served you as a dog, but rather than injure her, I –

Svengali You little fool! (*Takes him by the throat*) You, who owe everything to me – you, whom I picked out of the gutter when you were starving ... (*Puts hand to heart*) My heart – I faint – brandy, quick! I – what is this? I cannot see – my heart ... I will not die. God, do not let me die! Let me live another year! (*He gibbers*) I will repent – oh, God of Israel! Stemang Visreal adonai Eloheno Adonai Echod ...

(*Gecko gives him brandy*).

Ah – ah! I am not dying, eh, Gecko? Feel my heart, I am not dying ... I am young still – we will live, my Gecko, you and I, eh? We will wander eastward – you and Trilby and I – we will cage the songbird till it sings gold and pearls and diamonds and rubies, and we will be rich – I will ride in my carriage, and smoke the big Havanna cigar, and I will wear a big fur coat all the winter, and all the summer too.

Gecko She would never leave Paris.

Svengali We shall see – I have my power still. Trilby, come to me. She comes not ... Trilby, come to me!

Trilby enters, in a trance

Sit down in that chair – (*She does so*) Take that pen, Trilby. Write. 'My dear Taffy' –

Trilby 'My dear Taffy –'

(*Bells and organ music are heard from the church nearby*).

Svengali 'This is to say goodbye' –

Trilby '... to say goodbye ...'

Svengali 'Billee's mother is right – I shall never see him again –'

Trilby '... never see him again ...'

Svengali 'Tonight I leave Paris forever –'

Trilby '... Paris forever ...'

Svengali 'Do not try to find me; I am safe with friends –'

Trilby '... safe with friends ...'

(*Knocking is heard at the door*).

Svengali Write quick. 'Trilby O'Ferrall'.

Trilby '... Trilby O'Ferrall'.

Svengali You will go with Gecko in a carriage to the station, and you will wait with him till I join you. I wish it. I wish it.

Gecko And when she wakes?

Svengali She will be far from home. Quick – the back way

(Gecko takes Trilby off. Svengali unbolts the door and stands aside as Taffy, Laird and Mme Vinard rush in. Svengali instantly slips out unnoticed).

Laird What the devil – ? Who's been here ? Who locked the door ? And who let us in ?

Taffy Trilby! Trilby!

(The music rises)

Laird *(Seeing letter)* What's this ? *(Hands letter to Taffy)* Read.

Taffy *(Reads)* There'll be no marriage

Enter Billee

Billee Well, is everything all right ? Why, what's the matter ?

Taffy Bear it like a man, Billee. Trilby's gone.

Billee Gone! *(Reads letter)* '. . . leave Paris forever. Do not try to find me . . .' Oh, Taffy! Taffy!

(The organ peals out the 'Cantique de Noel'. Billee is comforted by Taffy; Svengali appears and laughs as the curtain falls)

Act 3

Five years later. Foyer of the Cirque des Bashibazouks. Mme Vinard in the dress of a theatrical box-keeper, is discovered.

Enter Colonel Kaw, the manager. Music is playing off stage

Kaw Ah, bong soir, Mme Vinard.
Mme Vinard Bon soir, M le Directeur.
Kaw Did you ever see such an audience in Paris before?
Mme Vinard Never.
Kaw Now, mind, if you allow anybody to enter when the music is going on, off goes your head my lady. (*Exit*)

Enter Zouzou and Dodor

Mme Vinard Ah, can it be? Is it possible?
Zouzou (*Loftily*) My good woman...?
Mme Vinard M Zouzou! M Dodor! Don't you remember Mme Vinard who was concierge? Five years ago?
Dodor Great Scott! How do!
Zouzou Ah! How do! How do! (*They all shake hands*).
Mme Vinard (*Showing them to their box*) M Zouzou talks Angliche now as well as an Englishman.
Zouzou Doosid deal better! I've married an American wife!
Mme Vinard (*Going*) Ah, may I felicitate...
Zouzou Thanks. Will you open my box? (*Hands her a ticket*).
(*Exit Mme Vinard chattering*) It's like old times to meet her.
Dodor You're too great a swell to think of old times now that you're a Duke.
Zouzou Bah! Am I not gathering the clans tonight for the express purpose of reviving them? Here come two of our party now.

Enter Anthony Oliver and Lorimer

Zouzou Anthony!
Dodor Lorimer!
(*Hearty greetings are exchanged*).

Zouzou What do you think? We just met Mother Vinard – she has turned box-keeper here.

Oliver Five years ago! (*Sighs*).

Zouzou It's just to rub up our memories that I asked you here to see Svengali.

All Svengali!

Zouzou Don't you know it's *our* Svengali who leads the orchestra tonight?

Dodor What? That damned blackguard?

Zouzou All the same, he married la Svengali, the greatest singer on earth.

Dodor I never heard of la Svengali. Enlighten me.

Zouzou Svengali, you remember, was always bragging about the 'bel canto', and how he found its secret in a dream. Well, somewhere in Poland he met a woman he could teach, and she's to make her first appearance in Paris tonight.

Dodor (*Reading programme*) Mme Svengali, the world renowned singer. First selection: 'Ben Bolt'. Why, that's a nursery rhyme!

Zouzou People declare she's not mortal at all. She's like an enchanted princess in a fairy tale. She makes you cry over the commonest tunes.

Dodor It's disgusting that a hog like Svengali should have found such a pearl.

Kaw (*Entering quickly*) Gentlemen, I must ask you not to linger in the foyer. The first two numbers are over, and we have a rule forbidding entrance while the music is being played. (*He ushers them off into their box*).

Enter Mme Vinard

Mme Vinard, let me know the instant Mme Svengali arrives. (*Exit*).

Mme Vinard Svengali? Why that's the name of – it can't possibly be the same, yet –

Gecko (*Off*) In a moment. I will see that the foyer is empty.

Mme Vinard Gecko! It is Gecko's voice! Then Svengali is – my money – !

Enter Gecko in Hungarian uniform; his hair is almost white

Gecko Mme Vinard!

Mme Vinard Yes, it is I, you little wretch! When you and your master Svengali ran away that Christmas you thought never to see me again, hein? Where is all the money he owes me for his rent?

Gecko He will pay, he will pay. He is now rich – his pockets are lined with gold. But no scene, I implore you – no scene! His wife, the great singer, is coming, and if you should excite his nerves –

Mme Vinard I'll excite – this time your master shall not run away from me. (*Exit*).

Gecko If Svengali meets her he will be all unstrung, and our bird will not sing tonight...

Enter Svengali in evening dress. He is noticeably older

Svengali Tell me when this number is finished. We are fifth on the programme

Enter Trilby, dressed in cloth of gold; her demeanour is normal except for her eyes

Trilby Oh, Taffy, have I kept you waiting? I am so sorry. I must look my best tonight, for the supper's in honour of Billee and me.

Svengali Always thinking of that miserable little painter still...

Trilby Mrs Bagot – won't you take my hand? Won't you take my hand? Sandy, Sandy, dear, you won't let him give me up...

Svengali If I could awake her – but it is too late. My life has passed into hers. And every note she sings I know that it is killing both her and me ... but tonight she will sing like a nightingale. (*His breathing is heavy; his hand is on his heart*).

Gecko You have been making her work too hard.

Svengali Have I spared myself? Would any doctor alive allow that I had a year to live?

Trilby Svengali, do not be cross with me. I am doing my best ... do not beat me.

Gecko You have beaten her?

Svengali Silence, dog.

Trilby Don't be cross with me ... don't scold me ... (*Shrinking*) don't beat –

Svengali Sleep...

Trilby (*Her voice dying out*) Don't beat ... beat ...

Enter Kaw

Kaw Ah, Svengali, bong soir. Bong soir. Your good lady is ready? Let me escort her to the stage.

(*Svengali nods; Kaw leads Trilby off*)

Gecko Svengali, you must listen to me. I have for years been your servant, your factotum – but if you ever raise your hand to strike Trilby, I will forget all. For Trilby I will go to the scaffold, and to the devil after.

Svengali (*Raising his hand*) Fool! (*His hand drops inert*).

Gecko Ah! You have just said your life is running out – you can no longer beat any but women. Go, make your song bird sing as never

George du
Maurier
(*Enthoven Collection*)

before. And remember – I will go to the scaffold to defend her

(*As Svengali goes out he attempts to strike Gecko with his baton, but falls forward slightly; exit*).

Gecko Merciful Heaven! He is killing her . . . (*Exit*)

Enter Taffy, the Laird and Little Billee arm in arm

Laird So this is the Cirque des Bashibazouks . . . don't think it existed in our time, eh, Taffy?

Taffy All Paris is changed! Doesn't seem like our Paris, does it, Billee?

Billee Ah, we'll never see that Paris again!

Enter Mme Vinard

461

Mme Vinard Mon Dieu! Les trois Angliches!

Billee It's Madame Vinard! Dear Madame Vinard!

Mme Vinard (*Hugging them each in turn*) Ah, mes garçons, what happiness to see you again.

Taffy Have you given up your lodge, Mme Vinard?

Mme Vinard No, messieurs, my husband keeps it now, and I earn a few sous as box-keeper.

Laird And our old studio – is that occupied?

Mme Vinard It has been three months to let. But you would not know it. Nothing is as it was but Trilby's foot – poor Trilby! So good – so pretty!

Laird Was – was nothing ever heard of her again?

Mme Vinard Nothing. I have nothing but this plain hair ring which she gave me to remember her.

Laird Mme Vinard, will you take fifty francs for that ring?

Mme Vinard Fifty? It's not worth two!

Laird Je prong. I'll give you fifty for Auld Lang Syne. (*Gives bank notes, she hands over the ring*).

Mme Vinard So the trois Angliches have not forgotten poor Trilby?

Billee (*Weeping*) I can't help it, Taffy. The mere mention of her name brings it all back to me. I loved her so – oh, God, I loved her so!

Taffy Brace up, old man, we loved her, too! Svengali may tell us something of her fate.

Laird Come, boys, we've just time to find our way to Zouzou's box.

Mme Vinard Ah, M Sandy, you are too late. They let no-one in when the conductor raises his baton. But you can hear this number from the window. There is Svengali – there!

Laird How sleek the villain looks, but pale as death.

Mme Vinard And Gecko, too. Can you pick him out?

Taffy How he has aged . . . but the woman, the prodigy – where is she?

Laird (*With opera glasses*) Two pages are pulling the curtain aside . . . there she is . . . and – here, Taffy, take these glasses: they make me see the queerest things

(*Orchestra starts playing 'Ben Bolt' introduction*).

Mme Vinard Why, what is it, M Taffy?

Billee Taffy, is it – is it – somebody we know?

Taffy Yes, dear lad. It's – it's Trilby.

Billee (*Seizing opera glasses*) Come back to life! La Svengali! His wife!

(*Trilby is heard singing distantly*).

Laird But by what miracle – ?

Billee Oh, listen, listen!

Laird Trilby – the tone-deaf! Preposterous!

Tuffy Svengali's eyes are rivetted on hers . . .

Billee Don't talk, boys, for heaven's sake, don't talk!

(*The song ends. Applause*).

Laird Now the bouquets – the air's thick with them. She is bowing, Svengali's hand in hers.

Taffy (*To Billee*) Come away, lad. We have seen enough

Enter Kaw; exit Mme Vinard

Kaw Gentlemen, I must ask you to withdraw. Mme Svengali is coming here to rest between her numbers. I must ask you

Enter Trilby on Svengali's arm, followed by Gecko carrying bouquets

Brava! Bravissima! (*Exit*).

Taffy Svengali!

Svengali Monsieur?

Taffy You recall me – Taffy. Talbot Wynne and my two friends the Laird and Little Billee?

Svengali Pardon me, sir, I have not the advantage of recollecting –

Billee But Madame Svengali – Trilby – she remembers us? Trilby, you know me, don't you, Trilby?

(*Trilby laughs*).

Trilby, don't laugh. Look at me – speak to me –

Svengali My wife, sir, never looks backward. To her the past is dead, and so are all who were in it.

Billee Tell me one thing, and I will ask no more. Was it really your regard for my mother's wish that made you give me up? Or was it your desire to be rich and famous with Svengali? Won't you answer? Don't you know that when you went away you broke my heart?

Trilby This time I will be strong, Mrs Bagot; I give you my promise. I will not marry your son.

Taffy Svengali has forbidden her to speak to us. But these were the words she used to your mother. She repeats them to show us why she ran away.

Billee You have been forbidden to speak to us?

Trilby No...

Billee Then you are doing this on your own responsibility?

(*She goes quietly on babbling*).

Why, then let us tell you how heartless we think you! And how we are convinced of what we long suspected, that you left me on the eve of our marriage, not because you cared for my mother, but because this devil (*Pointing to Svengali*) tempted you! For that you sold yourself! For that you betrayed me!

(*Trilby laughs softly*).

You laugh, all right. You are famous today. Great! The world is all at your feet, but if your conscience doesn't make you suffer when you think

463

of me, it's because you have no conscience; it's because you have bartered your soul for fame –

Kaw (*Entering*) Mme Svengali, we have a few minutes before your number – if I might have the honour to escort you to the stage? (*Takes her arm and goes out with her*) You're booming, madame, you're booming!

Svengali (*Following them*) You are brave, my young friend, but you shall not lack provocation

(*He strikes Billee in the face with one of Trilby's bouquets; Billee attempts to strike him but is restrained by Laird. Taffy hurls Svengali to the floor*).

Gecko Ah, you who beat women, let us see how you like to be beaten yourself.

Billee He struck Trilby?

Gecko I heard her say it just now – 'do not beat me, Svengali'.

Svengali (*Rising feebly and falling heavily into seat*) My heart – my heart!

Gecko He is killing her.

Billee Our Trilby?

Gecko No, it is not our Trilby – it is Svengali's Trilby.

Laird What do you mean, Gecko?

Gecko There are two Trilbys. There is the Trilby you know, who cannot sing one note in tune. That is the Trilby we love. And all at once this Svengali, this magician, can with one look of his eye, one wave of his hand, turn her into another Trilby, so that when his Trilby is singing our Trilby has ceased to exist

(*Music strikes up off stage*).

Taffy Then, Gecko, Trilby cannot sing unless Svengali is present.

Gecko Not a note.

Billee But think – the song she just went to sing...

Gecko Madre de misere – I forgot!

(*Music stops; sounds of riot in auditorium*).

Laird Look! The audience has risen to its feet! There's an uproar!

Enter Dodor, Zouzou and Lorimer

Dodor Ah, my friends, such a scene! Hideous! Grotesque!

Zouzou Oh, mes enfants! Pandemonium has broken loose – hisses, cat-calls –

Lorimer The curtain has been rung down

Enter Kaw

Kaw Svengali, Svengali, why didn't you come to my help? Damn you, sir, don't you know that your wife has gone mad! Yes, stark, staring mad upon the stage, Come to her at once. Do you hear, man? Are you drunk?

(Svengali rises slowly; he throws Taffy a horrible grin of hatred and attempts to leave; he then throws up his hands and falls forward on the table. Taffy listens to his heart and signals that he is dead. Trilby is heard off stage).

Trilby I won't sing – not a note

She enters

Where am I . . . ? Why, Billee! Taffy – Sandy! Why are you here? And Svengali? Where's Svengali?

(The others form a screen across Svengali's body).

Laird Svengali's gone home

(He takes her out on his arm)

Curtain

Act 4
Same as Acts 1 & 2

Taffy and Laird are decorating the room with holly and misteltoe

Taffy There – it looks quite like old times.
Laird Ha, yes! Those old times that will never come back. It was five years ago today that Trilby went away with Svengali

Enter Mme Vinard

Well, how is she ?
Mme Vinard Dr Oliver says she seems better

Enter Dodor

Laird Halloa, Dodor – how are you ?
Dodor I have come to wish our dear Trilby a merry Christmas. Mme Vinard, take in my card and ask if she is well enough to see me.
Mme Vinard Well, I will see – but mind, no chatter

Enter Oliver

N'est-ce pas, docteur ? N'est-ce pas ? There must be no chatter. (*Exit*).
All How is she, Oliver ?
Oliver Mending – but she must be kept quiet. What we fear is excitement – she is better since she came to the old studio.
Dodor But what on earth was the secret of Svengali's influence over her ?
Oliver Heaven only knows! My one object now is to make her forget him

Enter Zouzou

Hello, Zouzou!
Zouzou Bon jour, chéri. Oh, la, la!
Oliver What's the matter, my bold Zouzou ? One would think you had seen a ghost.
Zouzou So I have.

466

Dodor (*Laughing*) Ho, ho! Whose ghost have you seen, Zouzou?

Zouzou Svengali's.

(*All laugh*).

Dodor It was that Welsh rarebit last night at Brebaut's.

Zouzou It's no use, boys – ever since that fellow died across the table at the Bashibazouks, his eyes have haunted me. His voice has haunted me – his laugh has haunted me. I seem to meet him everywhere. Last night I was walking home from the Opera – it was a dark, gusty night – I was thinking of poor Trilby, and of Svengali's death. A big greasy creature with a worn overcoat and a muffler that half concealed his face was hurrying along. Under his arm he was carrying a large parcel; there was a sudden gust of wind, the covering was blown aside, and there I saw Svengali staring at me with his great big eyes.

Dodor And then –?

Zouzou He hurried away, and as he did so, it seemed to me he was carrying Svengali's head under his arm. Was it Svengali, or was it a picture?

Dodor It was the Welsh rarebit.

Zouzou It was a nightmare. Oh, la, la, la, la!

Oliver Hush! She is coming – not a word about Svengali and the picture, mind . . .

Enter Trilby supported by Mme Vinard

Trilby Zouzou . . . Dodor . . . dear friends.

(*Oliver talks quietly to Dodor and exits*).

No, don't touch me. I am quite strong enough to walk. (*Totters to sofa*).

Mme Vinard My poor lamb, I will bring your medicine. But do not let these magpies chatter. You hear, gredins de militaires? You may talk, but no chatter. (*Exit*).

Trilby Dear Madame Vinard! Ah, what it is to see you all again. It makes one glad to be alive! Ah, j'aime tant ca, c'est le ciel – I wonder I've a word of English left.

Zouzou Are you anxious to sing in an English theatre?

Trilby Sing in an English theatre? I never sang at any theatre, except a few nights ago – I'll take precious good care never to sing in a theatre again. How they howled! It all seemed like a bad dream. Was it a dream, I wonder?

Zouzou But the diamonds – the trinkets – the beautiful dress –

Trilby Svengali gave them to me – he made lots of money.

Zouzou Did he never try to teach you how to sing?

Trilby Oh, maie aie! Not he. I used to sing 'Ben Bolt' – just for fun; I'd no training, you know.

Dodor And nobody ever told you you were a famous singer?

467

Trilby   You are making fun of me, Dodor

Enter Gecko and Billee

Gecko   Ah, mes amis – Trilby, ma chérie, all is well ?
Billee   I have brought you these roses, dear.
Zouzou   Well, as you're in safe hands, we'll be toddling, Trilby.
Trilby   Don't go – stay and smoke a cigarette and talk over old times.
Zouzou   No, thanks – we've all appointments at – at –
Trilby   The Austrian Embassy ?
Zouzou   (*Confused*) Not at the Austrian Embassy, but – oh, la, la, la, la! Goodbye, Trilby – we'll come to see you every day – and don't forget to send us a bit of the wedding-cake.
Trilby   Wedding-cake ?
Zouzou   Goodbye!
Zouzou, Dodor, Oliver   A la mariee (*Exeunt*).
Trilby   Dear fellows . . . what do they mean ?
Laird   You've just had a peculiar sort of brain fever, and we are going to send you away from Paris.
Trilby   With Mme Vinard ?
Laird   No, with Billee – as his wife.
Trilby   With Billee as his wife ?
Laird   Yes, Trilby, as soon as you are strong and able to travel we want to pack you off happily as Billee's wife.
Trilby   Now I am sure it's a dream . . . dear Taffy!

(*Exeunt Taffy and Laird*).

Billee, it's real, is it not ? All is going to be as it used to be ? Oh, my love, my love I'm so happy! And I thought I was going to die.
Billee   Hush!
Trilby   Oh, Billee, if we could only wipe out all those five years !
Billee   See, here is the holly and mistletoe – just as it was five years ago.
Trilby   Just as it was five years ago . . . yes, everything is the same, except poor Trilby. You and the Laird and Taffy are just the same – but where is Svengali ?
Billee   Trilby, that shadow has passed from our lives.
Trilby   Ah, look at all my beautiful presents – (*Begins to open them*) See, this is from Zouzou – a cigarette case – and Billee, look at this.
Billee   Why, what's that ?
Trilby   It's from your mother – a little necklace, with a kind letter . . .

Enter Mme Vinard with picture, covered

Mme Vinard   Ah, Madame Trilby, see – here is another present.
Trilby   A picture – who brought it ?

Mme Vinard He did not stay – it was a man with a great big greasy coat – he said he had instructions to leave it with Madame Trilby at Christmas time.

Trilby Open it, dear Mme Vinard.

Mme Vinard Now, M Litrebili, now M Gecko. You must both say goodnight. Trilby is tired.

Gecko You permit? (*Kisses Trilby's hand and exits*).

Mme Vinard And M Sandy and M Taffy too, must say goodnight.

Trilby Go and fetch them, the dear boys

(*Billee kisses her, then exits*).

Mme Vinard See, here is a letter. (*Hands Trilby letter, and places picture on easel*).

Trilby Svengali's hand! (*Reads*) 'From Svengali to Trilby – souvenir of Christmas Day five years ago'. Ah, they told me he was dead – it is a message from the dead! (*Goes to easel and takes off the cover*)

(*Trilby shrieks and falls; Taffy enters just in time to catch her. Enter also Laird and Little Billee*).

Don't look at me, Svengali – turn your eyes away!

Billee Trilby, Trilby!

Trilby What? The whole song over again? Very well – not too quickly at first – I can hardly see – everything is so dark! (*She starts to sing 'Ben Bolt'*).

Billee Trilby – speak to me!

Trilby (*Continues singing, then stops suddenly*) Svengali, Svengali, Svengali! (*She falls lifeless into Billee's arms*)

Curtain

THE PRESS

The Manchester Guardian, September 9th, 1895:

Theatre Royal. Mr Beerbohm Tree and the Haymarket Company in Trilby

Saturday was one of the red-letter days in the history of the Theatre Royal – a new play for which all England is waiting, a first-rate performance, a great success, a thronged, excited, and fascinated house. In keeping such a primeur *for Manchester Mr Tree has laid us all under an obligation, and the audience was evidently glad to be able to acknowledge it in its own way. The applause was most hearty and spontaneous, and the success absolutely unequivocal. In a little speech which he made at the close of the performance Mr Tree referred lightly to the 'great effort' which had been put forth by all concerned to be ready in time, and we can well believe it. But the piece went without hitch, and the rollicking festivity of the second act was carried through with the greatest finish as well as animation. It was a great triumph for all concerned, primarily, of course, for Mr Du Maurier, but also for Mr Paul Potter, who dramatised the novel for the stage and whose appearance by the side of Mr Tree at the close was not the least interesting event of a very interesting night, for Mr Tree himself, for Miss Dorothea Baird, in whom he has found an almost ideal Trilby, and for a company in general excellently good.*

Trilby, *after captivating all America, is fast captivating all England, and an adaptation of it stands, therefore, in a very special case. On the one hand, it is bound to suffer by comparison with the diffused* bonhomie *and quaint fantasy of the novel – qualities almost impossible to give upon the stage; – but, on the other hand, a mere suggestion goes a long way, when a great part of the audience have the whole book present to their minds, and prevents what would be mere melodrama in an ordinary form sounding merely melodramatic in* Trilby. *Moreover, M Du Maurier's novel was a very special case in that he was able to possess his readers' imaginations in two ways, and to put his personages before them with the pencil as well as with the pen. The reader thus knows* Trilby *and* Svengali *and* Taffy *and the rest with them as he knows his own friends and acquaintances, and his interest in seeing them move and hearing them speak may confidently be counted on beforehand. It is one of the rare cases where it is a positive advantage, instead of as usual a drawback, that there is a book behind the play. Of course, this would not apply if the play were a coarse travesty of the book and nothing else. But the surprise – to be frank – of Saturday was that it was a good deal more than that. The first act is really skilful, and keeps to a remarkable degree the easy familiar tone, the mingled realism and romance of the original. The personages were at once firmly planted on their feet, and the difficult process of giving, by way of dialogue only, the necessary retrospects and explanations which the author is able to give at length in his own person in the novel, was successfully performed. Much of the second act was also good in the same way. It was only from the end of the second act onwards that the real or supposed demands of the stage victoriously asserted themselves, and that the piece dropped at times into ordinary melo-drama. If after reading* Trilby *we ask what interests us, the answer will be anything but 'the story'. It is the loveableness of* Trilby *herself, the kind, brave manliness of her three friends, the gusto and humour of the book, the 'realisation of the day-dream' which, far more than 'real life', is what so many of us want from art, and which M Du Maurier here pre-eminently supplies. As for the story, one sees that there are two. (a) The 'dame aux Camélias' in another setting; and (b) a melodrama with hypnotism for its* motif *– to be candid, what the French call a 'tale of Mother Goose'. Now the story in some form must – at all events till the stage has been a good deal further Ibsenised than it is at present – become the vital point as soon as there is any question of turning a book into a play. In this particular case the choice is only between (a) and (b). Shall we lay stress on this essentially tragic situation – that a woman, naturally good, has been guilty of grave lapses, is honourably loved and returns the affection, and is then called upon to sacrifice her happiness for her lover's sake, the irrevocable past coming up disastrously between him and her? There are two objections to that. One is that it is the classic situation of Dumas's famous play. Dumas by no means exhausts it, and some day it will be put on the stage again. But that will need courage. For the moment Dumas stands somewhat in the way. Also that situation means tragedy, psychology – all manner of great but difficult things. How much easier is (b)! Get the audience to grant to you this postulate – that a man can hypnotise a woman so as to give her a new self and cause her to forget her old one, and can make an unrivalled singer of her who could not sing a note in tune – and how easy every-thing becomes. Of course, there is a sacrifice. Tragedy becomes melo-drama, and mere arbitrary wonder-working takes the place of the difficult, tiresome things which we call psychology and literature and the development of character. But very few men in Mr Potter's place would have done differently. Probably, as the stage now is, his resolute avoidance of (a) (an avoidance carried much further than it is by Mr Du Maurier himself in the novel) and his resolute concentration of all the stress on (b), was the necessary condition of success. Of course, that comes* to the same thing as saying that the stage, 'as it now is', is an inferior form of art, and that the great masters would not have been thus content with the second best. Such considerations, however, are unpractical. Mr Potter did not make the modern stage, and there is no question of his being a great master. But he has the credit of having done a piece of journeyman's work in an uncommonly workmanlike manner, at least as well, if not better, than any piece of work of the kind has been done of late years in England.

The play ends, as in the novel, with the death of Trilby, hastened apparently by the portrait of Svengali. The merely marvellous, 'mother goose' element in the plot, which is present at this point even in the novel, is here disagreeably prominent. Why does Trilby die? Not because she loves Svengali – the play is clearer on that point than the novel. Is it because she cannot marry Billee? But that possibility almost vanishes in the play, and the excision of half a dozen words would remove it altogether. But, then, is this abrupt tragic ending necessary? No moral necessity binds her to the dead Svengali, whom she does not love and whose wife she has been in name only. But against a merely physical necessity – the man's hypnotic power over her brain – the mind of the spectator rebels, and rightly. The power of the dead man over her is merely repulsive and horrible, and would be felt at once to be so if we could commit ourselves to taking it seriously. Happy endings are often inept because in defiance of the moral and logical necessities of the situation. But a happy ending in this case is possible and justifiable – granted, of course, the abandonment of the (a) motif, and the exclusive stress that has been laid throughout on (b) – and we think that this last act, which even an excited and enthusiastic audience felt on Saturday to be disappointing, should be seriously reconsidered.

Mr Beerbohm Tree has found one of the great parts of his life – some, no doubt, will think it the greatest – in Svengali. He makes a very Mephistopheles of the part, indeed, it is clear that he would be a Mephistopheles of the first order. The facial play was masterly, and there was a short mirthless laugh and a kickout of the leg behind for Gecko's benefit, when Svengali thought himself unusually clever, which were miracles of uncanny realism. Particularly interesting was the scene with Mrs Bagot and the Rev Dr Bagot, in which the gesture of the hands by which it was conveyed that Trilby had sat for 'the altogether' was half comic and wholly sinister – a very triumph of expressiveness. This deeply studied, picturesque, and always interesting piece of acting was, of course, one of the great features of the performance. Hardly less important a one, however, was Miss Dorothea Baird's rendering of the part of Trilby. To have found such a Trilby is a piece of unheard of good fortune. Miss Baird looks the part almost to perfection: she has precisely the charming smile which Mr Du Maurier gives to Trilby; and by some *happy gift of nature or art or both, she is able to play the part with the unhackneyed freshness and candour which it before all required. It was a beautiful performance, with rare poetical qualities, and even the most hardened old playgoers could not watch it without a thrill of sympathy and pleasure. Mr Edmund Maurice's* Taffy *was a little disappointing. He looked the part admirably, and some of his byplay was excellent, but he failed to convey distinction, and* Taffy *was essentially distinguished. Mr Patrick Evans will make more of* Billee *with further experience; at present he has the* physique *and all the gallant youthful bearing of the part. Mr Lionel Brough made the* Laird *a little too farcical, and his Scotch was a little too middle-class; but it was a strongly individualised and humorous performance. Mr Herbert Ross's* Zouzou *was a first-rate sketch – nature itself in the second act, where he has taken rather more than is good for him, and not less in the third act, where his desperate, good-natured hurry in emergencies, and his little French ejaculations under his breath were excessively diverting. Mr Charles Allan delighted the audience with a wonderfully exact, but good-natured and un-exaggerated, reproduction of the parsonial manner, and Miss Annie Hughes was a fair* Madame Vinard, *though why she should talk broken English throughout was not apparent. Is that the only way in which it can be brought home to an English audience that a personage is French ?*

Despite having her performance damned as being only 'fair', Annie Hughes received excellent notices in other papers. She was, however, replaced by Rosina Filippi by the time the play reached London. Patrick Evans was very poorly reviewed, but was not re-placed until after the play had opened at the Haymarket the fol-lowing month; also in the cast was (Sir) Gerald Du Maurier, the son of the original author, and the father of another successful novelist, Dame Daphne Du Maurier.

The Era, November 2nd, 1895;

The triumph of Trilby *is the topic of the week. 'You're booming, madame, you're booming !' says Manager Kaw to the hypnotised singer in the third act of the play; and this remark exactly denotes the nature of the enthusiasm which prevailed at the Haymarket last Wednesday. The tidings of the success of the dramatisation of the novel in America, the reports of the performances of the play at Manchester, had whetted expectation to its sharpest; and the Haymarket Theatre was closely crowded with a brilliant audience, literally packed into the smallest possible space, but, figuratively, on the tiptoe of expectation. That the fancies thus formed were not illusory, that the adaptation was received with wildly enthusiastic fervour, proved the merit of Mr Du Maurier's novel and the adroitness of Mr Paul M Potter's adaptation. It is hardly necessary to retell the story of the tone-deaf artist's model into whom the*

473

musician breathes his talent; and who, when under what it used to be considered comic to call the 'fluence', warbles most divinely, and charms all Paris by her voice and beauty. How Svengali *expires as the result of his reckless expenditure of the mesmeric fluid; how* Trilby, *worn out, comes home to die merely from the shock of beholding her tyrant's portrait – has not all this been told in critiques, in reviews, and in the editions of Mr Du Maurier's novel? Mr Potter has done his work well. It was impossible, within the limits prescribed, to develop the minor characters elaborately; but still we get a glimpse of* Zouzou *and* Dodor, *the latter, in one of his exits, 'realising the picture' of the inebriated* militaire *on all fours. The* Rev Thomas Bagot *retains his ecclesiastical severity, plus the salacity of Mr Joskin Tubbs in* Pink Dominos. *As for the leading personages in the play, they seemed to have simply walked out of the pages of the novel. It was with a curious feeling of welcoming old friends that we saw* Taffy, The Laird, *and* Little Billee *successively present themselves at the entrances on Wednesday. By-the-bye, this production has some of the interest that attaches to a historical drama, and the actual embodiments of John Tenniel, Charles Keene, and Frederick Walker may well be looked upon with interest by all lovers of their country's art. As for* Svengali, *he was even more absorbing and impressive than in Mr Du Maurier's pages; and* Trilby *– oh! the daintily moulded feet! Oh! the fair, open face and the ingenuous eyes! The 'sweet, expressive she!' It was a delightful evening.*

As we have hinted, Mr Potter – assisted by Mr Beerbohm Tree, who has made, since the production of the piece at Manchester on September 7th last, some alterations which are essentially improvements – has dealt with his materials tenderly and judiciously. He has just brought a character into greater or less prominence, elaborated the hypnotic motive, and glided gently over some little bits of thinnish ice. The slight sketches of subordinate character are necessarily moved into the background, and Svengali *is made to loom up tremendously, Satanically. And wonderfully does Mr Beerbohm Tree depict the overpowering Jew. His make-up is a study in itself. This* Svengali *towers above his companions with the pride of Lucifer and the malice of Mephistopheles. In the first act his very old clothes are suggestive and poetic. And how weird are the bursts of this* Svengali's *merriment, what authority there is in his magic, what intensity in his rage, his agony, his ambition! Two scenes of Mr Tree's it is hard to erase from one's memory. The first is that in which* Svengali, *believing himself to be on the point of death, cries to the 'God of Israel' for mercy. The second is the awful death scene in the last act, with the talk of which all London is already ringing. We almost feel inclined to call the curtain down, to hurry over the epitaph pronounced by the* Laird, *so awful is the sight of that hideous corpse, half inverted on the table. Mr Tree's* Svengali *is so grand an impersonation that the question at once suggests itself – when will he play Shylock?*

Miss Dorothea Baird both looks and acts delightfully as Trilby. *The character is not a complex one, nor are the emotions expressed superfine, subtle, or heroic. The great thing – after the necessary talent and intelligence, of course – was to find a young lady who would not disappoint us, familiar as we all are with Du Maurier's picture heroine. And Miss Baird, besides being all that could be desired in the matter of teeth and 'extremities', is original. Her features are not of the still, regular, cold, classical class. She is better than beautiful – she is winning, fascinating, flesh-and-blood like. Whether she has capacity for greater things than her excellent interpretation of* Trilby's *mesmeric trances and* Trilby's *death is to be proved. What we have to record is that at no point of her performance did we feel the least shortcoming or inadequacy; that she charmed her audience as the real* Trilby *charmed the three students; and that the London stage is brighter by the addition of her presence. And as for her feet – well, Miss Baird has given the women a fresh cause of emulation; and, now that she has shown us how beautiful a thing is the female foot in its natural shape, perhaps it may become fashionable amongst ladies to wear boots to fit the feet, instead of torturing feet to fit boots – as is at present the custom. Mr Edmund Maurice played Talbot Wynne with the admirable repose and self-possession which are his best attributes; and Mr Lionel Brough hit off the oddities of McAlister with his wonted solid humour and grim pathos. Mr Patrick Evans, beyond looking like the* Billee *of the book, did little to help matters. His performance was decidedly amateurish; but he seems intelligent, and may with practice excel in his profession. Mr C M Hallard was earnest and dramatic as Gecko. Mr Herbert Ross as Zouzou and Mr Gerald Du Maurier as* Dodor *did all that was required. Mr Charles Allan indicated adroitly the sly pruriency of the parson, and gave to the Rev Thomas Bagot's delivery just the necessary pulpit twang. Mr Holman Clark did a neat bit of acting as* Manager Kaw. *Miss Frances Ivor was exactly the individual described and sketched by Du Maurier in the book; and Miss Rosina Filippi was sufficiently spirited as* Madame Vinard, *and gave a very effective representation of a bright, energetic Frenchwoman of the middle class. Miss Cicely Turner, Miss Agnes Russell, Miss Olive Owen, and Miss Sadie Wigley danced a lively but 'proper' can-can in the second act very briskly. The mounting was worthy of warm praise, not only on account of the liberality which was noticeable in the Cirque des Bashibazoucks scene in the third act, in which a very illusive effect of space and extent was obtained, but on account of the pains which had been taken to create the 'studio atmosphere', to supply the details and accessories. We must go out of our way to praise the orchestra, which, under the direction of Mr Raymond Roze, played selections from Schubert, Schumann, and Chopin with great finish and precision.*

Trilby *will be* the *success of the London season, into which we have little doubt it will run in July. It is not, of course, an 'epoch-making' work. But the playgoing public has been so sickened with gritty squalor and purposeless pessimism in plays that it is flying with eagerness to the fountain of fresh water at the Haymarket. What a relief it is, even though we may not go very deep down in psychological research, to associate for a while with loving, clean, and honest folk! Trilby has triumphed as it deserved to triumph. We owe a debt of gratitude to Mr Du Maurier and to Mr Tree; to the author-artist for his fair and bright conception and gay and tender fancy, to the manager for his conscientious labours in creating the tout ensemble, imperfection in which would have been as aggravating as the reverse is acceptable and agreeable. This play, with its atmosphere of friendship, love, and loving-kindness, its thrilling story, and its pathetic end, is very welcome to our stage. We congratulate Mr Tree on a success which is both opportune and well merited. For many months to come the box-offices of the Haymarket Theatre will be besieged by applicants eager to see Trilby. Mr Tree is thrice victorious – as manager, as actor, and as assistant-adapter. The 'Trilby boom' will not be due merely to a passing craze of society, to a prurient itch for forbidden fruit; but to the innate attractiveness of a charming and clever play, admirably acted.*

From William Archer's *The Theatrical 'World'* of 1895, published in 1896. This review, written on November 6th, commences with the usual lengthy recapitulation of the plot. Archer then continues:

We have here, then, a fantastic fairy-tale – a mixture of Mürger and Hoffmann. It appeals throughout to the imagination, not to the intelligence. I had almost said that it addresses itself to the child in us, not to the man; but children have a habit of asking, 'Is it true?' and that we deliberately refrain from doing. These things are told us, and we listen to them, not because they pretend to be actually or symbolically true, but because they somehow or other tickle the fancy. The lighter side of the picture charms us by its very familiarity. The 'primrose by the gutter's brim', spotless and virginal in the midst of corruption, is always gratifying to our passion for antithesis. (I am told that in the book she is not immaculate; but American chivalry has expunged her past). Familiar, too, are the three sworn friends, all in love with the same woman, two of whom remain her trusty champions after she has given her love to the third. These legendary figures are always agreeable to the imagination, and they are here presented with a good-humoured quaintness which lends them an air of novelty. As for the dark side of the picture, its charm is simply the sempiternal fascination of diablerie. Not for nothing does Svengali wear the features of a gargoyle from some mediaeval minster. He is lineally descended from the Devil of the Miracle Plays, own brother to Mephistopheles, and first cousin to the Pied Piper of Hamelin, and a whole tribe of demon musicians. Why this grotesque hocus-pocus should enchant us I really do not know, but, for my own part, I am not at all exempt from its influence. Our Gothic ancestors no doubt revive in us, and the terrors which made them what Stevenson calls 'midnight twitterers', coming down to us attenuated by scepticism, are found readily available as aesthetic motives. The Goth is not the highest element in our composition. He lives in our nerves, whereas the Greek lives in our intellect. But since the nerves respond automatically to the stimulus of theatrical effect, whereas the intellect responds only through a voluntary effort, when Goth meets Greek in the theatre there is practically no tug of war – the Goth holds the field. That is why Sir Henry Irving's Faust – *a vulgar piece of diablerie – outstripped in popularity his most distinguished and beautiful productions. That is why Mr Tree's* Svengali – *a performance not vulgar, indeed, but superficial and facile – will very likely prove the great success of his life, and become as closely associated with his name as Dundreary with Sothern's or Rip Van Winkle with Jefferson's. When I add that the heroine of the nursery-tale – the Beauty of this Beast – is a beauty indeed, with precisely the right quality of fresh and childlike loveliness, you will readily understand how wide, how universal, is its appeal. Its atmosphere of painting and music is also greatly in its favour. Three acts out of the four pass in a studio, than which there can be no more attractive scene – unless it be the* foyer *of a theatre, in which the remaining act is placed. Svengali's quality as a musician, too, makes 'slow music' an essential element in the action, and quite naturally converts a great part of the play into what the Germans call 'melodrame' – dialogue spoken through music. Thus all possible ingredients of popularity have, by chance or skill, been assembled in this play. Why, the very title,* Trilby, *with its bird-like quaver, acts as a lure to draw people together.*

Let me define my meaning with respect to Mr Tree's Svengali. *It is by no means a bad piece of acting – on the contrary, it is quite as good as the play requires or permits. But it stands on a low plane of art, because it is not an effort of observation or composition, but of sheer untrammelled fantasy. Mr Tree is simply doing what comes easiest to him, luxuriating in obvious and violent gestures and grimaces, expending no more thought on the matter than is involved in the adroit use of his personal advantages and the mechanical resources of stage effect. Please note that I say this without reproach; Mr Tree gives the character all the thought that it requires or admits of. He makes the most of his material; but his material is second-rate at best. When I was an idle schoolboy, I remember achieving a great reputation among my classmates by a knack of drawing just such figures as* Svengali – *spidery monstrosities, with flagrant hair and tentacle-limbs contorted in all sorts of extravagant postures. I had not the remotest talent for drawing, and never attempted to represent a man in natural proportions or conceivable attitudes; but by sheer unbridled whimsicality, I somehow managed to impress the schoolboy*

477

imagination and sense of humour. Mr Tree's Svengali *carries this art to its highest pitch; but its highest pitch is low as compared with the summits either of poetical acting, or of such true character-acting as Mr Tree himself has sometimes given us. To revert to a former illustration, the carvers of the Gothic gargoyles were artists in their way, but we do not class them with Michael Angelo, or even with Houdon. Miss Dorothea Baird, as* Trilby, *is not only beautiful, but intelligent and un-affected. She is not yet an accomplished actress; there were points, notably in the third act, where one felt that a touch of real inspiration would have transmuted the fairy-tale into tragedy, and thrilled us with terror and pity; but, on the fairy-tale level, Miss Baird made an absolutely ideal* Trilby. *Miss Rosina Filippi was an admirable* Madame Vinard. *Her recognition of the three artists in the third act was the most genuine piece of acting of the whole evening. The other parts were fairly well played, but the interest of the piece would certainly be heightened by a less insignificant* Little Billee *than Mr Patrick Evans.* Let me add – I don't know whether it is a confession or a boast – that so thoroughly did I enter into the innocent playfulness of the production that I can scarcely help laughing as I write at the recollection of the* Laird's *false nose.*

---

*This gentleman was presently replaced by Mr H V Esmond

Select Bibliography

English Theatrical Literature Published in 1970 by the Society for Theatre Research; a continuation & completion of Robert W Lowe's bibliography of 1888

Green Room Book 1907. Later *Who's Who in the Theatre*

Oxford Companion to the Theatre

Archer, William	*The Theatrical World* 5 vols 1893/7
	English Dramatists of Today 1882
Arliss, George	*On The Stage* 1928
Baker, H B	*History of the London Stage* 1904
Barrett, Wilson jr	*On Stage For Notes* 1954
Beerbohm, Max	*Around Theatres* 1924 (reprinted 1953)
	Herbert Beerbohm Tree 1920
Booth, Michael	*Hiss The Villain* 1964
	English Melodrama 1965
	English Plays of the Nineteenth Century 2 vols 1969
Brereton, Austin	*Henry Irving* 1883
Bunn, Alfred	*The Stage, Both Before and Behind The Curtain* 1840
Coleman, John	*Plays and Playwrights I have Known* 2 vols 1888
	Fifty Years Of An Actor's Life 2 vols 1904
Cook, Dutton	*Hours With the Players* 2 vols 1881
	Nights At The Play 2 vols 1883
	On The Stage 2 vols 1883
Dark, Sidney & Rowland Grey	*W S Gilbert: his life and letters* 1924
Darton, Harvey	*Vincent Crummles: his theatre and his times* 1926
Dickens, Charles	*The Amusements Of The People* (*Household Words* March 30th & April 15th 1850)
	The Theatrical Young Gentleman (*Sketches By Boz*, chapters 11 and 13 1836)
	Two Views of A Cheap Theatre (*The Uncommercial Traveller* 1860)
	Nicholas Nickleby chapters 22–30 (1838/39)

Donaldson, W A	*Recollections of an Actor* 1865
Doran, John	*Their Majesties' Servants: annals of the English Stage from Thomas Betterton to Edmund Kean* 3 vols 1888
Downer, Alan S	*Plays And Painted Stage – 19th century acting* P.L.M.A. vol LXI pp 522–576 1946
Disher, M Willson	*Blood And Thunder* 1949
	Melodrama – Plots That Thrilled 1954
Dye, William S	*A Study Of Melodrama in England from 1800/1840* 1919
Erle, Thomas W	*Letters From A Theatrical Scene-Painter* 1880
Filon, Augustin	*The English Stage: an account of the Victorian drama* 1897
Fitzball, Edward	*Thirty-five Years Of A Dramatic Actor's Life* 1859
Fitzgerald, Percy	*The World Behind The Scenes* 1881
	Life Of David Garrick 1899
Garcia, Gustav	*The Actor's Art* 1882
Gassner, J	*Masters Of The Drama* 1940
Genest, John	*Account of the English Stage* 10 vols 1832
Grein, J T	*Dramatic Criticism* 1899
Hamilton, Clayton	*Studies In Stage Craft* 1914
Hazlitt, William	*Hazlitt on Theatre* 1895 (reissued 1957) edited by William Archer and Robert W Lowe
	Collected Works 8 vols edited by A R Waller and A Glover 1902/4
	Liber Amoris and Dramatic Criticism edited by Charles Morgan 1948
	Criticism and Essays of the English Stage 1851
Hibbert, H G	*A Playgoer's Memories* 1920
Hunt, Leigh	*Dramatic Essays* edited by William Archer and Robert W Lowe 1894
	Critical Essays on Performers 1807
Jerome, Jerome K	*On the Stage – and Off* 1885
	Stage-Land 1889
Lamb, Charles	*Essays* 1823/33
Lennox, Lord William Pitt	*Plays, Players & Playhouses* 2 vols 1881
Lewes, George Henry	*On Actors and the Art of Acting* 1875
Morley, Henry	*The Journal of a London Playgoer 1851/1866* 1899

Newton, H Chance	*Crime And The Drama* 1927
Nicoll, Allardyce	Sundry works including *A History Of English Drama* 6 vols, the standard reference work
	English Drama 1900/1930 1973
Oxberry, Catherine & William	*Oxberry's Dramatic Biography and Histrionic Anecdotes* 1825
Pearson, Hesketh	*Tree* 1956
Planché, J R	*Recollections* 2 vols 1876
Publications	see below: Felix Sper and Carl J Stratman
Reynolds, Ernest	*Early Victorian Drama 1830/70* 1936
Rowell, George	*The Victorian Theatre* 1956 (includes a long bibliography)
	Nineteenth Century Plays 1953
	Late Victorian Plays 1968
Scott, Clement	*Thirty Years At The Play* 1891
Sharp, R F	*A Short History of the English Stage to 1908* 1909
Shaw, G B	*Advice to a Young Critic* letters 1894/1928, published in 1956
	Our Theatres in the Nineties 1932; 3 vols of pieces from the *Saturday Review* 1895/98
	Dramatic Opinions and Essays 1907
Sherson, Erroll	*London's Lost Theatres of the XIX Century* 1925
Southern, Richard	*Changeable Scenery* 1951
	Victorian Theatre – a Pictorial Survey 1970
Sper, Felix	*The Periodical Press of London 1800/1830* 1937
Stirling, Edward	*Old Drury Lane* 2 vols 1881
Stratman, Carl J	*Bibliography of British Dramatic Periodicals 1720/1960* 1962
Thompson, A R	*Melodrama and Tragedy* P.M.L.A. vol 43 Sept 1928 pp 810-35
Trewin, J C	*The Pomping Folk* 1968
	The Night has been Unruly 1957
	Journal of William Charles Macready 1832/51 abridged and edited 1967
Watson, E Bradlee	*Sheridan to Robertson* 1926
Whyte, Frederic	*Actors of the Century* 1898
Wills, Freeman	*W G Wills, dramatist and painter* 1898

Appendix A

The Patent theatres, the Theatres Royal at Covent Garden and Drury Lane, were granted the exclusive right to present 'straight' plays in 1660. This charter was abrogated in 1843, and the following extract from volume two of J R Planché's *Recollections* (pp 70–76), written thirty years later, shows an interesting reaction to this change, and displays an early (but not the first) concern for the idea of a National Theatre.

I say you're free to act where'er you please,
No longer pinioned by the patentees.
Need our immortal Shakespeare mute remain,
Fixed on the portico of Drury Lane;
Or the nine Muses mourn the drama's fall
Without relief on Covent Garden's wall?
Sheridan now at Islington may shine,
Marylebone echo 'Marlowe's mighty line;'
Otway may raise the waters Lambeth yields,
And Farquhar sparkle in St George's fields;
Whycherley, flutter a Whitechapel pit,
And Congreve wake all 'Westminster to wit'

The doubt implied by Punch *has been painfully illustrated. A recent writer in the* Quarterly Review, *commenting on this subject, says: 'Of what avail was it to multiply theatres and give them the right to perform the higher drama, unless you could also provide actors to keep pace with their demands? These are a commodity not to be turned out in any quantity to order. No amount of demand will produce a corresponding supply. Natural gifts and training must go to their production, and the only real training-school is a theatre of good actors, working together with a pride in their art, and under a system of intelligent discipline. But the change of system made the existence of such a school impossible: for how could such actors of ability and experience as then existed be kept together when they were being continually bribed away, by offers of increased salary and higher rank, to the host of competitive theatres which soon afterwards sprang into existence? Companies became of necessity broken up; actors, who by time and practice might have been tutored into excellence, were ruined by being lifted into positions far beyond their powers; every player became a law to himself; the traditions*

482

of the art were lost, the discipline which distinguished the old theatres was broken down, and the performance of a comedy of character or of a poetical play, as these used to be represented, became, as the elders of the craft had foretold, simply impossible'. *

These are sad truths. I quote them because I am desirous to show that writers of much more weight than I, feel as acutely the present position of our national stage and acknowledge the results of the shortsighted legislation which abolished the privileges of the patent theatres, to have been what the great actors predicted, and I ventured to hint, thirty years ago. I say shortsighted, because, in amending laws no longer suited to the age, not the slightest prevision was exercised by the reformers, who simply yielded to the outcry justly raised against the absurd, incongruous, and partial regulations that oppressed and degraded the profession, without providing for the security of its best interests and the encouragement of its noblest aspirations.

The present generation of play-goers can scarcely imagine the vexatious and anomalous state of affairs that existed in the theatrical world when I first became a member of it. The Theatres Royal Drury Lane and Covent Garden enjoyed, by their patents, the exclusive privilege of being open all the year round, *if their lessees so willed it, for the performance of any species of dramatic entertainment. 'Tragedy, comedy, history, pastoral', etc, as old Polonius had it, 'for the law of writ and the liberty' (to act it) 'they were the only men'. The little theatre in the Haymarket had a* limited licence, as a summer theatre, *for the performance of what is called the regular drama. With these exceptions, no theatre within the bills of mortality was safe from the common informer, did its company venture to enact any drama in which there was not a certain quantity of vocal or instrumental music. The Lyceum, a new establishment, was specially licensed for the performance of English opera and musical dramas, and the Adelphi and Olympic Theatres had the Lord Chamberlain's licence for the performance of burlettas* only, by which description, *after much controversy both in and out of court, we were desired to understand dramas containing not less than five pieces of vocal music in each act, and which were also, with one or two exceptions, not to be found in the* repertoire *of the patent houses. All beside the above-named six theatres were positively out of the pale of the law. There was no Act of Parliament which empowered the magistrates to license a building for* dramatic performances. *Astley's, the Surrey, the Victoria, Sadler's Wells etc, had, in common with Vauxhall, a licence 'for music and dancing' only, by which was originally meant public concerts and balls; gradually permitted to extend to ballets*

---

* *Quarterly Review* for January, 1872, p 13

and pantomimes and equestrian performances: but no one had a legal right to open his mouth on a stage unaccompanied by music; and the next step was to evade the law by the tinkling of a piano in the orchestra throughout the interdicted performances. There is perhaps no greater folly than permitting laws to exist which changes of times and circumstances have rendered so absurd that justice is obliged to wink at the breach of them. It being considered hard that the inhabitants of St George's Fields, Lambeth, Islington, Marylebone, etc, should be compelled to make a positive journey in order to enjoy the rational amusement of the theatre, the proprietors of the public places of 'entertainment for man and horse' in those vicinities were suffered to violate the law nightly with impunity; and the unwillingness of magistrates to convict, when occasionally compelled to notice the offence, became at last so notorious that the holders of the royal patents, who were most interested in suppressing the innovators, finding nothing but odium was to be gained by their opposition, after two or three ineffectual struggles, gave up the cause in despair, and regular dramas were soon acted as boldly and almost as well at the minors as at the majors. Still the law was not repealed. It existed and could be put in force at any moment; nay, what was more ridiculous, though the entire disregard of it was tolerated at the Surrey or in Tottenham Street, had Macbeth *or* The School for Scandal *been acted at the Adelphi or the Olympic Theatres, legally licensed for the performance of some description, at least, of the drama, the Lord Chamberlain would have pounced upon the audacious manager or lessees, and shut up his doors* instanter. *Notwithstanding this even, the Strand Theatre, which had been added to the number of dramatic establishments, was kept open for nearly two years in defiance of his lordship's authority, and the only way at last discovered was the petty one of common information against the poor actors.*

Lent arrived, and the theatres in the parish of St Paul, Covent Garden, were rigorously restricted from the performance of a moral or poetical play on Wednesdays or Fridays during that period; but a theatre that happened to be on the other side of Oxford Street or of Waterloo Bridge was unaffected by this prohibition, and though the manager of the Adelphi might not dream of playing the whole of one of the spectacular 'burlettas', which were at that period so popular there, no objection was made to his exhibiting tableaux from them, and adding any tomfoolery which was not *dramatic, by way of keeping holy the said Wednesdays and Fridays. The performers at Drury Lane and Covent Garden lost two nights' salary every week, but then they could go to Greenwich or Richmond, and act what they pleased there. Lent was only a sacred season within the circle described by the wand of the Lord Chamberlain. Passion Week itself was unknown in the theatres two or three miles from St James's Palace. Such was England during the first quarter of the nineteenth century ! At length the injustice became intolerable, and the regulations supremely ridiculous; but, in conceding what reason demanded, no precautions were taken against the almost inevitable misuse of the liberty accorded. The gates were recklessly thrown open, and the glorious drama of England, free to roam wherever she would, has never since found a permanent resting-place for the soles of her feet. A stage has not yet risen for her, and her true lovers are still 'sincerely wishing she may get it'.*

Appendix B

This passage is from volume one of J R Planché's *Recollections* (pp 46–51), and is a grand but unconvincing defence of the practice of theatre writers of borrowing source material from poets and novelists without permission or financial consideration. The passage also shows us contemporary ideas on the writing of the popular play. No mention is made of borrowing from other playwrights . . .

On the 3rd of December, 1822, was produced my first opera, Maid Marian, *the music by Bishop, the subject taken from a sparkling little tale of that name written by Mr Peacock, of the India House, author of* Headlong Hall *and two or three other similar 'novelettes', published by Hookham, in Bond Street. To Mr Hookham, as in duty bound, I offered the refusal of the libretto of my opera, which, be it observed, contained much original lyrical and other matter, besides two or three situations from* Ivanhoe, *a kindred subject, Mr Peacock's story being too slight to form the entire framework of a three-act opera. This offer Mr Hookham declined in terms it would be flattering to call courteous, and all but threatened to prevent the performance of the opera as an infringement of his copyright. Its great success afforded me the handsome revenge of putting a lump of money in his pocket by the sale not only of the novel of* Maid Marian, *but of all the other works by the same author, of which a second edition was speedily demanded, and the great gratification of making the public acquainted with the works of one of the most agreeable of writers which, like too many gems 'of purest ray serene', had remained for years unknown, and consequently unappreciated.*

And here I am desirous of making a few observations on a much contested subject. One of the many respecting which my favourite philosopher, Sir Roger de Coverley, remarks, 'much may be said on both sides', viz, the adaptation of novels or romances in prose or in verse to the stage. If we refer to usage, no one can deny that it has been the practice of the greatest dramatists in every age and every country to found their plays upon the popular tales of their own or of former times, and provided the fact was 'handsomely acknowledged', like the offence described by Sir Lucius O'Trigger, it 'became an obligation'. I question if any author felt otherwise than flattered by the proceeding. I know that Mr Charles

Kemble, when he placed Maid Marian *in my hands, never entertained
an idea of any objection being made by its writer; nor was there; for, in
consequence of Mr Hookham's behaviour, I called on Mr Peacock at the
India House, and was most cordially received by him. The objection
was solely that of the short-sighted publisher, who could not perceive
how greatly the value of his property would be increased till the gold
began to jingle in his own pocket, some of it, I trust, finding its way into
that of the amiable author. The great mass of writers of fiction are not
dramatists, and if they desire, as to my knowedge they nearly all do, to
see their works transferred to the stage, they must be indebted to the
playwrights. After the success of* Maid Marian, *I had piles of novels
sent me by not only authors but by their publishers, requesting my
acceptance of them for that purpose. They knew it was the finest
advertisement for a book in the world; and I have been even offered
money by some to obtain for them that advantage. The author was
especially on the safe side; for if the adaptation was good, and the piece
successful, he had the chief glory, and a brisk sale for his book; while
if it failed the dramatist was the sufferer in purse as well as reputation.
How few writers combine the diametrically opposite qualifications
required for success on the stage and popularity in the circulating
library ! The hackneyed quotation 'Poeta nascitur, non fit', is equally
applicable to the playwright, and it is remarkable that the greater the
novelist the less able has he proved himself to fulfil the requirements and
exigences of the theatre. The talent of the novelist is displayed in
elaboration; that of the dramatist is condensation. The former may waft
his reader from 'Indus to the Pole' at his pleasure; occupy pages with
the description of a country-house or the character of its proprietor;
dedicate a chapter to the development of his plot. Not so the modern
playwright; he can no longer, as in the early days of the English drama,
shift the scene from country to country, or direct the performer who has
just made his exit in one to walk on the next minute in the other, without
the fall of an act-drop, and an intimation of the time supposed to have
elapsed in the playbill; and at no time dared he ever to exceed a certain
limit in his dialogue, or substitute lengthy narrative for action. Walter
Scott was devoted to the theatre, but quite incapable of dramatising his
very dramatic novels and romances, and gladly contributed his valuable
aid to his friend Terry in their adaptation as operas, by writing for him
many charming characteristic lyrics. Dickens tried 'his 'prentice hand',
and never repeated the experiment. Thackeray sadly disappointed the
manager to whom he had promised a comedy, and which, when presented,
was pronounced unactable.*

*Mrs Charles Gore and Lord Lytton are the only examples, so far as I
can recollect, of novelists who have obtained any success on the stage;
and it is worthy of remark that they have never attempted to dramatise
their own most popular novels; but sought in history or the French*

drama for plots better suited to the purpose. *Mr Wilkie Collins appears likely to add his name as a third; but these are quite the exceptions that prove the rule, and I am aware of none other; for Mr Charles Reed was a dramatist before he was a novelist, having written for the stage at the commencement of his literary career, in conjunction with a master of his art, Tom Taylor. He cannot, therefore, be included in the category. On the other hand, I should be the last to dispute the right of the novelist to the full benefit of his own property, or think he should not be 'courteously entreated' previous to any meddling with it. He may have contemplated attempting to dramatise it himself, or be desirous to entrust another with the task, or have strong objections to its being dramatised at all, as Dickens had to the adaption of his* Pickwick Papers; *and no one with a grain of delicacy would disregard such objections. I simply contend that, except in special cases such as above mentioned, the complaint of injury to the interest of the novelist which has been recently so loudly expressed is utterly without foundation. And in any case who is the greatest criminal? The adapter, who violates the rights of property and the courtesies of society, or the manager who rewards him for the act, even if he have not, as is the case in nine instances out of ten, suggested and tempted him to commit it? Surely if the receiver be worse than the thief, the encourager of literary larceny is more blameable than the perpetrator. Were there not ready markets for stolen goods, depredation would speedily cease to be a trade worth following. Were there no theatres at which such pieces were acceptable, the least scrupulous dramatist would soon find honesty the best policy.*

Index

Titles of plays, books and journals are given in italics

491